In an area of vivid interaction between the EU and the national and regional levels, Martin Milán Csirszki provides a sharp analysis of the sustainability goal in the interface between agricultural law and competition law. I would recommend this book to anyone interested in EU and comparative economic law.

Bert Keirsbilck, ***Professor, KU Leuven, Belgium***

Csirszki's highly reflective, comparative, and comprehensive study on agricultural and competition policy objectives in a sustainable development setting is worth reading. Challenging a 'more-economic approach', this book suggests a novel food sovereignty-based take on agri-food cases and markets where agricultural objectives inform the application of antitrust law. *Agriculture, Sustainability and Competition Law: Policy Paradigms and Their Legal Implications* will inform the sustainable agriculture regulatory policy debate for years to come.

Ignacio Herrera Anchustegui, ***Professor, University of Bergen, Norway***

Agriculture, Sustainability and Competition Law

Through a detailed law-and-policy analysis, this book investigates competition law and policy in relation to agricultural producers, examining the topic in light of both the neoliberal agricultural policy and food sovereignty paradigms, with a focus on their differing approaches to competition and sustainability.

This book addresses the increasing pressures faced by agricultural producers, stemming from two major developments: the shift towards neoliberal economic policies in agri-food markets, and the growing recognition of the agricultural sector's role in environmental degradation due to unsustainable practices. These developments have provoked protests from farmers and prompted critical questions about how different agricultural and competition policy theories navigate the complex relationship between competition, agriculture and sustainability. By conceptualising the connections between each topic, the book comprehensively analyses their interdependence. While competition law experts frequently overlook the realities of the agricultural sector, agricultural scholars may not fully grasp the objectives of competition law. By bridging these divides, the book provides an integrated understanding of competition and agricultural policy, also with a particular focus on sustainability.

This book will be of interest to researchers in the field of agricultural law and policy, and competition law and policy, as well as those interested in sustainability.

Martin Milán Csirszki serves as Head of Unit at the Hungarian Competition Authority. Before joining the national competition agency, he worked as a researcher at the Ferenc Mádl Institute of Comparative Law. Besides his enforcement work, he is Adjunct Lecturer at the Budapest-based Ludovika University of Public Service, where he teaches courses on competition law and compliance. He completed his legal and PhD studies at the University of Miskolc, Hungary.

Routledge Research in Competition Law

Merger Control in Europe
The Gap in the ECMR and National Merger Legislations
Ioannis Kokkoris

Harmonising Regulatory and Antitrust Regimes for International Air Transport
Jan Walulik

Collective Redress and EU Competition Law
Eda Sahin

Competition Policy and Network Industries
Structural Separation in the Telecommunications Sector
Pierluigi Congedo

Competition Laws, National Interests and International Relations
Ko Unoki

Private Law and Competition Regulation
A Comparative Study
Alberto Brown

Competition Law in China and the EU
Institutional Dynamics and Theories of Harm
Xingyu Yan

Antitrust Law and Mergers
David Hansen

Agriculture, Sustainability and Competition Law
Policy Paradigms and Their Legal Implications
Martin Milán Csirszki

For more information about this series, please visit: www.routledge.com

Agriculture, Sustainability and Competition Law

Policy Paradigms and Their Legal Implications

Martin Milán Csirszki

Routledge
Taylor & Francis Group
LONDON AND NEW YORK

First published 2025
by Routledge
4 Park Square, Milton Park, Abingdon, Oxon OX14 4RN

and by Routledge
605 Third Avenue, New York, NY 10158

Routledge is an imprint of the Taylor & Francis Group, an informa business

British Library Cataloguing-in-Publication Data
A catalogue record for this book is available from the British Library

ISBN: 978-1-032-99087-3 (hbk)
ISBN: 978-1-032-99543-4 (pbk)
ISBN: 978-1-003-60474-7 (ebk)

DOI: 10.4324/9781003604747

Typeset in Times New Roman
by Apex CoVantage, LLC

To my amazing wife, Sára,
for her endless patience and support

Contents

Acknowledgements

Everyone I have met during my professional journey has shaped my thinking. Some do it every day; some did it for more than five years during my legal and PhD studies. The competition law postgraduate programme I attended in 2021–22 has also had a lasting impact on my views. I am grateful also to my colleagues, past and present, both in academia and at the Hungarian Competition Authority. Longer and shorter conversations, research trips, conferences in Hungary or abroad, or even a passing remark – these have all added to this book. As before, I remain open to everyone's professional thoughts, advice and suggestions. Without mentioning specific individuals, I am – to a greater or lesser extent – indebted to all academics, enforcers and private practitioners who I have met in the last eight years. However, the opinions expressed in the book are my own, and, furthermore, these cannot be treated as the official position of my current and former employers.

Part I

Introduction

1 Starting point

Many of us may have heard or read the shocking story of *Lee Kyung-hae*, a South Korean farmer and activist, who – in Cancún in September 2003 – took his own life by stabbing himself as an act of protest and resistance against the free market policies of the World Trade Organization (WTO).[1] Even academic publications recall this devastating event[2] to shed light on the utter difference between, on the one hand, farmers' way of thinking about the role of agriculture in a globalised world economy and, on the other hand, the market functioning that neoliberal policymakers see as ideal. In general, at least at the level of political communication, trends in the last few decades have pointed in the direction of less intervention and more market orientation in agri-food markets. In the 1990s, this was first realised by the Agreement on Agriculture within the WTO at the global level, by the MacSharry reforms in the European Union (EU),[3] and by cutting farm programme costs in the United States, which all happened under the aegis of the retrenchment of the agricultural welfare state.[4]

Other more or less moderate protests by agricultural producers are a common occurrence. These have happened for a number of different reasons: milk producers in the Czech Republic against prices that do not reach their production costs[5]; farmers from all over the EU against the declining prices of milk and pork[6]; Slovak producers against irregularities in EU farm subsidy payments[7]; livestock farmers in the Netherlands against the blame for nitrogen pollution and the proposal to limit

1 John Vidal, 'Farmer Commits Suicide at Protests' *The Guardian* (London, 11 September 2003).

2 Peter M. Rosset, *Food Is Different: Why We Must Get the WTO Out of Agriculture* (Fernwood Publishing 2006); Alana Mann, *Global Activism in Food Politics: Power Shift* (Palgrave Macmillan 2014) 33.

3 Arlindo Cunha and Alan Swinbank, *An Inside View of the CAP Reform Process: Explaining the MacSharry, Agenda 2000, and Fischler Reforms* (OUP 2011) 68–101.

4 Adam D. Sheingate, *The Rise of the Agricultural Welfare State: Institutions and Interest Group Power in the United States, France, and Japan* (Princeton University Press 2001) 200.

5 Jaroslav Hála, 'Farmers Protest as Czech Agriculture Declines' *Eurofound* (4 February 2010).

6 'EU Farmers Protest Low Milk Prices in Belgium' *AlJazeera* (7 September 2015).

7 Georgi Gotev, 'Slovak Farmers Drive Tractors into Capital to Protest Alleged EU Subsidy Fraud' *Euractiv* (20 June 2018).

DOI: 10.4324/9781003604747-2

the number of animals[8]; Spanish farmers against curbing water supplies for irrigation[9]; Greek producers against the spike in energy prices and the effects coming with it.[10] Unfortunately, producers could not even stay out of trade wars.[11]

2024 also came with a wave of farmers' protests all around the European continent. In early January, Germany fell victim to demonstrations against phasing out and cutting agricultural fuel state subsidies.[12] Then, French agricultural producers blocked roads with their tractors against new environmental regulations and high energy costs,[13] which even resulted in an accident causing the death of a farmer and her daughter after a car had unintentionally crashed into one of the roadblocks.[14] These protests spread to the Netherlands and Belgium, where farmers also blocked exit roads of highways as well as set fires along the roads.[15] Polish agricultural producers, too, demonstrated in Warsaw against EU climate policies and Ukrainian grain imports.[16] Greece, Spain, the Czech Republic and Hungary also experienced smaller and larger protests.[17] In all countries, the unrest usually roots in the same issues: higher costs of agricultural production, higher environmental obligations imposed on the sector, in parallel with lower incomes.

It tells a lot about the controversies surrounding these events that the *Economist* was not afraid of noting about the protests that

> [a] sector used to exorbitant privileges – roughly one-third of the EU's budget goes on subsidies to the common agricultural policy, after all – has felt them slip from its grasp. It is in many ways a familiar story, of a privileged caste sensing its status declining.

In a broader context, by mocking the EU, the weekly also mentioned that "[t]he decline of European farming typifies the continent's ever-dwindling relevance. Agriculture has been left in the dust by other sectors much as the broader

8 Stephanie van den Berg, Toby Sterling and Bart Meijer, 'Angry Farmers Cause Dutch Police to Close Off Parliament Square' *Reuters* (16 October 2019).
9 Raul Cadenas and Emma Pinedo, 'Spanish Farmers Protest against Plans to Curb Water Supply for Irrigation' *Reuters* (11 January 2023).
10 Costas Kantouris and Derek Gatopoulos, 'Greek Farm Protests Are a Sign of Europe's Inflation Anxiety' *AP News* (17 February 2022).
11 Peter Teffer, 'Why Are European Farmers Unhappy?' *EUobserver* (7 September 2015).
12 Kate Connolly, 'Thousands of Tractors Block Berlin as Farmers Protest Over Fuel Subsidy Cuts' *The Guardian* (Berlin, 15 January 2024).
13 'French Farmers Close in on Paris as Government Struggles to Calm Protests' *France24* (31 January 2024).
14 Chris Bockman and Paul Kirby, 'French Protests: Female Farmer and Daughter Killed as Car Hits French Protesters' *BBC News* (24 January 2024).
15 Bart Meijer and Geert De Clercq, 'Police Move to End Dutch Farmer Protests' *Reuters* (6 February 2024).
16 Alicja Ptak, 'Thousands of Farmers Protest in Warsaw against EU Climate Policies and Ukrainian Imports' *Notes from Poland* (27 February 2024).
17 Catarina Demony and Guillermo Martinez, 'Protesting Spanish Farmers Drive Hundreds of Tractors to Madrid' *Reuters* (21 February 2024).

European economy has been overtaken by its geopolitical rivals."[18] From a US perspective, without taking into account the different farm structure of the European Union and its Member States, it would be arduous to accept the reality of the Old Continent's agricultural sector. Emerging in the 1980s, the more market-oriented approach towards agricultural production reached two absolutely different setups as regards the sector's characteristics. Though concentrating on the varieties of conservativism, the utter contrast between the attitudes of the two sides of the Atlantic in this regard is analysed brilliantly by *Scruton*, and it is worth recalling in length:

> *Conservatives in America emphasize economic freedoms, and associate this emphasis with a rugged individualism and a belief in the virtues of risk-taking and enterprise. Conservatives in Europe have favoured tradition, custom and civil society, emphasizing the need to contain enterprise within a durable social order.* This difference of emphasis can lead to conflicting policies [emphasis added by the author]. *Thus there is a tendency in American conservatism to prefer "market solutions", whether or not they pose a threat to traditional forms of community and social equilibrium. Americans collectively possess an abundance of land and natural resources, and this has enabled them to put problems of scarcity and overpopulation out of mind, believing that there will always be space and resources for some new experiment. Europe is an assemblage of constricted states, settled throughout recorded history and with precious habitats, both human and animal, cared for and fought for over centuries. European conservatives are acutely aware of the constraints that surround them, and of the dangers of "breaking out". This does not mean that they reject market solutions. It means that they will pay more attention than their American counterparts to the things that make markets possible: to law, tradition and the moral life.*[19]

The reason I brought in *Scruton*'s claims about the different attitudes of the two continents is that these thoughts can be used beyond conservativism. *Scruton* builds his philosophical arguments upon such general geographic features and qualities that have determined significantly the economic reality of the continents and their regulatory attitudes within this context. Nevertheless, it is another question that agricultural producers are treated historically as conservatives,[20] and all current protests have been attributed to right-wing parties.[21]

18 'Europe's Grumpy Farmers Are a Symptom of Wider Malaise' *The Economist* (London, 1 February 2024).
19 Roger Scruton, *Green Philosophy* (Atlantic Books 2012).
20 Patrick Schröder and Tim Benton, 'European Farmers' Protests Show the Need for a Just Transition to Net Zero' *Chatham House* (London, 2 February 2024).
21 See: Jessica Parker in Berlin and Adam Robinson, 'Germany's Far Right Seek Revolution in Farmers' Protests' *BBC News* (15 January 2024); Ajit Niranjan, 'Why Europe's Farmers Are Protesting – and the Far Right Is Taking Note' *The Guardian* (London, 15 January 2024); Nicholas Vinocur

The fundamental philosophical distinction between the United States and Europe concerning environmental protection and its nexus with agriculture can be better understood through these reflections. In the United States, when the neoliberal turn reached the agricultural sector in the last quarter of the 20th century, US agricultural production was better prepared to adapt to free market forces because of its farm structure. On the contrary, European agriculture has been characterised by small and medium-sized agricultural holdings, which were – due to the European natural features and the sector's further functions beyond production – more unprepared for the retrenchment of the agricultural welfare state.

Anyway, for many, farmers' willingness to protest does not come as a surprise. Besides production risks related to climate and weather, agricultural producers have to cope with, and react to, a whole range of other factors. Personal, market, institutional and financial risks may all result in adverse outcomes for them, typically lower incomes and yields.[22]

Some suggest that the failures in agricultural markets have been worsened by globalisation and the neoliberal agricultural policy underpinning it.[23] Although neoliberalism is most frequently labelled as the enemy of farmers in developing countries, "[f]or years now, neoliberal policies have also threatened the agricultural model and livelihoods of small and medium-size farmers in the global North, who cannot compete with agribusinesses that keep growing."[24] This does not seem to change in the future. According to new research results, "under current development trajectories, the number of farms globally will probably decline from the current 616 million in 2020 to 272 million by the end of the twenty-first century, with average farm size doubling."[25] Without denying the benefits of globalisation, one must also take into account its dark side, such as the growing influence of transnational corporations (TNCs) with the difficulties in regulating them, the struggle of small producers lacking economies of scale, as well as monocultures causing environmental problems.[26]

In parallel with freer agricultural markets, another trend can be observed. Since the 1980s, an ever-higher emphasis has been put on environmental considerations, which was framed as the imperative of sustainability and of sustainable development.

Without going into more detail here, these two tendencies prima facie seem contradictory to one another as regards their consequences. Free agricultural markets

---

and Bartosz Brzeziński, 'How the Far Right Aims to Ride Farmers' Outrage to Power in Europe' *Politico* (26 January 2024).

22 Adam M. Komarek, Alessandro De Pinto and Vincent H. Smith, 'A Review of Types of Risks in Agriculture: What We Know and What We Need to Know' (2020) 178 Agricultural Systems, Article 102738.

23 See, for example: Valeria Sodano, 'Food Policy Beyond Neo-Liberalism' in Dennis Erasga (ed), *Sociological Landscape: Theories, Realities and Trends* (IntechOpen 2012) 375–402.

24 Peter Andree, Jeffrey Ayres, Michael Bosia and Marie-Josee Massicotte (eds), *Globalization and Food Sovereignty: Global and Local Change in the New Politics of Food* (University of Toronto Press 2014) 34.

25 Zia Mehrabi, 'Likely Decline in the Number of Farms Globally By the Middle of the Century' (2023) 6 Nature Sustainability 949.

26 Guy M. Robinson, 'Globalization of Agriculture' (2018) 10 Annual Review of Resource Economics 133.

that are built upon global food value chains do not help achieve the objectives of a sustainable agricultural sector and supply chain. Modern, industrialised agriculture that fits well in the globalised economy is rather at odds with the sustainability objectives formulated at different levels. Of course, academia is concerned with understanding the notion of sustainable globalisation and to measure the impact of globalisation on sustainability. However, the complexity[27] which scholars have to face in this regard is not easy. It is a common conclusion that one cannot automatically associate globalisation with "either positive or negative effects on environmental quality."[28] Nevertheless, the deeper understanding of this issue due to the lack of measurable overall outcomes and precise data is missing.

Thus, farmers increasingly face pressure from, at least, two notable directions. They do not only have to adapt to new environmental requirements, but also operate in a less protective regulatory framework. This is framed by *Daugbjerg and Swinbank* as "a stepwise process of dual policy layering," constituting "the twin trajectory of redesigning EU farm price support into WTO-compatible decoupled payments, together with the greening of the CAP."[29] American farmers are in a similar situation.

This book aims to delve into this atmosphere from a law and policy perspective, concentrating on the private law relations of producers and – with one exception – excluding the state aid-related part of the issue.[30] That is, I examine the relations when farmers appear in the marketplace as buyers of their production inputs or sellers of their produce, and do not touch upon state aid programmes and policies.

The problem this book aims to examine is that agricultural producers are continuously confronted with their stigmatic role in contributing to environmental degradation; however, they are also required to maintain their current productivity, be they small or medium-sized agricultural holdings, or more developed and vertically integrated agribusinesses. The topic generates fierce debates not only among but also within European Union institutions. For example, concerning pesticides reduction, the European Parliament's Committee on Agriculture and Rural Development is a great counterpower against the European Commission's ambitions to have the European Green Deal's objectives realised. Furthermore, even within the Parliament there are different interests, such as those of the Committee on the Environment, Public Health and Food Safety which has a strong voice in environment-related agricultural issues.[31]

27 Sai Tang, Zhuolin Wang, Gengqi Yang and Wenwen Tang, 'What Are the Implications of Globalization on Sustainability? – A Comprehensive Study' (2020) 12 Sustainability 3411.

28 Kevin P. Gallagher, 'Economic Globalization and the Environment' (2009) 34 Annual Review of Environment and Resources 279.

29 Carsten Daugbjerg and Alan Swinbank 'Three Decades of Policy Layering and Politically Sustainable Reform in the European Union's Agricultural Policy' (2016) 29 Governance 265.

30 See subheading 3 of chapter 10.

31 Bartosz Brzeziński and Paula Andrés, 'Meet the Farmers Who Control One-Third of the EU's Budget' *Politico* (6 October 2023).

A 2021 special report by the European Court of Auditors made worrisome conclusions. Despite the 100 billion euro of Common Agricultural Policy funds in the period 2014–2020 to tackle climate change, the juncture is not better as regards livestock emissions and greenhouse gas emissions from the use of chemical fertilisers and manure.[32] One must also bear in mind that the agricultural sector has been stagnating since 2005 regarding its performance related to the reduction of greenhouse gas emissions.[33] The United States approach towards the transition to a more sustainable agricultural sector is also dominated by government spendings based on farm bills' conservation programmes.

Thus, the question arises of, *beyond subsidies*, how agricultural producers could be helped to overcome this dual challenge, as well as how the legal framework assists them in this goal. The motivation to exclude the examination of different financial schemes and stay within the area of private initiatives between market participants came from this, as well as the observation that so far academic interest has been limited to whether regulation creates a supportive framework for agricultural producers, food processors and traders to operate in the supply chain as sustainability-focused market players. The latter is less true for the European Union than for the United States of America, because recently the antitrust scholars of the Old Continent deal quite a lot with the interaction between competition and sustainability, however, not in the context of the agricultural sector. In contrast, US literature as well as US antitrust enforcers are not truly concerned with the role of antitrust in solving environmental problems.

My hypothesis is that the prevailing and mainstream paradigm in economic, and in particular competition, policy as well as the broader neoliberal idea and model of market organisation dominating in the last four decades have reached their limits as regards the agricultural sector, meaning that the regulatory approach these paradigms offer to the sector cannot contribute better to the attainment of agricultural policy objectives, including that of sustainability. It is, therefore, necessary to put under scrutiny what the alternative paradigms in agricultural and competition policy provide to advance the system.

For the sake of academic straightforwardness, I share some personal insights about my initial beliefs that originate from several years ago when I started the research about the relationship between competition and the agricultural sector. I looked at agricultural producers as victims of the transition from an agricultural to an industrial world economy, whose situation has been significantly worsened with free markets pushed by pro-globalisation institutions and experts and whose legal protection are not given appropriate consideration within the current legal framework. The voices echoing the unfairness of agri-food markets, the demonstrations

32 European Court of Auditors, *Special Report: Common Agricultural Policy and Climate: Half of EU Climate Spending But Farm Emissions Are Not Decreasing* (Publications Office of the European Union 2021) 3.

33 European Environment Agency, *Progress and Prospects for Decarbonisation in the Agriculture Sector and Beyond* (6 October 2022).

of producers that are a common occurrence worldwide, and the emerging food sovereignty paradigm challenging the whole functioning of globalised agriculture all have influenced my assumptions, and I realised that the question begs for a comprehensive analysis deprived of populist rhetoric. With this in mind, I have begun the work to better understand the many strands of ideas that appear in the discourse.

The impetus to examine this topic has several further reasons. First, although deemed "peripheral to understanding the Union's future development,"[34] the Common Agricultural Policy still constitutes a significant proportion of the overall EU budget: it accounts for 31% for the period between 2021–2027 (though its share is declining because 40–50 years ago it was more than 60% of the overall budget).[35] Second, as *Grant* put it in 1997, "the interaction [of the Common Agricultural Policy] with other policy areas tends to be poorly developed."[36] This is also true for today, and in some respects, the situation has become even more complex with the intensifying emphasis on environmental considerations. The interrelationship of the agricultural sector with, on one hand, competition policy, and, on the other hand, sustainability is given limited attention in US academic circles, too. There, the connection between antitrust and sustainability has not been brought to the fore, except in very few academic writings. Conversely, the literature in the EU is continuously expanding in this regard with more activities and developments. This divergence between the two continents can be traced back to the approach of competition agencies. While the European Commission (EC), as the EU competition authority, has been dealing with sustainability considerations in the last few years, and this standpoint also appears in binding EU legal acts as well as soft law documents, the US enforcers – the Federal Trade Commission (FTC) and the Department of Justice (DoJ) – have not been actively engaged in these discussions.

The linkage between agriculture and sustainability runs on a different path. Scholarly literature is vast on both sides of the Atlantic, however, obviously, not by lawyers. Still, I am of the opinion that the legal viewpoint has relevance on this subject, taking into account the undeniable need of legal scholars to build upon extant academic literature beyond law, such as economics and environmental science.

The book, therefore, aims to fill this gap as regards these three areas: agriculture, sustainability and competition. The prerequisite for mapping their interdependence altogether is to explore and conceptualise the connection in pairs: between agriculture and sustainability, agriculture and competition and sustainability and competition. The complete understanding of the three can only come afterwards.

As a consequence of this positioning of the book, it may be useful to note the audience to whom I aim to address my discussions. Although seemingly a niche topic, the questions posed are of relevance to the representatives of several disciplines and policy areas.

34 Wyn Grant, *The Common Agricultural Policy* (Macmillan Press 1997) 1.

35 European Parliament, 'Financing of the CAP: Facts and Figures' (Fact Sheets on the European Union 2024).

36 Grant (n 34) 1.

First and foremost, I attempt to contribute to the debate of competition lawyers about sectoral regulations, antitrust exemptions and the boundaries of antitrust. In particular, my competition law-related aim lies in the better understanding of agricultural markets, their unique problems and the possible solutions thereof.

My discussion is centred around the market of primary agricultural production and the connection of this market with its input providers as well as its buyers. The reason for this is simple. At the core of agricultural policy are agricultural producers and farmers. I use these expressions as synonyms. As much as I can, I deliberately distance myself from using ideologically coloured phrases, such as the term 'peasants' by the food sovereignty movement. Of course, where this formulation adds to the meaning of the discussion, I do not avoid it, however, I would like to remain as neutral as possible to remain located outside the terrain of activist scholars. More generally, my modest contribution as regards antitrust law helps identify and analyse the century-long disputes about the interpretation of antitrust goals as well as certain practical enforcement questions for the sake of the assistance of competition agencies. The limited case law regarding agricultural markets could be broadened by certain steps and recommendations to competition authorities.

Second, food sovereignty advocates, scholars and experts can also use my discussions and arguments. In academia, there are not many, if any, legal scholars who aim to embed the food sovereignty paradigm in the legal system. There are some constitutions in the world,[37] in which food sovereignty is explicitly mentioned, giving some impetus for constitutional lawyers to scrutinise its legal implications. However, academics in economic law have not seized the opportunity to get engaged in food sovereignty-related research, despite the fact that the demands of this policy paradigm are, to a high extent, of economic nature. Food sovereignty proponents can only make their ideas operationalise, if these visions are brought down to the ground with legal proposals, for the law is what forms and affects any social and economic relations with binding force.

Third, as a potential target group, I must mention policy-makers, in particular agricultural and environmental policy-makers. They can draw from the analysis certain development directions that can be made use of in optimalising their respective areas. Furthermore, researchers of agricultural policy and sustainability whose methods are of social science nature can also find more or less connecting points with their research interests.

Overall, I hope that the book offers useful insights to the complex relationship between agriculture, competition policy and sustainability for both practitioners and theorists; not only for those who aim to influence legislative outcomes and who adopt laws, but also who are entitled to enforce them.

Sustainability has turned into a fashionable term in academia and politics.[38] There is no doubt that the transition to a more sustainable world is crucial

37 The most famous and groundbreaking was Ecuador in this regard.

38 See a brief but comprehensive overview: Harald Heinrichs and Frank Biermann, 'Sustainability: Politics and Governance' in Harald Heinrichs, Pim Martens, Gerd Michelsen and Arnim Wiek (eds), *Sustainability Science: An Introduction* (Springer 2016) 129–137.

for the 21st century. Different public policies cannot, and should not, avoid the need to integrate their possible contribution to the discourse on sustainability. Agricultural policy-makers could have felt this expectation since the emergence of intensive discussions on sustainability. The underlying reason is straightforward: agricultural production is attributed with a number of methods and processes that contribute to environmental degradation, and there are many ongoing initiatives aiming to address the likely negative environmental effects of agricultural production and animal husbandry. One example is the recent "nitrogen wars."[39]

The effects of agricultural production on sustainability are often framed within the debate on appropriate farm sizes. And, of course, the aspect of farm size brings with itself the question of productivity levels.[40]

However, there is no consensus whether small or large-scale cultivation is better for the planet. In popular science literature, the issue has been summarised laconically and in a manner, I think, too simplified: "Small farms are inefficient but are more likely to grow healthful foods and might be more environmentally friendly, while large farms are sometimes environmentally unfriendly but raise large amounts of food efficiently and affordably."[41] The reality, nevertheless, is more equivocal. In a literature review, as global average, it was found that yields of smaller farms (less than two hectares) are higher, along with the not so surprising, 'popular' fact that they come with higher biodiversity and crop diversity.[42] According to others, this inverse relationship between farm size and productivity has been proved to be true only for developing economies.[43] The reason behind this phenomenon in low-income countries is labour market transaction costs (the additional costs of hiring more workforce).[44]

Nevertheless, this may suggest that the popularised 'inefficiency' argument in connection with small farms is to be understood rather in terms of the inability of these holdings to provide an appropriate standard of living to their producers, and not necessarily their inability to generate quantities of yields proportionate to their size. This contention is underpinned by the fact that small-scale farmers in rural

39 Paul Tullis, 'Nitrogen Wars: The Dutch Farmers' Revolt That Turned a Nation Upside-Down' *The Guardian* (16 November 2023).

40 See, for example: Jay Dee Atwood and Arne Hallam, 'Farm Structure and Stewardship of the Environment' in Arne Hallam (ed), *Size, Structure, and the Changing Face of American Agriculture* (Routledge 1994) 561–586.

41 Tamar Haspel, 'Small vs. Large: Which Size Farm Is Better for the Planet?' *The Washington Post* (2 September 2014).

42 Vincent Ricciardi, Zia Mehrabi, Hannah Wittman, Dana James and Navin Ramankutty, 'Higher Yields and More Biodiversity on Smaller Farms' (2021) 4 Nature Sustainability 651–657.

43 P.A. Garzón Delvaux, L. Riesgo and S. Gomez y Paloma, 'Are Small Farms More Performant Than Larger Ones in Developing Countries?' (2020) 6 Science Advances 1–11.

44 Andrew D. Foster and Mark R. Rosenzweig, 'Are There Too Many Farms in the World? Labor Market Transaction Costs, Machine Capacities, and Optimal Farm Size' (2022) 130 Journal of Political Economy 636–680.

areas constitute a specific group at risk of poverty because of low incomes.[45] In developing countries, although not covered by the scope of this book, we know that statistics are alarming. "Half of all undernourished people in the world, three-quarters of Africa's malnourished children, and the majority of people living in absolute poverty can be found on small farms."[46]

The European setting is far from clear. Poverty of small-scale farmers is interpreted within the context of rural poverty in general. As put by *Bernard*, in European countries with a higher proportion of farmers, increased rural poverty can be observed, which is not only true for poorer countries but also richer ones, keeping also in mind the fact that in the former the situation is more tense.[47] Although there are different methods to measure poverty, based on 2003 data, 5–14% of the farms can be considered poor in the United States, which is the lowest number in the country's history.[48] Of course, these US data do not take farm size into account, and there are huge differences between the two sides of the Atlantic as well as developing countries.

The average farm size in the United States was approximately 180 hectares in 2019,[49] in the European Union a little bit more than 17 hectares in 2020,[50] and in the poorest 20% of countries worldwide 1.6 hectares.[51] As a general trend, it is found that

> average farm size decreased in most low and lower-middle income countries for which data are available from 1960 to 2000, whereas average farm sizes increased from 1960 to 2000 in some upper – middle – income countries and in nearly all high – income countries for which we have information.[52]

In light of these considerations, it would be too simplified to make general conclusions as regards the connection between farm size, poverty, productivity and the ecological consequences.

45 European Parliamentary Research Service, 'Rural Poverty in the European Union' (European Parliament 2017) 5.
46 International Food Policy Research Institute, 'The Future of Small Farms: Proceedings of a Research Workshop' (IFPRI 2005) vii.
47 Josef Bernard, 'Where Have All the Rural Poor Gone? Explaining the Rural–Urban Poverty Gap in European Countries' (2019) 59 Sociologia Ruralis 386–387.
48 Susan E. Offutt and Craig Gundersen, 'Farm Poverty Lowest in U.S. History' (United States Department of Agriculture, Economic Research Service 2005).
49 United States Department of Agriculture, 'Farms and Land in Farms: 2019 Summary' (National Agricultural Statistics Service 2020).
50 EuroStat, 'Farms and Farmland in the European Union – Statistics' (5 September 2023).
51 Tasso Adamopoulos and Diego Restuccia, 'The Size Distribution of Farms and International Productivity Differences' (2011) University of Toronto Department of Economics Working Paper 411, 2 <www.imf.org/external/np/seminars/eng/2013/spr/pdf/restuccia.pdf> accessed 26 June 2024.
52 Sarah K. Lowder, Jakob Skoet and Terri Raney, 'The Number, Size, and Distribution of Farms, Smallholder Farms, and Family Farms Worldwide' (2016) 87 World Development 16–29.

The scope of this book covers the European Union and the United States, and not developing countries. Although the paradigm of food sovereignty first came to the fore in the framework of the Global South, there have also been attempts recently to "translate and situate the ideologies and goals of food sovereignty into contexts in the global North."[53] This is attempted here in the framework of competition policy and sustainability, concentrating on the agricultural sector.

I have two reasons to delve into this issue as regards the EU and the United States. First, if the food sovereignty movement finds its tone and means to influence the policy-making in the Global North, and well-established methods are construed for the paradigm to become an unavoidable factor in developed countries, these may permeate developing countries, too. Second, and it may sound disappointing but honest, I do not possess the necessary knowledge about the functioning of policy-making in the Global South, my socialisation did not take place there, and a foreign standpoint may seem forced to those who actually live in the Southern Hemisphere and experience everyday life there. My vision would be that, if there is willingness on the side of local scholars, activists and policy-makers, and feasible and actually used policy tools in the spirit of food sovereignty become established in developed countries, with the inclusion of those locals, a kind of transfer process regarding both information and experience may begin, taking into account each and every characteristic of the respective country and adjusting the policy to these local attributes.

Regarding the mode of agricultural production, small farms are advocated by food sovereignty advocates, while large-scale cultivation is preferred by neoliberal policy-making. This would imply that – based on farm size differences – the demands of the food sovereignty movement are easier to get embedded in the European context, and US agriculture rather adheres to neoliberal policy objectives. *Patel*'s claim corresponds with this suggestion.[54]

This viewpoint would, however, be without regard to the organic development of the two continents' agriculture, which – for a long time – had been given before these two conceptual directions emerged at all. The question is not which of the two agricultural policy paradigms is closer to the current framework applied by the EU and the United States, but what better serves the attainment of agricultural policy objectives as well as competition policy objectives. As will be seen in Part II, this is not black and white, because the two public policies can have opposing goals. It is easier to perceive their relationship as a balancing scale. The more preference we add to agricultural policy objectives, the more we may distance ourselves from the attainment of general competition policy objectives, and vice versa. That is to say, trade-offs are necessary, and it would be folly to believe that the regulatory solution chosen will satisfy every need of all interested groups without hurting certain interests of other groups.

53 M. Jahi Chappell and Mindi Schneider, 'The New Three-Legged Stool: Agroecology, Food Sovereignty, and Food Justice' in Mary C. Rawlinson and Caleb Ward (eds), *The Routledge Handbook of Food Ethics* (Routledge 2017) 424.

54 Raj Patel, 'What Does Food Sovereignty Look Like?' (2009) 36 The Journal of Peasant Studies 663.

There are areas in competition policy where it has been supported by scholars and practitioners alike that the basic framework should be adjusted to the emerging trends. This is particularly true for the European Union in connection with the digital sector and sustainability in general. The former has been advanced with the adoption of the Digital Markets Act,[55] which "aims to complement the enforcement of competition law"[56] with fairness and contestability[57] considerations, while the latter is given consideration in a soft law document[58] that puts great emphasis on sustainability agreements in a separate chapter.[59] Not to mention that the agri-food sector has its own sustainability-related exemption from the prohibition of anticompetitive agreements,[60] accompanied by soft-law guidelines issued by the European Commission on the detailed interpretation of the new provisions.[61]

Although it can be regarded as part of the broader technology developments, it is also worth mentioning that the Court of Justice of the European Union (CJEU) was not afraid to find that competition authorities, in the context of abuse of dominance, can examine whether the "undertaking's general terms of use relating to the processing of personal data and the implementation thereof are not consistent with the [General Data Protection Regulation],"[62] where this analysis is necessary to establish the existence of an abuse of dominant position.[63]

Ezrachi points out that the "sense of purity" attributed to antitrust law, which idealistically builds upon only economic considerations, is an illusion. Antitrust law is porous and absorbent, therefore external social or political objectives are taken into account.[64] The examples provided, such as a fair digital sector, sustainability, data protection, underpin this statement.

55 Regulation (EU) 2022/1925 of the European Parliament and of the Council of 14 September 2022 on contestable and fair markets in the digital sector and amending Directives (EU) 2019/1937 and (EU) 2020/1828 [2022] OJ L265/1 (DMA).

56 DMA, preamble (10).

57 DMA, art 1(1).

58 Commission, 'Guidelines on the Applicability of Article 101 of the Treaty on the Functioning of the European Union to Horizontal Co-Operation Agreements' (Communication) [2023] OJ C259/1 (Horizontal Guidelines).

59 Horizontal Guidelines, ch 9.

60 Regulation (EU) No 1308/2013 of the European Parliament and of the Council of 17 December 2013 establishing a common organisation of the markets in agricultural products and repealing Council Regulations (EEC) No 922/72, (EEC) No 234/79, (EC) No 1037/2001 and (EC) No 1234/2007 [2013] OJ L347/671 (CMO Regulation), art 210a.

61 Commission, 'Guidelines on the Exclusion from Article 101 of the Treaty on the Functioning of the European Union for Sustainability Agreements of Agricultural Producers Pursuant to Article 210a of Regulation (EU) No 1308/2013' (Communication) [2023] OJ C/2023/1446 (Article 210a Guidelines).

62 Regulation (EU) 2016/679 of the European Parliament and of the Council of 27 April 2016 on the protection of natural persons with regard to the processing of personal data and on the free movement of such data, and repealing Directive 95/46/EC [2016] OJ L119/1 (GDPR).

63 Case C–252/21 *Meta Platforms Inc and Others v Bundeskartellamt* [2023] EU:C:2023:537.

64 Ariel Ezrachi, 'Sponge' (2017) 5 Journal of Antitrust Enforcement 49–75.

What adds to the question of sustainability is the consideration that, according to the neoliberal viewpoint, agricultural producers with limited financial resources and low income are unlikely to prioritise sustainable methods. Antitrust law alleviations for farmers and the additional protection enjoyed by them beyond antitrust aim to give a helping hand to producers to ensure their fair income, or – at least – this is the declared social objective. So the circle is as follows: if competition law alleviations are made available for farmers and they make use of these possibilities, they may be better off to channel sustainability considerations into their production methods. Given that "[e]nvironmental, social and income goals are inherently interwoven,"[65] one must analyse them in their complexity.

65 Robert Finger and Nadja El Benni, 'Farm Income in European Agriculture: New Perspectives on Measurement and Implications for Policy Evaluation' (2021) 48 European Review of Agricultural Economics 254.

2 Methodology

The methodology used in the book is, on one hand, the analysis of authoritative texts (legal sources, such as legislation and case law),[66] and, on the other hand, the examination of agricultural and competition policy behind them. Law and policy are strongly intertwined regarding the regulation of trade and competition in agricultural and food products, therefore regulation and the policy approaches appearing as the foundation of regulation cannot be sharply separated in all cases during the analysis.

The book is of doctrinal nature in Part IV, while Parts II, III and V are concerned with the two public policies from different perspectives.

By 'doctrinal', I mean that Part IV aims to analyse, define, redefine and systematise legal concepts related to agriculture-related competition law in its broad sense.[67] Legal research is to a great extent dominated by doctrinal research which seeks to answer the question of "what the law is in a particular area."[68] That is, as a lawyer, in the book I must cast my vote also in favour of a method which can be labelled as the "distinctly legal approach to research."[69] As put by *Busse*, it is advisable to collect and order an area of law before it is analysed in detail.[70]

The doctrinal analysis – which is of a hermeneutic and argumentative nature[71] – in Part IV is the basis of comparison between the United States and the European Union. A US–EU comparison shows us the similarities and differences between

66 Philip Langbroek, Kees van den Bos, Marc Simon Thomas, Michael Milo and Wibo van Rossum, 'Methodology of Legal Research: Challenges and Opportunites' (2017) 13 Utrecht Law Review 2.

67 See the critical acclaim of András Jakab to the book *Legal Doctrinal Scholarship* authored by Mátyás Bódig (published by Edward Elgar Publishing in 2021) <www.e-elgar.com/shop/gbp/legal-doctrinal-scholarship–9781788114059.html> accessed 29 June 2024.

68 Ian Dobinson and Francis Johns, 'Qualitative Legal Research' in Mike McConville and Wing Hong Chui (eds), *Research Methods for Law* (Edinburgh University Press 2007) 18–19.

69 Terry Hutchinson, 'Doctrinal Research – Researching the Jury' in Dawn Watkins and Mandy Burton (eds), *Research Methods in Law* (Routledge 2013) 7.

70 Christian Busse, 'Die Sonderrechtstheorie im Agrarrecht – Konzeptionelle Überlegungen zu ihrer Weiterentwicklung' in José Martínez (ed), *Reichweite und Grenzen des Agrarrechts: Gedächtnisschrift für Dr. Wolfgang Winkler* (Nomos 2018) 19.

71 Mark Van Hoecke, 'Legal Doctrine: Which Method(s) for What Kind of Discipline?' in Mark Van Hoecke (ed), *Methodologies of Legal Research: Which Kind of Method for What Kind of Discipline?* (Hart 2011) 4.

DOI: 10.4324/9781003604747-3

common law and civil law legal systems on the issue, being aware of the fact that the European Union has Member States dominantly with civil law legal systems deeply embedded in Roman law traditions. The comparison is analogical in nature (and not genealogical due to the lack of a common ancestor for them), which may result in weaker conclusions.[72]

By comparison, I mean the functional, structural and hermeneutical methods used in comparative law. The functional one, as the name implies, aims to examine which function a certain provision fulfills in a legal system, and how this function is fulfilled in another legal system. Functionality is "the basic methodological principle of all comparative law."[73] As put by *Husa*, "[i]nstead of concentrating on studying particular material and isolated provisions, emphasis should be on the comparison of those specific solutions that each state makes in situations that are practically identical."[74] The structural method is concerned with the question of to which structure a legal norm is embedded in a legal system, and how it differs from the structure of another legal system built around a similar legal norm. The hermeneutical method concentrates on textual interpretation of laws, nevertheless with having continuously in mind that the interpretation is necessarily situated when one turns to foreign legal systems. It is situated because I see legal provisions outside Hungarian law through the pre-understanding of law as I have absorbed my knowledge on law during Hungarian legal education. Furthermore, in a broad sense, my comparison is necessarily related to a given sociopolitical context[75] which shows similarities in all analysed jurisdictions: the market participants of the agricultural sector could successfully lobby for their competition-relevant alleviations because of their unique social role in guaranteeing the population the appropriate quantity of food of appropriate quality.

Of course, functional, structural and hermeneutical methods all interrelate in the course of comparison, therefore it may be difficult to draw a strict dividing line between the methods. The US–EU comparison is rather based on the functional and structural methods than the hermeneutical one.

In principle, I consider law as an instrument to realise policy objectives. This viewpoint comes with a shifted emphasis from extant legal problems rooted in technicalities (and their solutions) towards diverse policy approaches underlying the law: both *de lege lata* and *de lege ferenda*. It is crucial to explore the current legal framework, but not primarily for the sake of a clearer legal doctrine. There are not many conventional legal problems to be solved in this niche area: relevant

72 Geoffrey Samuel, *An Introduction to Comparative Law Theory and Method* (Hart 2014) 57–58, 65–120.

73 Konrad Zweigert and Hein Kötz, *An Introduction to Comparative Law* (3rd edn, OUP 1998) 34.

74 Jaakko Husa, 'Comparative Law, Legal Linguistics and Methodology of Legal Doctrine' in Mark Van Hoecke (ed), *Methodologies of Legal Research: Which Kind of Method for What Kind of Discipline?* (Hart 2011) 215–216.

75 Ioanna Tourkochoriti, 'Comparative Rights Jurisprudence: An Essay on Methodologies: Special Issue – Comparative Law' (2017) Law and Method 2 <https://doi.org/10.5553/REM/.000030> accessed 30 June 2024.

legal provisions and related case law are limited in number. The rules *de lege lata* and those few cases that have interpreted the scant legal norms concern me to the extent they appear as means of attaining communicated policy objectives. That is, the debate surrounding the issue is more abstract in nature, and broader than the pure amelioration of rules in force. This is the reason that a significant part of the book is about understanding the dynamics of divergent policy standpoints, both in the field of competition policy and of agricultural policy.

General competition policy trends necessarily influence all economic sectors, and the respective sector will, of course, adapt to, and process, these developments. Where sector-specific interests are more accentuated and even when there are derogations from general rules, such as in agriculture, changes in general policy directions may appear more intensively, because the general framework is modified, from which sectoral rules derive. This is seen, for example, as regards sustainability. The issue broke into the antitrust law discourse in the EU, and sectoral rules 'overtook in a bend'. To this day, there are no binding antitrust rules on sustainability considerations across sectors, only a soft law guidance that includes the issue. However, Article 210a of the CMO Regulation was adopted, which applies exclusively to the agri-food sector.

Conventional antitrust law tries hard to find its tone in connection with the assessment of sustainability agreements, although – at the EU level[76] – this has not come with the modification of horizontal competition rules, only that of the legally nonbinding evaluation framework in the form of a guidance.[77] Another example is the general direction change in the United States, where – with the arrival of the Neo-Brandeisian approach – competition issues in agriculture have been rediscovered, more intensively than in the four decades of the Chicago School. For example, Biden's Executive Order on Promoting Competition in the American Economy mentions farmers in the very first sentence as being threatened by excessive market concentration.[78] In March 2022, the first 'listening forum' of the two US antitrust agencies was held about the effects of mergers and acquisitions in the food and agriculture sector.[79] Federal Trade Commission Chair Lina Khan also submitted a written contribution to the Department of Agriculture's Advance Notice of Proposed Rulemaking titled "Poultry Growing Tournament Systems: Fairness and Related Concerns."[80] In September 2022, Assistant Attorney General Jonathan

76 On the contrary, see the modified section 2(1) of the Austrian antitrust act (*Bundesgesetz gegen Kartelle und andere Wettbewerbsbeschränkungen – Kartellgesetz 2005*) that declares the following: "Consumers also have a fair share when the benefits arising from improving the production or distribution of goods or promoting technical or economic progress contribute significantly to an environmentally sustainable or climate-neutral economy."

77 See Horizontal Guidelines.

78 President Joseph R. Biden Jr., 'Executive Order on Promoting Competition in the American Economy' (9 July 2021).

79 Federal Trade Commission, 'FTC and Justice Department Listening Forum on Firsthand Effects of Mergers and Acquisitions: Food and Agriculture' (28 March 2022).

80 Written Submission of Federal Trade Commission Chair Lina M. Khan, 'Poultry Growing Tournament Systems: Fairness and Related Concerns (Docket No. AMS-FTPP-22-046).

Kanter said that "the Department [of Justice] [was] committed to fighting for fairness in food systems and protecting American farmers, producers, workers, and consumers from the effects of consolidation throughout the food supply chain."[81] And the list may go on.

Given the broad formulation of antitrust laws, paradigm changes may bring about enforcement changes without legislative changes. This does not mean that legislative amendments never happen (see, for example, Article 210a of the CMO Regulation), but new policy objectives may result in a paradigm shift at the level of law enforcement. Therefore it is worth paying particular attention to new (agricultural and competition) policy developments that precede legislative modifications, if there is need for the latter at all. These are the considerations that have led me to place great emphasis on policy.

What catches the essence of my methodology is a kind of viewpoint attributed to socio-legal studies. As put by *Campbell and Wiles*, it is not the theoretically sophisticated sociology of law, but rather an anti-theoretical way of conducting research for the sake of social engineering.[82] Socio-legal studies seems to be an appropriate choice because of its strong engagement with political activism.[83] The countermovement against the neoliberal agricultural policy status quo, the food sovereignty movement strongly advocates for political and social change, and so does the Neo-Brandeisian school of thought in competition policy. Although the former has achieved so far more moderate results in its own area, the latter has already barged in on the established representatives of the Chicago School and their viewpoint in US competition policy.

Although formulated more than 40 years ago, *Schiff*'s brief summary on the nature of the socio-legal approach is as pertinent as it was in 1976:

> analysis of law is directly linked to the analysis of the social situation to which the law applies, and should be put into the perspective of that situation by seeing the part the law plays in the creation, maintenance and/or change of the situation.[84]

In our context, it is put under scrutiny from a reverse viewpoint, too. That is to say, on one hand, I take a look at the impact of the rules in force on the social situation of agricultural producers, and, on the other hand, at the social situation that called forth the sector-specific competition rules.

81 U.S. Department of Justice, 'Assistant Attorney General Jonathan Kanter Meets with National Farmers Union' (12 September 2022).

82 C.M. Campbell and Paul Wiles, 'The Study of Law in Society in Britain' (1976) 10 Law and Society Review 547–578.

83 Naomi Creutzfeldt, Marc Mason and Kirsten McConnachie, 'Socio-Legal Theory and Methods: Introduction' in Naomi Creutzfeldt, Marc Mason and Kirsten McConnachie (eds), *Routledge Handbook of Socio-Legal Theory and Methods* (Routledge 2020) 3.

84 David N. Schiff, 'Socio-Legal Theory: Social Structure and Law' (1976) 39 The Modern Law Review 287.

There are two facts that frame the economic reality of agricultural production: first, inelastic demand of agricultural products, and second, the lack of market power of agricultural producers. The former fact means that as soon as supply becomes higher than demand, the total revenue of the sector decreases because of falling prices. The latter fact comes from the fact that the level of competition is high between producers, however, processing, wholesale and retail markets are highly concentrated. When a producer wants to sell its products downstream, there are only a few alternatives as regards the buyer. On the contrary, the buyer can buy its input from a high number of competing producers, all resulting in producers being price takers and not price givers.[85] Consolidation takes place not only at processing, wholesale and retail markets, but also at the level of agricultural production because of mechanisation and economies of scale. There are fewer and fewer producers both in the United States and the European Union, and this does not seem to stop. It is worth repeating here that

> [u]nder current development trajectories, the number of farms globally will probably decline from the current 616 million in 2020 to 272 million by the end of the twenty-first century, with average farm size doubling. In some regions, such as Europe and North America, we will see a continued decline from recent history.[86]

Market exit by agricultural producers has a wide variety of drivers. To mention the most evident one: it is not worthwhile for many farmers to continue agricultural production because of low farm gate prices that do not provide an appropriate living for them, in other words, because of insufficient monetary returns.[87] There are limited empirical data, but, for example, local-level research in the United States showed that 15 of 64 dairy farms in Maine had said that their market exit from dairy farming had been imminent.[88] It has also been shown that technical inefficiency is positively correlated with firm exit.[89] Though of different nature, but after Finland's accession to the EU in 1995, exit from farming was encouraged in the country by subsidised early retirement programmes.[90] *Breustedt and Glauben*

85 John B. Penson, Oral Capps Jr., C. Parr Rosson III and Richard T. Woodward, *Introduction to Agricultural Economics* (7th edn, Pearson 2018) 204.

86 Zia Mehrabi, 'Likely Decline in the Number of Farms Globally by the Middle of the Century' (2023) 6 Nature Sustainability, 949–954.

87 Emmanuel Paroissien and Laure Latruffe-Laurent Piet, 'Early Exit from Business, Performance and Neighbours' Influence: A Study of Farmers in France' (2021) 48 European Review of Agricultural Economics 1132–1161.

88 L.A. Bragg and T.J. Dalton, 'Factors Affecting the Decision to Exit Dairy Farming: A Two-Stage Regression Analysis' (2004) 87 Journal of Dairy Science 3092–3098.

89 Simone Pieralli, Silke Hüttel and Martin Odening, 'Abandonment of Milk Production under Uncertainty and Inefficiency: The Case of Western German Farms' (2017) 44 European Review of Agricultural Economics 425–454.

90 Kyösti Pietola, Minna Väre and Alfons Oude Lansink, 'Timing and Type of Exit from Farming: Farmers' Early Retirement Programmes in Finland' (2003) 30 European Review of Agricultural Economics 99–116.

concluded concerning Western Europe that "exit rates are higher in regions with smaller farms and are closely related to production structures."[91]

Without going into more detail here, it is evident that the agricultural sector has been going through intensive concentration, and exit from farming has many reasons, including insufficient monetary returns. My simplifying viewpoint is that – ultimately – exit decisions are based on financial considerations (with the exception of succession and retirement). One can show that the driving force behind a firm's exit is, for example, technical inefficiency, and it will be true. However, it necessarily goes back to the consideration that as a technically inefficient agricultural producer, the respective business cannot compete with more technically developed firms and its revenue will decrease. If one makes a good living even as a technically inefficient farmer, they will not exit farming.

It is no accident that it is a deliberate choice of agricultural policy-makers to openly declare as a stated goal the ensuring of a fair standard of living that – by and in itself – tells a lot about the social situation in which many producers operate.

To narrow the broad spectrum of socio-legal studies, or what the term may entail at all, it must be emphasised that the issue that I examine is concerned with the market behaviour of undertakings.[92] That is, within the terrain of socio-legal studies, I concentrate on the social aspects of market behaviour, which may be "an important supplement to law and economics."[93] The discipline of law and economics dominated antitrust policy for four decades in the United States, thanks to the intellectual powerhouse located at Chicago University. What is interesting from my point of view, and this has its effects on methodology, is that while competition policy and its long-reigning underpinnings in the form of law and economics are associated with right-wing economists, socio-legal studies are considered rather left-leaning.[94]

And even this chosen methodology reflects my objective, which I mentioned earlier, that we should converge the viewpoints of different interest groups to one another, and not talk past each other.[95] This is accentuated also by *Donahue*, encouraging the representatives of socio-legal studies to pose the question of what they can learn from law and economics, and, of course, vice versa. Law-and-economics scholars should take also this kind of attitude towards the more socially oriented discipline.[96]

91 Gunnar Breustedt and Thomas Glauben, 'Driving Forces Behind Exiting from Farming in Western Europe' (2007) 58 Journal of Agricultural Economics 115–127.

92 The word "undertaking" is used here in its antitrust law sense.

93 Richard Craven, 'Socio-Legal Studies and Economics' in Naomi Creutzfeldt, Marc Mason and Kirsten McConnachie (eds), *Routledge Handbook of Socio-Legal Theory and Methods* (Routledge 2020) 182.

94 Craven (n 93) 182.

95 Lauren B. Edelman, 'Rivers of Law Contested Terrain: A Law and Society Approach to Economic Rationality' (2004) 38 Law & Society Review 182.

96 John J. Donohue III, 'Law and Economics: The Road Not Taken' (1988) 22 Law & Society Review 922.

Therefore, my objective in the book is to prevent both the under-socialised viewpoint of economics and the over-socialised viewpoint of sociology,[97] and in parallel with this approach, to analyse the legal implications of the results deriving from this balanced methodology. Ultimately, since I view law as an instrument to achieve policy objectives, my conclusions and proposals are necessarily of a legal nature. That is, they refer to the current functioning of law enforcement and the impact of the rules in force on this functioning, as well as the possible ways to ameliorate both legislation and enforcement, taking into consideration the endeavour to better contribute to sustainability and agriculture-related goals set by policy-makers.

Both public policies within the scope of the book display this tension, and I hope that the analysis on the social aspects of market behaviour may alleviate the strain, not only within the respective policy field, but also between them. Although this is a simplified approach, the paradigms extant in the two public policies may be summarised as regards their related prevailing method in the following way.

It seems that the policy paradigms characterised with a law-and-economics approach (neoliberal agricultural policy and the Chicago School of competition policy) are sieged by the policy paradigms characterised with a socio-legal-studies approach (the food sovereignty paradigm in agricultural policy and the Neo-Brandeisians in competition policy). While the breakthrough has happened in US competition policy, and there are some cracks in the more economic approach in EU competition policy, agricultural policy's food sovereignty paradigm awaits its more intense exploration. The 'challengers' with the desire and endeavour to implement social considerations in competition law analysis (in general) and in the agricultural sector (in particular) necessarily cause a shift of emphasis also in the relationship between the two public policies.

Taking into consideration my limitations in the field of economics, in this regard I rely exclusively on research results already published by esteemed economists, and I do not carry out any original economic analysis on my own. The purpose of this book is not, and cannot be, to elaborate on the incontestable economic foundations of competition in agri-food markets and their relationship towards sustainability. I leave this task to economists. The research underlying the book has been carried out through the prism of a lawyer's spectacles. It means that the book considers economics as crucially important to explore the issue, but the approach taken towards competition in agri-food markets is from the viewpoint of a lawyer who has in mind several noneconomic objectives beyond profit maximisation.

Borrowing from *Anchustegui*: "mindful of my limitations as a non-economist, I have decided to resort to an economically informed legal analysis," however, it does not imply that "economics should be used with a normative effect."[98]

97 See these terms: Mark Granovetter, 'Economic Action and Social Structure: The Problem of Embeddedness' (1985) 91 American Journal of Sociology 481–510.

98 Ignacio Herrera Anchustegui, *Buyer Power in EU Competition Law* (Concurrences 2017) 12.

During the research, I faced two difficulties. First, the quantity of academic scholarship that directly scrutinises competition rules (law or policy) applying to agri-food markets – be it doctrinal or practical analysis – is limited. Of course, there are some publications on unfair trading practices and agricultural antitrust exemptions, the findings of which have been used in this book, however, I must be honest: the issue plays a marginal role in competition law discourse. Second, the food sovereignty paradigm puts a great emphasis on fairer trade and competition in its agenda, but so far it has not elaborated the details of it, and moreover, its implications for *legal regulation*. The reason for this is simple. Food sovereignty proponents in academia are not lawyers; they are the representatives of other disciplines, such as sociology, political economy, agrarian studies, political science, development studies, etc. All of these could have resulted in the amount of scholarship cited – be it legal or nonlegal – in the book being relatively low, but quite the contrary. Besides the sources directly relevant to my issue, to a significant extent I have used general scholarship on competition law and policy, agricultural law and policy as well as food sovereignty, which have been of great use to my niche topic.

As a consequence of the limited amount of scholarship on competition issues in agri-food markets, I aim to provide a modest contribution to, on one hand, academic scholarship on agriculture-specific competition law and policy, and, on the other hand, the discourse on agricultural policy paradigms' competition perceptions.

3 Structure

The book consists of four main parts after the introduction and before the summarising and concluding remarks. These four parts all contribute to one or another aspect of the interrelationship between competition (law and policy), sustainability and the agricultural sector. To fully understand the uneasy complexity between the three areas, we must discover, first, the respective 'bilateral' connection between each of these aspects.

Parts II, III and IV concentrate on the currently dominant policy paradigms, with some brief exceptions in the form of references to food sovereignty, which are crucial to better frame the examination. This means that the analysis necessarily takes place in light of the prevailing neoliberal agricultural policy paradigm and the economic-centred competition policy paradigm. The competing agricultural policy paradigm in the form of the food sovereignty movement only comes to the picture in detail in Part V, where its diverse approach towards the existing problems is displayed.

Part II is concerned with the clash of public policies, meaning that I investigate the agricultural sector based on competition-related considerations, as well as the notion of competition from a sectoral perspective, that of the agricultural sector. The former aims to answer how the sector and its objectives are approached by general competition policy, while the latter section follows a reverse approach; it is interested in the way agricultural policy takes a look at competition.

The objective of Part II is to shed light on the dissonant standpoint that these public policies offer to one another. The clash of public policies, however, must be resolved. Borrowing from political economy analyses,[99] the resolution between these areas is necessarily cumbersome, because differences in viewpoints arise from contrasting interests and values. Agricultural policy-makers have their own interests and values and so do competition policy-makers. While diverging interests can be converged to each other through bargaining and trade-offs, values constitute such an established feature of one's identity that they are painful and challenging to give up in policy-making processes. That the debate between competition and agricultural

99 Koen Deconinck, 'Facts, Interests, and Values: Identifying Points of Convergence and Divergence for Food Systems' in Danielle Resnick and Johan Swinnen (eds), *The Political Economy of Food System Transformation: Pathways to Progress in a Polarized World* (OUP 2023) 32–53.

DOI: 10.4324/9781003604747-4

policy has not calmed down since the appearance of antitrust in the late 19th century can be explained by the distinctive values which each of the two represents. By the same token, I think that my primary task is not to force one viewpoint to the other group, but to delve into their different motivations and help policy-makers understand the incentives of other actors in the policy-making process, who probably aim to achieve various objectives. I do not offer a political economy analysis in this regard, nevertheless, I take into account the considerations that are extant in the literature. Moreover, at the end of Part II, I am obliged to scrutinise the state of play as regards the relationship between these two public policies. The current situation shows that the agricultural sector enjoys specific treatment from the viewpoint of competition policy and law, which is a justified, unambiguous and bespoke regime, at least partly, fit for the sector's needs from an agricultural policy perspective.

The policy choice and value judgment that gives preference to the agricultural sector over conventional competition considerations is obviously reflected in the regulation of agri-food markets. The laws in force governing competition in the agricultural sector are analysed in detail in Part IV.

Before the in-depth legal analysis of rules in force, in Part III there is a separate section dedicated to sustainability in general, as well as its relationship to, on one hand, the agricultural sector, and, on the other hand, to competition law and policy. Though not completely uncontested, the three-pillar approach towards sustainability serves as a basis to further investigate the notion's connections with agricultural and competition policy. To be more exact, this means that not only the ecological but also the social and economic pillar of sustainability are theorised within the framework of competition policy as well as of agricultural policy. Although ecological sustainability seems the most obvious to connect to competition law and policy and the agricultural sector, I also aim to interpret both the social and economic pillars in the context of these two areas. While the literature on sustainability and the agricultural sector is plentiful and dates back to the beginnings of the sustainability discourse of the 1980s, the possible contribution of antitrust law to sustainability efforts and objectives has only emerged in the last few years, and dominantly only in the European Union and its Member States, and not in the United States. American authors explain this reluctance of the US antitrust community (of both enforcers and academics) with two reasons: first, the 'politicised nature' of this debate, and, second, the prevalent Neo-Brandeisian viewpoint of antitrust agencies (Federal Trade Commission and the Antitrust Division of Department of Justice) that more competition necessarily comes with environmental and social benefits.[100] The latter suggests that the question of whether antitrust law should contribute to sustainability (at all) arises in a general context, and it does not bring with itself new (soft and hard) laws. That

100 Denise Hearn, Cynthia Hanawalt and Lisa Sachs, 'Antitrust and Sustainability: A Landscape Analysis' (2023) Columbia Center on Sustainable Investment and Sabin Center for Climate Change Law, 8 <https://ccsi.columbia.edu/content/antitrust-and-sustainability-landscape-analysis> accessed 22 June 2024.

is to say, the relationship between sustainability and antitrust is rather framed, if framed at all, in the context of antitrust law objectives.

With regard to the intersection of the three areas, it is worth noting that although not explicitly mentioned and communicated, social and economic sustainability also play a role in competition regulation of agri-food markets. By it, I mean that agricultural policy objectives are present concerning the sector's competition policy. What clearly appears at the level of legal regulation is the ecological pillar of sustainability in governing competition of agri-food markets.

Part IV investigates the regulation *de lege lata* in order to explore its strengths, weaknesses, opportunities and threats. First, I examine rules in force that are about competition in agri-food markets (without sustainability relevance), and second, this is complemented with the sustainability aspect. The latter, however, excludes the general (non-sectoral) laws at the intersection of competition law and sustainability, despite the fact that the European Commission has been active also in this regard. Although not only general but also agriculture-specific competition rules (including both legally binding norms and soft law) exist with sustainability considerations in the EU, I concentrate only on the sectoral laws. The situation is different in the United States, where there are sectoral antitrust rules dedicated to agriculture, but sustainability has not come to the fore as a likely factor that should be respected concerning the competitive process: neither in a sector-neutral, nor in a sector-specific way.

In Part IV it becomes visible that competition regulation in agri-food markets goes beyond the conventional realm of antitrust. Besides antitrust exemptions that are applicable to certain market participants of the agricultural supply chain, there are prohibitions to be taken into account and to be respected by buyers and sellers of agricultural produce. This additional protection provided typically for farmers are not efficiency based like antitrust, but fairness driven. Because of this very feature, the regulatory solution that is based upon a certain list of unfair trading practices is often criticised by antitrust lawyers for its inefficiency, which may run counter to antitrust objectives.

Part V aims to synthetise agricultural policy paradigms and competition law schools of thought. As can be seen in Part II, the dominant conceptual framework in agricultural policy is of neoliberal nature, which has prevailed since the 1980s. However, at the turn of the 21st century, a new paradigm started to emerge, namely that of food sovereignty. This movement contests the central tenets of neoliberal agricultural policy and attempts to appear as an alternative voice in the political arena, typically at the international level. In this Part, first, I display the perceptions of neoliberal policy-making on competition and sustainability, and, second, those of the food sovereignty advocates. Then, I scrutinise whether these perceptions can be brought into line with any of the extant competition law schools of thought. The approach these two agricultural policy paradigms take towards competition and its regulation can only be reconstructed through the careful perusal of their demands concerning agricultural markets, their recommended ways of dealing with farm problems as well as the policy means they campaign for. Of course, the analysis is much easier in connection with neoliberal policy-making, because it is a mature and developed conceptual framework not only for agricultural markets but also the whole economy in general. Nevertheless, there are valuable policy documents that shed light on food sovereignty's take on competition; the three food sovereignty definitions elaborated on earlier may also give a helping hand in this regard. One must not forget, however, that the paradigm of food sovereignty is still developing, and in many aspects it is theoretically underdeveloped. The analysis on the compatibility of agricultural policy paradigms with competition schools of thought is framed in the discourse on competition law objectives, given that they determine to a high extent the approach of competition law regimes to both economic and noneconomic issues. Ultimately, Part V is closed with a brief outlook on the ideas of ordoliberalism about agriculture.

It is extremely important to record that I refrain from supporting either side with an activist approach. My inquiry into these debates is purely of an academic nature. The issue of the relationship between the agricultural sector and markets is heavily politicised, and different political sides seize on the events to get sympathisers and, thus, votes. I lay down here that I do not use the expressions 'neoliberal policy-making' or 'food sovereignty paradigm' as stigma on their representatives; I only seek to delineate these two groups of ideas, concepts and patterns and to label them for the sake of easier understanding of the paradigms. The political borders, however, are not completely clear. Laconically and in a simplified manner, the neoliberal attitude towards markets (and their regulation, or – rather – their nonregulation) is of a right–wing nature. On the contrary, the food sovereignty paradigm is rather leftist. As regards the core ideals of these two ways of thinking, the antagonism can be perceived as the battle between efficiency and fairness. While neoliberalism, in general, argues for free market policies on the assumption that markets without state intervention tend to increase economic efficiency, and, thus, contribute to overall welfare, food sovereignty is concerned that (agricultural) markets without state intervention result in unfair outcomes.

With an example the strong political determinations of these paradigms may be illustrated well: the 'nitrogen war' in the Netherlands and the farmers' protest coming with it already mentioned previously was heavily criticised by food sovereignty advocate *Jan Douwe van der Ploeg*. He saw hypocrisy in the demonstration, for "Dutch farmers, especially the larger ones, who [were] out on the streets, are probably among the most cosseted on the planet: receiving mind-boggling subsidies from the European Union's Common Agricultural Policy." *Van der Ploeg* attributes the turmoil to right-wing demands by agribusinesses.[101] It goes beyond Europe to make a connection (an alliance) between rightist parties and farmers protesting against carbon reduction schemes; another example is New Zealand.[102] Furthermore, it is articulated in many cases that right-wing parties "piggyback on"

101 Jan Douwe van der Ploeg, 'Right Wing Farmers' Protests in the Netherlands' (*Agrarian Conservations*, 2 July 2022) <www.peasantjournal.org/news/jan-douwe-van-der-ploeg-on-right-wing-farmers%E2%80%99-protests-in-the-netherlands/> accessed 9 March 2024.

102 Lucy Craymer, 'New Zealand Farmers Set for Right-Wing Protest Vote over Climate Change Policies' *Reuters* (27 September 2023).

farmer protests.[103] It is not uncommon to make a link between these protests supported by right-wing populist parties and the neoliberal agenda that these parties may represent, as has been shown in the case of India.[104] The pioneers of neoliberal politics, Conservative prime minister of the United Kingdom Margaret Thatcher and Republican president of the United States Ronald Reagan were the leaders of right-wing parties, thus it comes as no surprise that

> [t]he Anglo-American scholarship has long assumed that right-wing political parties were the natural bedfellows of neoliberal reformers in their first entrée into politics, with third-way variants only emerging in a second phase as a kind of compromise gesture from the social democratic left.[105]

The discrepancy arises here. Though right-wing political parties following a neoliberal agenda are eager to bolster farmers' protests against environment-friendly policies that may decrease the financial support of agricultural producers, the ideology of those same parties rests on free market principles.

Although the food sovereignty movement is considered "left-wing progressive agrarian populism,"[106] which aims to contest the existing neoliberal agricultural policy agenda, still the right-wing parties that can be more easily associated with neoliberal policy-making are the ones that embrace farmers' protests. The overlap has already been identified, for right-wing politicians are apt to operate with a kind of agrarian phraseology expressing their support for smallholders, local supply chains as well as sustainability efforts, which are prima facie left-wing issues to address.[107] The blurred lines are even more evident, when it comes to the functioning of markets and competition. Not to mention that the food sovereignty movement's choice to include 'sovereignty' in its name makes it confusing to position the paradigm's side on the political spectrum.

Part V tries to disentangle all these factors, and provide an analysis about and a way out from the chaos of rhetoric and terminology. This is necessary to find which agricultural policy paradigm is suitable to cling to a certain competition law school of thought and find in it its ally in realising its objectives.

Part VI includes my general conclusions on agri-food markets and their regulation, the conceptualisation of the food sovereignty paradigm with ordoliberal

103 Camille Gijs and Bartosz Brzeziński, 'Europe's Right Wing Piggybacks on Dutch Farmer Protests' *Politico* (29 July 2022).

104 Rakib Akhtar, 'Protests, Neoliberalism and Right-Wing Populism amongst Farmers in India' (2022) 50 The Journal of Peasant Studies 2457–2477.

105 Damien Cahill, Melinda Cooper, Martijn Konings and David Primrose, 'Introduction: Approaches to Neoliberalism' in Damien Cahill, Melinda Cooper, Martijn Konings and David Primrose (eds), *The SAGE Handbook of Neoliberalim* (SAGE Publications 2018).

106 Natalia Mamonova and Jaume Franquesa, 'Right-Wing Populism in Rural Europe: Introduction to the Special Issue' (2020) 60 Sociologia Ruralis 704.

107 Mamonova and Franquesa (n 106) 706.

competition policy and some proposals on the regulation of competition in agri-food markets in light of the demands of the food sovereignty movement.

Another note must be made here. Being aware of the complexity of the issue that I aim to examine and the number of strands encompassing the relationship between agriculture, competition and sustainability, I attempt to navigate the readers through the multifaceted analysis by key takeaways of no more than three of four sentences after the end of chapters or subheadings. These important outcomes of the respective analyses provide simplified milestones, and constitute clear boundaries, to proceed in the later dissection of the issue. The milestones are built on those milestones that precede them. The takeaways do not fit perfectly into the structure, by which I mean that not every chapter or subheading is followed by them. I use them only when I feel that a key message should be delivered to provide the smooth continuance of the investigation.

4 Delimitation

Although I take a totally different approach from *Gerber*'s, his clarifying ambition is relevant here. As an analogy from him, "[m]y use of the term 'competition law' deserves comment."[108] Within the framework of the book, by 'competition law' not only those rules are understood which are connected to the restrictions of competition (antitrust rules) but also – to a certain extent – those which aim to ensure the fairness of competition and which regulate trade between undertakings. The reason for the inclusion of both antitrust and trade regulation within the book is that they are strongly intertwined and they complement each other to control and direct competition in agri-food markets.

This implies that throughout the book competition law is used in a broader sense than antitrust law. That is to say, in the book, the term 'competition law' includes both antitrust and regulation. By antitrust, I mean the provisions on anti-competitive agreements, abuse of dominance and merger control. By the term 'regulation', I mean those provisions which do not necessarily require evidence of negative effects on competition to be proved but which are strongly related to the competitive environment. One example of this is the regulation on unfair trading practices (UTPs).

Therefore, 'antitrust law' and 'competition law' are not used as synonyms in the book. Antitrust law covers a narrower scope of conduct, while competition law covers a broader one, also including antitrust.

These legal instruments are not analysed through their general provisions. The book seeks to find their sector-specific provisions behind which agricultural policy objectives emerge. Besides the vast number of academic literature as a possible explanation, this is also the reason why, beyond sector-specific rules, I do not delve into the general (sector-neutral) antitrust assessment of sustainability agreements in Part IV.

It is crucial to delimit the scope of the book as to what I understand by the term 'agri-food' products, for the examination is limited to those competition rules that are in connection with agricultural policy objectives, and thus, with agri-food products. One of the starting points when determining these products is the list referred to in

108 David J. Gerber, *Law and Competition in Twentieth Century Europe* (OUP 1998) 4–5.

DOI: 10.4324/9781003604747-5

Article 38 of the Treaty on the Functioning of the European Union (TFEU).[109] The products in this list are those that are subject to the Common Agricultural Policy (CAP).[110] The other starting point is the definition of food in Regulation (EC) No 178/2002: food (or foodstuff) means any substance or product, whether processed, partially processed or unprocessed, intended to be, or reasonably expected to be ingested by humans. It also includes drink, chewing gum and any substance, including water, intentionally incorporated into the food during its manufacture, preparation or treatment. Nevertheless, it does not cover feed, live animals unless they are prepared for placing on the market for human consumption,[111] plants prior to harvesting, medicinal products, cosmetics, tobacco and tobacco products, narcotic or psychotropic substances, residues and contaminants.[112] Although tobacco and tobacco products and those live animals which are not prepared for placing on the market for human consumption are not foodstuffs pursuant to Article 2 of Regulation (EC) No 178/2002, live animals in general, as well as unmanufactured tobacco and tobacco refuse can be found in Annex 1 of TFEU, therefore they are considered agri-food products and, thus, are included within the scope of the analysis.

There is a serious limitation this approach has. Agricultural and food sectors are so diverse and complex that it is difficult to make generalised conclusions for *the* agricultural and food sector. More plausible findings could be made on a certain subsector, because it is not irrelevant that the discussions are about, for example, the poultry, wheat, coffee or tomato sector. Each subsector, which can be deemed agricultural, has its own peculiarities. The intensity and forms of competition, the vulnerability of producers, the extent of vertical integration and that of horizontal concentration all vary subsector by subsector. And still, agricultural antitrust exemptions both in the EU and the United States apply to agriculture in general, and not a certain subsector of it. There is no differentiation between subsectors. The US exemption generally refers to "the persons engaged in the production of agricultural products," while the EU covers conducts related to "the production of, or trade in, agricultural products." That is to say, my generalised approach to *the* agricultural and food sectors is based on the standpoint antitrust legislation has chosen. It does not, however, mean that there are no provisions only applying to certain subsectors; it is enough to think of the Packers and Stockyards Act in the United States, or some provisions of the single common market organisation on the milk and milk products sector in the EU.

One further remark is of high importance. The terms 'agricultural producers' and 'farmers' are used as synonyms in the book. Law is necessarily generalising in nature,

109 Consolidated version of the Treaty on the Functioning of the European Union [2012] OJ C 326/47 (TFEU), Annex I.

110 TFEU, art 38(3).

111 For example, that is why the Packers and Stockyards Act is included in the analysis.

112 Regulation (EC) No 178/2002 of the European Parliament and of the Council of 28 January 2002 laying down the general principles and requirements of food law, establishing the European Food Safety Authority and laying down procedures in matters of food safety [2002] OJ L31/1 (Food Regulation), art 2.

therefore it is unfit to indicate, express and differentiate between the great variety of social groups which are covered by these terms. By the terms I mean people living in either rural or urban areas who make their living (completely or in part) from agricultural production, operate – typically – small and medium-scale farms, have their own land, market their produce for generating profit, irrespective of whether or not they employ labourers working for them. In general, this lax limitation refers to – small and mid-sized – family farms in the context of the Global North. My generalisation, however, evidently has defects, but legislation, law enforcement and legal doctrine are different from disciplines like agrarian political economy, political ecology, social anthropology, development studies or sociology. I need to treat producers as homogeneous to make the analysis easier, and I leave the task of scrutinising their heterogeneity for the previously mentioned disciplines.

The book does not address competition-related rules of public law nature, i.e., provisions on state aid. There is one exception in subheading 10.3 of Part III: this is reasonable to get included to demonstrate the primary means of greening agricultural policy – environmental criteria adopted in state aid schemes. That is to say, I engage in this analysis not because of competition relevance, but the better understanding of the relationship between agricultural policy and sustainability.

By using the terminology employed in EU law, the book encompasses competition rules applying to undertakings[113] and further competition-related regulation, but does not involve competition rules on aids granted by states.[114] The scope of the research covers exclusively sector-specific rules which regulate and control competition between undertakings and, in addition, behind which agricultural policy objectives appear. Therefore, rules on state aid with agricultural policy relevance are not discussed. The amount of legal literature has continuously been increasing on this topic, in contrast with the academic publications on agriculture-related competition rules of private law nature. It means also that those state measures which, for example, regulate the purchase of agricultural surplus by the state from producers are out of scope, too.

I must also mention that the book does not cover those provisions which are "crisis measures," that is to say, which only apply in crises (for example, the pandemic or serious animal diseases) with such impacts on markets that do not come to the fore under general economic circumstances, "in peacetime."[115]

Moreover, I neither deal with nor analyse the detailed rules on the recognition and functioning of producer organisations; I take it for granted that they are a means of significant importance to strengthen the bargaining power of agricultural producers when it comes to selling agri-food products downstream. I concentrate on those competition-related rules which are relevant for them when they appear

113 In German literature, it is expressed by the term "unternehmensbezogene Vorschriften." See Ines Härtel, '§ 7 Agrarrecht' in Mathias Ruffert (ed), *Europäisches Sektorales Wirtschaftsrecht* (1st edn, Nomos 2013) 437.

114 In German literature, it is expressed by the term "staatsbezogene Vorschriften." See Härtel (n 113) 437.

115 For a crisis cartel, see: C–209/07 *Competition Authority v Beef Industry Development Society Ltd and Barry Brothers (Carrigmore) Meats Ltd* [2008] EU:C:2008:643.

as suppliers on the relevant market. That is, I concentrate on substantial and not procedural provisions.

All of the aforementioned results in – based on the conduct covered by the research – the book aiming to position itself in a system which, on the one hand, addresses antitrust, and, on the other hand, regulation. Their relationship is not completely clear, for regulation has competition relevance, and vice versa, antitrust law is none other than a subsystem of regulation.

5 Doctrinal fundamentals

As the previous chapter shows, there are some overlaps between agricultural and food products. The material scope of sector-specific competition rules, that are analysed in detail in Part IV, not only cover the 'output' of primary agricultural production, that is to say agricultural produce without any processing, but also products that are processed for use as food using the agricultural produce. By this token, it is worth taking a look at some doctrinal fundamentals as regards agricultural and food law.

First, although these two areas of law were strictly separated in the past, nowadays "[t]his legal separation of spheres has been losing its clarity in the face of more complex interfacing in the field of foodstuffs (agricultural products and further processed foods)."[116] *Ines Härtel* consequently uses the term 'agri-food law' to include in her analysis both agricultural law and food law, as well as their intersections. The strong connection between agricultural law and food law can be illustrated from the viewpoint of food law. According to secondary EU law, 'food law' means the laws, regulations and administrative provisions governing food in general, and food safety in particular, whether at the community or national level; it covers *any stage of production*, processing and distribution of food, and also of feed produced for, or fed to, food-producing animals.[117] By looking at it through the lens of agricultural law, it is obvious that primary agricultural production is the first step towards food, and – in many cases – integrated value chains do not make the separation of vertical levels entirely possible.

However, it is a common standpoint, too, that food law is treated as one part of agricultural law.[118] An interface between agricultural and food law can be drawn up from the viewpoint of, for example, Hungarian agricultural law doctrine. It is generally accepted that Hungarian agricultural law distinguishes five subject matters of regulation. These are the following: (a) agricultural activity, (b) agricultural

116 Ines Härtel (ed), *Handbook of Agri-Food Law in China, Germany, European Union: Food Security, Food Safety, Sustainable Use of Resources in Agriculture* (Springer 2018) 2.

117 Food Regulation, art (3)1.

118 Horváth Gergely, 'A környezetjog és az agrárjog közeledése, találkozása és metszete a magyar jogrendszerben [The Approaching, Meeting and Overlapping of Environmental Law and Agricultural Law in the Hungarian Legal System]' (2007) 48 Állam- és Jogtudomány 2, 335.

DOI: 10.4324/9781003604747-6

producer, (c) agricultural holding, (d) agricultural product and food[119] as well as (e) rural areas.[120,121] As can be seen, agricultural products are in the same group as food products. These two categories are mentioned separately as one of the subject matters, but they have many overlaps.[122]

Going back to the EU level, pursuant to Article 38 TFEU, the term 'agricultural products' means the products of the soil, of stock farming and of fisheries and products of first-stage processing directly related to these products. Besides this definition, Annex I of the TFEU enumerates the products referred to in the CAP determined by the TFEU. As already mentioned, Regulation (EC) 178/2002 defines the term 'food'. It means any substance or product, whether processed, partially processed or unprocessed, intended to be, or reasonably expected to be ingested by humans.[123] As illustrated by, on one hand, these two definitions and, on the other hand, the list in Annex I, agricultural products and foodstuffs are overlapping categories. From the aforementioned, a clear conclusion can be made that handling agricultural law and food law under the common term 'agri-food law' is well founded both from the perspective of agricultural law and that of food law. This approach has strong EU law foundations, but it can also be underpinned from the perspective of national agricultural law doctrine. 'Agri-food law' is not an isolated expression. Among others, it has increasingly been used by Italian legal literature,[124] and the phrase has appeared in Germany, too.[125]

Also reserving the possibility of separating agricultural law and food law from each other is, however, a must. The common term 'agri-food products' is an appropriate term in the book because I aim to give insights to not only specific

119 Fodor László, *Agrárjog* [Agricultural Law] (Kossuth Egyetemi Kiadó 2005).

120 Szilágyi János Ede, 'Változások az agrárjog elméletében? [Changes in the Theory of Agricultural Law?]' (2016) 11 Miskolci Jogi Szemle 1, 41–42.

121 Defining agricultural law based on its subject matters is also used in Italian legal literature. See, for example: Antonio Carrozza, 'L'individuazione del diritto agrario per mezzo dei suoi istituti' (1975) 21 Rivista di diritto civile, 107–178 cited by Mariagrazia Alabrese, 'Agricultural Law from a Global Perspective: An Introduction' in Mariagrazia Alabrese, Margherita Brunori, Silvia Rolandi and Andrea Saba (eds) *Agricultural Law: Current Issues from a Global Perspective* (Springer 2017), 5.

122 Hojnyák Dávid, 'Az agrárszabályozási tárgyak megjelenése az EU tagállamainak alkotmányaiban, különös tekintettel a Magyar Alaptörvényben megjelenő agrárjogi szabályozási tárgyakra [Regulatory Objects of Agricultural Law in the Constitutions of EU Member States, in Particular in the Hungarian Fundamental Law]' (2019) 14 Miskolci Jogi Szemle 64.

123 Food Regulation, art 2.

124 See, for example: Donato Castronuovo, Antonio Doval Pais and Luigi Foffani, *La sicurezza agroalimentare nella prospettiva europea: Precauzione, prevenzione, repressione* (Giuffrè Francis Lefebvre 2014); Alberto Germanò, Maria Pia Ragionieri and Eva Rook Basile, *Diritto agroalimentare: Le regole del mercato degli alimenti e dell'informazione alimentare* (2nd edn, Giappichelli 2019); Ferdinando Albisinni, 'Diritto agroalimentare innanzi alle sfide dell'innovazione' (2020) Rivista di BioDiritto 2, 25–42; or see the academic journal entitled *Diritto agroalimentare* published by Giuffrè Francis Lefebvre.

125 During the European Congress on Rural Law held in Lucerne (Switzerland) on 11–14 September 2013, in the Commission III the term '*Agrarlebensmittelrecht*' was used in the German national report. Furthermore, see the academic journal entitled *Blätter für Agrarrecht* whose declared aim is to deal with the legal issues of '*Agrarlebensmittelrecht*'.

competition-related rules applying to agricultural products but also foodstuffs. In the literature it is a recognised proposition that both agricultural law and food law have to be maintained as autonomous from one another, but – in addition – it cannot be forgotten that their boundaries are getting more difficult to determine.[126] This statement is in parallel with that of *Härtel*, and by using the term 'agri-food products', I express my agreement with these findings. Regarding agri-food law, it must be noted that "agriculture also produces non-food products, which means that agricultural law cannot be dissolved into food law."[127]

As regards the definition of agricultural law, there are two approaches: on the one hand, the functional notion of agricultural law (*funktionaler Agrarrechtsbegriff*)[128] and, on the other hand, agricultural law as a special area of law (*Agrarrecht als Son derrechtsgebiet*).[129,130] The latter refers to a narrower box of rules than the former, yet none of the two standpoints provide clear-cut boundaries for agricultural law.[131] According to the Swiss literature, the choice is a value judgment rather than being based on strong theoretical foundations.[132]

Based on the functional notion of agricultural law, each and every provision can be considered being part of agricultural law which – from a functional point of view – has a specific effect with regard to agriculture and forestry, be it from an area of law determined by typical agricultural interests, or be it from an area of law which has or predominantly has interests other than agricultural ones. With this approach those norms are also pulled into the domain of agricultural law which have no specific nature.[133] For example, within the framework of this standpoint, the general social obligations of property ownership pursuant to Article 14 of German

126 Luigi Russo, 'Dal diritto agrario al diritto alimentare (e viceversa)' (2011) 5 Rivista di diritto alimentare 2 <www.rivistadirittoalimentare.it/rivista/2011-02/RUSSO> 18.

127 Alabrese (n 121) 10.

128 See the representatives of this approach cited by Roland Norer (ed), *Handbuch des Agrarrechts* (Springer 2005) 4: Maximilian Eichler, 'Land- und Forstwirtschaftsrecht' in Viktor Heller (ed), *Rechtskunde* (1st edn, Manz 1975) 9; Gottfried Holzer, 'Zum Begriff und Standort des Agrarrechts in der österreichischen Rechtsordnung' (1982) Juristische Blätter 11–12; Gottfried Holzer, 'Agrarrecht heute. Versuch einer Gegenstands- und Standortbestimmung' (1982) Agrarische Rundschau 1; Gottfried Holzer, *Agrar-Raumplanungsrecht* (Österreichischer Agrarverlag 1981) 20.

129 See the representatives of this approach cited by Norer (n 128) 4: Hans Karl Zeßner-Spitzenberg, *Das österreichische Agrarrecht für Studium und Praxis im Grundriss systematisch dargestellt samt Rechtsquellenverzeichnis* (Agrarverlag 1930); Wolfgang Winkler, 'Agrarrecht' in Volkmar Götz, Karl Kroeschell and Wolfgang Winkler (eds), *Handwörterbuch des Agrarrechts, Band I: Abfallbeseitigungsrecht* (Berlin 1981); Christian Grimm, *Agrarrecht* (3rd edn, C.H. Beck 2004); Rolf Steding, 'Das Agrarrecht: Bedenklichkeiten und Notwendigkeiten seiner Entwicklung' (1994) Neue Landwirtschaft: Briefe zum Agrarrecht 7.

130 Roland Norer, *Handbuch zum Agrarrecht* (Stämpfli Verlag 2017) 8.

131 Roland Norer, *Lebendiges Agrarrecht – Entwicklungslinien und Perspektiven des Rechts im ländlichen Raum* (Springer 2005) 136.

132 Adolf Pfenninger, 'Schweizerisches Agrarrecht: Begriff, Gliederung und Stellung in der Rechtsordnung' (1988) Blätter für Agrarrecht 2, 94.

133 Norer (n 128), 4–5.

Fundamental Law[134] are also important when one analyses the rules on agricultural holdings.[135]

By contrast, in the opinion of the representatives of the paradigm 'agricultural law as a special area of law', only those rules are included in agricultural law which primarily aim to regulate the relations connected to agriculture. These specific provisions applying to agriculture can be divided into two parts: exception norms (*Ausnahmenormen,* i.e., *ius singulare*) and specific norms (*Spezialnormen,* i.e., *ius proprium*). Exception norms are those provisions which deviate from general norms because of the particular circumstances of agriculture,[136] meanwhile specific norms are those provisions which are solely and exclusively adopted for agriculture.[137,138]

Furthermore, another interpretation must be noted from the Hungarian literature, which follows an instrumental approach. According to this, agricultural law is the aggregate of norms aiming to realise agricultural policy objectives. This definition refers to a factor which goes beyond law: agricultural policy. Therefore agricultural law is an instrument of realising agricultural policy objectives.[139]

My approach in the book corresponds to the viewpoint that perceives agricultural law as a special area of law (*Sonderrechtsgebiet*), which means that I analyse only exception norms (for example, the antitrust exemption from the prohibition of anticompetitive agreements) and specific norms (for example, the prohibition of unfair trading practices). Furthermore, I adopt the functional definition that treats law as a means to realise policy objectives. Since I limit the analysis to competition-related rules (both antitrust and regulation), the book is concerned exclusively with the aggregate of legal instruments aiming to realise agricultural policy objectives, created and maintained to regulate the behaviour of undertakings in and the competitive process of the agricultural and food market (see Chapters 12 and 14 of Part IV). As I show in subheading 10.2 of Part III, the current phase of agricultural post-exceptionalism necessarily includes environmental considerations, which strengthens the need to also cover the specific assessment criteria of sustainability agreements between agri-food market players from the viewpoint of antitrust law (Chapter 13 of Part IV).

134 Grundgesetz für die Bundesrepublik Deutschland, Artikel 14.

135 Grimm (n 129) 15.

136 For example VAT provisions applying to only agricultural producers which deviate from the general provisions on VAT.

137 For example land acts.

138 Grimm (n 129) 15.

139 Szilágyi János Ede (ed), *Agrárjog: A magyar agrár- és vidékfejlesztési jogi szabályozás lehetőségei a globalizálódó Európai Unióban* [Agricultural Law: Regulatory Possibilities of Hungarian Agricultural and Rural Development Law in the Globalising European Union] (Miskolci Egyetemi Kiadó 2017) 22.

Part II

The clash between agricultural and competition policy

Part II is the most fundamental building block in the analysis. This is so because the nature of the relationship between the agricultural sector and competition policy has a crucial impact also on how sustainability considerations are treated by competition policy within the context of the agricultural sector. By this, it is meant that – similarly to the liaison between agricultural and competition policy, in which the former is given preferential treatment as regards competition rules – the sector also enjoys competition-related privileges when sustainability considerations come to the picture. Instead of following the sector-neutral assessment criteria of competition law as to sustainability agreements, the agricultural sector's sustainability initiatives are evaluated in a less rigid way than any other sector's. This is analysed in detail in Chapter 13 of Part IV. That is to say, Part II sets the tone for the later examinations. Furthermore, it is necessary to note that the choice of analysing this relationship first is underpinned also by the fact that the interaction (the 'clash') between agriculture and competition policy was the first to emerge. Having in mind that this relationship is not a one-way street, Chapter 6 adds to the analysis by shedding light on the viewpoint of competition policy towards the agricultural sector, then Chapter 7 shows a reversed approach by delving into the standpoint of conventional agricultural policy towards competition. Chapter 8 takes stock of the status quo between these two public policy areas.

The meaning of public policy may vary, so it is reasonable to write a few words about my use of the term. Throughout the book, I mean by it a unique set of measures constructed as a unity within a specific area.[140]

Public policy on agriculture, or agricultural policy, consists of a wide variety of measures somehow related to the agricultural sector. Of course, there is an inexhaustible reservoir of problems and issues that are related to agriculture. Should we produce genetically modified crops? How can we increase the efficiency of irrigation? By what means should agricultural producers be supported in an economic sense? What are the social problems agricultural producers face in rural areas? And the list can go on endlessly.

140 Edward C. Page, 'The Origins of Policy' in Michael Moran, Martin Rein and Robert E. Goodin (eds), *The Oxford Handbook of Public Policy* (OUP 2008) 210.

DOI: 10.4324/9781003604747-7

What this book aims to explore in connection with agricultural policy cannot cover the whole spectrum of these issues, so some limits must be established. The focus is on the aspect of agricultural policy that reflects upon questions of competition, and relating to this, of sustainability considerations. When I speak of competition, I mean it in a microeconomic sense; I am interested in the competition between market actors, and not between countries, and in the way this is influenced by laws. Horizontal competition takes place between agricultural producers – a kind of textbook example of perfect competition. However, it is affected also, on the one hand, by the vertical relationship of producers with their input suppliers and output buyers, and, on the other hand, the intensity of competition between their input suppliers upstream and their output buyers downstream. The question is how agricultural policy imagines the optimal way of competing between producers and their vertical relationships with market actors one level up or down in the food supply chain. The other issue is that, in the given competitive structure, how agricultural producers can contribute better to sustainability objectives through private initiatives.

What must be emphasized is that it would be wrong to suggest an unbreakable consensus among agricultural policy-makers and their interest groups about the handling of these issues. There is a sharp dividing line between those who I call 'neoliberal policy-makers' and 'food sovereignty advocates'. Their deep difference of opinion is posed by many as a global conflict.[141] Neoliberal policy-makers believe rather in free markets than in the regulatory ability of, and necessity by, the state, while food sovereignty advocates would entrust the state with profound supervisory tasks over the proper functioning of agricultural markets. These two approaches, therefore, constitute an internal rupture in agricultural policy.

Turning our attention to competition policy sheds light on a likewise internal rupture in competition policy. When I speak of competition policy, I mean by it a broader area than the conventional framework of antitrust. My view is in accordance with that of *Shelanski* who distinguishes between antitrust and regulation as two possible means of shaping competition and the competitive structure.[142] In *Hovenkamp*'s opinion, limiting competition policy to antitrust rules would "seriously simplify reality." There are statutes outside antitrust that take into account competition policies directly or indirectly.[143] As regards agricultural markets, *Huffman*'s general contention seems fully acceptable and applicable that antitrust is a good alternative to oversee markets, "when efficient outcomes are consistent with larger

141 William D. Schanbacher, *The Politics of Food: The Global Conflict between Food Security and Food Sovereignty* (Praeger Security International 2010); María Elena Martínez-Torres and Peter M. Rosset, 'Diálogo de saberes in La Vía Campesina: Food Sovereignty and Agroecology' (2014) 41 The Journal of Peasant Studies 979–997; Philip McMichael, 'Historicizing Food Sovereignty' (2014) 41 The Journal of Peasant Studies 933–957; Joe J. Wills, *Contesting World Order? Socioeconomic Rights and Global Justice Movements* (CUP 2017).

142 Howard Shelanski, 'Antitrust and Deregulation' (2018) 127 The Yale Law Journal 1922–1960.

143 Herbert Hovenkamp, 'Antitrust's Place in Regulation' (2024) SSRN <https://papers.ssrn.com/sol3/papers.cfm?abstract_id=4841731> accessed 7 July 2024.

social, political, environmental – etc. – goals," while regulation prevails when these outcomes depart from the broader, noneconomic objectives of the society.[144] As can be seen later, the latter holds true for agricultural markets, for there are additional, in particular social and environmental, aims that are expected from the activity of agricultural production.

Conventional antitrust consists of the prohibition of anticompetitive agreements/collusions, of abuse of dominance/monopolisation, as well as merger control. These legal instruments traditionally operate with considerations of economic efficiency, including standards for consumer welfare or total welfare. What goes beyond antitrust but still falls within competition policy as a regulatory tool to influence competition is expressed by the term 'regulation'. The latter may include different kinds of legal interventions with diverse values in mind (see, for example, contestability and fairness in digital markets aimed to achieve the adoption and enforcement of the Digital Markets Act in the EU). What antitrust does not reach with its intervening hands can be addressed by some sort of regulation. Many antitrust lawyers contend the necessity of regulating competition beyond antitrust because of its possible non-efficiency-related goals that can run counter to the efficiency-enhancing ideal of antitrust. The mentioned rupture within competition policy comes to surface when the narrow antitrust framework concentrating on efficiency is attempted to broaden its scope also to reach social (for example, better working conditions) or political (for example, democracy) objectives. While the efficiency-centred antitrust law came to vivid life in the 1980s with the remarkable law and economics scholars of the Chicago School, their paradigm has started to get gradually contested 40 years later with the Neo-Brandeisian school of thought. This is what I call the internal rupture of competition policy.

What I label as the clash of public policies is that – beyond the internal ruptures within the respective public policy areas – there is also a confrontation between agricultural policy and competition policy as regards their general goals. Agricultural policy is primarily, among other things, concerned with the improvement of agricultural producers' standard of living – that is to say, it is producer focused. On the contrary, competition policy serves consumers. The antitrust law standards, however diverse they may be from one another, are aimed at ensuring lower prices, higher quality and a wider variety of consumer choices for end consumers. That is to say, these policy areas approach any interrelated issue between them, such as competition in agri-food markets, from a totally different standpoint.

If we follow the example of this book, the plain example for the confrontation is the following: competition in primary agricultural markets is intense, for there are many agricultural producers who farm the same products. However, who buys agricultural produce, i.e., market participants in the processing, wholesale and retail markets, compete in a much more concentrated situation. There are many farmers from whom processors, wholesalers and retailers can purchase their input.

144 Max Huffman, 'The Shifting Regulation and Competition Interface' (2024) 8 Market and Competition Law Review 15–32.

Conversely, there are only a few processors, wholesalers and retailers to whom farmers can sell their output, and these few potential buyers can pick the most appropriate sellers of farm produce. This, of course, results in an intense competition between producers with low farm gate prices; from a competition policy perspective, because of this intense competition buyers (typically intermediaries) can buy their input at lower cost, and, in theory, they, if pressured by their own horizontal competitors, also pass on this lower cost to their buyers (typically consumers). Competition policy deems this process fruitful because of lower consumer prices. On the contrary, if looked at from the viewpoint of agricultural policy, the process is devastating for agricultural producers whose income may not provide them with an appropriate standard of living. Simply put, while it is in the interest of competition policy to lower farm gate prices, agricultural policy stands in full opposition with it for the sake of higher incomes for producers.

There are shades, or rather ruptures, both in agricultural and competition policy, however, the basic determining factor will always be whether the respective policy area is producer or consumer oriented. The key is to find balance between competing interests.

The complexity of the issue is clearly demonstrated by this dual aspect of the system. On one hand, there are diffusions within the policy areas, and, on the other hand, the relationship between the two policy areas also involves a kind of general confrontation.

In the following chapters I will look into the state of play with regard to the latter aspect, that is, the clash between the public policies, and not the diffusions within the respective policy area. Internal diffusions are analysed both in Part IV with a pure competition law focus, as well as in Part V with a mixed approach covering both agricultural policy paradigms and their perceptions on the ideal way of competition.

6 The agricultural sector from the viewpoint of competition policy

6.1 General remarks

First and foremost, the most important attribute of antitrust policy is its primary focus on (end) consumers. The objectives of the mainstream consumer welfare paradigm are better (lower) prices, higher quality and more choice for consumers. Basically, this should determine the standpoint that antitrust policy also takes towards the agricultural sector, whose beneficiaries, as mentioned later in Chapter 7, are agricultural producers. That is to say, antitrust aims to contribute to consumers being able to buy, for example, apples at the best possible price, the highest quality and from the greatest range of choice. This leads us to antitrust's other highly relevant principle. It is sector neutral, which means that undertakings in each and every economic sector are subject to, and fall under the scope of, antitrust laws. For when agricultural producers carry out an economic activity, they are undertakings in an antitrust law sense, and, in principle, subject to the norms established by antitrust law.

Deriving from the sector neutrality of antitrust law, *Mestmäcker*, one of the most influential ordoliberal thinkers, asserted that sector-specific competition laws demonstrate desires of a certain part of the economy.[145] He also coined the term *verwalteter Wettbewerb*, which can be translated to English as 'administered competition'.[146] This is the antonym of free competition. Based on the concept of administered competition, *Pichler* harshly criticises, for example, the EU directive on the prohibition of unfair trading practices in the agricultural sector and its German implementation, which is labelled by him as a prime example of interest-based politics (*Interessenpolitik*).[147]

In my opinion, this viewpoint does not reflect the reality of policy-making. From a rigid legal standpoint, in particular through the lens of antitrust law, the criticism seems,

145 Ernst-Joachim Mestmäcker, '50 Jahre GWB. Die Erfolgsgeschichte eines unvollkommenen Gesetzes' (2008) 58 Wirtschaft und Wettbewerb 19.

146 Ernst-Joachim Mestmäcker, *Der verwaltete Wettbewerb: eine vergleichende Untersuchung über den Schutz von Freiheit und Lauterkeit im Wettbewerbsrecht* (Mohr Siebeck 1984).

147 Philipp Pichler, 'Die Umsetzung der UTP-Richtlinie ins deutsche Recht. Überblick über ein ordnungspolitisches Ungetüm' (2021) 9 Neue Zeitschrift für Kartellrecht 537.

DOI: 10.4324/9781003604747-8

and may be considered, justified. Nevertheless, the critique will necessarily correspond to the superiority of antitrust law characterised by a sense of purity. *Mestmäcker*'s argument, as a generalised position, against sectoral competition laws is forceful and future proof. Though, if pressed to its borders, it can disregard century-long economic realities that are charateristic of certain sectors, such as of primary agricultural production. It is not mere chance that the sector, since the birth of modern antitrust law, requires special treatment, on one hand, within the framework of antitrust (exemptions from the prohibition of anticompetitive agreements), and, on the other hand, beyond antitrust (regulation). The uniqueness of the sector from an antitrust perspective came to light almost as soon as enforcers started to apply the US antitrust statute, the Sherman Act. This will be analysed in more detail.

Moreover, a doctrinal standpoint to look at competing interests, which appear at the intersection of these two public policies, may also lead us to ignore the real way policy-making takes place at any level.

What is of crucial importance is to mention that in the first years of modern antitrust in the United States, there existed no privilege for the agricultural sector. It only appeared a few years later. The European Union is different in this regard, because even the first founding treaty[148] considered agriculture as part of the economy worthy of special antitrust law treatment.

I see two broad reasons, or rather tendencies, behind the continuous extension of the level of protection for the sector beyond antitrust with regulatory means. First, it is beyond doubt that – in general – the food supply chain has been going through a consolidation trend at many of its levels, in particular at processing and retail levels. Second, it is also evident that in the 1980s, because of its unsustainability that resulted in unmanageable agricultural surpluses, state aid coupled to production started to get abolished gradually. Decoupled state aid, which is calculated based on the area under cultivation and not on the quantity produced, means a predictable and fixed basis among the composition of agricultural income sources, however, above these predetermined amounts, the 'whims' of the market prevail. With this, agricultural producers have become more vulnerable to market forces than before.

My observation that the protection against market forces provided to farmers through state aid policy means before the liberalisation of agricultural markets is attempted to retain by the toolbox of competition policy, that is, by antitrust and regulation. However, the effects of these regulatory protective pillars are much less visible for agricultural producers because of their indirect nature. Still, they constitute a target for criticism by antitrust lawyers and policy-makers owing to the non-efficiency-based nature they represent.

From the viewpoint of the three pillars (prohibition of anticompetitive agreements, abuse of dominance, merger control) of antitrust law, competition problems can arise from different economic scenarios at the different levels of the food supply chain.

Given the large number of competitors at the level of primary agricultural production, agreements seem an appropriate solution to ease the competitive

148 Treaty establishing the European Economic Community.

pressure. In principle, these agreements between farmers, for example, to fix the selling prices of their produce would constitute the infringement of the legal prohibition of anticompetitive agreements. However insignificant their effects would be on the respective market, taking into consideration that price-fixing agreements are anticompetitive by object, these agreements could not be disregarded by the Commission based on the De Minimis Notice in EU antitrust law.[149] The US approach is similar. It establishes a safety zone "when the market shares of the collaboration and its participants collectively account for no more than twenty percent of each relevant market in which competition may be affected." Nevertheless, the safety zone does not apply to per se illegal collusions, such as price fixing.[150] This conflict is resolved by the agricultural antitrust exemptions analysed in detail in Part IV.

At the level of processing, wholesale and retail, markets are typically oligopolistic. There are three to six market players who are in a powerful position against agricultural producers. Nonetheless, within the conventional antitrust framework, these market actors most times do not reach a dominant position. For they are not dominant, the enforcement of abuse of dominance provisions are not set into motion. The threshold of monopolisation in US antitrust is even higher, so the same holds true. Abuse of dominance and monopolisation provisions are embedded, from the standpoint of antitrust agencies, in a setting of in-depth economic analysis concentrating on the exclusionary effects of the conduct under scrutiny. However, the question of whether exclusion has taken place is a concern as regards the competitors of the dominant undertaking. So even if abuse of dominance comes to the picture, it is not truly relevant that the sellers (i.e., agricultural producers) to that dominant undertaking were excluded from the market of primary agricultural production. For these reasons certain jurisdictions either introduced lower-level thresholds for the determination of a dominant position, or circumnavigated efficiency-based antitrust with the adoption of fairness-based intervention possibilities, such as the prohibition of certain unfair trading practices. And here comes the criticism by antitrust lawyers that efficiency (aimed to achieve by antitrust at the highest possible level) is sacrificed at the altar of sector-specific interests.

Merger control, as the ex ante intervention mechanism of antitrust, also does not provide much help to agricultural producers. It is unlikely that mergers and acquisitions at the level of production would reach the notification threshold, and, furthermore, these are quite irrelevant from the viewpoint of agricultural policy. As regards efficiency, bigger farms can be better off according to the basic neoclassical approach, so the fact that companies engaged in agricultural production can merge with one another or acquire each other without prior notification provides

149 Commission, 'Notice on Agreements of Minor Importance Which Do Not Appreciably Restrict Competition under Article 101(1) of the Treaty on the Functioning of the European Union' (Communication) [2014] OJ C291/1 (De Minimis Notice), I/2.

150 Federal Trade Commission and the U.S. Department of Justice, 'Antitrust Guidelines for Collaborations Among Competitors' (2000) 26.

a smooth way to expand. Recently there has been a trend toward consolidation at the production level, and there are fewer and fewer farms both in the EU[151] and the United States,[152] however, this does not arise from a conventional merger wave but rather the situation that inefficient farm holdings exit the market and their plots are bought by other producers.

What can actually raise the concerns of antitrust is the consolidation at processing, wholesale and retail levels. Consolidation of food retail has been in the spotlight in the last few decades,[153] and even certain processing markets have been given particular attention in this regard, in particular in the United States.[154] The merger wave taking place at the intermediary stages of the food supply chain creates worrisome scenarios for agricultural producers who fear that further consolidation weakens their bargaining position even more against their buyers. Added to this is the consolidation of input markets, such as fertilisers, seeds and machinery.[155] Thus, producers may find themselves in a situation where they must bargain with multinational market players operating in oligopolistic markets both downstream and upstream. They are stuck in a perfectly competitive market, but they must buy their input from markets consisting of powerful market actors, as well as sell their output to oligopolistic markets. Merger control could provide a helping hand for farmers, if competition agencies placed a much greater emphasis on the possible effects to the production markets of mergers taking place at the input as well as processing, wholesale and retail markets. This would mean an in-depth analysis of intensifying buyer power downstream and of selling power upstream *post-merger*.

6.2 Competition policy justifications for the intervention

As regards the justifications for the sector-specific competition-related rules applying to agri-food markets, a few thoughts are worth mentioning.

Agricultural antitrust exemptions are related to anticompetitive agreements, which make it possible for agricultural producers and their associations to combine forces and unite their economic power. This statutory possibility, both in the EU

151 Sebastian Neuenfeldt, Alexander Gocht, Thomas Heckelei and Pavel Ciaian, 'Explaining Farm Structural Change in the European Agriculture: A Novel Analytical Framework' (2019) 46 European Review of Agricultural Economics 713–768.

152 See: U.S. Department of Agriculture, 'The Number of U.S. Farms Continues Slow Decline' (2023) <www.ers.usda.gov/data-products/chart-gallery/gallery/chart-detail/?chartId=58268> accessed 16 March 2024.

153 Neil Wrigley, 'The Consolidation Wave in U.S. Food Retailing: A European Perspective' (2001) 17 Agribusiness 489–513; Eliana Zeballos, Xiao Dong and Ergys Islamaj, 'A Disaggregated View of Market Concentration in the Food Retail Industry' (U.S. Department of Agriculture 2023).

154 James M. MacDonald, Michael E. Ollinger, Kenneth E. Nelson and Charles R. Handy, 'Consolidation in U.S. Meatpacking' (U.S. Department of Agriculture 2000).

155 Rebecca Bratspies, 'Owning All the Seeds: Consolidation and Control in Agbiotech' (2017) 47 Environmental Law 583–560; Manuel A. Hernandez and Maximo Torero, 'Market Concentration and Pricing Behavior in the Fertilizer Industry: A Global Approach' (2013) 44 Agricultural Economics 723–734.

and the United States, is crucial for farmers to be able to have countervailing market power against their buyers.

As shown by *Anchustegui*, buyer power has two forms: monopsony power and bargaining power. While the former is inefficient in all cases because of its withholding effect, the latter requires a much more careful analysis whether it has adverse effects on competition.[156] Countervailing power established with the help of the exemption offsets monopsony power,[157] but the exemption is also applicable when farmers face bargaining power which does not necessarily constitute danger to efficiency. Therefore, it seems that the statutory exemption may create a possibility for agricultural producers to have market power against their buyers even in the case when this power faces nothing to countervail. It may be detrimental in a way that consumer prices increase. It is called supervailing power by *Baumer, Masson and Masson*. As can be seen later, for the sake of controlling supervailing power which may arise from the antitrust exemption, US antitrust has its control mechanism in the form of forbidding undue price enhancement.[158] This is missing in EU antitrust.

Based on *Carstensen*'s clustering which distinguishes five categories for antitrust exemptions,[159] three of them may prove to be useful regarding the agricultural sector: first, market or institutional failures, second, wealth transfers and protection from competition, and third, exemptions that improve the efficiency of the enforcement of competition policy. Of these three relevant justifications, only one group seems to be acceptable for contemporary antitrust. It is the group of market failures within which the aforementioned creation of countervailing power can be listed. Countervailing power, first coined by *Galbraith*, enabled by Section 6 of the Clayton Act and the Capper-Volstead Act in the United States and secondary law provisions in the EU, is different from the market power of industrial firms in that it is *the response* "to the power of those to whom they sold their [. . .] products."[160] The concept of countervailing power can be complemented with the consideration of reducing contracting costs.[161] Suppliers of agricultural products do not have market power even in the case when they negotiate terms and conditions jointly. The joint negotiation, however, reduces costs, and could control the business partner in engaging strategic conduct. Another theory, which is listed by *Carstensen* among

156 Anchustegui (n 98).

157 David L. Baumer, Robert T. Masson and Robin Abrahamson Masson, 'Curdling the Competition: An Economic and Legal Analysis of the Antitrust Exemption for Agriculture' (1986) 31 Villanova Law Review 198.

158 Baumer, Masson and Masson (n 157) 201.

159 1. Natural monopoly, 2. Market or institutional failure, 3. Wealth transfers and protection from competition, 4. Exemptions facilitating the transition of industry structure from state ownership or direct regulation to market orientation, 5. Exemptions that improve the efficiency of the enforcement of competition policy. See: Peter Carstensen, 'Economic Analysis of Antitrust Exemptions' in Roger D. Blair and D. Daniel Sokol (eds), *The Oxford Handbook of Antitrust Economics*, vol 1 (OUP 2015) 33–62.

160 John Kenneth Galbraith, *American Capitalism: The Concept of Countervailing Power* (Routledge 1993) 139.

161 Carstensen (n 159) 49.

the justifications to cure market or institutional failures and which is useful for agricultural producers, is the possibility for competitors to cooperate for the sake of creating an efficient market. This is embodied by agricultural cooperatives in the United States and producer organisations in the EU.

The considerations of the group 'wealth transfers and protection from competition' is not what antitrust tolerates and to what it wants to subscribe at all. Simply put, it is related to competition policy but it is not the field of antitrust. *Carstensen* mentions as one argument of this group the conferring of market power to achieve specific, in particular social, goals. Trade regulation provisions, such as the UTP Directive in the EU, aim to contribute to the attainment of increasing the individual earnings, and thus the standard of living, of agricultural producers. Besides this social goal, there are other arguments to appear within this group. The activity of agricultural producers, i.e., agricultural production, is supported because, as put by *Carstensen* in general, "the costs of protection are worth the benefit to some other socially desirable objective."[162] As to the agricultural sector, these other socially desirable goals are perfectly described by the concept of multifunctional agriculture. The protection of environment, the preservation of landscape, as well as rural employment and food security all are important pillars of the agricultural activity, which may be deemed as justifications for the intervention to the competition in agri-food markets. If policymakers are of the opinion that small and medium-sized agricultural enterprises better contribute to the preservation of landscape and environmental protection than large agribusinesses engaged in agricultural production, they may attempt to give a higher level of protection for smaller market participants not to be squeezed out of the market despite the fact that they may be (less) efficient. To this group, one can also add the wealth transfer considerations[163] provided for agricultural producers through sector-specific regulation. Regarding agriculture, it is closely related to the specific social objective of the increasing of producers' standard of living, which is pursued by agricultural policy.

Highly regulated sectors, such as agriculture, may require that not only antitrust agencies but also sectoral authorities have certain powers to contribute to the efficiency of the enforcement of competition policy.[164] A good example is the situation after the implementation of the UTP Directive in Germany, where an agriculture-specific authority (*Bundesanstalt für Landwirtschaft und Ernährung*) makes decisions on unfair trading practices committed against the suppliers of agri-food products.

All in all, it is reasonable to distinguish between, on the one hand, the economic arguments which are suitable to justify agricultural antitrust exemptions, and on the other hand, the arguments which can rather be called upon when one aims to justify other competition-related regulations in agri-food markets. The one and only acceptable antitrust argument for adopting exception norms for the agricultural

162 Carstensen (n 159) 56.
163 Carstensen (n 159) 56.
164 Carstensen (n 159) 58–59.

sector is related to the concept of countervailing power. Its creation by agricultural suppliers has to be made possible to offset monopsony power of buyers. From an efficiency-based viewpoint, it is only acceptable if the buyer power appears as monopsony and not bargaining power. Although the bargaining power of buyers may have adverse effects on competition, as put by *Anchustegui*, it is not harmful at first sight. However, there may be other arguments to be referred to when attempting to find the justification for competition-related regulations not falling under the scope of conventional antitrust. The prohibition of unfair trading practices is easier to be explained by arguments related to wealth transfers or socially desirable objectives to be pursued by other policies. Although wealth transfers to agricultural producers are economic in nature but do not play a role in antitrust enforcement, similarly to those agricultural policy objectives which aim to raise the standard of living of farmers. These latter types of arguments seem like interest group demands,[165] in which the power of agricultural lobby can be discovered.

In conclusion, competition policy in agricultural markets has two different groups of justifications. While the exemptions provided for the creation of countervailing power are accepted by antitrust policy, socially desirable objectives and wealth transfers come from the field of agricultural policy to influence competition in agri-food markets and do not fit the legal toolbox at the disposal of conventional antitrust law.

In the following, I analyse the historical trajectory of competition policy both in the United States and the European Union, concentrating on the agricultural sector. I start with the US because of its pioneering role in competition policy and the fact that modern antitrust's cradle is the US. The analysis proceeds chronologically. The difference between the two sides of the Atlantic is that in the first two decades of modern US antitrust there was no specific provision for the agricultural sector, while in the EU the special antitrust treatment of agriculture has been extant since the Treaty of Rome signed in 1957, which established the European Economic Community, the predecessor of the EU. The lack of sectoral rules up to 1914 is the reason that the early US developments are zoomed in through the possible agriculture-related motivations and events that led to the adoption of the first and second federal antitrust statutes (the Sherman and Clayton Acts).

6.3 The United States

The modern origins of antitrust date back to the end of the 19th century, when the Sherman Act was passed in the United States of America. The Sherman Act was signed into law by President Benjamin Harrison on 2 July 1890 and was the first federal law to address anticompetitive practices as we know them today.

The word 'antitrust' itself derives from the fact that the primary form of the creation of monopoly was the legal institution of trust, a specific construct of

165 R. Shyam Khemani, 'Application of Competition Law: Exemptions and Exceptions' (2003) UNCTAD Series on Issues in Competition Law and Policy 32.

common-law jurisdictions. Nevertheless, *Collins* notes that the era's state and federal antitrust legislation was aimed not against large firms but the combinations of competitors, and "[r]egardless of their technical legal form, these combinations came at the time to be called trusts."[166]

The Sherman Act came into public consciousness as a reaction against the trust created by S.C.T. Dodd in 1882. Dodd was an attorney-at-law for Rockefeller's Standard Oil Company and sought to create through the trust a close association of oil refiners able to influence prices and supply in the marketplace while avoiding state taxes and corporate regulation. Although many economists at this time opposed the adoption of a federal antitrust statute, saying that it would adversely affect rising real wages and falling prices, the camp of opponents refused to give up their belief in fair competition. However, the question of how to achieve undistorted and fair competition remained unresolved on their side. In agriculture, for example, technological progress has made it impossible for individual producers and small businesses to keep pace with their larger competitors. The populist tendency of the last third of the 1800s, often identified with the Granger movement that emerged in the decade following the American Civil War, accelerated the emergence of antitrust.[167] The mastermind behind the Granger movement was *Oliver Hudson Kelley*, an employee of the Department of Agriculture, who founded the organisation known as 'The Patrons of Husbandry' in 1867. The organisation was made up of local units called 'Granges'. Most adherents were attracted to the movement by the need to take action against the monopoly of railway companies and grain elevators (often owned by the railway companies), which charged farmers exorbitant fees for handling and transporting grain and other agricultural products.[168]

In one of the Granger cases, *Munn v. Illinois*, the US Supreme Court ruled that within the limits of the powers inherent in its sovereignty, the government may regulate the conduct of its citizens towards each other and, where the public good so requires, the manner in which individual citizens should use their property. In order to clarify the ratio decidendi, declared in principle, the facts of the case may be summarised as follows. The Illinois state legislation, influenced by the Granger movement, set maximum rates that grain elevators could charge for storage and transportation.[169]

166 Wayne D. Collins, 'Trusts and the Origins of Antitrust Legislation' (2013) 81 Fordham Law Review 2280.

167 Laura Phillips Sawyer, 'US Antitrust Law and Policy in Historical Perspective' (2019) Harvard Business School Working Paper 19–110, 2 <www.hbs.edu/ris/Publication%20Files/19-110_e21447ad-d98a-451f-8ef0-ba42209018e6.pdf> accessed 13 January 2024.

168 The Editors of Encyclopaedia Britannica, 'Granger Movement: American Farm Coalition' <www.britannica.com/event/Granger-movement> accessed 13 January 2024.

169 The General Assembly of Illinois – An Act to regulate public warehouses and the warehousing and inspection of grain, and to give effect to art. 13 of the Constitution of this State (approved April 25, 1871), Section 15: "The maximum charge of storage and handling of grain, including the cost of receiving and delivering, shall be for the first thirty days or part thereof two cents per bushel, and for each fifteen days or part thereof, after the first thirty days, one-half of one cent per bushel; provided, however, that grain damp or liable to early damage, as indicated by its inspection when received, may be subject to two cents per bushel storage for the first ten days, and for each additional five days or part thereof, not exceeding one-half of one per cent per bushel."

After Munn & Scott was fined under the legislative act, and the Illinois Supreme Court upheld the ruling, the company appealed to the US Supreme Court, arguing that the Illinois regulation violated the US Constitution because it unconstitutionally restricted the right holder's exercise of his property rights, thus infringing the right to property. This argument was rejected by the Supreme Court, and the essence of the ruling was that the states' regulatory power extends to the relations of private corporations when they have an impact on the public interest. Since the granaries were also intended for use in the public interest, charges imposed by them could be regulated by the state.[170] This holding highlights and confirms the possibility for states to take action by means of certain legal instruments in order to ensure fair competition, even though this means the imposition of property restrictions on certain entities through the determination of how they should operate in the market.

Although the administration emphasised that the Sherman Act was necessary because of the Standard Oil Trust's unscrupulous and – in many cases – unlawful trading practices,[171] as well as the exploitation of the agricultural sector by industry,[172] some authors argued that it was wrong to regard the agricultural sector's vulnerability as an impetus behind antitrust legislation,[173] for agriculture is not a sector that is exclusively exposed to industry, and the facts show that the practices of railroad companies stabilised and increased the income of farmers.[174] Furthermore, there are authors who see Sherman's personal motives behind the passage of the act. It was Russell A. Alger who helped Benjamin Harrison get the Republican Party nomination for president, which Sherman resented, so Sherman targeted Alger's trust, 'Diamond Match'. This was done by means of the Sherman Act of 1890. It is also argued that Sherman, as the most influential member of the Senate's Committee on Finance, directly supported a policy of high tariffs, which is in inextricable contrast to his efforts to limit trusts.[175] In view of these considerations, it is believed that there were more personal motivations behind the Sherman Act.

However, it is better to choose a middle way and not to overemphasise the power of a personal motif. If Sherman's individual "desire for revenge" had been the sole basis for the act's adoption, Congress would not have voted for it. In any case, the exploited agricultural sector in general, including the Granger movement and the vulnerable agricultural producers, played a decisive role on the road to the passage of the Sherman Act. The Standard Oil Company having been in a monopolistic position and causing resentment because of governmental manifestations combined with the belief in free competition, which dominated the views of all parties, led to the passage of the Sherman Act. The extent to which Sherman's personal motivation played

170 U.S. Supreme Court, *Munn v. Illinois*, 94 U.S. 113 (1876).

171 Hans Thorelli, *The Federal Antitrust Policy: Origination of an American Tradition* (Johns Hopkins University Press 1955) 92.

172 William Letwin, *Law and Economic Policy in America: The Evolution of the Sherman Antitrust Act* (Randon House 1965) 67–68.

173 Robert L. Bradley Jr., 'On the Origins of the Sherman Antitrust Act' (1990) 9 Cato Journal 739.

174 George Stigler, 'The Origin of the Sherman Act' (1985) 14 The Journal of Legal Studies 1–12.

175 Bradley Jr. (n 173) 739–740.

a role in this is irrelevant, as the act could not have been passed without the then current anticompetitive and distortive trade practices that had preceded it and the public outcry against them. This brief memento shows that the need to protect farmers was an important starting point for the Sherman Act's adoption. Equally important is the principle enunciated in *Munn v. Illinois*, which had agricultural relevance and which provided case law justification for competition rules and a solid basis for the creation of federal antitrust laws in the United States.

Although the adoption of the Sherman Act was seen as a major breakthrough, events in the late 19th and early 20th centuries proved that it did not provide fully adequate protection against distortions and restrictions of competition. This period also saw the so-called *Merger Movement*, during which corporate empires were created in spite of the Sherman Act, by using other legal constructions instead of trusts. As early as 1899, the seriousness of the problem was felt, and the *Civic Federation of Chicago* convened and held a conference to address the problem of trusts. Here, some already expressed their fear for agricultural regions, as the *Merger Movement* had created companies with market power that could raise the price of manufactured goods while lowering the price of raw materials.[176] The need for a new law was already mooted by *John Bates Clark*, which was very similar to the provisions of the Clayton Act passed fifteen years later.[177]

One of the notable differences between the Sherman Act and the Clayton Act is that the former does not and the latter does contain a direct provision for the agricultural sector. The Sherman Act did not differentiate between sectors, and there was a widespread public perception that the first federal antitrust law was in part enacted with the intention of cracking down on large agricultural cooperatives. On the other hand, it was also suggested that the Sherman Act's provisions could be interpreted as meaning that mutual assistance between local farmers managing small farms violated the act. Around the 1890s, there were already about a thousand agricultural cooperatives in the United States, which brought together producers and sought to coordinate their activities in order to reduce the vulnerability of farmers and improve their competitive position.[178] They were, however, covered by the Sherman Act in the same way as any other undertaking engaged in any other activity. There are authors in the literature who describe the Sherman Act as simply bad law,[179] and given that many see it as a response to the defencelessness of the agricultural sector and yet it does not contain specific rules for certain sectors with different needs, such as agriculture, there may have been some basis for negative opinions. And if not bad, it can certainly be described as an oversimplified legislative product.

The Clayton Act of 1914 attempted to change this, already seeking to place a differentiated emphasis on sectors where there was a specific need to do so. The

176 David Dale Martin, *Mergers and the Clayton Act* (University of California Press 1959) 6.

177 Martin (n 176) 7.

178 Christine A. Varney, 'The Capper-Volstead Act, Agricultural Cooperatives, and Antitrust Immunity' (2010) *The Antitrust Source* 1.

179 Bradley Jr. (n 173) 741.

Sherman Act was not repealed by the Clayton Act, the latter merely supplemented and strengthened the former. There are authors who have seen the Clayton Act as an excellent attempt to increase the strength of the Sherman Act,[180] and we can agree that the Clayton Act's provisions, a quarter of a century later, can be thought of as improvement. Approached from the other direction, one could not necessarily have expected more from the Sherman Act, for it lacked background experience which legislation could gain from case law in the decades that followed its adoption.

The Clayton Act declares that

> [n]othing contained in the antitrust laws shall be construed to forbid the existence and operation of labor, agricultural, or horticultural organizations, instituted for the purposes of mutual help, and not having capital stock or conducted for profit, or to forbid or restrain individual members of such organizations from lawfully carrying out the legitimate objects thereof; nor shall such organizations, or the members thereof, be held or construed to be illegal combinations or conspiracies in restraint of trade, under the antitrust laws.[181]

Prior to the adoption of the Clayton Act's Section 6, the position of agricultural cooperatives was not unambiguous in case law. Some state courts drew parallels between cartels and agricultural cooperatives by applying antitrust provisions to them; still others were much more tolerant.[182]

One of the most striking examples of questionable judicial application of antitrust laws was the *Ford v. Chicago Milk Shippers' Association* ruling, in which the Illinois Supreme Court held that the cooperative had influenced milk prices in a way that had restricted competition, and both the cooperative itself and its members had achieved this goal in parallel to the detriment of retailers.[183] Dairy farmers in Chicago formed a cooperative marketing association to determine prices that farmers would receive for milk and other dairy products. A milk trader entered into a purchase agreement with the cooperative but subsequently refused to pay the purchase price. When the cooperative brought an action to enforce payment, the trader relied on an 1891 Illinois state law that allowed buyers "who signed a contract to buy goods from a participant in a combination that violated the law could refuse to pay for the goods." The Illinois Supreme Court, without reference to the Sherman Act, ruled in favour of the dealer, holding that the cooperative was formed for the purpose of fixing prices and influencing and limiting the amount of milk that could be marketed. It is unlawful for the cooperative to pursue these objectives. Although the cooperative sought to argue that the cooperative itself and its members are a single legal entity, making it incapable

180 Charles Nagel, 'The Origin and Purpose of the Sherman Act' (1930) 15 St. Louis Law Review 323.

181 15 U.S. Code § 17.

182 Chris Sagers and Peter Cartensen, *Federal Statutory Exemptions from Antitrust Law* (American Bar Association 2007) 97.

183 Charles Fisk Beach, *A Treatise on the Law of Monopolies and Industrial Trusts: As Administered in England and in the United States of America* (The Lawbook Exchange 2007) 245.

for the cooperative to conspire with itself to restrict competition, the Illinois Supreme Court broke the unity between the cooperative and its members.[184]

In general, in the early cases dating back to before the adoption of state cooperative laws, state courts ruled predominantly against cooperatives. This trend was later reversed and cooperatives were considered as specific market actors. Not only was it realised that the vulnerability of farmers to market conditions could be alleviated through cooperatives, but also that their operation had to be balanced with antitrust law. This could not be done in another way than by exempting them from the scope *rationae personae* of antitrust law, thus placing them in a privileged position. However, this finding was realised almost 25 years after the passage of the Sherman Act. This realisation can be described as the first resolution of the conflicts between agricultural and competition policy, which set in motion the trend in antitrust law that has continued to this day: treating the agricultural sector specially in relation to competition-related provisions.

After the adoption of Clayton Act's Section 6, the development of agricultural cooperatives began, but two problems remained unresolved. On one hand, cooperatives covered by the exemption could not issue capital stock, since the exemption only applied to agricultural cooperatives without it. However, capital stock would have been essential to balance the power of middle-class producers. On the other hand, the question arose as to what was meant by the expression of 'lawfully carrying out the cooperative's legitimate objects'. To resolve these problems, the Capper-Volstead Act was passed in 1922.[185]

The Capper-Volstead Act directly and exclusively imposes conditions on agricultural cooperatives which, if met by cooperatives, result in them not being completely subjected to the antitrust regime. Whereas Section 6 of the Clayton Act contains a mere provision on the issue – a general declaration that certain agricultural cooperatives are exempt from the scope of antitrust law, the Capper-Volstead Act establishes a complex regime.[186] Originally, the draft of the Clayton Act did not include agricultural cooperatives in the list of its exceptions; it only intended to give priority to trade unions, but later agricultural cooperatives got involved among the exceptions. This raised the problem of how to interpret the expression 'lawfully carrying out the cooperative's legitimate objects'.[187]

184 Donald A. Frederick, *Antitrust Status of Farmer Cooperatives: The Story of the Capper-Volstead Act* (U.S. Department of Agriculture 2002) 68.

185 Baumer, Masson and Masson (n 157) 190–191.

186 See its critique: William E. Peters, 'Agricultural Cooperatives and the Antitrust Laws' (1963) 43 Nebraska Law Review 73–104. He concludes: "The law relative to agricultural cooperatives can be succinctly described by one word – uncertainty. Agricultural cooperatives are in the anomalous situation of not knowing what is right or wrong. As a consequence, they are faced with a continual threat of costly criminal and civil prosecutions. It is undesirable public policy to place any societal group in a position where it must risk extensive litigation in order to determine its rights."

187 L. Gene Lemon, 'The Capper-Volstead Act: Will It Ever Grow Up?' (1970) 22 Administrative Law Review 443–444.

The overall purpose of the Capper-Volstead Act is to enable farmers to compete more effectively and market their products more efficiently.[188] Although in public consciousness the act bears the names of its two most prominent proponents, its original title is as follows: An Act to authorize association of producers of agricultural products. The act can be divided into two distinct parts: the first sets out the conditions under which a cooperative may be covered by the act, and the second describes the procedure to be followed in the event a cooperative would commit an antitrust violation. The immunity granted by the act is limited. Farmers can be held liable under antitrust law, if they abuse the tools available to them.

Under the first provision of the act, the conditions can be summarised as follows: (1) only those who are engaged in the production of agricultural products, such as farmers, planters, ranchmen, dairymen, nut or fruit growers, may be members of a cooperative or an association; (2) they may act together in associations, corporate or otherwise, with or without capital stock, in collectively processing, preparing for market, handling, and marketing in interstate and foreign commerce; (3) such associations may have marketing agencies in common; and such associations and their members may make the necessary contracts and agreements to effect such purposes; (4) such associations are operated for the mutual benefit of the members thereof, as such producers; (5) no member of the association is allowed more than one vote because of the amount of stock or membership capital he may own therein, or the association does not pay dividends on stock or membership capital in excess of 8 per centum per annum; (6) the association shall not deal in the products of nonmembers to an amount greater in value than such as are handled by it for members.[189] As can be seen, the Capper-Volstead Act sets out an extensive set of conditions. The two sub-conditions set out in point 5 are in an alternative relationship to each other, so it is sufficient to satisfy only one of the two.

The first part, which establishes exact criteria to be followed by agricultural cooperatives, is complemented by complex procedural rules in the second part of the act.[190]

Beyond the Capper-Volstead Act, the Unfair Trade Practices Affecting Producers of Agricultural Products Act of 1968 is also worth mentioning. It was, among others, adopted to fill a gap in the enforcement of the Capper-Volstead Act. In certain agricultural sectors, farmers are not able to cooperate. A prime example of this is poultry growers.

> They provide housing for the chickens that the integrator owns. The integrator, also, provides the feed, medicine, etc. Hence, such growers cannot engage in collective action as a farm cooperative because they are hired only to grow the poultry belonging to others and, probably, because the owners of the birds do not qualify as "farmers" under Capper-Volstead this would also void the exemption.[191]

188 Varney (n 178) 3.
189 7 U.S. Code § 291.
190 7 U.S. Code § 292.
191 Peter C. Carstensen, 'Controlling Unfairness in American Agriculture' in Ignacio Herrera Anchustegui, Ronny Gjendemsjø, Peter C. Carstensen, Johan Hedelin and Antonio Miño López (eds), *Unfair Trading Practices in the Food Supply Chain* (Concurrences 2019) 7.

The Unfair Trade Practices Affecting Producers of Agricultural Products Act enumerates prohibited practices related to the collective action of agricultural producers.[192] Enabling agricultural producers to cooperate with one another for strengthening their bargaining power, as well as ensuring antitrust exemption for these cooperatives are two pillars of great importance to agri-food markets. The act provides protection for producers against the retaliation of their buyers. Retaliation is a common occurrence in the business relationship between agricultural producers and their buyers with (relative) market power.

Another important milestone in the history of competition policy is the passage of the Packers and Stockyards Act. It does not only provide for an exception (a derogation) under (from) general antitrust rules like the Clayton Act's Section 6 and the Capper-Volstead Act, but also establishes a special statutory regime for handling sector-specific anomalies in the market of live animals. The development of this market in the United States and its regulatory attempts/regulation will lead me to a crucial conclusion on the importance of regulating agri-food markets both with appropriate general and sector-specific rules and the finding that the harmonious relationship between these two pillars shall be established.

During the act's debate, Congressmen talked about 'food dictators'. A parallel was made between dictators and food dictators, and it was claimed that having a dictator as the head of government is as inadvisable as having a food dictator on top of the food system.[193]

The journey to the adoption of the Packers and Stockyards Act, which was passed on 15 August 1921 and amended on 14 August 1935 to also cover live poultry dealers and handlers,[194] started with the Federal Trade Commission (hereinafter

192 7 U.S. Code § 2303:

> It shall be unlawful for any handler knowingly to engage or permit any employee or agent to engage in the following practices:
>
> (a) To coerce any producer in the exercise of his right to join and belong to or to refrain from joining or belonging to an association of producers, or to refuse to deal with any producer because of the exercise of his right to join and belong to such an association; or
> (b) To discriminate against any producer with respect to price, quantity, quality, or other terms of purchase, acquisition, or other handling of agricultural products because of his membership in or contract with an association of producers; or
> (c) To coerce or intimidate any producer to enter into, maintain, breach, cancel, or terminate a membership agreement or marketing contract with an association of producers or a contract with a handler; or
> (d) To pay or loan money, give any thing of value, or offer any other inducement or reward to a producer for refusing to or ceasing to belong to an association of producers; or
> (e) To make false reports about the finances, management, or activities of associations of producers or handlers; or
> (f) To conspire, combine, agree, or arrange with any other person to do, or aid or abet the doing of, any act made unlawful by this chapter.

193 William E. Rosales, 'Dethroning Economic Kings: The Packers and Stockyards Act of 1921 and Its Modern Awakening' (2004) Wisconsin Law Review 1497–1498.

194 Harry Aubrey Toulmin, *A Treatise on the Anti-Trust Laws of the United States: And Including All Related Trade Regulatory Laws*, vol. 3 (W.H. Anderson 1949) 215.

referred to as the FTC) and the Department of Agriculture (hereinafter referred to as the DoA) receiving appropriations for conducting research on "whether there was reason to believe that the production, preparation, storage distribution and sale of foodstuffs were subject to control or manipulation."[195] Based on the inquiry,[196,197] it was found that the five largest meat-packing companies had conspired to control "the purchases of livestock, the preparation of meat and meat products and the distribution thereof in this country and abroad."[198] The most important finding of the FTC report is reproduced here in full:

> Five corporations – Armour & Co., Swift & Co., Morris & Co., Wilson & Co., Inc., and the Cudahy Packing Co. – hereafter referred to as the "Big Five" or "The Packers," together with their subsidiaries and affiliated companies, not only have a monopolistic control over the American meat industry, but have secured control, similar in purpose if not yet in extent, over the principal substitutes for meat, such as eggs, cheese, and vegetable-oil products, and are rapidly extending their power to cover fish and nearly every kind of foodstuff.[199]

The FTC report also posited that the Big Five used, in an unfair and illegal way, their powers

> to manipulate live-stock markets, restrict interstate and international supplies of foods, control the prices of dressed meats and other foods, defraud both the producers of food and consumers, crush effective competition, secure special privileges from railroads, stockyard companies, and municipalities, and profiteer.[200]

The report not only resulted in the Packers and Stockyards Act's passage but also – in February 1920 – in a consent decree in which the government settled an antitrust lawsuit under the Sherman Act with the major packers. The consent decree "enjoined and restrained the meat-packers from owning any public stockyard company and further required those that did to divest themselves of such ownership interests."[201] As a consequence of the divestiture, the concentration ratio of the four largest

195 William B. Colver, 'The Federal Trade Commission and the Meat-Packing Industry' (1919) 82 The Annals of the American Academy of Political and Social Science 170.

196 Federal Trade Commission, *Report of the Federal Trade Commission on the Meat-Packing Industry: Summary and Part I* (Government Printing Office 1919).

197 For an in-depth analysis of the investigation, see: G.O. Virtue, 'The Meat-Packing Investigation' (1920) 34 The Quarterly Journal of Economics 626–685.

198 Thomas J. Flavin, 'The Packers and Stockyards Act, 1921' (1958) 26 The George Washington Law Review 161.

199 Federal Trade Commission (n 196) 31.

200 Federal Trade Commission (n 196) 32–33.

201 Bill Bullard, 'Under Siege: The U.S. Live Cattle Industry' (2013) 58 South Datoka Law Review 562.

meat-packers dropped from about 45% to 20% until the late 1970s.[202] Although there were several attempts to modify and/or eliminate the consent decree,[203] ultimately it only happened in 1981, when it was "terminated on the joint motion of the Justice Department and Swift Independent Packing Company."[204] No surprise that after the repeal of the consent decree, the concentration ratio of the four largest meat-packers started to increase through mergers and acquisitions, and by the early 1990s it rose to over 80%.[205] This sheds light on the importance of harmonious co-existence between general antitrust rules and sectoral regulation in handling sector-specific problems. Without appropriate merger control, the sectoral regulation, the Packers and Stockyards Act has not been sufficient in the last four decades to halt the consolidation of live market animals in the United States, contrary to the period when the consent decree was in force. This historical experience is key to my later findings.

Another important legal source of US competition policy is the Perishable Agricultural Commodities Act of 1930. Its section titled 'Unfair conduct' consists of practices which, on one hand, are similar to general unfair competition conducts applying to all sectors,[206] and which, on the other hand, can be regarded as the

202 C. Robert Taylor, 'Buyer Power Litigation in Agriculture: Pickett v. Tyson Fresh Meats, Inc.' (2008) 55 Antitrust Bulletin 457.

203 Robert M. Aduddell and Louis P. Cain, 'The Consent Decree in the Meatpacking Industry, 1920–1956' (1981) 55 The Business History Review 359–378.

204 Robert M. Aduddell and Louis P. Cain, 'A Strange Sense of Deja Vu: The Packers and the Feds, 1915–82' (1982) 11 Business and Economic History 49.

205 Taylor (n 202) 457.

206 7 U.S. Code § 499b – Unfair conduct:

It shall be unlawful in or in connection with any transaction in interstate or foreign commerce:

(1) For any commission merchant, dealer, or broker to engage in or use any unfair, unreasonable, discriminatory, or deceptive practice in connection with the weighing, counting, or in any way determining the quantity of any perishable agricultural commodity received, bought, sold, shipped, or handled in interstate or foreign commerce.

(2) For any dealer to reject or fail to deliver in accordance with the terms of the contract without reasonable cause any perishable agricultural commodity bought or sold or contracted to be bought, sold, or consigned in interstate or foreign commerce by such dealer.

(3) For any commission merchant to discard, dump, or destroy without reasonable cause, any perishable agricultural commodity received by such commission merchant in interstate or foreign commerce.

(4) For any commission merchant, dealer, or broker to make, for a fraudulent purpose, any false or misleading statement in connection with any transaction involving any perishable agricultural commodity which is received in interstate or foreign commerce by such commission merchant, or bought or sold, or contracted to be bought, sold, or consigned, in such commerce by such dealer, or the purchase or sale of which in such commerce is negotiated by such broker; or to fail or refuse truly and correctly to account and make full payment promptly in respect of any transaction in any such commodity to the person with whom such transaction is had; or to fail, without reasonable cause, to perform any specification or duty, express or implied, arising out of any undertaking in connection with any such transaction; or to fail to maintain the trust as required under section 499e(c) of this title. However, this paragraph shall not be considered to make the good faith offer, solicitation, payment, or receipt of collateral fees and expenses, in and of itself, unlawful under this chapter.

consequence of superior bargaining power of buyers. To mention some examples of the latter: failing or refusing truly and correctly to account and make full payment promptly in respect of any transaction in any such commodity to the person with whom such transaction is had; or failing, without reasonable cause, to perform any specification or duty, express or implied, arising out of any undertaking in connection with any such transaction.[207]

6.4 The European Union

Antitrust law and the Common Agricultural Policy have been of primary importance to the European Economic Community since the Treaty of Rome of 25 March 1957.[208] The Treaty of Rome, already in its preamble, acknowledged the priority of fair competition. The purpose of establishing a common market presupposes a system ensuring that competition in the common market is not distorted.[209] The Treaty of Rome declared that Member States would develop the Common Agricultural

---

(5) For any commission merchant, dealer, or broker to misrepresent by word, act, mark, stencil, label, statement, or deed, the character, kind, grade, quality, quantity, size, pack, weight, condition, degree of maturity, or State, country, or region of origin of any perishable agricultural commodity received, shipped, sold, or offered to be sold in interstate or foreign commerce. However, any commission merchant, dealer, or broker who has violated –

(A) any provision of this paragraph may, with the consent of the Secretary, admit the violation or violations; or

(B) any provision of this paragraph relating to a misrepresentation by mark, stencil, or label shall be permitted by the Secretary to admit the violation or violations if such violation or violations are not repeated or flagrant; and pay, in the case of a violation under either clause (A) or (B) of this paragraph, a monetary penalty not to exceed $2,000 in lieu of a formal proceeding for the suspension or revocation of license, any payment so made to be deposited into the Treasury of the United States as miscellaneous receipts. A person other than the first licensee handling misbranded perishable agricultural commodities shall not be held liable for a violation of this paragraph by reason of the conduct of another if the person did not have knowledge of the violation or lacked the ability to correct the violation.

(6) For any commission merchant, dealer, or broker, for a fraudulent purpose, to remove, alter, or tamper with any card, stencil, stamp, tag, or other notice placed upon any container or railroad car containing any perishable agricultural commodity, if such card, stencil, stamp, tag, or other notice contains a certificate or statement under authority of any Federal or State inspector or in compliance with any Federal or State law or regulation as to the grade or quality of the commodity contained in such container or railroad car or the State or country in which such commodity was produced.

(7) For any commission merchant, dealer or broker, without the consent of an inspector, to make, cause, or permit to be made any change by way of substitution or otherwise in the contents of a load or lot of any perishable agricultural commodity after it has been officially inspected for grading and certification, but this shall not prohibit re-sorting and discarding inferior produce.

207 7 U.S. Code § 499b, 4.

208 It is, however, worth mentioning that the Treaty establishing the European Coal and Steel Community (known also as the Treaty of Paris of 18 April 1951) also included rules in connection with competition. Articles 4, 60 and 65–67 set out the basic aspects of Community competition policy for the key sectors covered.

209 Treaty establishing the European Economic Community, art 2 and art 3f.

Policy by degrees during the transitional period and would bring it into force by the end of that period at the latest.[210] The objectives of the Common Agricultural Policy were listed in Article 39: (a) to increase agricultural productivity by promoting technical progress and by ensuring the rational development of agricultural production and the optimum utilisation of the factors of production, in particular labour; (b) thus to ensure a fair standard of living for the agricultural community, in particular by increasing the individual earnings of persons engaged in agriculture; (c) to stabilise markets; (d) to assure the availability of supplies; (e) to ensure that supplies reach consumers at reasonable prices.[211]

The Treaty of Rome recognised the special characteristics of agriculture. During the elaboration of the Common Agricultural Policy, the following considerations had to be taken into account: (a) the particular nature of agricultural activity, which results from the social structure of agriculture and from structural and natural disparities between the various agricultural regions; (b) the need to effect the appropriate adjustments by degrees; (c) the fact that in the Member States agriculture constitutes a sector closely linked with the economy as a whole.[212] This provision and the objectives of the CAP were adopted as a consequence of powerful German interests. "[T]he objectives of the CAP are an almost faithful reflection of the aims as contained in Germany's Agricultural Act,[213] passed in September 1955, which institutionalised the generally-held view that *agriculture deserves special treatment*."[214]

The basis for the priority of Common Agricultural Policy over competition rules was established in Article 42: The provisions of the Chapter relating to rules on competition shall apply to production of and trade in agricultural products only to the extent determined by the Council within the framework of Article 43(2) and (3) and in accordance with the procedure laid down therein, account being taken of the objectives set out in Article 39.[215] Articles 43(2) and (3) laid down the procedural rules of working out the Common Agricultural Policy and the decision-making therein.[216]

210 Treaty establishing the European Economic Community, art 40(1).

211 Treaty establishing the European Economic Community, art 39(1).

212 Treaty establishing the European Economic Community, art 39(2).

213 See *Landwirtschaftsgesetz vom 5. September 1955*. It is still in force. Section 1 declares the following: In order to enable agriculture to participate in the progressive development of the German economy and to ensure the best possible supply of foodstuffs for the population, agriculture must be enabled by means of general economic and agricultural policy – in particular trade, tax, credit and price policy – to compensate for the natural and economic disadvantages it suffers compared with other sectors of the economy and to increase its productivity. At the same time, the social situation of people working in agriculture is to be brought into line with that of comparable occupational groups.

214 Rasmus Kjeldahl and Michael Tracy, *Renationalisation of the Common Agricultural Policy?* (Institute of Agricultural Economics 1994) 59 cited by Wyn Grant, *The Common Agricultural Policy* (Macmillan Press 1997) 64.

215 Treaty establishing the European Economic Community, art 42.

216 Treaty establishing the European Economic Community, art 43(2) and (3).

The detailed objectives, problems, principles and instruments of the Common Agricultural Policy were discussed during the Stresa Conference taking place from 3 to 12 July 1958.[217] In his opening speech, *Professor Hallstein* strengthened the justification for the special treatment of agriculture in relation to competition rules:

> The rules of competition which the Treaty has laid down in all economic sectors will only be applied to agriculture in so far as the Council so decides, in the light of the objectives of a Common Agricultural Policy. They will recur in the various forms which we will have to develop for the joint organisation of agricultural markets. Naturally, fixed rules of competition must also exist for production and trade in respect of agricultural commodities. In its final form the Common Market will operate on rules of competition based on the principle of equal rights. We know that agriculture is subject to special conditions for which allowance must be made.[218]

As can be seen from this quote, the privileged position of the Common Agricultural Policy over competition rules due to the structural characteristics of primary agricultural production[219] has accompanied the development of the European Union and its predecessors from the beginnings to the present day.

The birth of the CAP dates back to the first common market organisation in the cereal sector in 1962, although regarding the common prices, it entered into force in the 1967/68 crop year.[220] 1962 not only saw the launch of the Common Agricultural Policy but also the adoption of detailed rules on agriculture-related derogations from competition rules.[221] Though the Common Agricultural Policy has undergone a number of major and minor reforms over the past 60 years,[222] one factor seems to have remained constant and has not changed to date: the production and trade of agricultural products are subject to competition rules only to a limited extent. As *Blockx and Vandenberghe* put it, "[d]espite successive Treaty

217 C. Folmer, M.A. Keyzer, M.D. Merbis, H.J.J. Stolwijk and P.J.J. Veenendaal, *The Common Agricultural Policy Beyond the Macsharry Reform* (Elsevier 1995) 12.

218 Address by Professor Walter Hallstein, President of the Commission of the European Economic Community, at the opening of the Conference of the Member States of the European Economic Community. Stresa, 3 July 1958, VI/2.

219 Halmai Péter (ed), *A Közös Agrárpolitika rendszere* (Dialóg Campus 2020) 17.

220 Grant (n 190) 67.

221 EEC Council Regulation No 26 applying certain rules of competition to production of and trade in agricultural products [1962] OJ L993/129.

222 See details on the reforms: Franz Fischler, 'Reform of the Common Agricultural Policy' (2001) 36 Intereconomics 115–118; Peter Nedergaard, 'The 2003 Reform of the Common Agricultural Policy: Against All Odds or Rational Explanations?' (2006) 28 Journal of European Integration 203–223; Isabelle Garzon, *Reforming the Common Agricultural Policy: History of a Paradigm Change* (Palgrave Macmillan 2007); Robert Ackrill, Adrian Kay and Wyn Morgan, 'The Common Agricultural Policy and Its Reform: The Problem of Reconciling Budget and Trade Concerns' (2008) 56 Canadian Journal of Agricultural Economics/Revue Canadienne D'agroeconomie 393–411; Peter Nedergaard, 'The Reform of the 2003 Common Agricultural Policy: An Advocacy Coalition Explanation' (2008) 29 Policy Studies 179–195.

reforms, this agricultural exemption has never been profoundly touched upon and has remained in substance unaltered since 1957."[223]

Regulation No 26, in its preamble, made it clear that competition rules shall be made applicable to agricultural markets, however, these had to be adapted to the development of the common agricultural policy. The rules on the prohibition of anticompetitive agreements and abuse of dominance could not impede either the functioning of national market organisations or the attainment of common agricultural policy objectives. It must be borne in mind that at the time of the adoption of Regulation No 26, national market organisations had a crucial role in ensuring the proper functioning of agricultural markets.

Takeaway 1

The dominant neoliberal paradigm that handles antitrust law based on neoclassical economics as the ideal of supervising market forces looks at the agricultural sector's privileges in competition policy with great suspicion. Though the agriculture-related exemption from the prohibition of anticompetitive agreements can be – more or less – justified by analysis embedded in economic efficiency (the theory of countervailing power), other sectoral competition policy means, such as the prohibition of unfair trading practices by buyers of agricultural produce against farmers, which go beyond antitrust, are not seen as justified intervention thanks to the lax fairness rhetoric they constitute.

223 Jan Blockx and Jan Vandenberghe, 'Rebalancing Commercial Relations Along the Food Supply Chain: The Agricultural Exemption from EU Competition Law after Regulation 1308/2013' (2014) 10 European Competition Journal 390.

7 Competition from the viewpoint of agricultural policy

First and foremost, the most important attribute of conventional agricultural policy, in harsh contrast with antitrust policy, is its primary focus on agricultural producers. The objectives of the mainstream agricultural policy paradigm are better (higher) farm gate prices, higher income and standard of living for agricultural producers. As displayed in Part III, in the last few decades these goals have been complemented by other considerations to take into account, however, raising farm income has remained the most dominant aim of agricultural policy. That is to say, agricultural policy aims to contribute to agricultural producers being able to sell their produce at the highest possible price, and thus, have an appropriate standard of living thanks to the fair income they make. Furthermore, agricultural policy attempts to provide stability to farmers who suffer from the natural characteristics of agricultural production. Another self-evident feature of agricultural policy is its sector-specific nature, unlike antitrust policy. The way of thinking about these principles (farm income centred and sector specific) is in strong connection with the possible intervention approaches to agricultural markets and – through this – with the mode of competition that seems ideal for the proponents of the different schools of thought.

Novak, Sanders and Hagerman provide a multifaceted analysis on government intervention into agricultural markets, differentiating five archetypes for the possible approaches to the agricultural sector: free marketer with an attitude towards nonintervention for the sake of higher efficiency; humanitarian with the mindset that no one can starve; physiocratic with the emphasis on social sustainability[224]; stabilizer with the fight against volatility; and last but not least, regulator with the mandate to rationally coordinate and control human greed.[225]

Of course, these archetypes do not appear with clear boundaries in real-life scenarios. Neoliberal agricultural policy, which came into existence in the 1980s, is the closest to the free-marketer approach, however, the humanitarian rhetoric (the elimination of poverty and hunger) is intense, too. In the neoliberal paradigm, the

224 See my interpretation in this regard in subheading 4 of chapter 10.
225 James L. Novak, Larry D. Sanders and Amy D. Hagerman, *Agricultural Policy in the United States: Evolution and Economics* (2nd edn, Routledge 2022) 4.

DOI: 10.4324/9781003604747-9

achievement of *free competition* with no artificial (government) obstacles is seen as ideal, which will necessarily result in higher efficiency, higher economic welfare and, thus, the eradication of hunger. The contesting food sovereignty paradigm takes a strong physiocratic approach with a regulatory requirement in order to establish stabilised agricultural markets. This is much closer to the objective of *fair competition*, within the framework of which the state cannot lose sight of the vulnerable producers and must tame the powerful market actors who operate to the detriment of farmers. While globally (for example, within the World Trade Organization) and in the United States, the former approach also dominates thanks to its farm structure, the European Union rather represents the latter with its fragmented production system. Furthermore, these policy approaches cannot be interpreted independently from the period in which we live. For example, the COVID-19 pandemic intensified the humanitarian aspect after global food supply chains had been disrupted and concerns had arisen that – in certain regions – consumers' access to food had deteriorated significantly. The neoliberal approach emphasised the need for free markets to ensure the undisturbed flow of food supplies globally.[226] Obviously, the representatives of the food sovereignty paradigm made totally different conclusions as regards the necessary steps to handle the effects of the pandemic on food supply chains, emphasising the pivotal role small-scale farmers play in food production and, thus, the need to let local markets and short supply chains function and flourish.[227]

Speaking in terms of economics, what is of utter importance is that agricultural production markets have been – for a long time – treated as the textbook example of perfect competition. As formulated in one of the most well-known agricultural economics textbooks, "[t]he farm sector comes closer than any other sector of the economy to satisfying the conditions of perfect competition."[228] Perfect competition is characterised by four conditions: large numbers of buyers and sellers, homogeneous product, freedom of entry and exit, perfect information.[229] Nevertheless, others are much more critical as regards the nature of competition in agricultural markets. *Sexton*, for example, claims that he does not know any modern agricultural market that would meet all these characteristics attributed to competitive markets.[230]

Both in the United States and the European Union, the greatest attention was dedicated to those levels of the food supply chain where the (intermediate) buyers of agri-food products operate: research shows that processing and retail markets

226 Organisation for Economic Co-Operation and Development, *Food Supply Chains and COVID-19: Impacts and Policy Lessons* (OECD 2020).

227 La Via Campesina, 'The Corona Crisis Harms Those Who Feed Us' (28 April 2020) <https://viacampesina.org/en/the-corona-crisis-harms-those-who-feed-us/> accessed 29 June 2024; Philip McMichael, 'COVID-19 Implications on Our Broken Food System' (2020) <www.isa-agrifood.com/post/covid-19-implications-on-our-broken-food-system> accessed 29 June 2024.

228 Penson, Capps Jr., Rosson III and Woodward (n 85) 107.

229 Andrew Barkley and Paul W. Barkley, *Principles of Agricultural Economics* (Routledge 2013) 86.

230 Richard J. Sexton, 'Market Power, Misconceptions, and Modern Agricultural Markets' (2012) 95 American Journal of Agricultural Economics 209–219.

have gradually become more and more concentrated.[231] This, of course, has its own problematic effects from the viewpoint of agricultural producers who can sell their produce to only a few buyers. So, theoretically, the first condition requiring a large number of buyers is not realised. *Hendrickson and Harvey* argue that the economic pressure put on agricultural producers resulted in industrialisation, which necessarily comes with consolidation and concentration, creates constrained choice for farmers and, thus, increases the likeliness of unethical behaviour.[232] Later, they improved their theory that the constrained choice of producers violates the principle of justice, and should necessarily constitute an assessment element of fairness in agricultural markets. Their framework is proposed to recalibrate competition policy.[233] A constrained choice arises, for example, when agricultural producers have limited marketing options. It is quite clear-cut in literature that the high costs of transporting agricultural products limit "farmers' access to spatially distributed buyers, creating procurement markets that are natural oligopsonies."[234]

In some cases, research also shows that another crucial feature of perfect competition, perfect information, is also missing, for example, to the detriment of Polish apple growers; it was argued that information asymmetry constitutes "one of the most important constraints" in the supply chain.[235] However, *Perloff and Rausser* earlier arrived at a surprising conclusion: they claim that an increase in information sometimes decreases, sometimes increases the distortions in agricultural markets.[236]

Another focus of recent research has been on pricing strategies of intermediaries with market power. Asymmetric price transmission has been demonstrated by several authors: when the farm gate price increases, it is followed by a rapid and complete pass-through of costs by powerful companies to consumers, however, when the farm gate price decreases, the pass-through is slow and incomplete. Though it would go against common sense, perfectly competitive markets (or, at least,

231 In connection with the United States, see: Richard J. Sexton, 'Industrialization and Consolidation in the U.S. Food Sector: Implications for Competition and Welfare' (2000) 82 American Journal of Agricultural Economics 1087–1104; Richard J. Sexton and Mingxia Zhang, 'An Assessment of the Impact of Food Industry Market Power on U.S. Consumers' (2001) 17 Agribusiness 59–79. In connection with Europe, see: Paul W. Dobson, Michael Waterson and Stephen W. Davies, 'The Patterns and Implications of Increasing Concentration in European Food Retailing' (2003) 54 Journal of Agricultural Economics 111–125.

232 Mary K. Hendrickson and Harvey S. James Jr., 'The Ethics of Constrained Choice: How the Industrialization of Agriculture Impacts Farming and Farmer Behavior' (2005) 18 Journal of Agricultural and Environmental Ethics 269–291.

233 Mary K. Hendrickson and Harvey S. James Jr., 'Power, Fairness and Constrained Choice in Agricultural Markets: A Synthesizing Framework' (2016) 29 Journal of Agricultural and Environmental Ethics 945–967.

234 Marten Graubner and Richard J. Sexton, 'More Competitive Than You Think? Pricing and Location of Processing Firms in Agricultural Markets' (2023) 105 American Journal of Agricultural Economics 784.

235 Michał Pietrzak, Aleksandra Chlebicka, Paweł Kraciński and Agata Malak-Rawlikowska, 'Information Asymmetry as a Barrier in Upgrading the Position of Local Producers in the Global Value Chain – Evidence from the Apple Sector in Poland' (2020) 12 Sustainability, Article 7857.

236 Jeffrey M. Perloff and Gordon C. Rausser, 'The Effect of Asymmetrically Held Information and Market Power in Agricultural Markets' (1983) 65 American Journal of Agricultural Economics 371–372.

markets that are theorised as perfectly competitive) can also experience asymmetric price transmission.[237] The review of *Meyer and von Cramon-Taubadel* points to the fact that in most cases the noncompetitive market structure is used as an explanation for asymmetry, but other reasons also appear, such as adjustment costs or price support in the form of floor prices.[238]

As regards market entry in a narrow sense, agricultural production has no barriers: there are not any government obstacles or financial limitations de jure. However, de facto the high costs of land and equipment are to be considered obstacles.[239] What has substantial effects on the competition between agricultural producers are the high entry barriers present in food manufacturing and retailing. In the latter, significant investments must be carried out for the sake of distribution centres and logistics networks, and it is needless to say that economies of scope and of scale are of utter importance, too.[240] Within the sector of food manufacturing, regarding the cereal sector, *Schmalensee* concluded that reductions in the rivalry as to advertising and brand introduction facilitated the market entry of new competitors.[241] In a later work, it was also pointed out that the high entry barriers prevalent in food processing are because of expenditures on advertising and product development which have cumulative effects.[242] These findings are strengthened also by *Chaddad and Mondelli* who analysed firm performance in the US food economy.[243] So, as can be seen, it is widely held that advertising can be used to create future entry barriers. Furthermore, evidently, these erected barriers support firms in pursuing even greater power,[244] which – at sectoral level – creates greater concentration. In the long run, it is a vicious circle: firms in highly concentrated industries are in an easier position to prevent new entry.[245] Moreover, vertical integration, too, is a common phenomenon in the food supply chain, and although vertical mergers do not

237 Dejene Gizaw, Øystein Myrland and Jinghua Xie, 'Asymmetric Price Transmission in a Changing Food Supply Chain' (2021) 25 Aquaculture Economics & Management 89–105.

238 Jochen Meyer and Stephan von Cramon-Taubadel, 'Asymmetric Price Transmission: A Survey' (2004) 55 Journal of Agricultural Economics 581–611.

239 Barkley and Barkley (n 229) 87.

240 Reena Das Nair and Shingie Chisoro, 'Competition, Barriers to Entry and Inclusive Growth: Case Study on Fruit and Veg City' (2015) CCRED Working Paper Series 2015/9 <https://doi.org/10.13140/RG.2.1.1417.8321> accessed 20 January 2024.

241 Richard Schmalensee, 'Entry Deterrence in the Ready-to-Eat Breakfast Cereal Industry' (1978) 9 The Bell Journal of Economics 322.

242 J.M. Connor, R.T. Rogers, B.W. Marion and W.F. Mueller, *The Food Manufacturing Industries: Structures, Strategies, Performance, and Policies* (D.C. Heath 1985).

243 Fabio R. Chaddad and Mario P. Mondelli, 'Sources of Firm Performance Differences in the US Food Economy' (2012) 64 Journal of Agricultural Economics 382–404.

244 Kyle W. Stiegert, Shinn-Shyr Wang and Richard Rogers, 'Structural Change and Market Power in the US Food Manufacturing Sector' (2009) 25 Agribusiness 164–180.

245 Stefan Hirsch and Adelina Gschwandtner, 'Profit Persistence in the Food Industry: Evidence from Five European Countries' (2013) 40 European Review of Agricultural Economics 752.

directly affect the number of competing firms, entry barriers may arise due to their effects on creating limits to essential inputs or resale channels.[246]

In sum, the juncture from the viewpoint of agricultural producers is far from perfect. Though the market of agricultural production has been for a long time treated as the textbook example for perfect competition, thanks to the limited number of buyers of agri-food products at processing and retail levels (caused by consolidation and vertical integration) as well as the high entry barriers to these markets and the lack of perfect information for producers and asymmetric price transmission, the reality rather mirrors imperfect competition conditions, which determines to a significant extent the possibilities of agricultural producers.

Of course, horizontal competition between farmers is intense, since there are lots of competing market actors in all product markets. However, when they wish to sell their produce, the concentrated sectors at intermediary stage may function to the detriment of producers. Nevertheless, as the saying goes, even the slightest competition is ruinous for the weakest and least efficient market participants, who can perceive this in a way that competition is 'unfair'. The dividing line is extremely thin, and the perception on the functioning of the competition in a given market is always determined by the position of those who form an opinion. Competing paradigms take totally different approaches towards the desirable market functioning and the values that markets shall represent. Any policy means chosen will give an impression about the decision-makers' standpoint and will reflect their value judgment.

Takeaway 2

Though the neoliberal agricultural policy agenda emerging since the 1980s encouraged, and managed to bring forward, the more market orientation approach towards agri-food supply chains, the market of primary agricultural production is far from perfect competition. The problems of the sector do not come from ruinous horizontal competition between producers, but are rooted in upstream and downstream markets that have become more concentrated at their own horizontal level (e.g., processing and retail) and more integrated vertically with one another. As a consequence of these, agricultural producers suffer from the lack of bargaining power, and are price takers when it comes to buying input for production or selling their output (agricultural produce).

246 Paolo Buccirossi, Stéphan Marette and Alessandra Schiavina, 'Competition Policy and the Agribusiness Sector in the European Union' (2002) 29 European Review of Agricultural Economics 376.

8 The winner of the clash

Currently, the winner of the clash between these two public policies is agricultural policy beyond doubt. That it is demonstrated and labelled as a clash, and not as a bargain achieved through compromises, originates from the different values these policies represent and the different target groups they give preference to. There is an *insoluble discrepancy* between the two approaches, which cannot be cured by more evidence. Facts become relative among the value judgments taken by these two policies. Fruitless disputes may arise as to whether the status quo of the sector is efficient in economic terms, and based on these findings, how competition and antitrust policy can contribute to the sector's development. More evidence on, for example, small farms' inability to keep up with agribusiness based on economies of scale and of scope in terms of efficiency will not convince people who consider small and medium-scale family farming as an intrinsic value to be preserved. On the contrary, research results that small-scale farming is environmentally sustainable will not convince people who seek ways to improve giant agribusinesses' sustainability that small-scale diversified farming is the key to a better and more environment-friendly future.

I do not suggest that these research results are not valuable; they are. Policymaking and legislation shall be oriented with up-to-date evidence. However, from a practical point of view, values will prevail and determine outcomes in this area.

The victory of agricultural policy over competition rules is, first and foremost, translated into legal norms. On the one hand, the agricultural sector enjoys several derogations from general antitrust rules. Antitrust has had to give up its sector-neutral viewpoint as regards agriculture. The purity of its framework characterised by sector neutrality free from vested interests is wounded, however, it may find some relief with the economic theory of countervailing power. On the other hand, when legislation steps out of the antitrust framework and – under the flag of competition regulation – sets objectives other than those of antitrust, the whole belief system of antitrust is attacked with non-efficiency-based goals, generating disdain in antitrust circles. One example of this is the prohibition of unfair trading practices against agricultural producers.

Second, as a result of the victory of agricultural policy, one may experience a certain reluctance of antitrust agencies to delve into the economic realities of the sector and to enforce the (general and sector-specific) provisions intensively.

DOI: 10.4324/9781003604747-10

Antitrust case law is, to put it mildly, limited in this regard. It may have three underlying reasons. Firstly, as will be seen in Part IV, the legal framework is based on the voluntary assessment of otherwise anticompetitive agreements. There is no need for undertakings to notify the agency of an agreement to get exempted under the prohibition of anticompetitive agreements. Secondly, thanks to the intense competition between producers engaged in agricultural production, it is unlikely that an agreement between a few market actors would have significant effects on competition, which is worthy of the attention of antitrust authorities to allocate their scarce resources to deal with that agreement at all. Furthermore, antitrust enforcement is rarely set into motion by the competitive conditions of – typically oligopolistic – markets upstream and downstream in relation to agricultural production. Thirdly, even if an authority initiated proceedings, it would be quite ill suited to assess the different objectives formulated in agricultural policy as well as analyse these in relation to antitrust standards. This is an unfamiliar territory for antitrust agencies.

Takeaway 3

Despite the neoliberal mode of market organisation coming to the fore more than four decades ago, and still prevailing, the relationship between antitrust law and the agricultural sector has retained its more than one-century-long original nexus. Irrespective of the neoliberal economic setting, the objectives of agricultural policy maintain their precedence over the goals of antitrust. The winner of the clash is agricultural policy.

Part III

Sustainability in agricultural and competition policy

After having analysed the relationship between agricultural and competition policy, which is the basis for all further scrutiny, it is reasonable to separate them once again, but only for the sake of dealing with their independent connection with sustainability considerations. Their century-long nexus, however, cannot be forgotten for a long time, because after Part III, in Parts IV and V all three rejoin one another.

Nevertheless, before their reconnection, Part III contains three chapters that are concerned, respectively, with sustainability in general, sustainability in agricultural policy and, last but not least, sustainability in competition policy. I proceed from general considerations to specific ones, on one hand, and chronologically, on the other hand. By the latter I mean that the emergence of sustainability considerations in agricultural policy took place approximately three decades earlier (in the 1990s) than in competition policy.

The discussion on the clash between agricultural and competition policy (Part II) precedes the analysis of sustainability considerations in the respective policy areas because chronologically the conflict of interest between them has existed since the adoption of antitrust laws, that is, before any sustainability demands have been formulated at all. Thus, the nature and system of their relationship, i.e., the basic setup of their nexus, is demonstrated first, into which the new sustainability requirements have arrived later.

It is worth noting at the outset that the appearance of sustainability considerations in competition policy followed the general track that has been characteristic of the relationship between agricultural and competition policy. As seen in Part II, in a general setup, agricultural objectives are given preference over competition, and in particular antitrust, rules in the form of exemptions. When sustainability appeared on the horizon of competition law, the same happened in two aspects. First, in the European Union there exists no other antitrust law exemption of binding force for sustainability agreements than the special one for the agricultural sector codified in Article 210a of the CMO Regulation. Second, even the test for exempting agri-food related sustainability agreements under the prohibition of anticompetitive agreements consists of less difficult application criteria than the general test under soft law. So it becomes clear that agricultural policy-makers were able to hijack the general evaluation system of sustainability agreements under antitrust law, which

DOI: 10.4324/9781003604747-11

has been in the making in the last few years, and could direct the exception rules towards a solution that is easier to fulfil than the general test for exemption.

The following chapters on sustainability in agricultural and competition policy investigate policy integration. Because of the dominant environmental pillar of sustainability, the analysis of environmental policy integration prevails in literature. Environmental policy integration is a tool for sustainable development.[247] By the same token, I consider environmental policy integration as part of sustainability policy integration, and rely heavily on these analyses. Though I am aware that sustainability covers much more than the protection and preservation of the environment, there are certain trends, for example, in competition policy, that use environmentally advantageous agreements and sustainability agreements as synonyms. It would be more precise to speak of environmental policy integration in antitrust policy, despite the fact that the community of antitrust experts uses the term 'sustainability agreements'. It is misleading because antitrust policy aims to distance itself from social considerations that – as we know – are also part of the sustainability discourse. Social aspects, nevertheless, appear in antitrust policy, not as a crucial aspect of the falsely labelled sustainability policy integration, but – implicitly – in the crosscutting area between the agricultural sector and competition rules, where the latter are derogated through socially coloured agricultural objectives, such as the ensuring of a fair standard of living for the agricultural community.

Daugbjerg and Swinbank label the penetration of new issues (food safety, energy supplies, environmental protection, development aid, etc.) into the agricultural policy domain as the 'new' politics of agriculture and food. They also claim that "[n]o longer is 'farm income' the prime focus."[248] This statement is questionable, in my opinion. Beyond any doubt, new issues have emerged in agricultural policy-making, however, the primary objective of agricultural policy remains intact: continuously looking for policy solutions that help producers make higher income or, at least as a minimum standard, preserve their level of income irrespective of any type of imminent (and new) value and objective that should be taken into account in the opinion of nonagricultural policy-makers.

As defined by *Cejudo and Trein*,

> policy integration is a political process that entails the coordination of actors and agencies across policy subsystems, the combination of instruments from different policy sectors, as well as arrangements for their consistent implementation and evaluation, as a response to a complex policy problem that not one policy sector, policy instrument, or agency can solve.[249]

247 William Lafferty and Eivind Hovden, 'Environmental Policy Integration: Towards an Analytical Framework' (2003) 12 Environmental Politics 1–22.

248 Carsten Daugbjerg and Alan Swinbank, 'An Introduction to the "New" Politics of Agriculture and Food' (2012) 31 Policy and Society 259–260.

249 Guillermo M. Cejudo and Philipp Trein, 'Pathways to Policy Integration: A Subsystem Approach' (2023) 56 Policy Sciences 9.

Societal problems, such as environmental protection and climate change, have become increasingly complex and their solution requires integrated approaches,[250] meaning that other sectoral policies may also come to play a certain role in fixing them. Differing from this definition, *Candel* rather conceives policy integration as "the attempt to align policy variables (e.g. goals and instruments)", and not as coordination.[251] My use of the term is nearer to this latter conceptualisation, where, in our case, sustainability objectives are to be brought into line with, on one hand, agricultural policy objectives, and, on the other hand, competition policy objectives.

There are adjacent areas, such as agriculture and the environment, where one may imagine it's easier to find integrated solutions, however, the reality is different, and success depends on a number of factors (institutions, ideas, policy objectives, policy networks, etc.) characteristic of the respective policies. In areas further apart from each other, such as competition policy and sustainability, different types of difficulties may arise. The question may be posed in one policy area as to whether there is anything to be gained from solving the problems of another area that is completely different in its problems to be solved, in its objectives and approach. For example, what does competition policy, which has the objective of protecting free competition and increasing economic efficiency, have to do with environmental concerns at all? At least, the agricultural sector has a double-edged role in relation to certain environmental questions: the sector is not only responsible for emissions but also suffers heavily from climate change[252] caused by a range of other polluting sectors, meaning that agricultural policy-makers, in theory, should seem more inclined to integrate sustainability, and in particular environmental, aspects in their policy means, for the sake of the well-being of producers. On the contrary, competition policy-makers could put their hands up and say "we have nothing to do with the environment, we are here to ensure the level playing field for market participants."

The trends for sustainability policy integration, presented and scrutinised shortly, do not look like they reflect this basic assumption. The expediency of policy integration is put under scrutiny by *Candel* through its desirability and feasibility. It is assumed by him that some public policy scholars automatically presuppose that, for example, environmental policy integration is desirable.[253] I am of the opinion that the picture should be more nuanced. In certain cases, i.e., in areas where problems necessarily touch upon more public policies (although with diverse emphasis), and, thus, the respective problem makes these subsectors closely related in one way or another, one can presuppose the desirability

250 Jeroen J.L. Candel, 'The Expediency of Policy Integration' (2021) 42 Policy Studies 346.

251 Candel (n 250) 357.

252 Nicole M. Schmidt, 'Late Bloomer? Agricultural Policy Integration and Coordination Patterns in Climate Policies' (2019) 27 Journal of European Public Policy 893–911.

253 Candel (n 250) 346. He cites Karl Hogl, Daniela Kleinschmit and Jeremy Rayner, 'Achieving Policy Integration Across Fragmented Policy Domains: Forests, Agriculture, Climate and Energy' (2016) 34 Environment and Planning C: Government and Policy 399–414.

of policy integration. This is the situation between the agricultural sector and environmental policy integration. The feasibility of this desirable and necessary policy integration is another question. Nevertheless, by contrast, the examination of the *pure* desirability of sustainability, and in particular environmental, policy integration into competition policy seems a valid point, where there is no room for the assumption of expediency.

9 Some clarifications on sustainability and sustainable development

Based on the widely cited definition, sustainable development is "meeting the needs of the present without compromising the ability of future generations to meet their own needs."[254] Although used by many scholars as synonyms, sustainable development and sustainability are not the same. *Ruggerio*'s review sheds light on the fact that there are authors who signal the inherent limitation of the 'sustainable development' concept, taking into account our planet's limited resources and the continuous growth that this expression entails.[255] In contrast with sustainable development that concentrates on the process, the term 'sustainability' appears as a desirable outcome. It does not presuppose the seamless flow of growth, but may constitute a normative framework for our public policies.

The relationship between sustainability and environmental protection is quite straightforward. Sustainability is a wider concept that includes primarily environmental considerations. Environmental protection and the improvement of environmental conditions dominate the sustainability discourse to such a great extent that they are used by many as interchangeable notions.[256] This restrictive understanding of the 'sustainability' concept is clearly reflected in competition policy, where the professional community (both scholars and enforcers) is inclined to use the expression of sustainability agreements for environment-enhancing and/or -protecting cooperation forms. On the contrary, in the agricultural policy domain, environmental cross-compliance measures and greening conditions may also cover the area of rural development, within which the social sustainability of rural areas and the rural community are of great importance. That is to say, though it is clear that sustainability is much more than the protection of the environment and the amelioration of environmental conditions, the term is – in many cases – limited to the ecological pillar, neglecting the other two constituting elements in the form of economic and social aspects. For the sake of clarity, I will distinguish these three areas

254 United Nations Brundtland Commission, 'Report of the World Commission on Environment and Development: Our Common Future' (1987) 27.

255 Carlos Alberto Ruggerio, 'Sustainability and Sustainable Development: A Review of Principles and Definitions' (2021) 786 Science of the Total Environment, Article 147481.

256 Lucia Corsini and James Moultrie, 'What Is Design for Social Sustainability? A Systematic Literature Review for Designers of Product-Service Systems' (2021) 13 Sustainability, Article 5963.

DOI: 10.4324/9781003604747-12

in both policy domains as much as I can, bearing in mind that – in its pure textual sense – the discourse on agricultural state aid programmes is mainly dominated by environmental policy integration despite the emphasis put on the broader term of sustainability in practice, as well as the fact that competition policy explicitly voices sustainability as its new lighthouse but – in reality – it does not speak about it other than environmental considerations.

Based on these considerations, I use the three-pillar system of sustainability because it shows precisely the likely trade-offs that are necessary to balancing the different aspects. I do not contend that all sustainability initiatives and programmes come at the cost of one or two pillars that are not directly targeted, but situations may arise when, for example, economic sustainability is sacrificed at the altar of the environment.

Here, in this general part, I do not aim to define and circumscribe each of the three pillars separately. The more general the definition of the sustainability concept itself or of any of its pillar aims to be, the more difficulties we are to face. As early as 1992, *Holmberg and Sandbrook* identified more than 70 definitions of sustainable development,[257] and this was only five years after the publication of the influential Brundtland Report. Instead of defining sustainable development, sustainability and/or its three pillars, in Chapters 10 and 11 I attempt to shed light on the likely relevance and the connections of the environmental, social and economic sustainability aspects of agricultural policy and competition policy, respectively. In these chapters, the question is how we should interpret environmental, social and economic sustainability in agricultural policy and competition policy, in particular which aspects of these public policies are affected by the inclusion of the three-pillar sustainability concept.

To better understand what social sustainability is, *Vallance, Perkins and Dixon* provide a useful conceptualisation on which I rely in the subsequent chapters. Emphasising the chaos that surrounds social sustainability and pointing out the limitations that this chaos causes in the concept's usefulness, they distinguish a 'threefold schema' for social sustainability. It involves

> (a) "development sustainability" addressing basic needs, the creation of social capital, justice, equity and so on; (b) "bridge sustainability" concerning changes in behaviour so as to achieve bio-physical environmental goals; and (c) "maintenance sustainability" referring to the preservation – or what can be sustained – of socio-cultural characteristics in the face of change, and the ways in which people actively embrace or resist those changes.[258]

This is particularly useful in the context of both public policies, because – as regards the social sustainability proposals and ideas – agricultural policy and competition policy consist of different emphases.

257 Johan Holmberg and Richard Sandbrook, 'Sustainable Development: What Is to Be Done?' in Johan Holmberg (ed), *Policies for a Small Planet* (Earthscan 1992) 19–38.

258 Suzanne Vallance, Harvey C. Perkins and Jennifer E. Dixon, 'What Is Social Sustainability? A Clarification of Concepts' (2011) 42 Geoforum 342–343.

10 Sustainability in agricultural policy

10.1 General remarks

Agriculture-related industries – not only production itself but also processing activities – have been transformed significantly since the 1950s, resulting in adverse effects on the environment. A lacuna of problems have arrived in parallel with the post-World War II need for producing more food for lower costs. Excessive use of fertilisers poses both environmental and geopolitical complications, such as "nutrient imbalances, leaching of nutrients from crops to environment and the associated impacts, and increasing cost of fertilizers with serious geopolitical and economic problems for the food security in poor countries."[259] Certain intensification practices during production increase heavy metal contents in soil, water and, thus, in plants, affecting human health and resulting in reduced soil quality in the long term.[260] Environmental contamination as well as health risks may also be caused by inadequate agricultural waste management.[261] Worldwide water abstraction's 70% is generated by agriculture, and beyond this fact, "[f]arms discharge large quantities of agrochemicals, organic matter, drug residues, sediments and saline drainage into water bodies," playing a key role in water pollution.[262] According to some estimates, the livestock sector's contribution to total anthropogenic greenhouse gas emissions, typically in the form of methane and nitrous oxide produced by enteric fermentation and manure storage, is 14,5%.[263] These all contribute to climate change and have detrimental impacts on environmental ecosystems.

259 Josep Penuelas, Fernando Coello and Jordi Sardans, 'A Better Use of Fertilizers Is Needed for Global Food Security and Environmental Sustainability' (2023) 12 Agriculture & Food Security, Article 5.

260 Carlos Gil, Rafael Boluda, José Antonio Rodríguez Martín, Miguel Guzmán, Fernando del Moral and Joaquín Ramos-Miras, 'Assessing Soil Contamination and Temporal Trends of Heavy Metal Contents in Greenhouses on Semiarid Land' (2018) 29 Land Degradation and Development 3344–3354.

261 Resego Phiri, Sanjay Mavinkere Rangappa and Suchart Siengchin, 'Agro-Waste for Renewable and Sustainable Green Production: A Review' (2024) 434 Journal of Cleaner Production, Article 139989.

262 Food and Agriculture Organization of the United Nations, 'Water Pollution from Agriculture: A Global Review: Executive Summary' (FAO 2017) 2.

263 Giampiero Grossi, Pietro Goglio, Andrea Vitali and Adrian G. Williams, 'Livestock and Climate Change: Impact of Livestock on Climate and Mitigation Strategies' (2019) 9 Animal Frontiers 69–76.

DOI: 10.4324/9781003604747-13

Even in light of the aforementioned sketchy examples of limited number, it is no surprise that in the past half century, both EU and US agricultural policies have been increasingly pressured to take into account sustainability considerations when adopting policy means to achieve their objectives.

The question arises as to which policy tools sustainability has infiltrated into agricultural policy. The answer is straightforward. In the beginning, it has not happened by opening the door for private initiatives based on cooperation between market actors. Sustainability considerations, in particular environmental aspects, appeared in the 1980s in agricultural state aid programmes as conditions to be fulfilled by market players so that they could become eligible for certain payments. Initially, voluntary programmes were adopted, that is agricultural producers were free to choose whether they intended to participate in these programmes. Later, the environmental conditionalities have pervaded most of the agricultural state aid types, and not meeting the requirements results in the exclusion of the beneficiary from the respective programme and/ or in administrative fines.

This development trajectory since the 1980s serves as the reason to examine the evolution of agricultural state aids on the path to becoming green payments in the next chapter.

10.2 Environmental policy integration in agriculture

It is a principle of utmost importance that sustainability appears as an additional factor to be considered during the review of established agricultural policy means, and not vice versa. That is to say, sustainability is not the primary goal in the context of agricultural policy, but – now – an unavoidable aspect to be respected in policy-making processes, which is brought into the picture by environmentalists. At the core of agricultural policy is farm income support, which has been shaken up by further values.[264]

As early as 2000, *Lowe and Baldock* saw the problem in the low prioritisation of environmental issues, which has now definitely changed. What has remained intact is another factor mentioned by them: a closed agricultural policy network that attempts to filter and counterbalance environmental considerations.[265] In the first decades of the Common Agricultural Policy, the environment was subsumed "under the long-standing belief that what was good for farming would necessarily be good for the countryside."[266] Some authors argue that the greater emphasis on the environment has come to the fore intensively only in the last three decades

264 Daugbjerg and Swinbank (n 248) 259–270.

265 P. Lowe and D. Baldock, 'Integration of Environmental Objectives into Agricultural Policy Making' in F. Brouwer and P. Lowe (eds), *CAP Regimes and the European Countryside* (CAB International 2000) 31–52.

266 Henry Buller, 'Integrating EU Environmental and Agricultural Policy' in Andrea Lenschow (ed), *Environmental Policy Integration: Greening Sectoral Policies in Europe* (Earthscan 2001) 103.

despite the fact that the issue appeared as early as the 1970s.[267] Among others, the door for the greening process was opened by "the gradual decline of farmers' power."[268] Of course, one can also look at it from this direction, however, I see it more reasonable to emphasise not the power loss of farmers but the further fragmentation of different interests in policy-making through, for example, the appearance of environmental advocates.[269] There is a gradual trend that shows the increasing, but not uninterrupted, integration of environmental considerations in the US farm bills as well as during the periodic revision of the EU common agricultural policy. In the United States, the breakthrough happened with the 1990 farm bill that included a separate climate change title.[270] In the European Union, the Maastricht Treaty signed in 1992 signalled the enhanced commitment of the Community to environmental protection,[271] then – in agricultural policy context – the 1992 MacSharry reforms brought new environmental obligations for farmers. However, these did not meet the early expectations of reversing inimical trends for the environment.[272]

In the EU, the integration of environmental policy into agricultural policy is nevertheless limited because of, according to *Alons*, the incomplete transformation of the CAP from exceptionalism to post-exceptionalism.[273] *Daugbjerg and Feindt* are of the opinion that post-exceptionalism is the outcome of struggles between the conventional exceptionalist attitude towards the agricultural sector and the "market-oriented and performance-based" neoliberal approach. The neoliberal mode of market organisation, which emerged in the 1980s, confronted the exceptionalist ideas about agricultural production,[274] which was prevalent after World War II. The policy literature seems to agree that the state of play of agricultural policy-making is of post-exceptionalist nature, meaning that both continuity and change can be identified as regards ideas, institutions, interests and policy instruments. As formulated by *Daugbjerg and Feindt*, "partial departure" can be seen from "compartmentalized, exclusive and exceptionalist policies and politics, which, however,

267 As regards the United States: J.F. Parr and S.B. Hornick, 'The Evolution of Sustainable Agriculture in the United States: A Recent Historical Perspective' (U.S. Department of Agriculture) <www.infrc.or.jp/knf/PDF%20KNF%20Conf%20Data/C3-8-102.pdf> accessed 23 March 2024.

268 Yannis E. Doukas, Luca Salvati and Ioannis Vardopoulos, 'Unraveling the European Agricultural Policy Sustainable Development Trajectory' (2023) 12 Land, Article 1749.

269 Daugbjerg and Swinbank (n 248) 259–270.

270 Jonathan Coppess, 'Climate Change and the Farm Bill: A Brief History' (2022) 12 Farmdoc Daily 149.

271 David Wilkinson, 'Maastricht and the Environment: The Implications for the EC's Environment Policy of the Treaty on European Union' (1992) 4 Journal of Environmental Law 221.

272 Michael Winter, 'Strong Policy or Weak Policy? The Environmental Impact of the 1992 Reforms to the CAP Arable Regime in Great Britain' (2000) 16 Journal of Rural Studies 47–59.

273 Gerry Alons, 'Environmental Policy Integration in the EU's Common Agricultural Policy: Greening or Greenwashing?' in Carsten Daugbjerg and Peter Feindt (eds), *Transforming Food and Agricultural Policy: Post-Exceptionalism in Public Policy* (Routledge 2018) ch 3.

274 Carsten Daugbjerg and Peter H. Feindt, 'Post-Exceptionalism in Public Policy: Transforming Food and Agricultural Policy' in Carsten Daugbjerg and Peter Feindt (eds), *Transforming Food and Agricultural Policy: Post-Exceptionalism in Public Policy* (Routledge 2018) ch 1.

preserves some exceptionalist features and has not led to a complete transformation to market-oriented and performance-based policies," carrying "a significant legacy from past policy."[275]

Greer identifies a shallow post-exceptionalism, by which he means that the "historically persistent agricultural policy subsystem has opened up to new actors, incorporated some programme change but left the ideational framework largely intact."[276] Sustainability is one of these new objectives to take into account within the framework of the post-exceptionalist agricultural policy-making.

Exceptionalism was still palpable also as regards the environmental regulation of the agricultural sector around the turn of the century,[277] however, the process of greening agricultural policy, in particular the subsidy regimes of the EU and the United States, started to take shape in the late 1980s and early 1990s. The next subheading explores this road.

10.3 Greening the CAP and US agricultural policy

The aim of this subheading is not to analyse in detail the general agricultural policy reforms and environment-related agricultural subsidy programmes in the United States and the European Union, but to chronologically present and scrutinise the main principles and development trends that have proceeded since the 1980s and resulted in the current framework of agricultural and agri-environmental policy on the two sides of the Atlantic. The reason for choosing the 1980s as the starting point of examination is that the two phenomena mentioned already in the introductory remarks – more market orientation and more environment friendliness of the agricultural sector – began to unfold around this time.

What is an obvious method of the incorporation of environmental concerns into agricultural policy is the introduction of "greening" conditions to subsidy programmes, meaning that producers are entitled to certain agricultural state aid, only if they fulfil predetermined criteria aiming to develop the state of the environment. In the beginning, voluntary agri-environmental schemes appeared, whose success – the achievement of the policy objective of a more environment-friendly agricultural sector – is determined to a high extent by farmers' willingness to participate.[278] Later, aid programmes have gradually become obligatory in nature, within the framework of which direct payments are linked to complying with predetermined environmental criteria, and farmers are required to partake in these programmes in order to receive the payment. Both the design and scope of agri-environmental

275 Daugbjerg and Feindt (n 274) 3.

276 Alan Greer, 'Post-Exceptional Politics in Agriculture: An Examination of the 2013 CAP Reform' (2017) 24 Journal of European Public Policy 1585–1603.

277 J.B. Ruhl, 'Farms, Their Environmental Harms, and Environmental Laws' (2000) 27 Ecology Law Quarterly 263–350.

278 Maria Espinosa-Goded, Jesús Barreiro-Hurlé and Eric Ruto, 'What Do Farmers Want From Agri-Environmental Scheme Design? A Choice Experiment Approach' (2010) 61 Journal of Agricultural Economics 259–273.

schemes are diverse. Action-based programmes require farmers to implement an environmentally friendly agricultural practice, while result-based ones are built upon the condition to deliver certain outcomes.[279]

As regards the differences between the EU and US approach towards addressing environmental externalities generated by the agricultural sector, *Baylis, Rausser and Simon* identify three key distinctions. First and foremost, they contend that while the policy-makers in the United States treat agricultural production and environmental protection as conflicting notions, the European viewpoint is characterised by the fact that the expansion of agricultural production may help attain the objectives of environmental protection. Second, the focus of EU agricultural policy is on negative externalities resulting from intensification (for example, intensified use of pesticides or more livestock density); at the same time, the US is concerned rather with environmental harms induced by extensification (for example, the use of highly erodible soil). Third, US programmes

> focus on the anticipated environmental outputs (e.g. soil erosion, water quality) associated with certain agricultural activities, so that competing proposals for funding under these programmes are ranked in accordance with their potential for either mitigating the negative, or enhancing the positive, impacts of these outputs. In order to receive agri-environmental payments in the EU, by contrast, it is typically sufficient to commit to using agricultural inputs, or farming practices, that have been designated as environmentally friendly (e.g. organic production methods, livestock practices that respect animal welfare).[280]

US agricultural policy started the last two decades of the 20th century in a completely different setting than the European Communities. The then-new US farm bill preceded the MacSharry reforms by two years.[281] Its antecedent, the 1985 farm bill, was a great success: it meant a step towards the competitive agriculture paradigm, promoted exports, could maintain and even increase farmers' income, despite the sharp decrease in federal farm programme expenditures. This, as well as the erratic Uruguay Round concerning agricultural questions, resulted in the demand and possibility of preserving the status quo in the new 1990 farm bill. There were no external and internal pressures to radically divert the evolving US

279 Sergei Schaub, Jaboury Ghazoul, Robert Huber, Wei Zhang, Adelaide Sander, Charles Rees, Simanti Banerjee and Robert Finger, 'The Role of Behavioural Factors and Opportunity Costs in Farmers' Participation in Voluntary Agri-Environmental Schemes: A Systematic Review' (2023) 74 Journal of Agricultural Economics 617–660.

280 Kathy Baylis, Gordon C. Rausser and Leo K. Simon, 'Including Non-Trade Concerns: The Environment in EU and US Agricultural Policy' (2005) 4 International Journal of Agricultural Resources Governance and Ecology 264.

281 Food, Agriculture, Conservation, and Trade Act of 1990.

agricultural policy means from the path already started much earlier, characterised by incremental steps of decoupling.[282]

In the late 1980s, beside the economic needs of agriculture, there were more and more discussions on environmental issues in the House and Senate agriculture committees.[283] This does not mean that the 1985 farm bill was not concerned with environmental stewardship. Already on the path towards the 1985 legislation, the so-called Conservation Coalition not only embraced the adoption of the Conservation Reserve Program (a ten-year land retirement programme), but also succeeded in stimulating the introduction of environment-friendly measures, such as the Sodbuster, Swampbuster and Conservation Compliance.[284]

The 1990 farm bill, on one hand, expanded the existing conservation reserve programmes and, on the other hand, established several new ones. However, it also weakened the enforcement of the Sodbuster and Swampbuster programmes,[285] which were intended to prevent soil loss on lands prone to erosion and to conserve wetlands.

The remarkable novelty of these two farm bills was the regulatory approach of their conservation programmes. As put by *Roberts and Dean*, "penalties are prescribed if the desired behavior is not forthcoming rather than enticing the desired behavior with voluntary incentives, as has been traditional in agricultural legislation."[286] Both the Sodbuster and Swampbuster programmes, if the farmer violates the obligatons, create ineligibility for commodity programmes. The provisions on highly erodible land and wetland conservation oblige persons to "comply with established soil and water conservation practices." If these are not satisfied, farmers do not "receive certain benefits administered by the United States Department of Agriculture." These measures target at least five different objectives:

> (1) reduction of soil loss due to wind and water erosion; (2) protection of the Nation's long term capability to produce food and fiber; (3) production of sedimentation and improvement of water quality; (4) preservation of the Nation's wetlands; and (5) reduction of surplus commodities production.[287]

Swampbuster provisions aim to prevent wetlands from being converted for agricultural use. The mechanism behind it is similar to that of the Sodbuster programme: no compliance results in ineligibility. As was emphasised in Congress: the

282 Wayne Moyer and Tim Josling, *Agricultural Policy Reform: Politics and Process in the EU and US in the 1990s* (Ashgate 2002).

283 Robert L. Meyers, 'Greening of the Farm Bill' *Washington Watch* (October 1989) 599.

284 R. Robert and L.E.R. Dean, 'An Inquiry into Lowi's Policy Typology: The Conservation Coalition and the 1985 and 1990 Farm Bills' (1994) 12 Environment and Planning C: Politics and Space 71.

285 Linda A. Malone, 'The Conservation Title of the 1990 Farm Bill' *Agricultural Law Update* (May 1991) 4.

286 Robert and Dean (n 284) 71.

287 Galen Fountain, 'Land Use Related Restrictions and the Conservation Provisions of the Food Security Act of 1985: Sodbuster and Swampbuster' (1988) 11 University of Arkansas at Little Rock Law Review 554.

> purpose [of the measure] will be realized by limiting an agricultural producer's access to various price support, production adjustment, Federal crop insurance, Federal disaster loans and payments, and various other programs carried out by the Federal Government if the producer drains and plants crops on a natural wetland.[288]

Contrary to the situation in the United States, the 1992 MacSharry reform was not a resounding success, however, it was definitely a step forward to reforming the traditional functioning of the Common Agricultural Policy of the European Union.[289] On the road to the reform, Commissioner *MacSharry* emphasised that the proposals, which consisted of intervention price cuts as well as area and animal number-based compensatory direct payments, are the only way

> to preserve the natural environment, traditional landscape and a model of agriculture based on the family farm. The policy must now recognize that the farmer fulfils a double function of producing food and of protecting the environment and the countryside.[290]

The cereals and beef sectors were the ones most heavily affected, where intervention prices were lowered but the revenue loss of farmers were compensated by payments based on acreage and headage.[291]

Experts disagree whether the reform was effective, and if so, to what extent, in terms of its budgetary impacts as well as (at least partly) solving the problems underlying agricultural policy. It was not a policy paradigm change, but can be understood as a premonition of larger-scale reform attempts. It is another question that the need for changing EU agricultural policy is attributed, in part, to the external pressure created by multilateral trade negotiations within the framework of the Uruguay Round of the General Agreement on Tariffs and Trade (GATT).[292] The internal pressure to reforming the CAP can be derived from the fact that the highly priced agricultural support policy having been realised earlier in the EU generated a situation in which European producers were paid for their produce more than global price levels, causing oversupply (surpluses) that had to be sold on the international market with increasing export subsidies.[293] This meant a huge financial burden for the European community. *Lovec*, in his comprehensive analysis on

288 Daryn McBeth, 'Wetlands Conservation and Federal Regulation: Analysis of the Food Security Act's Swampbuster Provisions as Amended by the Federal Agriculture Improvement and Reform Act of 1996' (1997) 21 Harvard Environmental Law Review 221.

289 Joseph A. McMahon, 'The Common Agricultural Policy: From Quantity to Quality?' (2001) 53 Northern Ireland Legal Quarterly 15.

290 Agra Europe (25 January 1991) 1–2.

291 Alan Swinbank, 'New Direct Payments Scheme: Targeting and Redistribution in the Future CAP' (Directorate-General for Internal Policies 2012).

292 Grant (n 34) 77–79.

293 Moyer and Josling (n 282).

CAP reforms, also handles the 1992 MacSharry reform (as well as Agenda 2000) as the means to adjust EU agricultural policy to the new trade and budget context.[294] According to *Garzon*, unlike market and price policy means, there were, however, issues, such as the environmental incentives, that did not bring with them any concerns throughout the reform process. The reason was that it was recognised that certain measures are necessary to make the EU's agricultural policy more acceptable.[295] So although the environmental considerations appeared as (marginal) arguments during the process, the main reasons behind the policy change can be found rather in budget constraints and the need to bringing the CAP into accordance with international trade requirements posed by the Uruguay Round.

Of the environment-related means of the MacSharry reforms, two are worth mentioning: the obligatory set-aside of arable land and the voluntary agri-environment measures. The set-aside requirement within the general scheme was fixed at 15%, and all producers applying for compensatory payments had to comply with it.[296] Small producers were an exception, who could apply for these payments without the requirement within the simplified scheme.[297] Set-aside was not a new phenomenon,[298] however; as general obligation it had not existed earlier. Nevertheless, it must be borne in mind that the requirement does not bring with it unquestionable environmental improvements. Its effects are rather mixed, mainly depending on the quality of the respective plots set aside. Furthermore, these schemes incentivise farmers to fulfil the obligation with their lowest-quality and least-profitable land.[299] A *European Court of Auditors* report noted that although it has high environmental potential, its post-1992 application by the EU Member States left much room for better implementation. Certain requirements prescribed by Member States within the set-aside scheme were detrimental to the environment rather than advantageous.[300]

Similarly to the means of set-aside, agri-environmental measures had also been extant in different forms before the adoption of the new regulation within the MacSharry package, however, the difference could be found in that the Member States were obliged to establish and implement, in accordance with their specific needs, aid schemes that are coherent with the objectives formulated at the EU level.[301]

294 Marko Lovec, *The European Union's Common Agricultural Policy Reforms* (Palgrave Macmillan 2016) 93.

295 Garzon (n 222) 69.

296 Council Regulation (EEC) No 1765/92 of 30 June 1992 establishing a support system for producers of certain arable crops [1992] OJ L181/12, art 7.

297 Council Regulation (EEC) (n 296) art 8.

298 See, for example: Council Regulation (EEC) No 2328/91 of 15 July 1991 on improving the efficiency of agricultural structures [1991] OJ L218/1, art 2.

299 Organisation for Economic Co-Operation and Development, 'Agriculture and the Environment: Lessons Learned from a Decade of OECD Work' (2004) 21.

300 European Court of Auditors, 'Special Report No 14/2000 on "Greening the CAP" Together with the Commission's Replies' (2000) 17–18.

301 See: Council Regulation (EEC) No 2078/92 of 30 June 1992 on agricultural production methods compatible with the requirements of the protection of the environment and the maintenance of the countryside [1992] OJ L215/85, arts 1–2.

Farmers' participation still remained voluntary. *Buller* formulated harsh critique on the effectiveness of these measures. In his opinion, farmers – in most cases – participated in these programmes for economic considerations, i.e., supplementary income sources. Moreover, the policy failed to achieve a real breakthrough in environmental protection due to the lack of adequately addressing, for example, pesticide and nitrate pollution. It could, nevertheless, be considered as an important first step to integrate environmental policy into the agricultural sector, but significant problems to be addressed remained.[302]

The reform of US agricultural policy signed into law in 1996[303] was dominated so strongly by the competitive agriculture paradigm as never before. It was "a clear and unambiguous signal that the US is committed to the full liberalisation of farm policy."[304] The 1996 farm bill came to the fore with the establishment of decoupled commodity payments from production decisions,[305] long preceding the EU in this regard.

Though budgetary constraints surfaced early during the legislative process, the feedback from international developments after the Uruguay Round and the implementation of the Agreement on Agriculture was positive from the viewpoint of the United States.[306] It was an important achievement of the 1996 farm bill that despite the budget cuts, serious environmental problems to be addressed were given proper funding.[307] Departing from earlier farm bills, according to *Poe*, the FAIR Act of 1996 constituted a paradigm shift that builds upon the maximisation of environmental benefits per dollar spent.[308] The Sodbuster, Swampbuster and conservation reserve programmes all remained with some technical and/or substantial changes. Although area reduction programmes (set-aside) and base acreage controls were eliminated, as well as deficiency payment programmes ceasing to exist, thus creating significant changes in the structure of US agricultural policy, the actual effects of these alterations were prognosed to be small on agricultural production.[309]

302 Henry Buller, 'The Agri-Environmental Measures (2078/92)' in Floor Brouwer and Philip Lowe (eds), *CAP Regimes and the European Countryside: Prospects for Integration between Agricultural, Regional and Environmental Policies* (CABI Publishing 2000) 216.

303 Federal Agriculture Improvement and Reform (FAIR) Act of 1996.

304 David R. Harvey, 'The US Farm Act: "Fair" or "Foul"? An Evolutionary Perspective from East of the Atlantic' (Conference Paper 1998) <www.staff.ncl.ac.uk/david.harvey/AEF811/AEF811.5/FAIR1.pdf> accessed 29 June 2024.

305 Nigel Key, Ruben Lubowski and Michael J. Roberts, 'The 1996 Federal Agriculture Improvement and Reform Act: Correcting a Distortion?' (Annual Meeting of the AAEA, Denver, Colorado, August 2004) <https://core.ac.uk/download/pdf/6522852.pdf> accessed 27 January 2024.

306 Moyer and Josling (n 282).

307 Peter J. Kuch and Clayton W. Ogg, 'The 1995 Farm Bill and Natural Resource Conservation: Major New Opportunities' (1996) 78 American Journal of Agricultural Economics 1212.

308 Gregory L. Poe, 'Maximizing the Environmental Benefits Per Dollar Expended: An Economic Interpretation and Review of Agricultural Environmental Benefits and Costs' (1999) 12 Society & Natural Resources: An International Journal 571.

309 Vincent H. Smith and Joseph W. Glauber, 'The Effects of the 1996 Farm Bill on Food and Feed Grains' (1997) Policy Issues Paper 3 <https://ageconsearch.umn.edu/record/29170/?v=pdf> accessed 27 June 2024.

In the European Union, after the MacSharry package the next step that also contained crucial changes in agricultural policy was the Agenda 2000 reform adopted in 1999. Within this, the most far-reaching improvement was the creation of Pillar II within the Common Agricultural Policy. Pillar II still constitutes the European Union's rural development policy. Though it seems quite groundbreaking, the new two-pillar system could not be considered radical at that time. Agenda 2000 went further on the road of the MacSharry reforms, because – contrary to the juncture of the early 1990s – there was no crisis such as the one before the new era of the CAP. As formulated by *Moyer and Josling*, "[p]ursuing the MacSharry path was attractive in that the bargaining costs of incremental change appeared manageable, implementation was feasible and the consequences were predictable."[310]

Agenda 2000 aimed at updating the European model of agriculture, meaning the several functions that are fulfilled by the sector: economic and environmental development, preserving rural life and the landscapes of the countryside. Though a continued commitment to stable farm incomes and the need to lower guaranteed prices remained, EU primary law within the Treaty of Amsterdam also established the obligation of environmental policy integration into all other sectoral policies, which constituted an enhanced responsibility to greening the Common Agricultural Policy. As summarised by the document itself,

> [t]he new reform will help to develop a genuinely multi-functional, sustainable and competitive agricultural sector, which will also help to secure the future of the more fragile rural regions. It recognises that agriculture has a key role to play in preserving the countryside and natural spaces and in the vitality of rural life.[311]

As regards environmental protection, a novelty of Agenda 2000 was cross-compliance, "the practice of granting public payments to farmers only if they comply with certain environmental standards."[312] This policy mechanism was taken over from the United States, where it had appeared within the context of, for example, Sodbuster and Swampbuster programmes.[313] In the European Union, the 1999 reforms introduced this tool as a voluntary measure[314]; Member States had the option to link direct payments to certain environmental requirements. Nevertheless,

310 Moyer and Josling (n 282).

311 European Commission, 'Europe's Agenda 2000: Strengthening and Widening the European Union' (Office for Official Publications of the European Communities 1999) 4–10.

312 Stefan Mann, 'Different Perspectives on Cross-Compliance' (2005) 14 Environmental Values 471.

313 Claas Meyer, Bettina Matzdorf, Klaus Müller and Christian Schleyer, 'Cross Compliance as Payment for Public Goods? Understanding EU and US Agricultural Policies' (2014) 107 Ecological Economics 185.

314 Council Regulation (EC) No 1259/1999 of 17 May 1999 establishing common rules for direct support schemes under the common agricultural policy [1999] OJ L160/113, art 3.

only a limited number of countries introduced the mechanism.[315] Another development featured in the Agenda 2000 reforms is the introduction of modulation, which has indirect environmental consequences. Compensation payments by the Member States, at most 20% of them, could be voluntarily distracted and rendered to address, for example, agri-environmental concerns within Pillar II.[316]

In general, the 2002 US farm bill[317] reversed several forward-looking trends of the FAIR Act of 1996. The Doha Development Round was still in its early stage, and Congress managed to adopt the bill when the federal budget surpluses were still present in order to capture them. Payment limitations were removed, coupled payments came back. Futhermore, it "created new farm programs for commodities that had never before had them (small legumes); resurrected programs for wool, mohair, and honey that had been terminated in earlier legislation; increased benefits to sugar producers; and created another dairy program."[318] That is, there were neither budget constraints nor international pressure from the WTO to limit the spending of the 2002 farm bill, and to counteract, in part, agricultural lobby.[319] As regards its environmental protection effects, the bill was considered a small step in agri-environmental policy, however, it was emphasised that income support provisions still constitute unnecessary environmental harm. Although the dedication to support environmental protection continued, there was a lack of comprehensiveness in the programmes, and the voluntary nature of application derogated the bill's potential environmental effects.[320] Nevertheless, *Davis* still calls it "the greenest farm bill in history."[321] Simply put, 2002 marked a step forward concerning the aim of environment-friendly agriculture but a step backward in connection with market orientation.

What was brought about by the 1996 farm bill in the United States, i.e., a decoupled system of agricultural subsidies, only took place in the European Union thanks to the 2003 Fischler reform. Commissioner *Franz Fischler* explicitly declared in his mid-2001 publication in *Intereconomics* that the adaptation of the Common Agricultural Policy to the "society's evolving expectations" was inevitable. He was particularly keen to emphasise the need for sustainable agriculture and rural development.[322]

315 Martin Farmer and Vicki Swales, *The Development and Implementation of Cross-Compliance in the EU-15: An Analysis* (Institute for European Environmental Policy 2004) 4.
316 Katherine Falconer and Neil Ward, 'Using Modulation to Green the CAP: The UK Case' (2000) 17 Land Use Policy 270.
317 Farm Security and Rural Investment Act of 2002.
318 Robert L. Thompson, 'The US Farm Bill and the Doha Negotiations: On Parallel Tracks or a Collision Course?' (September 2005) IPC Issue Brief 5.
319 David Orden, 'Reform's Stunted Crop' (Spring 2002) Regulation 32.
320 Jesse Ratcliffe, 'A Small Step Forward: Environmental Protection Provisions in the 2002 Farm Bill' (2003) 30 Ecology Law Quarterly 637–659.
321 Todd D. Davis, 'Private Decisions and Public Goods: Trade-Offs in the Conservation Programs in the New Farm Bill: Discussion' (2004) 36 Journal of Agricultural and Applied Economics 435.
322 Franz Fischler, 'Reform of the Common Agricultural Policy' (May/June 2001) Intereconomics 115–118.

Although the year 2003 should have only been a midterm review of the agricultural policy of the European Union, it resulted in a comprehensive reform. *Swinnen* argues that the then-new qualified majority voting, external changes and an enthusiastic, agenda-setter European Commission all contributed to the "radical" reform.[323]

The legitimacy of the whole agricultural system of the EU had to be strengthened, and there were serious concerns that the EU would be isolated again during the international trade negotiations of the Doha Round, if the Common Agricultural Policy remained unchanged or slightly modified. This had happened in the early 1990s before the MacSharry reforms. Beyond the international pressures, budget constraints were not extant, however, a strong political need was formulated among the diversifying actors of EU agricultural policy to adapt the system to the society's evolving requirements. Of course, income support for farmers still constituted the most important issue, but it was strongly emphasised that direct compensatory payments can ensure the fair standard of living of farmers as well as shelter the producers from market instability. Decoupling emerged as a powerful alternative as never before in the EU,[324] establishing – according to some – the most radical reform in the history of the Common Agricultural Policy.[325] On the contrary, *Nedergaard* is of the opinion that the reforms meant only moderate policy changes, and the idea of protecting producers from market forces was unaltered.[326]

Regarding the agri-environmental aspects of the reform, the notable development took place in connection with a revitalised[327] cross-compliance and modulation, which became compulsory.[328] The freshly introduced Single Payment Scheme (SPS) was decoupled from the obligation to produce, as well as subject to certain environment-related conditions. Under the notion of cross-compliance, farmers were obliged to keep their land in good agricultural and environmental conditions (GAEC) and they had to comply with statutory management requirements (SMRs). The SPS "replaced most existing direct aid payments."[329] While SMRs were determined by Community legislation, the defining of GAEC was entrusted to Member States on the basis of the framework set up in one of the annexes of the respective regulation, taking into account the specific characteristics of the areas concerned, including soil and climatic condition, existing farming systems, land use,

323 Johan Swinnen, *The Perfect Storm: The Political Economy of the Fischler Reforms of the Common Agricultural Policy* (Centre for European Policy Studies 2008).

324 Garzon (n 222) 100–107.

325 Arlindo Cunha and Alan Swinbank, *An Inside View of the CAP Reform Process: Explaining the MacSharry, Agenda 2000, and Fischler Reforms* (OUP 2011) 125–149.

326 Peter Nedergaard, 'The 2003 Reform of the Common Agricultural Policy: Against All Odds or Rational Explanations?' (2006) 28 Journal of European Integration 213.

327 Farmer and Swales (n 315) 4.

328 Alons (n 273).

329 European Court of Auditors, 'Single Payment Scheme (SPS): Issues to Be Addressed to Improve Its Sound Financial Management' (2011) Special Report No 5, 11–14.

crop rotation, farming practices and farm structures.[330] Of the eighteen SMRs, five are concerned with the environment in a wide variety of issues: protection of wild birds, groundwater protection, soil protection against sewage sludge, water pollution against nitrates, protection of natural habitats as well as wild flora and fauna.[331] It is of utter importance that noncompliance with either SMRs or the GAEC criteria resulted in the reduction or exclusion from payments.[332] The other backbone of the 2003 Fischler reform was modulation that allocated a certain amount of direct payments to the rural development pillar.[333]

Nevertheless, in the opinion of *Scown, Brady and Nicholas*, after 2003, among others, the problem of inadequately addressing sustainability concerns within EU agricultural policy remained on the surface.[334] Using spatial agent-based modelling, research has demonstrated that the method of decoupling can adversely affect the landscape, because in extensive regions the GAEC criteria – through incentivising homogenous land use – do not constitute sufficient protection to avoid environmental consequences. Furthermore, in more intensive regions, "GAEC is generally redundant as market prices are sufficient to keep land in commodity production and hence meet payment obligations."[335] It is, however, a surprising finding that although cross-compliance resulted in reduced fertiliser and pesticide expenditure, this was also true for the voluntary participants of agri-environmental schemes. Moreover, quite interestingly, those farmers who relied more heavily on public payments had no stronger motivation to enhance their environmental performance.[336]

A few months apart in 2008, both the US farm bill and the EU's Common Agricultural Policy were revised. Practically, the so-called Health Check of EU agricultural policy came as an extension of the 2003 reforms.[337] The simplification of existing rules (for example, of the single payment scheme and of cross-compliance) was a declared objective.[338] One of the most important measures of the reform was

330 Council Regulation (EC) No 1782/2003 of 29 September 2003 establishing common rules for direct support schemes under the common agricultural policy and establishing certain support schemes for farmers and amending Regulations (EEC) No 2019/93, (EC) No 1452/2001, (EC) No 1453/2001, (EC) No 1454/2001, (EC) 1868/94, (EC) No 1251/1999, (EC) No 1254/1999, (EC) No 1673/2000, (EEC) No 2358/71 and (EC) No 2529/2001 [2003] OJ L270/1, arts 4–5.

331 Council Regulation (EC) No 1782/2003, Annex III.

332 Council Regulation (EC) No 1782/2003, art 6.

333 Council Regulation (EC) No 1782/2003, art 10.

334 Murray W. Scown, Mark V. Brady and Kimberly A. Nicholas, 'Billions in Misspent EU Agricultural Subsidies Could Support the Sustainable Development Goals' (2020) 3 One Earth 237–250.

335 Mark Brady, Konrad Kellermann, Christoph Sahrbacher and Ladislav Jelinek, 'Impacts of Decoupled Agricultural Support on Farm Structure, Biodiversity and Landscape Mosaic: Some EU Results' (2009) 60 Journal of Agricultural Economics 580.

336 Jūratė Jaraitė and Andrius Kažukauskas, 'The Effect of Mandatory Agro-Environmental Policy on Farm Fertiliser and Pesticide Expenditure' (2012) 63 Journal of Agricultural Economics 656–676.

337 Lovec (n 294) 148.

338 Commission, 'Preparing for the "Health Check" of the CAP reform' (Communication) COM/2007/0722 final, 2.1. and 2.2.

the 'soft landing policy' as regards milk quotas[339] that were gradually increased on the way towards their phasing out due in 2015, complementing the earlier measures adopted in 2003 in the form of declining intervention prices and the decoupling of premiums.[340] Moreover, decoupling was extended to further products that could have been supported earlier with coupled payments by Member States. Modulation, i.e., shifting certain amounts from direct aid to rural development, was also given a boost in the form of a possible higher percentage to be modulated. However, it must be taken into account that this is not in direct connection with increased environmental protection, because Pillar II also includes non-environmental policies.[341] The abolition of set-aside was also realised for arable crops, meaning that producers were no longer required to leave 10% of their land fallow.[342]

The 2008 US farm bill[343] increased the spending on conservation programmes. It not only changed certain details of existing schemes (eligibility requirements, programme definitions, enrollment and payment limits, etc.) but also introduced new ones.

> The majority of the agriculture and farmland conservation groups have responded favorably to the expanded provisions and increased funding for programs in the conservation title of the 2008 farm bill. However, a few wildlife groups have expressed concern about changes to some provisions during the conference negotiations, which are perceived as providing fewer benefits for the protection of wildlife and wildlife habitat.[344]

Thanks to the 2013 *Cioloş* reform, the Common Agricultural Policy 2014–2020 differed to a quite significant extent from its predecessors. After the 2009 Lisbon Treaty, the rules under which the reform process had to be carried out changed fundamentally. Co-decision has been required since then between the Council and the European Parliament on the basis of the proposal of the Commission, which at the same time plays the role of facilitator in case of nonagreement between the decision-makers. As a consequence of the reform, with the aim to achieve a more equal distribution of subsidies between Member States on one hand (external convergence), and between farmers within a Member State on the other hand (internal convergence), the Single Payment Scheme was changed to a totally different system. The new regulation established three obligatory programmes: a basic payment

339 See more: Lukáš Čechura, Zdeňka Žáková Kroupová and Irena Benešová, 'Productivity and Efficiency in European Milk Production: Can We Observe the Effects of Abolishing Milk Quotas?' (2021) 11 Agriculture 835.

340 Roel Jongeneel, Siemen van Berkum, Cees de Bont, Cees van Bruchem, John Helming and Jacob Jager, 'European Dairy Policy in the Years to Come; Quota Abolition and Competitiveness' (LEI report 2010) 9.

341 Alons (n 273).

342 Ruta Landgrebe, Timo Kaphengst and Susanne Friedrich, 'German Perspectives on the Current CAP Reform' (Policy Brief for the German Marshall Fund of the United States 2009) 4.

343 Food, Conservation, and Energy Act of 2008.

344 CRS Report for Congress, 'The 2008 Farm Bill: A Summary of Major Provisions and Legislative Action' (2008) CRS-14.

for farmers, a payment for farmers observing agricultural practices beneficial for the climate and the environment, as well as a payment for young farmers commencing their agricultural activity. Beyond these schemes, voluntary payments could also be set up at the discretion of Member States.[345]

The obligatory green payment was linked to the basic payment in such a way that only those could become eligible for the former who were entitled to a payment under the latter. The regulation determined three groups of practices that can be beneficial for the climate and the environment: crop diversification, permanent grassland and ecological focus area. Cross-compliance, of course, remained even among the eligibility criteria for basic payments (GAEC and SMRs).[346] The interconnectedness of these schemes, as well as a short transition period meant that

> not satisfying "green" payment requirements w[ould] imply that, in the worst case scenario, in the first two years of the new regime the farm w[ould] lose only the "green" payment, while from 2017 onwards it w[ould] also suffer a reduction in the other direct payments.

This constellation derogated the green payment scheme to the level of a voluntary measure in 2015 and 2016, and only as of 2017 has it become de facto mandatory with the possibility of imposing an administrative penalty in case of noncompliance.[347] Others were critical, too, of the new green payment scheme. *Bureau and Mahé* were of the opinion that – due to the lax eligibility criteria – almost all farms would be entitled to the 30% green payment premium, making it a "windfall gain."[348] Still others labelled the 2014–2020 CAP system as greenwashing and policy failure; the communication of the Commission was not in line with the measures adopted, which were weakened with exceptions and a wide discretion to allocate resources to non-environmental schemes.[349] The weakening took

345 Regulation (EU) No 1307/2013 of the European Parliament and of the Council of 17 December 2013 establishing rules for direct payments to farmers under support schemes within the framework of the common agricultural policy and repealing Council Regulation (EC) No 637/2008 and Council Regulation (EC) No 73/2009 [2013] OJ L347/608, art 1.

346 Regulation (EU) No 1306/2013 of the European Parliament and of the Council of 17 December 2013 on the financing, management and monitoring of the common agricultural policy and repealing Council Regulations (EEC) No 352/78, (EC) No 165/94, (EC) No 2799/98, (EC) No 814/2000, (EC) No 1290/2005 and (EC) No 485/2008 [2013] OJ L347/549, arts 91–93 and Annex II.

347 Giovannia Anania and Maria Rosaria Pupo d'Andrea, 'The 2013 Reform of the Common Agricultural Policy' in Johan Swinnen (ed), *The Political Economy of the 2014–2020 Common Agricultural Policy: An Imperfect Stom* (Centre for European Policy Studies 2015).

348 Jean-Christophe Bureau and Louis-Pascal Mahé, 'Was the CAP Reform a Success?' in Johan Swinnen (ed), *The Political Economy of the 2014–2020 Common Agricultural Policy: An Imperfect Stom* (Centre for European Policy Studies 2015).

349 Emil Erjavec, Marko Lovec and Karmen Erjavec, 'From '"Greening" to '"Greenwash": Drivers and Discourses of the CAP 2020 '"Reform"' in Johan Swinnen (ed), *The Political Economy of the 2014–2020 Common Agricultural Policy: An Imperfect Stom* (Centre for European Policy Studies 2015).

place during the political negotiation within both the Council and the European Parliament.[350]

The opinion about US developments was similarly critical.

> [T]he United States, which pioneered the move to decoupled payments, has undergone a complete turnaround. In its recent farm bills, the USA reverted to instruments that are more linked to market conditions and yields, and the proposals tabled by Congress for the 2012 Farm Bill go further to protect farmers from adverse situations.[351]

After 24 years of continuous expansion of conservation programmes between 1990 and 2014,[352] the main aim was to simplify and consolidate the framework. Though twelve programmes were repealed, two new ones were established, as well as two others that were merged into one. Overall, the funding for conservation decreased.[353]

Four years later, in 2018,[354] mandatory funding for conservation programmes increased slightly by approximately 2% between 2019 and 2023.[355] This slight increase came only with modest changes in programme funding.[356] As of 2008, a shift has been discernible – in terms of funding – from land retirement programmes (for example, Conservation Reserve Program – CRP) to programmes aimed at developing lands in production (for example, Conservation Stewardship Program – CSP and Environmental Quality Incentives Program – EQIP).[357] In 2018, there were funding rearrangements also within working land programmes. "The allocation of funds could shift focus away from farms already engaged in and committed to conservation, particularly in terms of supporting and enhancing ongoing conservation efforts."[358] As regards advances in soil protection, the 2018 Farm Bill was, however, praised.[359]

350 Kaley Hart, 'The Fate of Green Direct Payments in the CAP Reform Negotiations' in Johan Swinnen (ed), *The Political Economy of the 2014–2020 Common Agricultural Policy: An Imperfect Stom* (Centre for European Policy Studies 2015).

351 Jean-Christophe Bureau, Christophe Crombez, Louise Knops, Alan Matthews, Johan Swinnen, Stefan Tangermann and Davide Viaggi, 'The Common Agricultural Policy After 2013' (2012) 47 Intereconomics 316–342.

352 Laurie Ristino and Gabriela Steier, 'Losing Ground: A Clarion Call for Farm Bill Reform to Ensure a Food Secure Future' (2016) 42 Columbia Journal of Environmental Law 92.

353 Megan Stubbs, 'Conservation Provisions in the 2014 Farm Bill' (Congressional Research Service, April 2014).

354 Agriculture Improvement Act of 2018.

355 See: www.ers.usda.gov/topics/farm-bill/2018-farm-bill/conservation/.

356 Roger Claassen, Daniel Hellerstein and Steven Wallander, '2018 Farm Act Retains Conservation Programs But Could Reduce Payments for Land Retirement' (2019) <www.ers.usda.gov/amber-waves/2019/december/2018-farm-act-retains-conservation-programs-but-could-reduce-payments-for-land-retirement/> accessed 30 December 2023.

357 Megan Stubbs, 'Agricultural Conservation in the 2018 Farm Bill' (Congressional Research Service, April 2019).

358 Claassen, Hellerstein and Wallander (n 356).

359 Katie Harrigan and Alyssa Charney, 'Impact of 2018 Farm Bill Provisions on Soil Health' (Soil Health Institute National Sustainable Agriculture Coalition, August 2019).

Currently, until 30 September 2024, the "lifetime" of the 2018 Farm Bill was extended by the Further Continuing Appropriations and Other Extensions Act signed by President Biden.[360]

The current framework of the revised Common Agricultural Policy was adopted formally in late 2021 and entered into force on 1 January 2023 (there was a two-year-long transitional period in 2021 and 2022, because no new CAP framework could be adopted before the expiry of the earlier system). The CAP has been built around ten crucial objectives, which in part resonate from earlier efforts. At least three are related to the environmental pillar of sustainability, such as climate change action, environmental care and the preservation of landscapes and biodiversity. Conventional agricultural policy objectives, such as fair income for producers and the strengthening of farmers' position in the supply chain, also appear.[361]

After the Lisbon Treaty, of the two revisions, this was "the second anti-reform development" in the Common Agricultural Policy. *Lovec, Rac and Erjavec* argue that the parallel process of decision-making on the Multiannual Financial Framework and the CAP results in structural bias to retain the extant framework, and the institutional environment supports conservative actors in (re-)enforcing their interests.[362] As regards environmental considerations, academic literature formulated criticism that the new regime will still fail to achieve significant advances.[363] This has been strengthened by the war in Ukraine and the reaction to it by the Commission. A number of environmental commitments were relaxed in the short and medium term to counterbalance the likely shortages caused by the breaks in supply chains. *Morales et al.* are of the opinion that "these changes in policy may sacrifice long term biodiversity and agricultural sustainability in Europe, in favour of modest increases in current agricultural production and alleged improvements of food security."[364] Furthermore, it was argued that the conditionalities and voluntary schemes of the new CAP were not in line functionally with the European Green Deal, which hinders the possible success of the policy. Unfortunately, "[t]he majority of monetary resources is still pooled into payments that encourage input-intensive and high-emission systems, whereas the economic and environmental added value from ecosystem services provided by low-input agricultural areas has been largely overlooked."[365] In other authors' opinion, however, the CAP has made

360 See: www.ers.usda.gov/topics/farm-bill/2024-farm-bill/.

361 See: https://agriculture.ec.europa.eu/common-agricultural-policy/cap-overview/cap-2023–27/key-policy-objectives-cap-2023–27_en#nineobjectives.

362 Marko Lovec, Ilona Rac and Emil Erjavec, 'External Shocks, Policy Spillovers, and Veto Players: Post(Exceptionalist) Common Agricultural Policy and the Case of the 2023–2027 Reform' (2024) 46 Journal of European Integration 433–453.

363 Herve Guyomard, Cécile Détang-Dessendre, Pierre Dupraz, Luc Delaby, Christian Huyghe, Jean-Louis Peyraud, Xavier Reboud and Clélia Sirami, 'How the Green Architecture of the 2023–2027 Common Agricultural Policy Could Have Been Greener' (2023) 52 Ambio 1327–1338.

364 Manuel B. Morales et al., 'Protect European Green Agricultural Policies for Future Food Security' (2022) 3 Communications Earth & Environment, Article 217.

365 Ivon Cuadros-Casanova et al., 'Opportunities and Challenges for Common Agricultural Policy Reform to Support the European Green Deal' (2023) 37 Conservation Biology 10.

a significant shift towards sustainable agriculture. Nevertheless, through implementation, Member States are to play a crucial role in achieving the determined objectives.[366]

As of 2023, the CAP is based on a new delivery model that builds upon national strategic plans formulated and implemented by each Member State. With this, the main aim has been to better take into account the characteristics of the Member States' agricultural sector, in parallel with providing a common set of objectives deriving from the EU level. As formulated by the relevant regulation,

> [t]he delivery model should not lead to a situation in which there are 27 different national agricultural policies, thus endangering the common nature of the CAP and the internal market. It should, however, leave to Member States a certain degree of flexibility within a strong common regulatory framework.[367]

Based on the analysis of strategic plans, it can be concluded that most of the CAP budget is used by Member States states to contribute to the income of producers as well as to achieve environmental developments.[368]

One of the most important novelties in the CAP 2023–2027 is the introduction of eco-schemes into Pillar I. The new instrument constitutes 25% of the resources of the pillar. Meanwhile Pillar II has remained largely unchanged.[369] Eco-schemes are voluntary tools for farmers, however, Member States are obliged to adopt a framework for them.[370] Moreover, the earlier basic payment scheme and the Single Area Payment Scheme were replaced by the basic income support for sustainability (BISS). Eligibility to the BISS is a precondition for other direct payment schemes, such as the complementary redistributive income support for sustainability (CRISS), the complementary income support for young farmers (CISYF), the payment for small farmers (PSF), the eco-schemes.[371]

366 Yannis E. Doukas, Ioannis Vardopoulos and Pavlos Petides, 'Challenging the Status Quo: A Critical Analysis of the Common Agricultural Policy's Shift Toward Sustainability' in Andrea Ribeiro Hoffmann, Paula Sandrin and Yannis E. Doukas (eds), *Climate Change in Regional Perspective: European Union and Latin American Initiatives, Challenges, and Solutions* (Springer 2024) 128.

367 Regulation (EU) 2021/2115 of the European Parliament and of the Council of 2 December 2021 establishing rules on support for strategic plans to be drawn up by Member States under the common agricultural policy (CAP Strategic Plans) and financed by the European Agricultural Guarantee Fund (EAGF) and by the European Agricultural Fund for Rural Development (EAFRD) and repealing Regulations (EU) No 1305/2013 and (EU) No 1307/2013 [2021] OJ L435/1, recital (27).

368 Commission, 'Mapping and Analysis of CAP Strategic Plans: Assessment of Joint Efforts for 2023–2027' (Publications Office of the European Union 2023) 963.

369 Stéphanie Barral and Cecile Detang-Dessendre, 'Reforming the Common Agricultural Policy (2023–2027): Multidisciplinary Views' (2023) 104 Review of Agricultural, Food and Environmental Studies 47.

370 Regulation (EU) 2021/2115, art 31(1)–(2).

371 See: https://agriculture.ec.europa.eu/common-agricultural-policy/income-support/biss_en#singleareapaymentscheme.

Based on this broad outline, a few remarks can be made. The United States has always been one step ahead the European Union as regards the introduction of 'green' agricultural payments. The EU reforms within the framework of the Common Agricultural Policy started later with the 1992 MacSharry package. Nevertheless, US programmes are built upon voluntary participation by farmers. On the contrary, by now the European Union has arrived at a stage where if a producer aims to receive any financial support, certain basic environmental criteria must be fulfilled because of the connectedness of direct, decoupled payments to greening conditionalities (see the new CAP 2023–2027 and the *Cioloş* reform). It is also evident that the post-exceptionalism, which started in the late 1980s, slowed down in the 2010s. The US farm bills and the CAP reforms of the previous decade were harshly criticised due to not only their inadequate developments in the area of environmental protection but also the (limited) reversal towards some coupled support schemes. On both sides of the Atlantic, decision-makers struggled to reach an agreement on the revised framework of agricultural policy. In the EU, there was a two-year-long transitional period in 2021 and 2022, because the negotiations were not successfully closed, up to the end of the earlier CAP period in 2020. In the United States, President Biden also had to sign a transitional act to extend the temporal authorisation of the earlier farm bill.

In sum, the promising first two decades of environmental policy integration into agricultural state aid policy did not culminate in a great breakthrough in the 2010s. Rather, a slowdown took place in this policy area.

However, in parallel with this, in the 2020s policy-makers discovered competition policy as a possible intervention area for environmental policy integration. This trend has, nonetheless, received greater attention in the European Union, where policy-makers together with the academic sphere intensified the discussions about the ways to incorporate an environment-friendly approach within antitrust law. As soon as it has emerged that the market conduct of undertakings should be regulated to support private sustainability initiatives, the European Union started to lead the "regulatory competition" ahead of the United States. The latter has much more trust in the market behaviour of firms, and as seen in Chapter 13, takes a totally different viewpoint as to how antitrust enforcement can deliver advantageous outcomes in environmental protection.

10.4 Agriculture and the three-pillar system of sustainability

It is reasonable to approach the sustainability of agriculture through the conventional three-pillar system of the sustainability model because it may help us shed light on the necessary trade-offs to realise the objectives of agricultural policy.

Of the three pillars of sustainability, the environmental one is the most emphasised aspect in connection with agricultural production and the agricultural sector. The social and economic pillars are rather neglected, however, in implicit ways they appear in agricultural policy objectives. For example, since the beginnings, an interrelated social and economic (sustainability) objective of the Common Agricultural Policy in the European Union is the fair standard of living for the agricultural community, in particular by increasing the individual earnings of persons engaged in agriculture.[372] The US farm bills from 1977 and 1990 also mentioned the "enhanc[ing] of the quality of life for farmers and society as a whole" as a goal to be implemented within sustainable agriculture.[373] Since then, this has been perpetuated in the U.S. Code as part of the explicit definition of sustainable agriculture.[374] Nevertheless, the ambitious EU Green Deal does not actually contain references to the social aspects of agricultural sustainability. Nor does the Farm to Fork Strategy, with the exception of certain vague references.[375] Nevertheless, the EU Biodiversity Strategy for 2030 declares that farmers are guardians of our land, and "are an essential part of the EU's future and must continue to be the *social* and *economic* hub of many communities."[376]

In 2021, a comprehensive strategy was adopted by the Commission as regards the rural areas of the European Union. Although not specifically concentrating on the agricultural sector, the strategy acknowledges that

> [f]or centuries, "rural" meant "agricultural" with millions of farmers nurturing European society. Life in many rural areas, especially in more remote and peripheral parts, remains intrinsically linked to agriculture – over 40% of land in rural areas is used for agriculture.[377]

The long-term vision is for stronger, connected, resilient and prosperous rural areas by 2040. Stronger rural areas are characterised by empowered communities, access to services and social innovation, while connectedness means digital connectivity as well as transport links and new mobilities. It is straightforward that these features all constitute important aspects of, and keys to, the social sustainability of the agricultural sector. Prosperity with diverse economic activities and sustainable food production appears as a building block for the economic and environmental sustainability of the agricultural sector. Furthermore, resilience that is interpretable in relation to climate change and the environment as well as to social factors plays a key role in preserving and developing both the environmental and social pillars of sustainability.

Social sustainability in agriculture means, in my understanding, a commitment to rural communities, a desire to preserve the lifestyle and traditions of agricultural producers who are close to the nature and have inherent values that are not characteristic of the urban way of living. This approach situates the social sustainability pillar of agriculture within the so-called 'maintenance sustainability'. This does

372 TFEU, art 39(1)(b).

373 Section 1404(17) of the National Agricultural Research, Extension, and Teaching Policy Act of 1977 (7 U.S.C. 3103(17) and the Food, Agriculture, Conservation, and Trade Act of 1990 (FACTA), Public Law 101–624. Title XVI, Subtitle A, Section 1603, GPO, Washington, D.C., 1990 NAL Call#KF1692.A31 1990.

374 7 USC § 3103(19).

375 Commission, 'A Farm to Fork Strategy for a Fair, Healthy and Environmentally-Friendly Food System' (Communication) COM/2020/381 final.

376 Commission, 'EU Biodiversity Strategy for 2030: Bringing Nature Back Into Our Lives' (Communication) COM/2020/380 final, 2.2.2.

377 Commission, 'A Long-Term Vision for the EU's Rural Areas: Towards Stronger, Connected, Resilient and Prosperous Rural Areas By 2040' (Communication) COM/2021/345 final.

not mean that the other two types of social sustainability are not present, but with less relevance. In the context of social sustainability, the mainstream discourse in agricultural policy is about the preservation of rural values and communities.

By this token, the social pillar of sustainability necessarily has connections with agricultural fundamentalism or, as also mentioned in the United States, farm fundamentalism and agrarianism.

However, preserving rural communities necessarily requires, from the viewpoint of the agricultural sector, appropriate farm income that provides a way of living meeting the everyday needs of producers to avoid rural exodus. As a consequence of this, obviously, viable farm incomes can be interpreted not only as a crucial factor for social but also economic sustainability, so the pillars necessarily interact with one another.[378] This correlation has also been identified in numerical terms. Research that evaluated EU Member States based on certain indicators showed that "the countries that topped the economic ranking also occupied high positions in the social ranking."[379] One could also say that the economic objective of providing higher income for agricultural producers is an important means to achieve the social sustainability of agriculture, for the latter inevitably constitutes the precondition of the former. If the level of income of farmers does not meet the expectations of producers, they will turn their attention to other, more profitable areas of the economy. Since there are less job opportunities in rural areas, where farming typically takes place, producers who exit the agricultural sector will be encouraged to move to towns and cities. That is to say, if economic sustainability is not ensured at the household level, social sustainability of the agricultural sector will unquestionably suffer.

This is the reason that the economic pillar of sustainability stands on common ground with the notion of agricultural (post-)exceptionalism.

What must be emphasised is the distinction between rational and romantic agrarianism.[380] The sustainability discourse heavily rooted in a neoliberal setting attempts to maintain a fully rational and quantifying approach[381] towards a socially sustainable agricultural sector,[382] as well as aims to break the chains of the possible romantic strains of agrarianism. As put by *Danbom*, the latter displays an

378 See: https://agriculture.ec.europa.eu/sustainability/economic-sustainability/cap-measures_en.

379 Francisco José Castillo-Díaz, Luis J. Belmonte-Urena, María J. López-Serrano and Francisco Camacho-Ferre, 'Assessment of the Sustainability of the European Agri-Food Sector in the Context of the Circular Economy' (2023) 40 Sustainable Production and Consumption 408.

380 David D. Danbom, 'Romantic Agrarianism in Twentieth-Century America' (1991) 65 Agricultural History 1–12.

381 See, for example: Castillo-Díaz et al. (n 379) 398–411.

382 See, for example: Christina Umstätter, Stefan Mann and Jessica Werner, 'A Simple Measure for Workload as a Social Sustainability Indicator for Family Farms' (2022) 14 Environmental and Sustainability Indicators, Article 100180; Laure Latruffe, Ambre Diazabakana, Christian Bockstaller, Yann Desjeux, John Finn, Edel Kelly, Mary Ryan and Sandra Uthes, 'Measurement of Sustainability in Agriculture: A Review of Indicators' (2016) 118 Studies in Agricultural Economics 123–130; Anna Gaviglio, Mattia Bertocchi, Maria Elena Marescotti, Eugenio Demartini and Alberto Pirani, 'The Social Pillar of Sustainability: A Quantitative Approach at the Farm Level' (2016) 4 Agricultural and Food Economics, Article 15.

"emphasi[s on] the moral, emotional, and spiritual benefits agriculture and rural life convey to the individual."[383] This viewpoint is prevalent in the alternative posed by the food sovereignty paradigm against neoliberal agricultural policy.

The reason I claim that the economic pillar of sustainability is connected to agricultural (post-)exceptionalism is simple. Though there are a wide variety of definitions used for economic sustainability, when it adopts a firm-level approach, it revolves around the question of how to stay in business with profitability[384] but without further harming the environment. The same is true for those analyses that examine the economic sustainability of certain economic sectors: staying profitable but environmentally acceptable is the framework to be respected. While the exceptionalist agricultural policy agenda was concerned with individual farm households to be able to sustain an appropriate standard of living, post-exceptionalism has brought with itself a broader aspect that concentrates also on the sector's environmental impact. So, as globalisation hit the sector in the late 1980s and 1990s, the horizon started to become wider, and the firm-level (individual household) approach in an exceptionalist setting transformed to a sectoral approach in a post-exceptionalist setting. While economic sustainability was significant at the individual level within the framework of exceptionalism, post-exceptionalism allocated greater emphasis on the sectoral level as regards economic sustainability. The former sought the answer to the question of how to provide a fair standard of living for the individual producer, while the latter aims to find ways of building up an agricultural policy that contributes to the sector's environmental and economic sustainability without giving up the household-level support mechanisms to provide the producers with a fair standard of living. This is the neoliberal way of thinking in agricultural policy-making. The contesting paradigm in the form of the food sovereignty movement differs in its viewpoint: the food sovereignty advocates place back the emphasis on the individual level, as regards both environmental and economic sustainability.

Takeaway 4

With the appearance of sustainability, in particular the intensifying efforts to increase environmental protection since the 1990s, agricultural policy has (incompletely) transformed from an exceptionalist (strictly producer-focused) view towards a post-exceptionalist standpoint that places greater emphasis on issues beyond production, such as the environment. Environmental policy integration has culminated in a significant change of agri-food state aid schemes, and – in parallel – direct payments decoupled from production have also become dominant, later intertwined with, and conditioned on, greening criteria.

383 Danbom (n 380) 1.

384 Eila Jeronen, 'Economic Sustainability' in Samuel O. Idowu, René Schmidpeter, Nicholas Capaldi, Liangrong Zu, Mara Del Baldo and Rute Abreu (eds), *Encyclopedia of Sustainable Management* (Springer 2023) 1257–1263.

11 Sustainability in competition policy

Although the contemporary and mainstream antitrust is based on the methods of neoclassical economics and dominated by efficiency-based considerations typically in the form of consumer welfare, as seen in Chapter 18, the quest for a more inclusive antitrust framework is permanent both in literature and practice.

The sustainability discourse in competition policy has been emerging gradually. The intensity of discussions about the issue increased in the second part of the 2010s and grew to an even higher level in the 2020s. Before 2015, only sporadically could one find scholarly publications and comments of policy-makers in connection with the implementation of environmental considerations into competition law.[385] The debates are more present in the European Union than in the United States. US antitrust experts approach the issue rather from a general (and indirect) viewpoint, meaning that by following an active and strong enforcement agenda in accordance with the established (now Neo-Brandeisian) antitrust objectives, competitive markets will bring themselves the green innovations that are necessary for a sustainable future.

This chapter aims to delve into the theoretical backgrounds of the issue based on the three-pillar system of sustainability, similarly to the analysis on agricultural policy in the previous chapter. The regulation in force is examined in Part IV, therefore I do not deal with the legal implications at this point.

After a few repulsive opinions,[386] the competition law and policy community of the European Union seems to accept the inevitability of the inclusion of competition laws in the common good of helping the environment. Terminologically speaking, it is straightforward that by the expression 'sustainability agreements',

385 See, for example, before 2015: H.H.B. Vedder, 'Competition Law and Environmental Protection in Europe; Towards Sustainability?' (PhD thesis 2003); Markus W. Gehring, 'Competition for Sustainability: Sustainable Development Concerns in National and EC Competition Law' (2006) 15 Review of European Community & International Environmental Law 172–184; Thomas Lübbig, 'Sustainable Development and Competition Policy' (2013) 4 Journal of European Competition Law & Practice 1–2.

386 Maarten Pieter Schinkel and Leonard Treuren, 'Green Antitrust: (More) Friendly Fire in the Fight against Climate Change' (2020) SSRN <https://ssrn.com/abstract=3749147> accessed 29 June 2024; Luc Peeperkorn, 'Competition Policy Is Not a Stopgap!' (2021) 12 Journal of European Competition Law & Practice 415–418; Cento Veljanovski, 'The Case against Green Antitrust' (2022) 18 European Competition Journal 501–513.

DOI: 10.4324/9781003604747-14

antitrust lawyers mean agreements that aim to develop the level of environmental protection and/or are advantageous to some aspect of the environment.

The social and economic pillars of sustainability are 'no-go zones' for conventional antitrust law. The appearance of both notions could suggest that antitrust law does not only protect competition but also competitors.[387]

That is to say, although competition policy uses the term 'sustainability', it means nothing other than environmental considerations. Nevertheless, for antitrust policy, on one hand, it would be better to operate only with the term 'environmental agreements', since by thematising sustainability in its discourse it unavoidably steps into the area of social considerations, which it has wanted to avoid for decades in mainstream circles. On the other hand, the infiltration of the term 'sustainability' into antitrust policy and its favourable reception by antitrust law and policy professionals create a fancy area for the community to demonstrate its keen commitment to contribute to solving the most acute crisis of our time.

Of the three pillars of antitrust law (anticompetitive agreements, abuse of dominance, merger control), the inclusion of environmental considerations has been given the most attention in connection with the provisions on anticompetitive agreements. The basic dilemma and assumption is that the prohibition of anticompetitive agreements constitutes a significant obstacle for undertakings that attempt with their cooperation to contribute to the protection of the environment and the increase in environmental quality. The question of whether certain unilateral conducts by dominant undertakings can take the form of an abuse (to be captured by Article 102 TFEU) which harms the environment has received much less attention than the relationship between environmental considerations and the prohibition of anticompetitive agreements.[388] In the area of merger control, research also lags

387 Eleanor M. Fox, '"We Protect Competition, You Protect Competitors"' (2003) 26 World Competition 149–165.

388 Marios C Iacovides and Christos Vrettos, 'Falling Through the Cracks No More? Article 102 TFEU and Sustainability: The Relation between Dominance, Environmental Degradation, and Social Injustice' (2021) 10 Journal of Antitrust Enforcement 32–62; Valentin Mauboussin, 'Environmental Defences as a Shield from Article 102 TFEU' (2022) 3 Concurrences 30–41; Simon Holmes and Michelle Meagher, 'A Sustainable Future: How Can Control of Monopoly Power Play a Part?' (2022) <www.ebcam.eu/images/SSRN-id4099796.pdf> accessed 29 June 2024; Helen Lindenberg, 'Will Sustainability and Environmental Considerations Be the Next Big Hit for Shaping the Application of Article 102 TFEU?' (2022) 20 Zeitschrift für Wettbewerbsrecht 320–332; Matthias Uffer, 'Competition Law: Sustainability Through Competition and Participation' in Birgit Peters and Eva Julia Lohse (eds), *Sustainability through Participation? Perspectives from National, European and International Law* (Brill 2023) 275–280; Simon Holmes, Nicole Kar and Lucinda Cunningham, 'Sustainability and Competition Law in the United Kingdom' in Pranvera Këllezi, Pierre Kobel and Bruce Kilpatrick (eds), *Sustainability Objectives in Competition and Intellectual Property Law* (Springer 2024) 219–234; Marios C. Iacovides and Valentin Mauboussin, 'Sustainability Considerations in the Application of Article 102 TFEU: State of the Art and Proposals for a More Sustainable Competition Law' in Julian Nowag (ed), *Research Handbook on Sustainability and Competition Law* (Edward Elgar 2024); Roman Inderst and Stefan Thomas, 'Abuse of Dominance and Sustainability' (2024) 15 Journal of European Competition Law & Practice 48–56.

behind,[389] comparing with the vast quantity of scholarly and enforcement attention given to collusive practices.

The reasons I labelled the social pillar of sustainability as no-go zones for antitrust policy are the following. Although there have been continuous attempts to complement the goals of antitrust policy with social objectives, the mainstream of antitrust law resists this temptation. One cannot find competition proceedings and cases in which the social considerations of an anticompetitive agreement, an abusive unilateral conduct or a merger played a significant and substantial role. The pressure of the inclusion of social aspects into competition law has always come from academia. The administrability of these proposals raises, however, several questions.

It is reasonable to approach social sustainability in antitrust policy from the viewpoint of those (academic) proposals which call for a more inclusive antitrust and competition law and policy. The scale is wide. Although the issue of wealth equality sits uncomfortably in the context of antitrust law,[390] antitrust undeniably influences wealth distribution,[391] therefore academic debate continuously brings the matter to the fore. It does this despite the fact that moving away from efficiency is, and would be, a "daunting" assignment for antitrust,[392] as well as antitrust being ill suited to directly engage in the attainment of goals related to income equality.[393] *Waked*, however, is of the opinion that antitrust is "malleable to achieve goals far beyond the narrow efficiency-based goals."[394]

The narrow efficiency-based antitrust framework is also contested in the context of developing countries.[395] It has become common to connect antitrust and competition policy with social issues, such as inequality, for the sake of enhancing antitrust's role in redistributional tasks,[396] at least as a complementing

389 Markus Röhrig, Lukas Ritzenhoff and Malcolm Tiffin-Richards, 'Green Deal and Merger Control Sustainability: A Killer Deal Rationale?' *Brussels à Jour Newsletter* (March 2021); Emanuela Lecchi, 'Sustainability and EU Merger Control' (2023) 44 European Competition Law Review 70–80; Suzanne Kingston, 'Greening Merger Control? The Role of Environmental Considerations in Merger Analysis' in Ioannis Kokkoris and Nicholas Levy (eds), *Research Handbook on Global Merger Control* (Edward Elgar 2023) 383–401; Elias Deutscher and Stavros Makris, 'Sustainability Concerns in EU Merger Control: From Output-Maximising to Polycentric Innovation Competition' (2023) 11 Journal of Antitrust Enforcement 350–399.

390 Daniel A. Crane, 'Antitrust and Wealth Inequality' (2016) 101 Cornell Law Review 1228.

391 Herbert J. Hovenkamp, 'Antitrust Policy and Inequality of Wealth' (2017) Faculty Scholarship at Penn Law <https://bit.ly/3t6leB4> accessed 29 June 2024.

392 Shi-Ling Hsu, 'Antitrust and Inequality: The Problem of Super-Firms' (2018) 63 The Antitrust Bulletin 112.

393 Carl Shapiro, 'Antitrust in a Time of Populism' (2018) 61 International Journal of Industrial Organization 714–748.

394 Dina I. Waked, 'Antitrust as Public Interest Law: Redistribution, Equity, and Social Justice' (2020) 65 The Antitrust Bulletin 87.

395 Eleanor M. Fox, 'Economic Development, Poverty and Antitrust: The Other Path' (2007) 13 Southwestern Journal of Law and Trade in the Americas 211–236.

396 Anthony B. Atkinson, *Inequality: What Can Be Done?* (Harvard University Press 2015) 126–127.

and supporting policy beside tax, labour and trade policies.[397] It may be more reasonable and realistic, however, to address the issue in a way that redistribution should not be an explicit objective of antitrust, but antitrust – through its failure to retain competitive markets – contributes to an unequal form of income distribution.[398]

A more inclusive antitrust framework is related to the approach that antitrust should be polycentric, because the monocentric viewpoint – which only concentrates on economic efficiency – ignores that "[a] 'complex economy' is characterised by the existence of overlapping and interpenetrating domains of economic networks, political networks, and social/kinship networks."[399] *Lianos* proposed a fairness-driven antitrust with complex equality at its centre, which is suitable to step out of the current paradigm exclusively focusing on market power as well as fit to concentrate on all sources of power through certain legal instruments, such as the prohibition of the abuse of relative market power.[400]

In the context of the European Union, *Kornezov* calls for a more socially sensitive antitrust enforcement based on the assumption that the EU Treaties – Articles 2 and 3 TEU as well as Article 9 TFEU – put a great emphasis on social considerations, which should also govern the competition policy.[401] In the United States, *Miazad* brings to the fore the notion of prosocial antitrust which challenges the current framework preventing undertakings from collaborating to meet, among others, social demands.[402]

These social proposals are to be interpreted within *Vallance, Perkins and Dixon*'s notion of 'development sustainability'. They aim to reform competition policy in a way that the enforcement of competition laws result in a more equitable and/or equal society. The administrability of most of these proposals is underdeveloped. It is no coincidence that competition authorities are not enthusiastic about this kind of approach; they aim to avoid opening Pandora's box in general.

Nevertheless, as regards the agricultural sector, they are entitled to do the opposite. With a firm legal basis, both the United States and the European Union treat agricultural production differently. The social sustainability aspect of antitrust policy implicitly appears in the European Union's primary law: long-determined agricultural policy objectives are given priority over competition rules. Of these objectives, the ensuring of a fair standard of living for the agricultural community, in particular by increasing the individual earnings of persons engaged in agriculture, can clearly be handled as social aspects to be taken into account in competition

397 Jonathan B. Baker and Steven C. Salop, 'Antitrust, Competition Policy, and Inequality' (2015–2016) 104 Georgetown Law Journal Online 27.

398 Lina M. Khan and Sandeep Vaheesan, 'Market Power and Inequality: The Antitrust Counterrevolution and Its Discontents' (2017) 11 Harvard Law and Policy Review 294.

399 Ioannis Lianos, 'Polycentric Competition Law' (2019) 71 Current Legal Problems 206.

400 Ioannis Lianos, 'Competition Law as a Form of Social Regulation' (2020) 65 The Antitrust Bulletin 83.

401 Alexander Kornezov, 'For a Socially Sensitive Competition Law Enforcement' (2020) 11 Journal of European Competition Law & Practice 399–403.

402 Amelia Miazad, 'Prosocial Antitrust' (2022) 73 Hastings Law Journal 1637–1696.

enforcement. A fair standard of living, no matter how elusive this expression, is a cornerstone for a just and equitable society.

As already mentioned also in connection with agricultural policy, this social aspect is strongly linked with economic sustainability, taking into account that staying in the market of agricultural production by producers is dependent upon how much individual profits they can obtain.

Turning our attention to the economic pillar of sustainability as a no-go zone for antitrust policy, the following remarks are worth considering. A firm-level approach in connection with the economic sustainability of antitrust policy would lead us to protect "competitors" and not competition in and of itself. Contrary to social sustainability, this approach is much more prevalent in law enforcement as well. While the importance of including social considerations into antitrust policy are emphasised only within academic circles, creating a level playing field for smaller competitors is an existing issue as regards legislation and law enforcement, too. Although mainstream antitrust law aims to distance itself from the objective of protecting small and medium-sized enterprises, sometimes this infiltrates into law enforcement. Proponents of this approach usually refer back to earlier case law on both sides of the Atlantic, arguing that with the consumer welfare standard and the more economic approach, antitrust has lost its original objective. These cases typically date back to the period before the 1980s in the United States and before the 2000s in the European Union.

The issue has surfaced with renewed power recently in the United States. Progressive antitrust with the appearance of the Neo-Brandeis movement has come to the fore also within the US federal antitrust agencies. Both Lina Khan and Jonathan Kanter support an agenda that goes beyond a narrow consumer welfare approach towards antitrust laws.

Lande is of the opinion that, among others, the protection of small businesses – connected to the opportunity to compete – as a goal is revealed in connection with all relevant US antitrust acts (Sherman, Federal Trade Commission and Clayton Acts).[403] Nevertheless, *Grimes* argues that antitrust has a systemic bias against small businesses: on one hand, it does not tolerate collective action of small firms for the sake of offsetting power, and, on the other hand, antitrust raises obstacles to enforce power abuses against small firms.[404] *Hovenkamp* begins the argument with the other side of the coin: if antitrust takes a 'bigness' approach, which rejects big firms based on absolute size, it is easily translated into the protection of small businesses.[405]

The market players of the agricultural sector, however, are given preferential treatment also in this respect. The exemption under the prohibition of anticompetitive agreement has been adopted both in the United States and the European

403 Robert H. Lande, 'Wealth Transfers as the Original and Primary Concern of Antitrust: The Efficiency Interpretation Challenged' (1999) 50 Hastings Law Journal 907–910, 925–926, 945.

404 Warren S. Grimes, 'Antitrust and the Systemic Bias against Small Business: Kodak, Strategic Conduct, and Strategic Conduct, and Leverage Theory' (2001) 52 Case Western Reserve Law Review 233.

405 Herbert Hovenkamp, 'The Slogans and Goals of Antitrust Law' (2022) 25 Legislation and Public Policy 705.

Union in view of the fact that, taking into account the perfect competition at the level of production and the oligopolistic structure of the processing and retail levels, producers should be ensured with some kind of countervailing power against their buyers. This implicitly means the objective to contribute to the economic sustainability of agricultural producers. Through the possibility of combining forces without violating antitrust law's prohibition of collusion, in theory producers have better bargaining power to determine their own selling prices.

If we broaden the viewpoint and look at the economic sustainability of the agricultural sector in general, two paths are available theoretically. If economic sustainability is interpreted in strong connection with environmental sustainability, the policy path chosen may be directed towards a kind of farm structure and those farm sizes which better contribute to an environment-friendly agriculture. Research results are mixed in this regard; however, the common assumption is that small farms are more environment friendly. If economic sustainability is interpreted on its own, the policy path may lead decision-makers to favour larger and more efficient farm holdings that operate based on economies of scale and of scope. These two theoretical directions are important as to the economic sustainability pillar of antitrust law, because competition policy has unequivocally chosen the first path in the agricultural sector, but the second one in general. It means that the mainstream approach of competition policy is to preserve the economic sustainability of a certain sector or – using antitrust law terminology – of the respective market, and not that of individual undertakings. However, as regards the agricultural sector, it changes perspective and puts great emphasis also on the economic sustainability of individual farm holdings.

In sum, the following broad findings are worth mentioning. Environmental sustainability is invited to antitrust policy with open arms. While general antitrust law takes a more moderate stance in this regard, as to the agricultural sector, the methodology to consider environmental aspects has been widened. Social sustainability is a 'no-go zone' for antitrust policy, but it has been given some relevance within the competition rules applying to the agricultural sector. With economic sustainability, general antitrust policy is only concerned with the sectoral level; on the contrary, competition rules of the agricultural sector put a much greater emphasis on economic sustainability at the level of individual undertakings, too.

All these conclusions lead us to the recognition that in competition law and policy there is only one economic sector where each and every pillar of sustainability is taken into account, either explicitly or implicitly. While an explicit legal framework is established as to environmental sustainability with a sector-specific assessment methodology, implicit considerations can be found regarding economic and social sustainability. These latter considerations follow from the justification of the sectoral exemption under the prohibition of anticompetitive agreements as well as the additional protection that is provided to agricultural producers through prohibiting certain unfair trading practices imposed on them by their buyers.

However, it is quite strange that the alleviations agricultural producers enjoy within the framework of antitrust law are in many cases under attack by referring to the inefficiency these provisions represent from the viewpoint of conventional antitrust law. Nevertheless, if one disentangles these provisions, the additional protection of farmers can be easily placed within the pillars of, and under the aegis of, social and economic sustainability. And it is clear-cut that sustainability, used in this extremely broad sense by the antitrust law community, has become an issue that deserves (almost) unconditional support from antitrust policy-makers and lawyers. This is a contradiction which is difficult to explain, if one looks beyond the "lobbying agricultural producers and their interest groups but advantageous and supportable sustainability advocates" rhetoric. It seems that the sustainability rhetoric in antitrust policy, in light of the urgent need to save our planet, has transformed the acceptance of these issues, but only until one starts using the terminology of the pre-sustainability period.

Takeaway 5

In the last few years, with a bespoke legal assessment method, environmental policy integration – under the misleading expression of sustainability agreements – has also appeared in the framework of antitrust law, in particular in the European Union. The EU even has sui generis antitrust provisions exclusively applicable to the sustainability agreements of the agri-food supply chain. Nevertheless, the other two pillars of sustainability (economic and social) are also implicitly present in the agriculture-specific antitrust regime of the EU, in the form of the obligation to take into consideration the specific socio-economic objective of ensuring producers a fair standard of living within antitrust law.

Part IV

Competition rules applying to agri-food markets and to sustainability agreements of agri-food market players

After setting the tone of policy-makers in Part II as regards agricultural and competition policy as well as in Part III concerning the emergence of sustainability in, on one hand, agricultural policy, and, on the other hand, competition policy, Part IV adds to the analysis by elucidating the legal implications of these policy nexuses.

Part IV includes four main chapters. The first and second deal with the analysis of agriculture-specific antitrust law, the third with that of the agriculture-specific competition-related rules beyond antitrust, and the fourth with my conclusions that flow from the previous examination. While the first main chapter is only engaged in the nexus between antitrust and the agricultural sector, the second supplements this two-component analysis with an additional third layer: sustainability.

As put by *Shelanski*, the means to influence competition policy may include both antitrust law and other types of (economic) regulation. These two ways of supervising competition by the state sometimes complement and sometimes derogate each other.[406] Their underlying objectives, which they aim to achieve, are different in nature. While mainstream antitrust is concerned with the objective of economic efficiency in the form of consumer welfare, economic regulation typically follows a distinct path, in many cases, with sector-specific goals. That is the reason *Mestmäcker* criticised these regulations as representing sectoral interests. Because of these considerations, it is justifiable to break up the scrutiny into two parts.

At the level of legal doctrine, antitrust rules exclusively applying to the agricultural sector are exception norms (*Ausnahmenormen, i.e., ius singulare*). These provisions deviate from general norms because of the particular circumstances of agriculture. If general rules were applied to agriculture without exceptions, producers would, and should, operate – because of the characteristics of the sector – in a more difficult economic setting than with the existence of *ius singulare*. Competition-related rules beyond antitrust constitute in the agricultural sector special norms (*Spezialnormen, i.e., ius proprium*) that are solely and exclusively adopted for agriculture.[407] This means that these kinds of rules have no general equivalent.

406 Shelanski (n 142).
407 Christian Grimm, *Agrarrecht* (3rd edn, C.H. Beck 2004) 15.

DOI: 10.4324/9781003604747-15

12 Antitrust and the agricultural sector[408]

This chapter disentangles those rules that are treated as part of antitrust law. The chapter is divided into two subheadings concerning, on one hand, the European Union, and, on the other hand, the United States. Of the three pillars of antitrust law, only the prohibition of anticompetitive agreements comes with some exception norms applying to the agricultural sector. Within abuse of dominance and merger control provisions, exemptions are not established for the favour of agricultural producers.

What is different between the EU and the US is that the former adopted exception norms as regards agriculture-related sustainability agreements, too. These will not be scrutinised here, but in Chapter 13.

12.1 The European Union

In the European Union, both the primary and secondary law must be examined to receive a complete picture of the nexus between the agricultural sector and antitrust law.

When addressing the primary law of the EU, the analysis must start with the Treaty on the Functioning of the European Union, in particular its Articles 38–44 on the common agricultural policy. The Treaty on European Union includes no specific provisions regarding the issue.

In principle, the EU defines its common agricultural and fisheries policy, which – according to *Whish and Bailey* – has its own philosophy.[409] The internal market shall extend to agriculture, fisheries and trade in agricultural products.[410] Therefore, the common agricultural and fisheries policy is part of the internal market. Except when otherwise provided in Articles 39 to 44 TFEU, the rules laid down for the establishment and functioning of the internal market shall also apply to agricultural

408 This chapter is, in part, based on Martin Milán Csirszki, 'The Comparison of the US and EU Agricultural Antitrust Exemption' (2022) 15 Yearbook of Antitrust and Regulatory Studies 137–173.

409 Richard Whish and David Bailey, *Competition Law* (7th edn, OUP 2012) 963.

410 TFEU, art 38(1).

DOI: 10.4324/9781003604747-16

products.[411] Rules on competition, being positioned in Chapter 1[412] of Title VII of the TFEU from Article 101 to 109, form a part of the internal market.[413] However, even since the beginning of European integration, European agricultural markets have not been fully exposed to free competition.[414] *Schweizer* posits that the introduction of common competition rules for agricultural markets has a negative and a positive component. The negative component relates to the application of competition rules in Articles 101 et seq. TFEU to agriculture. The positive component opens the way for the European Parliament and the Council to independently regulate competition issues in the agricultural sector.[415]

The basic system and derogation is provided by an exception norm codified in Article 42 TFEU which declares:

> The provisions of the Chapter relating to rules on competition shall apply to production of and trade in agricultural products only to the extent determined by the European Parliament and the Council within the framework of Article 43(2) and in accordance with the procedure laid down therein, account being taken of the objectives set out in Article 39.[416,417]

This provision establishes a primacy of agricultural policy over general antitrust law.[418]

Article 39 TFEU comprises the objectives of the Common Agricultural Policy, which have to be taken into consideration when deciding on the extent of the application of competition rules to the production and trade in agricultural products:

> (a) to increase agricultural productivity by promoting technical progress and by ensuring the rational development of agricultural production and the optimum utilisation of the factors of production, in particular labour; (b) thus to ensure a fair standard of living for the agricultural community, in particular by increasing the individual earnings of persons engaged in agriculture; (c) to stabilise markets; (d) to assure the availability of supplies; (e) to ensure that supplies reach consumers at reasonable prices.[419]

For the attainment of the objectives of common agricultural policy, a common organisation of agricultural markets shall be established. The organisation can take

411 TFEU, art 38(2).

412 Section 1 of Chapter 1 (from Article 101 to 106) deals with rules applying to undertakings, while Section 2 of Chapter 1 deals with rules on state aids (from Article 107 to 109).

413 TFEU, art 3(1)(b). See: Walter Frenz, 'Agrarwettbewerbsrecht' (2010) 40 Agrar- und Umweltrecht 193.

414 Härtel (n 113) 437.

415 Dieter Schweizer, 'Art. 42 AEUV' in Torsten Körber, Heike Schweitzer and Daniel Zimmer (eds), *Wettbewerbsrecht – Band 1: EU. Kommentar zum Europäischen Kartellrecht* (6th edn, C.H. Beck 2019).

416 TFEU, art 42.

417 See also: Philipp Groteloh, 'Grundzüge des Agrarkartellrechts' in Matthias Dombert and Karsten Witt (eds), *Münchener Anwaltshandbuch Agrarrecht* (2nd edn, C.H. Beck 2016).

418 Härtel (n 113) 438.

419 TFEU, art 39(1).

the form of common competition rules, compulsory coordination of the various national market organisations, and/or a European market organisation. The question may arise as to how the common organisation of agricultural markets affects national jurisdiction. Although the most significant ruling on the issue was made before the adoption of the first single common market organisation, its finding on jurisdiction still prevails. The common market organisation (in the milk and milk products sector) does not mean that national competition authorities cannot apply competition laws to a (milk) producer's cooperative, holding a powerful position on the national market. The jurisdiction of national authorities in principle remains unaffected by the common organisation of a product's market,[420] however it has its limits. National authorities shall refrain from "adopting any measure which might undermine or create exceptions to that common organisation." The measure adopted shall be in line with the objectives of the Common Agricultural Policy, and the respective measure shall not result in any of the CAP objectives listed being impossible to be realised because of giving priority to another objective, that is to say, authorities shall find a balance between the attainment of CAP objectives without giving any of them unnecessary weight.[421]

Article 43(2) TFEU lays down procedural rules which have to be respected during the decision-making process: the European Parliament and the Council, acting in accordance with the ordinary legislative procedure and after consulting the Economic and Social Committee, shall establish[422] those rules which provide for the possibility of derogation from general competition rules and, thus, the special treatment of agriculture.

By declaring the priority of CAP objectives over competition rules in the TFEU and its earlier versions, the attainment of CAP objectives shall be ensured through regulatory instruments, for – from a competition perspective – an uncontrolled and unregulated agricultural market within the EU is not able to realise and fulfil the objectives for which it was entrusted. For example, the objective of ensuring a fair standard of living for the agricultural community, in particular by increasing the individual earnings of persons engaged in agriculture, cannot be expected to be realised by general antitrust rules, given that the CAP objective mentioned is social in nature, unlike antitrust law which is primarily concerned with efficiency considerations.

The main problems faced by the agricultural sector, such as

> the problem of fluctuation of incomes from year to year; the problem of low incomes in certain sectors of the industry, which become manifest in poverty among families occupying small farms; and poor comparability between the rewards earned in agriculture and in the rest of the economy,[423]

420 Case C–137/00 *The Queen v The Competition Commission, Secretary of State for Trade and Industry and The Director General of Fair Trading, ex parte Milk Marque Ltd and National Farmers' Union* [2003] EU:C:2003:429, para 67.

421 Case C–137/00 (n 420) para 94.

422 TFEU, art 43(2).

423 Berkeley Hill, *Understanding the Common Agricultural Policy* (Earthscan 2012) 33.

may require stronger intervention to agri-food markets beyond the reach of antitrust rules. By stronger intervention, I mean that legislation – in certain cases – may have to provide additional rules to protect market players with weak bargaining positions. Additional rules can take the form of either exception norms or specific norms.

EU case law has not failed to state that the Common Agricultural Policy takes precedence over competition rules,[424] thereby strengthening the power of this policy choice present in EU primary law. There have been relatively few cases on the application of competition provisions to the agricultural sector, however these take us closer to the better understanding of the relationship between competition law and the agricultural sector.

Although the priority of agricultural policy objectives over competition rules has been declared several times, there is a limited number of rulings which provide us with some clarifications on the current exemption system.[425]

The possibility for derogations established by the TFEU is realised in secondary legal acts. The following two regulations constitute the pillars of EU secondary legislation:

1 Council Regulation (EC) No 1184/2006 of 24 July 2006 applying certain rules of competition to the production of, and trade in, agricultural products (Agri-Food Competition Regulation)[426]; and
2 Regulation (EU) No 1308/2013 of the European Parliament and of the Council of 17 December 2013 establishing a common organisation of the markets in agricultural products and repealing Council Regulations (EEC) No 922/72, (EEC) No 234/79, (EC) No 1037/2001 and (EC) No 1234/2007 (CMO Regulation).[427]

The regulatory pillar of EU competition policy applicable to the sector is based on the

424 Case 139/79 *Maizena GmbH v Council of the European Communities* [1980] EU:C:1980:250, para 23; Case C–280/93 *Federal Republic of Germany v Council of the European Union* [1994] EU:C:1994:367, para 61; Case C–311/94 *IJssel-Vliet Combinatie BV v Minister van Economische Zaken* [1996] EU:C:1996:383, para 31; Case C–456/00 *French Republic v Commission of the European Communities* [2002] EU:C:2002:753, para 33; Case C–137/00 *The Queen v The Competition Commission, Secretary of State for Trade and Industry and The Director General of Fair Trading, ex parte Milk Marque Ltd and National Farmers' Union* [2003] EU:C:2003:429, para 81; Case C–671/15 *Président de l'Autorité de la concurrence v Association des producteurs vendeurs d'endives (APVE) and Others* [2017] EU:C:2017:860, para 37.

425 Cases C–456/00 and C–311/94 are related to state aid, Case C–280/93 to the issue of an import regime, Case C–137/00 to jurisdiction issues, while Case 139/79 to a production quota.

426 Council Regulation (EC) No 1184/2006 of 24 July 2006 applying certain rules of competition to the production of, and trade in, agricultural products [2006] OJ L214/7 (Agri-Food Competition Regulation).

427 Regulation (EU) No 1308/2013 of the European Parliament and of the Council of 17 December 2013 establishing a common organisation of the markets in agricultural products and repealing Council Regulations (EEC) No 922/72, (EEC) No 234/79, (EC) No 1037/2001 and (EC) No 1234/2007 [2013] OJ L347/671 (CMO Regulation).

3 Directive (EU) 2019/633 of the European Parliament and of the Council of 17 April 2019 on unfair trading practices in business-to-business relationships in the agricultural and food supply chain (UTP Directive).[428]

Both the relevant articles of the CMO Regulation and the Agri-Food Competition Regulation are exception norms (*ius singulare*); the UTP Directive consists of specific norms (*ius proprium*) by establishing a sui generis system which has no general equivalent.

The Agri-Food Competition Regulation replaced – with minor changes – the Council Regulation No 26 of 4 April 1962. The replacement took place because of clarity and rationality requirements.[429] The policy behind its adoption is derivable from the general objectives of the Common Agricultural Policy.

Although pursuant to Article 1 of the Agri-Food Competition Regulation, Articles 101 to 106 TFEU and provisions adopted for their implementation shall apply to all agreements, decisions and practices referred to in Articles 101(1) and 102 TFEU which relate to the production of, or the trade in, the products listed in Annex I to the TFEU; these conducts are also subject to Article 2 of the Agri-Food Competition Regulation.[430]

The meaning of agricultural products is elaborated in CJEU case law.[431] Given that the following examples are not agricultural products listed in Annex I, special provisions do not apply to them: products obtained by further processing made from original products listed in Annex I, such as cognac brandies[432]; primary but non-Annex I agricultural products used as auxiliary substances for Annex I products[433]; primary but non-Annex I agricultural products, such as fur skins.[434] Insofar as

428 Directive (EU) 2019/633 of the European Parliament and of the Council of 17 April 2019 on unfair trading practices in business-to-business relationships in the agricultural and food supply chain [2019] OJ L111/59 (UTP Directive).

429 Agri-Food Competition Regulation, recital (1) and art 5.

430 Agri-Food Competition Regulation, art 1.

431 Dieter Schweizer, 'GWB § 28 Landwirtschaft' in Torsten Körber, Heike Schweitzer and Daniel Zimmer (eds), *Wettbewerbsrecht – Band 2: GWB. Kommentar zum Deutschen Kartellrecht* (6th edn, C.H. Beck 2020).

432 Case 123/83 *Bureau national interprofessionnel du cognac v Guy Clair* [1985] EU:C:1985:33, para 15: "potable spirits are expressly excluded from the category of agricultural products."

433 Case 61/80 *Coöperatieve Stremsel- en Kleurselfabriek v Commission of the European Communities* [1981] EU:C:1981:75, paras 20–21: The applicant's fifth submission was that animal rennet for cheese making is agricultural product despite the fact that it is not included in the Annex of agricultural products (then: Annex II, now: Annex I). According to the Court, "in order for the Regulation to be applicable to rennet, that product must therefore itself come under Annex II to the Treaty. It follows that Regulation No 26/62 can have no application in this case and that the applicant's fifth submission must be rejected."

434 Case T-61/89 *Dansk Pelsdyravlerforening v Commission of the European Communities* [1992] EU:T:1992:79, para 2: "The scope of Regulation No 26 applying certain rules of competition to production of and trade in agricultural products was limited in Article 1 thereof to the production of and trade in the products listed in Annex II to the Treaty. Consequently, that regulation may not be applied to the production of or trade in products, such as furskins, which do not come under

primary products have already been treated or processed, they are only covered by the special competition regime if the treated or processed product is listed in Annex I.[435]

Article 2 includes the exceptions to Article 101(1) TFEU. In *Whish*'s words, these exceptions are the so-called derogations.[436] Of the two pillars of EU antitrust law applying to undertakings regulated in the TFEU,[437] the Agri-Food Competition Regulation only sets out derogations with regard to the prohibition of anti-competitive agreements; it does not recognise any derogation regarding abuse of dominance.[438] That is, the Agri-Food Competition Regulation does not affect the prohibition of abuse of dominance under 102 TFEU; this, therefore, applies in full to the agricultural sector.[439]

The two main derogations in relation to Article 101(1) TFEU may be called upon when agreements, decisions and practices

a form an integral part of a national market organisation; or
b are necessary for attainment of the objectives set out in Article 39 of the TFEU.[440]

Sentence 2 of Article 2(1) also includes an example. The wording 'in particular' reflects the indicative/illustrative nature of the provision: *In particular*, Article 101(1) TFEU shall not apply to agreements, decisions and practices of farmers, farmers' associations, or associations of such associations belonging to a single Member State which concern the production or sale of agricultural products or the use of joint facilities for the storage, treatment or processing of agricultural products. Nevertheless, there are also negative criteria determined as regards this provision. On the one hand, there is an absolute requirement that under the agreement, decision or practice of farmers, farmers' associations or associations of such associations, there shall be no obligation to charge identical prices, and on the other hand, there are two further requirements formulated being in an alternative relation to each other, and being individually in a cumulative relation to the prohibition of charging identical prices. These two requirements are the following: (a) competition shall not be excluded, or (b) the objectives of the Common Agricultural Policy shall not be jeopardised. This means that for an agreement, decision or practice

Annex II to the Treaty even if they are ancillary to the production of another product which itself comes under that annex."

435 Schweizer (n 431).

436 Whish and Bailey (n 409) 964.

437 The third pillar, merger control, is not covered directly by the TFEU.

438 Whish and Bailey (n 409) 964.

439 Ines Härtel, 'AEUV Art. 42 [Eingeschränkte Anwendung der Wettbewerbs- und Beihilferegeln]' in Rudolf Streinz (ed), *EUV/AEUV – Vertrag über die Europäische Union, Vertrag über die Arbeitsweise der Europäischen Union, Charta der Grundrechte der Europäischen Union* (3rd edn, C.H. Beck 2018).

440 Agri-Food Competition Regulation, art 2(1).

being exempted from Article 101(1) TFEU, the following prohibitions shall be respected cumulatively: (a) the prohibition on charging identical prices, (b) the prohibition on exclusion of competition and (c) the prohibition on jeopardising CAP objectives.[441] From a reversed point of view, it is sufficient to return to the application of Article 101(1) if any of the three aforementioned prohibitions are violated.

Paragraphs 2 and 3 of Article 2 consist of procedural rules. The European Commission has sole power, subject to review by the General Court and the Court of Justice of the European Union, to determine which agreements, decisions and practices fulfil the substantive conditions. The decision shall be made after consulting the Member States and hearing the undertakings or associations of undertakings concerned, and any other natural or legal person that it considers should be heard. The decision shall be published. Determining so may take place (a) on the own initiative of the Commission; (b) at the request of a competent authority of a Member State; or (c) at the request of an interested undertaking or association of undertakings.[442] The publication of the determination shall state the names of the parties and the main content of the decision. It shall have regard to the legitimate interest of undertakings in the protection of their business secrets.[443] Nevertheless, it is important to note that

> "as farmers assess the applicability of the derogation to the agreement themselves without informing the Members States or the Commission, the Commission has no data on how often farmers relied on this derogation. In competition investigations, parties rarely referred to [this derogation]."[444]

The two derogations included in Article 2 of the Agri-Food Competition Regulation have a doubtful relationship. Although the wording shows that they are formulated as alternative conditions (the word '*or*' implies this finding),[445] earlier case law suggests otherwise. In a 1974 Court judgment, the term 'national market organisation' was defined. On the basis of Articles 43(3) and 45(1) of the Treaty establishing the European Economic Community, the Court found that the objectives of national market organisations are analogous at national level to those pursued by the common market organisations at Community level. It means that

> the national organization can thus be defined as a totality of legal devices placing the regulation of the market in the products in question under the control of the public authority, with a view to ensuring, by means of an increase in

441 Agri-Food Competition Regulation, art 2(1).

442 Agri-Food Competition Regulation, art 2(2).

443 Agri-Food Competition Regulation, art 2(3).

444 Commission, 'The Application of the Union Competition Rules to the Agricultural Sector' (Report) COM(2018) 706 final, 17.

445 See: Those agreements are exempted from the general cartel prohibition which form an integral part of a national market organisation *or* are necessary for attainment of the Common Agricultural Policy objectives.

> productivity and of optimum utilization of the factors of production, in particular of manpower, a fair standard of living for producers, the stabilization of markets, the assurance of supplies and reasonable prices to consumers.[446]

By defining national market organisations based on the objectives of the Common Agricultural Policy, thereby drawing analogy between national and common market organisations, the second condition in Article 2 of the Agri-Food Competition Regulation has been merged into the first condition. That is, based on case law, the first derogation can only apply to an agreement, if it also fulfils the second condition. It is insufficient that the agreement in case is an integral part of a national market organisation, because that agreement shall also be necessary for the attainment of Common Agricultural Policy objectives. It was reiterated later in a Commission Decision which found that the agreements and decisions of various French producers groups in the new potatoes market are exempted because they meet both criteria: not only do they constitute an integral part of a national market organisation but they also are necessary for the objectives of the Common Agricultural Policy.[447] Here a further condition must be mentioned: the first derogation can only be applied, if there is no common market organisation regarding the respective product.[448] It results that the significance of the derogation provided for national market organisations in Article 2 of the Agri-Food Competition Regulation is limited, given that "the majority of national marketing organisations have ceased to exist"[449] thanks to the system of single common market organisation.

The second derogation refers to the possibility for exempting agreements, decisions or concerted practices, if they are necessary for the attainment of Common Agricultural Policy objectives. The most significant clarification of case law regarding this provision is that the respective agreement shall contribute to the achievement of all five CAP objectives.[450] An agreement cannot be exempted from the general prohibition, if it does not satisfy each and every objective listed in Article 39 TFEU.[451]

The Commission's careful consideration of whether an agreement realises all CAP objectives is clearly shown, for example, in one of its 2003 decisions. The enforcement authority thoroughly screened whether the five goals of the Common Agricultural Policy had all been attained respectively. The Commission found that the agreement in case, which – in the French beef market – intended to fix a minimum price higher than

446 Case 48/74 *Charmasson v Minister for Economic Affairs and Finance* [1974] EU:C:1974:137, paras 24 and 26.

447 *New potatoes* (Case IV/31.735) Commission Decision 88/109/EEC [1987] OJ L59/25.

448 Whish and Bailey (n 409) 965–966, mentions *Scottish Salmon Board* (Case IV/33.494) Commission Decision 92/444/EC [1992] OJ L246/37: "as there was a common organisation of the market in fishery products, the Scottish Salmon Board could not rely on the national market organisation defence."

449 Whish and Bailey (n 409) 965.

450 Case 71/74 *Nederlandse Vereniging voor de fruit- en groentenimporthandel, Nederlandse Bond van grossiers in zuidvruchten en ander geimporteerd fruit "Frubo" v Commission of the European Communities and Vereniging de Fruitunie* [1975] EU:C:1975:61, paras 24–26; Case C–399/93 *Oude Luttikhuis and others v Verenigde Coöperatieve Melkindustrie Coberco BA* [1995] EU:C:1995:434, para 25.

451 Whish and Bailey (n 409) 965.

the market price, did not in any way increase agricultural productivity [Article 39(1)(a)]. It was not necessary to stabilise markets [Article 39(1)(c)], given that

> [t]he crisis in the beef sector was due primarily to a massive imbalance between supply and demand. Fixing a minimum purchase price does nothing to remedy such a situation. It does not affect the volume of supply, of which there was a large surplus; an increase in minimum prices might even cause demand to fall, thus widening the gap between supply and demand.

Furthermore, taking into account that there is no shortage of supply in the beef market, it was not necessary to assure the availability of supplies [Article 39(1)(d)]. The goal of supplies reaching consumers at reasonable prices was not realised [Article 39(1)(e)], by finding that "[e]specially in the case of consumption via restaurant and catering services, which are a major user of cheaper, imported meat, the suspension of imports could only have the effect of increasing prices." All in all, the Commission found that

> the agreement is not necessary in order to achieve at least four of the five objectives of the Common Agricultural Policy. Even if the view were to be taken that it did indeed fall within the scope of the objective "ensuring a fair standard of living for the agricultural community, in particular by increasing the individual earnings of persons engaged in agriculture", nevertheless, when that objective is weighed against the other four objectives [. . .], which it would not help to achieve, it has to be concluded that the derogation in Regulation No 26 does not apply here.

The Commission, for the sake of strengthening its findings, also declared that if the respective agreement would have actually contributed to the attainment of all CAP objectives, the word 'necessary' in the provision means that the taken measure shall be proportionate, that is to say, there would be no less restrictive measure to be taken to realise the objectives. This requirement of proportionality was not met.[452]

Another remark must be noted. The wording of Article 2 of the Agri-Food Competition Regulation is formulated in such a way that it seems that after the first two derogations, an example is mentioned by way of illustration. However, case law treats 'this example' as the third separate derogation from Article 101(1) TFEU. In *Oude Luttikhuis* the doctrinal elements of this third derogation are greatly summarised:

> The third derogation is subject to three cumulative conditions. For that derogation to be applicable, it must be confirmed, firstly, that the agreements in question concern cooperative associations belonging to a single Member

452 *French beef* (Case COMP/C.38.279/F3) Commission Decision 2003/600/EC [2003] OJ L209/12, paras 135–149. See also the rejected appeals before the EU Courts: Case T–217/03 *FNCBV and Others v Commission* [2006] EU:T:2006:391 and Case C–101/07 P *Coop de France bétail and viande v Commission* [2008] EU:C:2008:741.

> State, secondly that they do not cover prices but concern rather the production or sale of agricultural products or the use of joint facilities for the storage, treatment or processing of such products, and thirdly that they do not exclude competition or jeopardize the objectives of the Common Agricultural Policy.[453]

The most recent judgment of the Grand Chamber of the Court of Justice of the European Union has established simplified benchmarks to decide whether antitrust rules shall apply to the activities of producer organisations and associations of producer organisations. The prohibition in Article 101 TFEU shall apply to agreements, decisions and concerted practices, if

(1) they are not agreed/made *within* a producer organisation or an association of producer organisations, in other words, if they are not agreed/made between the members of *the same* producer organisation or *the same* association of producer organisations; or
(2) any of the parties subject thereto is not *legally recognised* by the Member State; or
(3) they are not *strictly necessary* for the pursuit of at least one objective assigned to the producer organisation or the association of producer organisations.[454]

If any of the three criteria is not fulfilled, Article 101 TFEU shall apply to the respective agreement, decision or concerted practice.

These three requirements have been determined regarding the assessment of the following types of conducts: (1) collective fixing of minimum sale prices, (2) concentration on quantities put on the market and (3) exchanges of strategic information. That is, the Court ruled that the collective fixing of minimum sale prices escapes the prohibition in Article 101 TFEU, if it is agreed on between the members of a legally recognised producer organisation or a legally recognised association of producer organisations and strictly necessary to reach the objective pursued by the respective PO or APO. The question arises as to what the prohibition on charging identical prices in Article 2 of the Agri-Food Regulation actually means, if a legally recognised PO or APO – to the extent of pursuing one of its objectives which is strictly necessary – can decide to determine a minimum sale price. It possibly means that the respective PO or APO shall ensure its members can sell their own products themselves below the minimum sale price determined by the PO or APO.[455]

453 Case C–399/93 *Oude Luttikhuis and others v Verenigde Coöperatieve Melkindustrie Coberco BA* [1995] EU:C:1995:434, para 27.

454 Case C–671/15 *Président de l'Autorité de la concurrence v Association des producteurs vendeurs d'endives (APVE) and Others* [2017] EU:C:2017:860, para 67.

455 Case C–671/15 *Président de l'Autorité de la concurrence v Association des producteurs vendeurs d'endives (APVE) and Others* [2017] EU:C:2017:860, para 66.

The CMO Regulation has a separate part on competition rules.[456] Part IV is divided into two chapters: Chapter I is concerned with rules applying to undertakings, while Chapter II contains provisions on state aids.

First and foremost, it is worth mentioning that the provisions of Agri-Food Competition Regulation and the provisions of Chapter I of Part IV of the CMO Regulation are – in most aspects – identical. In its Article 1, the Agri-Food Competition Regulation declares that it does not apply to the products covered by Council Regulation (EC) No 1234/2007. Since references to Regulation (EC) No 1234/2007 shall be construed as references to the CMO Regulation,[457] the declaration of the Agri-Food Competition Regulation on its material scope still applies and is in force in relation to the CMO Regulation. The *ratione materiae* of Agri-Food Competition does not cover those Annex I products which are covered by the CMO Regulation. However, it does not have too much practical significance, given that both the material scope of Agri-Food Competition Regulation and of CMO Regulation are established in Annex I to the TFEU. Because most Annex I products are covered by the CMO Regulation, the latter leaves little room for the Agri-Food Competition Regulation to be applied.

The CMO Regulation, contrary to the Agri-Food Competition Regulation, includes definitions on the relevant product and geographic market. Product market means the market comprising all those products which are regarded as interchangeable or substitutable by the consumer by reason of the products' characteristics, their prices and their intended use.[458] Geographic market means the market comprising the area in which the undertakings concerned are involved in the supply of the relevant products, in which the conditions of competition are sufficiently homogeneous and which can be distinguished from neighbouring areas, particularly because the conditions of competition are appreciably different in those areas.[459] These definitions do not say anything new compared with what can be read in case law. The definitions are also in line with the Commission Notice on the definition of relevant market for the purposes of Community competition law.[460]

Another definition of the CMO Regulation may cause a slight contradiction. Although there are no special rules applying to the agricultural and food sector as to Article 102 TFEU, the CMO Regulation provides for a definition of dominant position: a position of economic strength enjoyed by an undertaking which enables it to prevent effective competition being maintained in the relevant market by giving it the power to behave to an appreciable extent independently of its competitors, of its suppliers or customers and ultimately of consumers.[461] It is unclear why Article 208 of the CMO Regulation repeats, word for word, the case-law definition of the dominant

456 See Part IV of the CMO Regulation.
457 CMO Regulation, art 230(2).
458 CMO Regulation, art 207(a).
459 CMO Regulation, art 207(b).
460 Commission, 'The Definition of Relevant Market for the Purposes of Community Competition Law' (Notice) 97/C 372/03, II./7–8.
461 CMO Regulation, art 208.

position formulated in the cases *United Brands*[462] and *Hoffmann-La Roche*.[463] The definition embedded in this provision lacks reason and has no function at all.

Although the core meaning of the exceptions formulated in the Agri-Food Competition Regulation and in the CMO Regulation is the same, there are two small differences between the provisions. Pursuant to Article 2(1) of the Agri-Food Competition Regulation, the prohibition of anticompetitive agreements shall not apply to agreements, decisions and practices of farmers, farmers' associations or associations of such associations *belonging to a single Member State*. The CMO Regulation complements this list with producer organisations recognised under Article 152 or Article 161 of the CMO Regulation, or associations of producer organisations recognised under Article 156 of the CMO Regulation; however, as to the associations of farmers' associations it does not mention the requirement 'belonging to a single Member State'. The latter difference may be based on the fact that associations of farmers' associations must be recognised under national law, the rules of which only apply to organisations which belong to the same Member State. The expansion of the list with producer organisations can be perceived as the concretisation of farmers' associations. Every producer organisation is a farmers' association but not every farmers' association is a producer organisation. The dividing line is whether the entity in question is recognised by a Member State in accordance with EU law. If it is, it is called a producer organisation, if it is not, it is called a farmers' association. It shows that 'calling up' the exemption does not necessarily require recognition in legal sense.

Furthermore, by way of derogation from Article 101(1) TFEU, a recognised producer organisation may plan production, optimise the production costs, place on the market and negotiate contracts for the supply of agricultural products, on behalf of its members for all or part of their total production. There are five cumulative requirements to do so.

(a) One or more of the following activities is/are genuinely exercised jointly: processing; distribution; packaging, labelling or promotion; organising quality control; use of equipment or storage facilities; management of waste directly related to production. These activities contribute to the fulfilment of the CAP objectives.
(b) The producer organisation concentrates on supply and places the products of its members on the market, whether or not there is a transfer of ownership of agricultural products by the producers to the producer organisation.
(c) It is irrelevant whether or not the price negotiated is the same as regards the aggregate production of some or all of the members.

462 Case 27/76 *United Brands Company and United Brands Continentaal BV v Commission of the European Communities* [1978] EU:C:1978:22, para 65.

463 Case 85/76 *Hoffmann-La Roche & Co. AG v Commission of the European Communities* [1979] EU:C:1979:36, para 38.

(d) The producers concerned are not members of any other producer organisation. This can be ignored in duly justified cases where producer members hold two distinct production units located in different geographical areas.
(e) The agricultural product is not covered by an obligation to deliver arising from the farmer's membership of a cooperative, which is not itself a member of the producer organisations concerned, in accordance with the conditions set out in the cooperative's statutes or the rules and decisions provided for in or derived from those statutes.[464]

There are further procedural rules in the CMO Regulation which do not appear in the Agri-Food Competition Regulation. The listed entities, which can be subjected to the exception, may request an opinion from the Commission on the compatibility of the respective agreements, decisions and concerted practices with the objectives set out in Article 39 TFEU.[465] The burden of proof is also established: the burden of proving an infringement of Article 101(1) TFEU shall rest on the party or the authority alleging the infringement; on the contrary, the party claiming the benefit of the exemptions shall bear the burden of proving that the conditions are fulfilled.[466] As can be seen, the agricultural exception follows the same logic regarding the burden of proof as in the case of the individual exception under Article 101(3) TFEU.

Contrariwise, when speaking of interbranch organisations, for them to be exempted, they shall be recognised. Recognition not only has general rules[467] but also special rules for the milk and milk products sector[468] and for the olive oil and table olives and tobacco sectors.[469] The exception provided for interbranch organisations is based also on self-assessment. However, an opinion may be requested from the Commission concerning the compatibility of the agreement, and the Commission is obliged to send the requesting interbranch organisation its opinion within four months of receipt of a complete request. If the Commission finds at any time after issuing an opinion that the conditions to be exempted are no longer met, it shall declare that Article 101(1) TFEU shall apply in the future to the agreement, decision or concerted practice in question and inform the interbranch organisation accordingly. The Commission may change the content of an opinion at its own initiative or at the request of a Member State, in particular if the requesting interbranch organisation has provided inaccurate information or misused the opinion.[470] There are five

464 CMO Regulation, art 152(1a).
465 CMO Regulation, art 209(2). The provision also declares that the Commission shall deal with requests for opinions promptly and shall send the applicant its opinion within four months of receipt of a complete request. The Commission may, at its own initiative or at the request of a Member State, change the content of an opinion, in particular if the applicant has provided inaccurate information or misused the opinion.
466 CMO Regulation, art 209(2).
467 CMO Regulation, arts 157–158.
468 CMO Regulation, art 163.
469 CMO Regulation, art 162.
470 CMO Regulation, art 210(2).

conditions determined which leads to the incompatibility of these agreements with EU law. Three of them are quite similar to the previously mentioned case of exception: the respective agreement, decision or concerted practice shall not create distortions of competition which are not essential to achieving the objectives of the CAP pursued by the activity of the interbranch organisation (similar to the jeopardisation of CAP objectives); they shall not entail price fixing or quota fixing (similar to charging identical prices); they shall not create discrimination or eliminate competition in respect of a substantial proportion of the products in question (similar to the exclusion of competition). Besides these, agreements, decisions and concerted practices shall not lead to the partitioning of markets within the Union in any form and shall not affect the sound operation of the market organisation.[471]

In the CMO Regulation, there are derogations which only apply to a certain subsector of agriculture. These are mostly related to contractual negotiations. Pursuant to Article 149(1), a producer organisation or an association of producer organisations[472] in the milk and milk products sector – in case it is recognised under Article 161(1) – may negotiate on behalf of its farmer members, in respect of part or all of their joint production, contracts for the delivery of raw milk by a farmer to a processor of raw milk, or to a collector.[473,474] However, to do so, there are quantity restrictions determined: (a) the volume of raw milk covered by such negotiations shall not exceed 3,5% of total Union production, (b) the volume of raw milk covered by such negotiations which is produced in any particular Member State does not exceed 33% of the total national production of that Member State, and (c) the volume of raw milk covered by such negotiations which is delivered in any particular Member State does not exceed 33% of the total national production of that Member State.[475,476] There are three further conditions to be fulfilled: (a) the farmers concerned shall not be members of any other producer organisation which also negotiates such contracts on their behalf,[477] (b) the raw milk shall not be covered by an obligation to deliver arising from the farmer's membership of a cooperative in accordance with the conditions set out in the cooperative's statutes or the rules and decisions provided for in or derived from these statutes, and (c) the producer organisation shall notify the competent authorities of the Member State or Member States in which it operates of the volume of raw milk covered by

471 CMO Regulation, art 210(4).
472 CMO Regulation, art 149(4).
473 A 'collector' is understood as defined by the CMO Regulation, art 148(1).
474 CMO Regulation, art 149(1).
475 CMO Regulation, art 149(2)(c).
476 The threshold of 33% does not apply to cases when the volume of raw milk covered by the negotiations is produced in or delivered in a Member State having a total annual raw milk production of less than 500.000 tonnes. In this case, the volume of raw milk covered by the negotiations shall not exceed 45% of the total national production of that Member State, that is a privileged threshold shall apply. See: CMO Regulation, art 149(3).
477 However, Member States may derogate from this condition in duly justified cases where farmers hold two distinct production units located in different geographic areas.

such negotiations.[478] This possibility of the producer organisations is irrespective of whether there is a transfer of ownership of the raw milk by the farmers to the producer organisation and whether the price negotiated is the same as regards the joint production of some or all of the farmer members.[479]

It is also worth mentioning that earlier, Articles 169–171 of the CMO Regulation included similar derogations applying to the olive oil, beef and veal and arable crops sector, but these provisions were repealed as of 1 January 2018.[480]

12.2 The United States of America

Agriculture-related federal antitrust rules, as unravelled in subheading 3 of Chapter 6, have a long history. These provisions have not been amended significantly since then but have developed through case-law interpretation. The pillars of this area are to be found in Section 6 of the Clayton Act and the Capper-Volstead Act. It is reasonable to interpret these legal sources hand in hand with one other, taking into account that the Capper-Volstead Act – labelled as the Magna Charta of farmers[481] – was adopted as a result of the deficiencies in Clayton Act's Section 6.[482] Basically, the Capper-Volstead Act extends the scope of Clayton Act's Section 6.[483]

It would be wrong to assume that antitrust laws do not apply to agricultural cooperatives at all: they are not completely immune.[484] The scope of exemption entitled to them under antitrust laws is limited,[485] however its exact extent is unclear.[486]

The essence of Clayton Act's Section 6 is to permit "the operation of agricultural or horticultural mutual assistance organizations when such organizations do not have capital stock or are not conducted for profit."[487] The reason behind this is clear: the Sherman Act's provisions can be interpreted in such a way that they cover mutual assistance between local farmers managing small farms which violate the act through the joint pricing and marketing of agricultural products by resulting in the elimination of competition.[488] This was ceased by Section 6, however, only with

478 CMO Regulation, art 149(2)(d)–(f).

479 CMO Regulation, art 149(2)(a)–(b).

480 Commission, 'The Application of the Union Competition Rules to the Agricultural Sector' (Report) COM(2018) 706 final, 25.

481 Ewell Paul Roy, *Cooperatives: Today and Tomorrow* (2nd edn, Interstate Printers & Publishers 1969) 215.

482 Varney (n 202) 2.

483 Stephen D. Hawke, 'Antitrust Implications of Agricultural Cooperatives' (1984) 73 Kentucky Law Journal 1035.

484 T.O., 'Agricultural Cooperatives and the Antitrust Laws: Clayton, Capper-Volstead, and Common Sense' (1958) 44 Virginia Law Review 63.

485 Alice Schumacher Horneber, 'Agricultural Cooperatives: Gain of Market Power and the Antitrust Exemption' (1982) 27 South Dakota Law Review 476.

486 William E. Peters, 'Agricultural Cooperatives and the Antitrust Laws' (1963) 43 Nebraska Law Review 103.

487 U.S. Department of Justice, *Antitrust Division Manual* (5th edn, DOJ 2021) II–13.

488 Hawke (n 483) 1036–1037.

significant limitations: capital stock and for-profit organisations are not covered by the provision.

First of all, a distinction has to be made: while the activities *below* cooperative level, such as marketing agreements between farmers and cooperatives and joint marketing contracts among affiliated cooperatives, are exempt from antitrust laws, the activities *on* cooperative level, such as the ones mentioned in the next two cases, are not.[489] In its 1939 landmark judgment of the *United States v. Borden* case, the US Supreme Court emphasised that agricultural cooperatives do not enjoy full exemption under antitrust laws.[490] The *Borden* judgment clearly shows that cooperatives shall not combine with nonexempt persons in restraint of trade.[491] In 1960 – as a continuation of this restrictive analysis[492] – the *Borden* holding was clarified and expanded in the *Maryland and Virginia Milk Producers Assn., Inc. v. United States* case.[493] With this judgment

> the Supreme Court established that the agricultural cooperative exemption does not extend to unilateral competition-stifling practices. The Court condemned a cooperative's coercive and predatory trade practices which were so far outside the legitimate objectives of agricultural cooperatives as to be clear violations of the Sherman Act.[494]

The 'predatory action' test was developed by the Supreme Court in light of the legislative history of Clayton Act's Section 6 and the Capper-Volstead Act.[495] The Capper-Volstead immunity is granted to a cooperative, if it has a legitimate object to be attained when engaged in agricultural business activities and no predatory trade practices are used by the cooperative to achieve this goal. It means that an ends–means analysis can be carried out consisting of four patterns: (a) legitimate goal – non-predatory action, (b) legitimate goal – predatory action, (c) illegitimate goal – non-predatory action, and (d) illegitimate goal – predatory action.[496] Obviously, only the first pattern is exempted. Although it is established in Supreme Court case law that antitrust law exemptions shall be interpreted narrowly,[497] the Capper-Volstead

489 Alan M. Anderson, 'Agricultural Cooperative Antitrust Exemption-Fairdale Farms Inc. v. Yankee Milk Inc.' (1981–1982) 67 Cornell Law Review 401–402.

490 U.S. Supreme Court: *United States v. Borden Co.*, 308 U.S. 188 (1939).

491 Schumacher Horneber (n 485) 480.

492 Hawke (n 483) 1044.

493 U.S. Supreme Court: *Maryland and Virginia Milk Producers Assn., Inc. v. United States*, 362 U.S. 458 (1960).

494 Schumacher Horneber (n 485) 480.

495 Hawke (n 483) 1045.

496 Hawke (n 483) 1047–1048.

497 See the cited cases in footnote 155 of Alison Peck, 'The Cost of Cutting Agricultural Output: Interpreting the Capper-Volstead Act' (2015) 80 Missouri Law Review 473: "Union Labor Life Ins. Co. v. Pireno, 458 U.S. 119, 126 (1982); see also Bankamerica Corp. v. United States, 462 U.S. 122, 147–48 (1983); Grp. Life & Health Ins. Co. v. Royal Drug Co., 440 U.S. 205, 231 (1979); Abbott Labs. v. Portland Retail Druggists Ass'n, Inc., 425 U.S. 1, 11 (1976); Fed. Mar. Comm'n v. Seatrain

act's protection has been even extended to price-fixing agreements,[498] despite the fact that the act's wording does not mention it *expressis verbis*. Some say that price-fixing is the most effective tool of achieving bargaining balance and has to be interpreted as an aspect to be included in the term 'marketing'.[499] This also shows us the likely interpretation problems emerging from Section 6 of the Clayton Act: what is meant by 'legitimate objects'? Besides collective processing, preparing for market and handling, Section 1 of the Capper-Volstead Act declares that marketing is also a possible legitimate object to be carried out by a cooperative, however, the boundaries of these terms leave room for different interpretations.

Furthermore, one must neither forget the express requirements of the Capper-Volstead Act which are greatly summarised by *Hawke*: producing agricultural products by the cooperative's members; operating for the mutual benefit of members; the volume of nonmember business not exceeding that of member business; structured so that each and every member has one vote irrespective of the capital owned or the dividends paid per year not does not exceed 8% on stock or membership capital; voluntary membership; performing of at least one of the statute's enumerated acts before the immunity. "Most of these requirements are inherent in an agricultural cooperative's basic structure and, therefore, should present little problem for the eligible cooperative."[500] It was explicitly held by the Supreme Court that even one nonfarmer member in a cooperative deprives that cooperative of the exemption provided by the Capper-Volstead Act.[501] This approach has also been adopted by district courts judgments recently.[502] The inadvertent nature of the inclusion is irrelevant, so is the good faith belief of members in being part of a properly constituted cooperative.[503]

Today, the Capper-Volstead Act is under fire from critics. Many argue that cooperatives have grown to such a size that their protection under the act is unjustified. It is an opinion too general. These voices fail to take into account that not only have cooperatives grown, but so have their buyers, particularly retail chains, and thus the imbalance in bargaining power has stayed but has to be decided through case-by-case analysis. Due to the small number of court cases interpreting the

Lines, Inc., 411 U.S. 726, 733 (1973); United States v. McKesson & Robbins, Inc., 351 U.S. 305, 316 (1956); United States v. Masonite Corp., 316 U.S. 265, 280 (1942)."

498 Donald M. Barnes and Jay L. Levine, 'Farmer Cooperatives "Take Cover": The Capper-Volstead Exemption is Under Siege' (2021) 74 Arkansas Law Review 16.

499 Charles Edward Black and Ronald Kent Sufrin, 'Agricultural Cooperatives: Price-Fixing and the Antitrust Exemption' (1978) 11 U.C.D. Law Review 553–554.

500 Hawke (n 483) 1039–1040.

501 U.S. Supreme Court: *Case-Swayne Co., Inc. v. Sunkist Growers, Inc.*, 389 U.S. 384 (1967); U.S. Supreme Court: *National Broiler Marketing Association, Petitioner, v. United States*, 436 U.S. 816 (1978).

502 John C. Monica, Jr. and Jetta C. Sandin, 'Agricultural Antitrust Pitfalls' (2017) 50 Maryland Bar Journal 19. See: United States District Court, E.D. Pennsylvania: In Re Mushroom Direct Purchaser Antitrust Litigation, 621 F. Supp. 2d 274 (2008); United States District Court, E.D. Pennsylvania: In Re Processed Egg Products Antitrust Litigation, 206 F. Supp. 3d 1033 (2016).

503 Barnes and Levine (n 498) 10 and 13.

Capper-Volstead Act, there are still many unanswered questions about the law. There are conflicting views as to whether the exemption covers supply management in the form of production restriction, as well as whether vertical integration of farmers nullifies the exemption. Moreover, in many cases, even deciding on who qualifies as a farmer may be a challenging question.[504] The issue of immunity for production and supply restrictions under the act is manifold, and arguments can be raised both pro and contra.[505] A comprehensive and in-depth analysis of the question concludes that

> Congress did give agriculture certain exemptions because of inherent difficulties endemic to agricultural markets, but those exemptions extend only as far as Congress intended. Output limitations – however effective in controlling supply and fixing prices – do not appear to be among the tools that Congress intended to exempt in passing the Capper-Volstead Act.[506]

The provision on jurisdiction in Section 2 of the Capper-Volstead Act is also noteworthy for a few comments. It gives authorisation to the Secretary of Agriculture "to obtain a cease and desist order if he finds that an association has monopolized or restrained trade to such an extent that the price of any agricultural product is unduly enhanced."[507] The main issue is the extent and scope of this jurisdiction: is it exclusive or primary in relation to that of the FTC and the Department of Justice? The question was answered in the *Borden* case whose relevant findings on this are reproduced here in full:

> We find no ground for saying that this limited procedure is a substitute for the provisions of the Sherman Act, or has the result of permitting the sort of combinations and conspiracies here charged unless or until the Secretary of Agriculture takes action. That this provision of the Capper-Volstead Act does not cover the entire field of the Sherman Act is sufficiently clear. The Sherman Act authorizes criminal prosecutions and penalties. The Capper-Volstead Act provides only for a civil proceeding. The Sherman Act hits at attempts to monopolize as well as actual monopolization. And § 2 of the Capper-Volstead Act contains no provision giving immunity from the Sherman Act in the absence of a proceeding by the Secretary. We think that the procedure under § 2 of the Capper-Volstead Act is auxiliary, and was intended merely as a qualification of the authorization given to cooperative agricultural producers by § 1, so that, if the collective action of such producers, as there permitted, results in the opinion of the Secretary in monopolization or unduly enhanced prices, he may intervene and seek to control the action thus

504 Barnes and Levine (n 498) 16–19, 19–23, and 23–24.
505 See the arguments summarised by Varney (n 202) 5–8.
506 Peck (n 497) 498.
507 Barnes and Levine (n 498) 8.

> taken under § 1. But as § 1 cannot be regarded as authorizing the sort of conspiracies between producers and others that are charged in this indictment, the qualifying procedure for which § 2 provides is not to be deemed to be designed to take the place of, or to postpone or prevent, prosecution under § 1 of the Sherman Act for the purpose of punishing such conspiracies.[508]

It means that the Secretary of Agriculture has neither exclusive nor primary jurisdiction over antitrust offenses of agricultural cooperatives.[509] Actually, "[t]he Secretary of Agriculture has never been called upon to determine whether an association has restrained trade to such an extent that it has unduly enhanced prices."[510]

Besides the Capper-Volstead Act, another piece of agricultural legislation must be noted: as an expansion to the former one, the Cooperative Marketing Act of 1926 was passed to provide further protection for agricultural cooperatives. It authorises farmers to acquire, exchange, interpret and disseminate past, present and prospective crop, market, statistical, economic and other similar information by direct exchange between them, and/or their associations or federations and/or by and through a common agent created or selected by them.[511,512] This law creates the possibility that no court action could be brought against farmers because of anticompetitive exchange of information.

Takeaway 6

Though there are differences in details, both the European Union and the United States regulate antitrust exemptions for agricultural producers, who enjoy some alleviations as regards the prohibition of anticompetitive agreements, in recognition of the fact that they are to be provided with countervailing power through making them possible to join forces against their buyers without the threat to violate antitrust rules.

508 See: U.S. Supreme Court (1939) *United States v. Borden Co.*, 308 U. S. 206.

509 Ralph H. Folsom, 'Antitrust Enforcement under the Secretaries of Agriculture and Commerce' (1980) 80 Columbia Law Review 1634.

510 United States Department of Agriculture, 'The Story of the Capper-Volstead Act' Cooperative Information Report (2002) 281.

511 7 U.S. Code § 455.

512 As *Mahaffie* put it: "Elements of the exemption are also contained in the Cooperative Marketing Act of 1926." See: Charles D. Mahaffie Jr., 'Cooperative Exemptions under the Antitrust Laws: A Prosecutor's View' (1970) 22 Administrative Law Review 436.

13 Antitrust, sustainability and the agricultural sector

The recent appearance of the sustainability discourse in antitrust policy has had its effect also on the decade-long relationship between antitrust and the agricultural sector. In the European Union, it culminated in the world-first, legally binding sustainability exemption exclusively applicable to the agri-food supply chain. The US has not stepped onto the path of legislation neither in general antitrust nor as regards sectoral antitrust provisions. The interesting fact is that the European Union's engagement in the discourse about sustainability and antitrust resulted in legally binding rules only in connection with the agri-food supply chain; in general regarding antitrust, only soft law guidelines appeared about the Commission's approach towards the antitrust assessment of sustainability agreements. These provisions, which are only binding to the Commission itself, constitute part of the general guidelines of the Commission on the applicability of Article 101 to horizontal co-operation agreements.[513] The general (not agriculture-specific) antitrust assessment of sustainability agreements, however, does not form part of my current analysis.

13.1 The European Union[514]

Globally, Article 210a of the CMO Regulation includes the one and only explicit provision dedicated to the interrelationship between agriculture, sustainability and antitrust law. The new rules have been incorporated into Chapter I of Part IV of the CMO Regulation.[515] As stated earlier, this chapter of the CMO Regulation comprises, firstly, a horizontal derogation for producers and their associations, regardless of their recognition under national law,[516] and secondly, a vertical derogation for recognised interbranch organisations.[517] The new provision in Article 210a conflates horizontal

513 See Horizontal Guidelines.

514 This subheading is, in part, based on the author's earlier research. The published version has been developed and put into broader context in the book. See the earlier version: Martin Milán Csirszki, 'Competition Law, Sustainability, and Agriculture: Uneasy Complexity' (in press by the Institute of Justice in Warsaw).

515 CMO Regulation, arts 206–210a.

516 CMO Regulation, art 209.

517 CMO Regulation, art 210.

DOI: 10.4324/9781003604747-17

and vertical elements, regulating them within a single article, resulting in – through the legislative process itself – a considerable incoherence in its wording.[518]

The Commission's initial proposal for the new framework of the Common Agricultural Policy would not have introduced any new provisions concerning antitrust law.[519] Subsequently, however, the European Parliament, through its Committee on Agriculture and Rural Development,[520] proposed an amendment that exclusively encompassed the exemption of vertical agreements, omitting any reference to horizontal ones.[521] This version resembled that of early Article 210, whereby the relevant interbranch organisation was required to inform the Commission of its agreement to secure the Commission's approval through a declaration of compatibility. Conversely, alongside these proposals, a modification of the original notification system in Article 210 was proposed, eliminating the necessity for notification to obtain the exemption.[522]

In a subsequent phase, the European Parliament pushed for horizontal agreements to be also incorporated into the sustainability-related exemption framework, thus allowing both vertical and horizontal agreements to benefit from the exemption without the requirement for market participants to notify the Commission.[523] The

518 CMO Regulation, art 210a.

519 Commission, 'Proposal for a Regulation of the European Parliament and of the Council Amending Regulations (EU) No 1308/2013 Establishing a Common Organisation of the Markets in Agricultural Products, (EU) No 1151/2012 on Quality Schemes for Agricultural Products and Foodstuffs, (EU) No 251/2014 on the Definition, Description, Presentation, Labelling and the Protection of Geographical Indications of Aromatised Wine Products, (EU) No 228/2013 Laying Down Specific Measures for Agriculture in the Outermost Regions of the Union and (EU) No 229/2013 Laying Down Specific Measures for Agriculture in Favour of the Smaller Aegean Islands', COM(2018) 394 final.

520 Committee on Agriculture and Rural Development, 'On the Proposal for a Regulation of the European Parliament and of the Council Amending Regulations (EU) No 1308/2013 Establishing a Common Organisation of the Markets in Agricultural Products, (EU) No 1151/2012 on Quality Schemes for Agricultural Products and Foodstuffs, (EU) No 251/2014 on the Definition, Description, Presentation, Labelling and the Protection of Geographical Indications of Aromatised Wine Products, (EU) No 228/2013 Laying Down Specific Measures for Agriculture in the Outermost Regions of the Union and (EU) No 229/2013 Laying Down Specific Measures for Agriculture in Favour of the Smaller Aegean Islands' (A8–0198/2019), Amendment 144.

521 Amendments adopted by the European Parliament on 23 October 2020 on the proposal for a regulation of the European Parliament and of the Council amending Regulations (EU) No 1308/2013 establishing a common organisation of the markets in agricultural products, (EU) No 1151/2012 on quality schemes for agricultural products and foodstuffs, (EU) No 251/2014 on the definition, description, presentation, labelling and the protection of geographical indications of aromatised wine products, (EU) No 228/2013 laying down specific measures for agriculture in the outermost regions of the Union and (EU) No 229/2013 laying down specific measures for agriculture in favour of the smaller Aegean islands, P9_TA(2020)0289, Amendment 144.

522 Amendments (n 521) Amendment 143.

523 Position of the European Parliament adopted at first reading on 23 November 2021 with a view to the adoption of Regulation (EU) 2021/. . . of the European Parliament and of the Council amending Regulations (EU) No 1308/2013 establishing a common organisation of the markets in agricultural products, (EU) No 1151/2012 on quality schemes for agricultural products and foodstuffs, (EU) No 251/2014 on the definition, description, presentation, labelling and the protection of geographical indications of aromatised wine products and (EU) No 228/2013 laying down specific measures for agriculture in the outermost regions of the Union (EP-PE_TC1-COD(2018)0218).

definitive version states that neither horizontal nor vertical sustainability-related agreements are prohibited, and no prior decision is necessary.[524] The ambiguity of the provisions' wording is caused by a reference in paragraph (2) to paragraph (1). While the former applies to horizontal, the latter applies to vertical agreements. Nevertheless, it is of utmost importance that vertical agreements can benefit from the exemption also in the case when parties to that agreement are *one* agricultural producer alongside one or more operators from other levels of the food supply chain, such as processing and trade. The reference in paragraph (2) to paragraph (1) suggests that only agricultural producers are exempt from Article 101 TFEU concerning vertical sustainability initiatives, while the prohibition still applies to operators that are also party to the agreement. This is caused by the fact that paragraph (1) is only concerned with *exempting producers* from the prohibition of anticompetitive agreements (since it applies to horizontal agreements between producers), while paragraph (2) brings nonproducing entities to the framework, too. This solution would be clearly unreasonable. A more reasonable explanation, supported by the Guidelines, is that a vertical initiative must include at least one party that is a producer and another that is not, but this does not influence the exemption of the whole agreement, if other criteria are met.

The recent exemption has expanded the existing agriculture-related derogation regime into a three-pillar system. Pillar I in Article 209 and Pillar II in Article 210 are general provisions applicable to all agriculture-related agreements. In contrast, Pillar III serves as a *lex specialis*, addressing sustainability-related agreements among agricultural market participants. Article 152(1a), which predates Article 210a, plays a significant role in supporting recognised producer organisations and associations of producer organisations. It facilitates their ability to plan production, optimise production costs, market products, and negotiate contracts for the supply of agricultural products on behalf of their members for all or part of their total production, without the risk of violating anticompetitive agreement prohibitions.[525] This derogation, categorised as a Pillar I exemption due to its relevance to horizontal agreements, is restricted to legally recognized entities,[526] in contrast to Article 209.

If a horizontal agreement does not meet the criteria outlined in Article 210a, it may still qualify for exemption under Article 209.[527] Since all the pillars of the derogation regime rely on voluntary assessment, potentially leading to latency, this situation may create uncertainty for undertakings regarding the legal evaluation of their initiatives, and may impede enforcement authorities in investigating greenwashing practices. To cure this, a system based on comfort letters or the creation of a regulatory sandbox could enhance the visibility of initiatives. It would necessitate increased institutional resources from agencies due to the additional

524 CMO Regulation, art 210a(4).

525 CMO Regulation, art 152(1a)–(1b).

526 Autoriteit Consument & Market, 'Guidelines Regarding Collaborations between Farmers' (22 September 2023) 7.

527 Article 210a Guidelines, recital (17).

workload; however, this investment would be justified in the pursuit of a commendable objective. As seen later, the new exemption indicates that there are counterweights (higher sustainability standard and indispensability) to the agricultural market participants' possibility to enter into sustainability agreements consisting of competition restrictions. However, if Article 210a requirements fail to be fulfilled, by having the chance to go back to the analysis in light of the general derogations in Articles 152(1a), 209 and 210, the purpose of the new exemption can become obsolete, because other provisions may still give the green light for the exemption of these agreements anyway. If the agreement is still referred to as a sustainability agreement, it might actually be viewed as greenwashing. The fact that the Guidelines also refer to agreements that do not meet the requirements of Article 210a as sustainability agreements – as these agreements can only be exempted under other exception rules – creates an inherent contradiction.

A notable distinction between the new exemption and previous ones lies in the personal scope. The novel sustainability-related provisions do not specify any particular organisational form[528]; it solely refers to 'producers of agricultural products' concerning horizontal initiatives, and this is further complemented by the general term 'operators' in relation to vertical initiatives. This approach is novel.

The first two pillars of the agricultural exemption system operate in a distinct manner. A prerequisite for the application of Article 152(1a) and Article 210 is the legal recognition of producer organisations and interbranch organisations, respectively. The complexity of the situation concerning Article 209 is notable. While legislation may not explicitly mandate the established form of producer organisation, case law in *Endives* indicates a different interpretation.[529] The regulation identifies not only producer organisations and associations of producer organisations but also farmers, farmers' associations, and associations of such associations. The last two forms represent informal cooperations among farmers that lack recognition under Article 154 of the CMO Regulation. Conversely, in *Endives*, the Court of Justice ruled that the derogation is inapplicable in instances where non-recognised persons are also party to the agreement.[530] The personal scope of the new exemption is

528 Article 210 Guidelines, recital (11).

529 Although the judgment in Case C–671/15 *Président de l'Autorité de la concurrence v Association des producteurs vendeurs d'endives (APVE) and Others* [2017] EU:C:2017:860 is concerned with the Agri-Food Competition Regulation, this legal act – similarly to Article 209 of CMO Regulation – is formulated as also applying to non-recognised entities. The Court, however, ruled that anti-competitive practices could only be exempted, if they were applied within a recognised producer organisation. Because of the similarity between Article 2 of Agri-Food Competition Regulation and Article 209 of CMO Regulation, this finding of the Court can, in my opinion, be applied to Article 209 based on analogy.

530 See: Case C–671/15 *Président de l'Autorité de la concurrence v Association des producteurs vendeurs d'endives (APVE) and Others* [2017] EU:C:2017:860. See a brief analysis: Jan Blockx, 'The ECJ Preliminary Ruling in French Endives: Two (Too?) Simple Rules to Attune Article 101 TFEU to the Common Agricultural Policy' (Kluwer Competition Law Blog, 2017) <http://competitionlawblog.kluwercompetitionlaw.com/2017/11/15/ecj-preliminary-ruling-french-endives-two-simple-rules-attune-article-101-tfeu-common-agricultural-policy/> accessed 30 December 2023.

broader than that of the earlier derogations, allowing for greater flexibility in legal interpretation and potential for misuse.

The sustainability-related derogation from Article 101 TFEU aligns with the agricultural exemption system regarding the voluntary assessment method. However, its personal scope diverges from the established framework in the CMO Regulation and does not necessitate a legally recognized form of organisation, such as producer or interbranch organisations. This may lead to increased instances of arbitrary and unbounded legal interpretation.

As regards the counterweights to the new exemption not to be limitless, there are two crucial concepts: a higher sustainability standard than required by law and the indispensability of the cooperation to achieve that standard with indispensable competition restrictions.

It is worth mentioning that stakeholders have raised numerous concerns regarding the condition of indispensability. Many would appreciate the clarification of the criterion,[531] while others recognise its importance in balancing benefits and harms.[532] ClientEarth contends that the interpretation should not be overly stringent, allowing producers the opportunity to enhance profitability and avoid financial distress.[533] Some argue that elevated sustainability standards inherently result in increased costs.[534]

The indispensability standard is defined in the Commission's guidelines on Article 101(3) TFEU.[535] It indicates that the sustainability agreement should not impose restrictions that are not essential for achieving the efficiencies generated by the agreement. This interpretation suggests that efficiencies, defined as enhanced sustainability – such as reduced food waste, decreased pesticide use and improved animal welfare – require collaboration among market participants. Its assessment method regarding consumers' willingness to pay has been subject to significant debate.[536] For instance, the Dutch Competition Authority determined that the actions undertaken by participants in the well-known initiative 'Chicken of Tomorrow' are not essential for achieving an enhanced level of animal welfare.[537] The desired efficiencies could have been attained through methods less severe than collusion.

531 LTO Nederland, 'Response to Call for Evidene: Sustainability Agreements in Agriculture – Guidelines on Antitrust Derogation' (2022) 4; EuroCommerce, 'Guidelines on Antitrust Derogations for Sustainability Agreements in Agriculture: Call for Evidence' (2022) 3.

532 BEUC – The European Consumer Organisation, 'European Commission's Consultation on Sustainability Agreements in Agriculture: BEUC's Comments on the Guidelines on the Antitrust Derogation in Article 210a CMO' (2022).

533 ClientEarth, 'Sustainability Agreements in Agriculture – Guidelines on Antitrust Derogation' (2022) 4.

534 Association of Dutch Flower Auctions, 'Consultation on Sustainability Agreements in Agriculture – Guidelines on the Antitrust Derogation' (2022); COPA-COGECA, 'Contribution to the Commission Public Consultation on Sustainability Agreements in Agriculture Guidelines on Antitrust Derogation' (2022).

535 Commission, 'Guidelines on the Application of Article 81(3) of the Treaty' (Communication) OJ C101/97, paras 73–82.

536 Simon Holmes, 'Climate Change, Sustainability, and Competition Law' (2020) 8 Journal of Antitrust Enforcement 379–380.

537 See the ACM's analysis of the sustainability arrangements concerning the 'Chicken of Tomorrow' (2015) <www.acm.nl/sites/default/files/old_publication/publicaties/13789_analysis-chicken-of-tomorrow-acm-2015-01-26.pdf.pdf> accessed 1 September 2023.

The indispensability of the relevant agreement in achieving the objectives is at least as significant as the necessity for a higher sustainability standard than what is legally required, among the two protective pillars related to Article 210a. The two-factor test regarding indispensability is crucial for determining whether a sustainability-related agreement can achieve the anticipated results. The realisation of both standards – no efficiencies without agreement and no efficiencies without competition restriction[538] – should be evaluated rigorously to qualify for an exemption under Article 210a.

The evaluation of indispensability should align with the assessment conducted under Article 101(3) TFEU. In contrast, the Guidelines indicate that the Guidelines on the application of Article 101(3) TFEU serve merely as a useful starting point for evaluating indispensability in the context of sustainability agreements. However, due to significant differences in the articles, the standard for indispensability is inherently distinct between the two.[539] The finalised Guidelines omitted this claim; however, the Draft Guidelines included it, noting that sustainability agreements in the agricultural sector extend beyond merely providing a fair share of benefits to consumers.[540]

I would address the question from a different perspective. The indispensability test remains consistent across both cases. The distinguishing factor is the objective to be attained through a specific agreement. Achieving a higher level of sustainability may necessitate, at least initially, a more accommodating stance regarding restrictions. Nonetheless, this does not imply that the core of the indispensability test would alter. The factual circumstances relevant to the application of the indispensability test are dissimilar; however, the same procedural steps must be followed regarding the test: first, assessing the indispensability of the agreement, and second, evaluating the indispensability of the competition restrictions in that agreement. The fair share of benefits to consumers, which the Draft Guidelines mentioned here, is a distinct assessment criterion, and should not play a role in the assessment of indispensability. An agreement can be essential for attaining specific efficiencies; however, it may inadequately ensure a fair distribution of benefits to consumers. These two should remain separate. I believe that the (Draft) Guidelines should not suggest the existence of varying indispensability tests for different categories of restrictive agreements.

Obviously, "sustainability does not come at zero cost."[541] In my opinion, if consumers still have the option to choose the less expensive, non-sustainable product, then the indispensability criterion can tolerate higher prices. That is to say, unlike in *Chicken of Tomorrow*, the initiative (agreement) that seeks to achieve a higher

538 Commission, 'Guidelines on the Application of Article 81(3) of the Treaty' (Communication) OJ C101/97, para 73.

539 Article 210a Guidelines, recital (87).

540 Draft Guidelines, Recital (83).

541 'Collective Initiatives and Sustainability Agreements in an Organic Farming Association: The Case of Bioland e.V.' (2022) 4 <https://enrd.ec.europa.eu/sites/default/files/enrd_publications/case_study_bioland.pdf> accessed 1 September 2023.

sustainability standard does not cover the entire product market; rather, it gives consumers the right of decision with different alternatives. This also accounts for those who are unable to purchase the more costly product that results from factoring in the costs associated with sustainability. However, higher costs may be necessary not because the indispensability test is altered per se, but rather because the goal of the agreement may call for solutions that appear more restrictive than our common understanding of what is acceptable.

The other central component of the new exemption is the definition of the sustainability standard. Adopted by private entities, it must exceed the requirements set by EU or national legislation. This suggests that it is inadequate for entities seeking to utilise the exemption to merely agree on terms that are already mandated by legally binding regulations. If a specific pesticide is prohibited in the European Union, and market participants collectively decide not to buy agricultural products treated with that pesticide, they do not meet the criteria for the derogation. This decreases the potential for greenwashing. The parties may seek to conceal anticompetitive collusion through their agreement, presenting it as a sustainability initiative.

This position appears to conflict with the case of garden centers in the Netherlands. They have reached an agreement to limit the use of illegal pesticides by refraining from marketing plants treated with such substances.[542] In my view, this commitment does not surpass the legally mandated sustainability standard. To determine if a standard exceeds the requirements set by EU and/or national law, the benchmark must be interpreted restrictively. The Guidelines specify that the exception rule no longer applies to the agreement once equivalent standards come into effect.[543] The regulation concerning the illegal use of specific pesticides places obligations on individuals who market or utilise these substances, rather than on those who sell products treated with them. However, this does not alter the reality that the law sets a sustainability standard that must be adhered to at every level of the vertical chain. The 2013 judgment of the Court of Justice is noteworthy in this aspect, as it determined that the alleged illegal operation of an undertaking affected by a competition-restricting agreement at the time of its conclusion does not impact the assessment of whether the agreement constitutes an infringement of the relevant provision.[544] In the Dutch case, the fact that the agreement among the garden centres imposes restrictions on suppliers engaging in unlawful practices, such as the use of prohibited pesticides, does not imply that the garden centres are authorised to enforce the laws through their anticompetitive agreement. The illegal nature of the suppliers' actions does not alter the anticompetitive nature of the buyers' agreement. Furthermore, it does not exceed the sustainability standards required by law.

542 See: ACM agrees to arrangements of garden centers to curtail use of illegal pesticides, available at: www.acm.nl/en/publications/acm-agrees-arrangements-garden-centers-curtail-use-illegal-pesticides.

543 Article 210a Guidelines, recital (64).

544 Case C-68/12 *Protimonopolný úrad Slovenskej republiky v Slovenská sporiteľňa a.s.* [2013] EU:C:2013:71, para 37.

Sustainability standards may encompass a wide range of phenomena, including climate change mitigation, sustainable water use, food waste reduction, decreased pesticide application and animal welfare.[545] This perspective is both progressive and potentially hazardous. Market participants can collaborate on various issues to enhance sustainability, which is beneficial. Though plant health is not included, nor do the Guidelines mention it, it would be prudent to clarify its potential inclusion within the objectives outlined in Article 210(3)(a). However, animal health and welfare are addressed separately, indicating that certain sustainability agreements may be exempted in relation to these factors.[546] Animal welfare has begun to permeate scholarly[547] and policy discussions[548] as a contributing factor to sustainability. Nonetheless, a significant breakthrough demonstrating its concrete positive impacts on sustainability has yet to occur. Numerous prominent statements advocate for the inclusion of animal welfare in sustainable initiatives; however, a direct causal link appears to be lacking. I acknowledge the importance of animal welfare; however, I claim that it is underdeveloped as to sustainability. The significant contributions of soil and water protection, reduced pesticide use and biodiversity to sustainability cannot be overemphasised, while the same is difficult to say in connection with animal welfare, which appears to be more distant in consideration. Antitrust policy should reflect this distinction. Regarding the exception rule in Article 101(3) TFEU, it is agreed that the causal link between the restrictive agreement and the asserted efficiencies must be direct, and claims based on indirect effects are generally considered too uncertain and too remote to be considered.[549] The primary

545 CMO Regulation, art 210a(3).

546 CMO Regulation, art 210a(3)(c).

547 See, for example: M. Baumgartner and others, 'Improving Horse Welfare and Environmental Sustainability in Horse Husbandry: Linkage between Turnout and Nitrogen Surplus' (2021) 13 Sustainability <https://doi.org/10.3390/su13168991> accessed 1 September 2023; G. Olmos Antillón and others, 'Animal Welfare and the United Nations' Sustainable Development Goals – Broadening Students' Perspectives' (2021) 13 Sustainability <https://doi.org/10.3390/su13063328> accessed 1 September 2023; Y. Sun and others, 'Determinants of Animal Welfare Disclosure Practices: Evidence from China' (2021) 13 Sustainability <https://doi.org/10.3390/su13042200> accessed 1 September 2023; O. Torpman and H. Röcklinsberg, 'Reinterpreting the SDGs: Taking Animals into Direct Consideration' (2021) 13 Sustainability <https://doi.org/10.3390/su13020843> accessed 1 September 2023; L. Friedrich and others, 'Iceberg Indicators for Sow and Piglet Welfare' (2021) 12 Sustainability <https://doi.org/10.3390/su12218967> accessed 1 September 2023; L. Keeling and others, 'Animal Welfare and the United Nations Sustainable Development Goals' (2019) Frontiers in Veterinary Science, Article 336; H. Buller and others, 'Towards Farm Animal Welfare and Sustainability' (2018) 8 Animals <https://doi.org/10.3390/ani8060081> accessed 1 September 2023.

548 C. Verkuijl and others, 'Mainstreaming Animal Welfare in Sustainable Development: A Policy Agenda' (2022) <https://euagenda.eu/upload/publications/animal-welfare-stockholm50backgroundpaper.pdf> accessed 1 September 2023; S. Weimer, 'Being Sustainable Doesn't Equate to a Free Pass on Animal Welfare' (2020) <www.thepoultrysite.com/articles/being-sustainable-doesnt-equate-to-a-free-pass-on-animal-welfare> accessed 1 September 2023; United Nations Environment Programme, 'Why Is Animal Welfare Important for Sustainable Consumption and Production?' (2019); World Society for the Protection of Animals, 'Animals: Helping Us Achieve the Future We Want' (2013).

549 Commission, 'Guidelines on the Application of Article 81(3) of the Treaty' (Communication) OJ C101/97, recital (54).

objective of the sustainability agreement is to enhance efficiency in sustainability practices. The efficiencies require verification, and the actual impact of animal welfare measures, such as larger cages, on sustainability is yet to be determined. I reiterate: I support animal welfare; however, I oppose the use of antitrust law exemptions for the purpose of achieving sustainability, which remains unattainable even with legally permissible competition restrictions due to the absence of a direct causal link between the means employed and the efficiencies expected. This undermines the fundamental purpose of the exemption: permitting a restriction to attain efficiencies. The invocation of antitrust law should occur only when the justification for the exception is adequately supported.

It is important to recognise that sustainable practices may conflict with other dimensions of sustainability. For instance, if intensively farmed animals were transitioned to extensive farming systems, there would be a significant increase in the demand for currently unfarmed land. While this may enhance animal welfare, it could also result in habitat degradation and soil loss.[550] These cases necessitate a careful assessment of whether the agreement in question ultimately promotes sustainability. Legal certainty, particularly regarding the establishment of a clear and effective definition of sustainability standards, is essential for entities within the food supply chain to identify agreements eligible for exemption.[551]

As previously indicated, an agreement can only be exempted if its goal is to meet a higher standard of sustainability than those required by EU or national law. According to the Guidelines, producers and operators operating in a Member State shall respect the higher national standard, if a mandatory national standard is more stringent or ambitious than the corresponding EU standard.[552] The Guidelines interpret this clause in a way that does not apply uniform standards across the EU. Because of stronger national laws, a sustainability standard may be adequate in one Member State but insufficient in another. It is incompatible with the global (and cross-border) nature of environmental issues and the growing number of global food value chains. The exemption stems from the directly applicable CMO Regulation, so the sustainability standards mandated by EU law should be used as the benchmark when evaluating an agreement. This current approach results in market participants from various Member States not being treated equally at the EU level.

The Guidelines indicate that an agreement may be exempted if it involves only one party that is an agricultural producer.[553] The requirement for a provision adopted within the framework of the CAP is not excessively high, as it aims to enhance the individual earnings of individuals involved in agriculture.

550 D.M. Broom, 'Animal Welfare Complementing or Conflicting with Other Sustainability Issues' (2019) Applied Animal Behaviour Science <https://doi.org/10.1016/j.applanim.2019.06.010> accessed 1 September 2023.

551 BEUC – The European Consumer Organisation, 'European Commission's Consultation on Sustainability Agreements in Agriculture: BEUC's Comments on the Guidelines on the Antitrust Derogation in Article 210a CMO' (2022).

552 Article 210a Guidelines, recital (60).

553 Article 210a Guidelines, recital (27).

The new exemption primarily focuses not on the fair standard of living for agricultural producers, but rather on promoting sustainability agreements that align with the objectives of the EU Green Deal. However, the selected method and legal foundation, specifically Article 42 TFEU, appears unusual. It is theoretically feasible for a single agricultural producer to enter into an agreement with multiple food processors and/or retailers, as the product in question is listed in Annex I of the TFEU.

Although Article 42 TFEU references the trade in agricultural products as an activity subject to potential limitations on competition rules as determined by the European Parliament and the Council, the fundamental purpose and intrinsic characteristic of the Common Agricultural Policy is the safeguarding of producers. Article 40(1) TFEU reinforces that the unique characteristics of agricultural activity, stemming from the social structure of agriculture, must be considered in the formulation of the CAP. In other words, it appears that the resources intended to assist agricultural producers also benefit other industrial and commercial stakeholders. Article 210a employs the term 'operator'. Exemptions apply not only to food processors, wholesalers and retailers but also to entities within the hotel, restaurant and catering sector (HoReCa). Regrettably, this is not the inaugural instance in which the CAP, grounded in its legal framework, has been employed to safeguard market participants who do not engage in farming. The primary aim of the UTP Directive, examined in subheading 1 of Chapter 14, is to address unfair trading practices (UTPs) directed at agricultural producers; however, the definition of a supplier entitled to protection encompasses any natural or legal entity that sells agricultural and food products. Not solely agricultural producers. I believe that EU legislation should exercise caution in utilising the CAP to assist market participants beyond agricultural producers. This trend starkly contrasts with the purpose of agricultural policy.

Enforcing the new provisions will present challenges, despite the Guidelines pointing out that the threshold of jeopardising Common Agricultural Policy objectives is high.[554] Without the assistance of regulatory agencies focusing on agriculture and possessing knowledge about the environment and agri-food markets, I predict that competition authorities will find it difficult to resolve these issues. The challenges of balancing conflicting public policy interests clearly emerge when enforcing the new provisions by competition authorities.

Despite the introduction of a new exemption related to sustainability in the agricultural sector, I do not believe that there will be any major changes. Even in the absence of these provisions, competition authorities could have evaluated the sustainability agreement under the parameters of the individual exemption. The requirement of a higher sustainability standard than required by law could be included in the analysis of whether the agreement contributes to improving the production or distribution of goods or to promoting technical or economic progress.

554 Article 210a Guidelines, recital (181).

The indispensability criterion is also part of the assessment of the individual exemption.[555]

The relief of the agricultural policy community stems from the fact that – in antitrust terms – consumers should not receive a fair share of benefits resulting from the sustainability agreements. Nevertheless, the requirement of the higher sustainability standard than required by law as well as indispensability may have pitfalls; still, the new exemption appears less strict.[556]

The aforementioned clarifications and modifications have the potential to facilitate the attainment of the objectives of the new antitrust exemption. However, the operationalisation of the exemption would necessitate close collaboration between competition authorities and agricultural regulatory agencies.

13.2 The United States

As mentioned earlier, the antitrust agencies, policy-makers and academics of the United States do not pay particular attention to the issue of sustainability in antitrust law and policy. This also holds true for the antitrust assessment of the agricultural sector's sustainability initiatives. Thanks to its different approach, which addresses these topics in an indirect manner that a pro-enforcement agenda will necessarily deliver desirable outcomes also in this regard, the United States lags behind in terms of nuanced frameworks that could constitute an assessment scheme for sustainability agreements.

The lack of explicit (and direct) legal framework is telling in itself. On the one hand, it shows that antitrust policy in the US does not accept noneconomic considerations directly. This was particularly accurate in the period from the emergence of the Chicago School in the 1980s until the Neo-Brandeisian paradigm change in the 2020s. The latter change, however, has not brought to the fore that within antitrust enforcement noneconomic concerns should be given direct and intensified attention. These noneconomic concerns only get cured as a consequence of effective and interventionist antitrust enforcement. The conclusions of *Crane*, one of the leading voices of the new school of thought, demonstrate this vision perfectly. He declares that antitrust cannot and should not become "a self-conscious instrument of democracy in its doctrines or operations. An antitrust policy focused on mitigating market power and preserving competition is more helpful to the democratic cause."[557] This is no different when it comes to sustainability. The key players in federal antitrust enforcement, FTC Chairperson *Lina Khan* and the DOJ's Assistant

555 See the ACM's Analysis of the Sustainability Arrangements Concerning the 'Chicken of Tomorrow' (2015) 5–6 <www.acm.nl/sites/default/files/old_publication/publicaties/13789_analysis-chicken-of-tomorrow-acm-2015-01-26.pdf.pdf> accessed 1 September 2023.

556 Ioannis Lianos, 'Agriculture & Competition Law: An Overview of EU and National Case Law' (2022) Concurrences.

557 Daniel A. Crane, 'Antitrust as an Instrument of Democracy' (2022) 72 Duke Law Journal Online 40.

Attorney General *Jonathan Kanter*, are of the opinion that increased competition leads to better environmental outcomes.[558]

On the other hand, it also displays that, unlike the European Union, the United States does not immediately, or at all, attempt to regulate a newly emerging issue. Instead, it has much more trust in market participants to deliver favourable outcomes. On the contrary, the European legislators feel the urge to define the boundaries in order to orient undertakings towards market behaviours that are accepted as lawful by the decision-makers. This mirrors the general free-marketer approach of the United States.

Takeaway 7

In contrast with the relationship between the agricultural sector and antitrust, when it comes to sustainability and antitrust, the paths taken by the EU and the US are different. The European Union follows a direct (ready-to-innovate) approach towards sustainability agreements with special legal provisions and assessment methods. It holds particularly true in the agricultural sector, which – following the century-long tradition of helping agricultural producers through antitrust means – enjoys even further alleviations in the antitrust regime, compared to the non-agriculture-related sustainability agreements.

558 Denise Hearn, Cynthia Hanawalt and Lisa Sachs, 'Antitrust and Sustainability: A Landscape Analysis' (2023) 22 Columbia Center on Sustainable Investment and Sabin Center for Climate Change Law.

14 Beyond antitrust

14.1 The European Union

14.1.1 UTP Directive: the road to and the policy behind its adoption

The UTP Directive was adopted on 17 April 2019 by the European Parliament and the Council after more than ten years of preparatory work.[559] Before analysing the directive in detail, presenting the path towards its adoption[560] is necessary since it gives insights into the agricultural policy objectives behind the legal act. Where appropriate, reference is made to legal literature, but I rely primarily on documents adopted within the framework of the European Union. Both *Ackermann* and *Paredis and Keirsbilck* consider the opinion adopted by the European Social and Economic Committee in 2005 as the first EU document dealing with unfair trading practices.[561,562] In its first sentence, the opinion mentions that changes over the past 20 years have led to the emergence of supermarkets and hypermarkets, the main drivers of changing consumer demands.[563] Structural changes in the retail market have led to increasing market concentration: "the market share of the top five food retailers has increased on average by 21.7% reaching an average of 69.2% in the [then-]EU 15."[564] One of the most important findings of the opinion is the following:

559 Victoria Daskalova, 'The New Directive on Unfair Trading Practices in Food and EU Competition Law: Complementary or Divergent Normative Frameworks?' (2019) 10 Journal of European Competition Law & Practice 281.

560 The antecedents of the UTP Directive's adoption are analysed in German by Jan Ackermann, *Wohlgeordnetes Agrarwettbewerbsrecht mit Blick auf Erzeugerorganisationen und unlautere Handelspraktiken* (Nomos 2020) 192–215. The issue is dealt with in English by Elisa Paredis and Bert Keirsbilck, 'Run-Up, Legal Basis and Scope of Application' in Bert Keirsbilck and Evelyne Terryn (eds), *Unfair Trading Practices in the Food Supply Chain: Implications of Directive (EU) 2019/633* (Intersentia 2020) 7–12.

561 Ackermann (n 560) 192; Paredis and Keirsbilck (n 560) 9.

562 European Economic and Social Committee, 'Opinion on the Large Retail Sector: Trends and Impacts on Farmers and Consumers' (2005/C 255/08).

563 European Economic and Social Committee (n 562) 1.1.

564 European Economic and Social Committee (n 562) 5.1.

DOI: 10.4324/9781003604747-18

> since consumers attach great importance to price and given that consumers' demand also influences the offer, there is considerable pressure on retailers to lower prices. In their determination to provide low prices to the consumer, the [retail chains] put pressure on suppliers to reduce prices. This is true in the food sector and primarily in markets where the concentration is very high.[565]

This more than 15-year-old finding implies that retail chains acting as intermediaries in the food chain have to choose whether to benefit their suppliers or consumers. Since there is significant competition for consumers in the retail market, retail chains can only compete with each other by lowering the prices they pay to suppliers, by taking advantage of their relative market power vis-à-vis suppliers. The opinion not only declares that "[i]f over a period farmers are subject to falling incomes and increasing costs, more farmers will go out of business,"[566] but also concludes that the Member States and EU institutions "must avoid a total liberalisation of the market that would lead to further concentration,"[567] which can mean "that in the future food retailing would be in the hands of a very small number of players, which could lead to less consumer choice and higher prices."[568]

The 2009 EC Communication already distinguished between unfair trading practices as possible outcomes of the bargaining power asymmetries of contracting parties and anticompetitive practices. On the former ones, the Communication notes that

> [c]ontractual imbalances associated with unequal bargaining power have a negative impact on the competitiveness of the food supply chain as smaller but efficient actors may be obliged to operate under reduced profitability, limiting their ability and incentives to invest in improved product quality and innovation of production processes. A better awareness of contractual rights and stronger action against unfair contractual practices could contribute to preventing these drawbacks since actors with limited bargaining power suffer from a lack of information on their rights. Moreover, they may hesitate to contest contract clauses for fear of losing the contract altogether.[569]

Furthermore, the Commission's statements on the latter issue suggest that it assesses anticompetitive practices solely in terms of consumer harm. As regards anticompetitive practices, the Commission uses the expression "distort[ing] competition *to the detriment of consumers*."[570] This would seem to suggest that the 2009 EC Communication views antitrust law enforcement solely in terms

565 European Economic and Social Committee (n 562) 7.1.
566 European Economic and Social Committee (n 562) 9.2.
567 European Economic and Social Committee (n 562) 11.2.
568 European Economic and Social Committee (n 562) 11.6.
569 Commission, 'A Better Functioning Food Supply Chain in Europe' (Communication), COM(2009) 591, 3.1.1.
570 Commission (n 569) 3.1.2.

of the objective of consumer welfare taken over from the Chicago School of thought; however, EU antitrust law is designed to achieve much more than that. *Stylianou* and *Iacovides* have explored in their research at least seven different goals of the Union competition law: efficiency, welfare, freedom/competitors, market structure, fairness, European integration and competition process, that is, "EU competition law is not monothematic but pursues a multitude of goals."[571]

Following the Commission Communication, in 2012 the European Parliament gave its resolution on imbalances in the food supply chain.[572] The EP divided the practices complained of by producers into two groups and provided a non-exhaustive list. On the one hand, there are practices which restrict the producers' access to retailers; on the other hand, there are unfair contractual conditions or unilateral changes to contract terms.[573] The former arise mainly in the pre-contractual phase, while the latter arise when the parties are already in a contractual relationship. According to the European Parliament, addressing imbalances in the food supply chain not only requires self-regulatory solutions but also normative regulation in the form of *adjustments to competition law*.[574]

In 2013, the European Commission published its Green Paper on the issue in order to stimulate discussion on different aspects of the problem.[575] The Green Paper not only deals with unfair trading practices in the food supply chain but also in the nonfood supply chains in general. It stipulates that only a subset of unfair trading practices falls within the scope of antitrust law,[576] of which – to a limited extent – abuse of dominance can serve as a legal instrument to handle these practices. Besides the toolbox of antitrust law, the Green Paper also mentions the possible treatment of unfair trading practices within the framework of civil/commercial law and of special legislation.[577] Legal instruments related to relative market power, i.e., other abuse-type conducts constitute no part of antitrust law in its conventional sense. At the EU level, Article 102 TFEU covers some UTPs, but – because of the limits of EU antitrust law in this regard[578] – there are other regulatory solutions to handle these practices. For example, the Directive 2005/29/EC can be

571 Konstantinos Stylianou and Marios C. Iacovides, 'The Goals of EU Competition Law: A Comprehensive Empirical Investigation' (2019) SSRN <https://ssrn.com/abstract=3735795> accessed 7 October 2023.

572 European Parliament, 'Imbalances in the Food Supply Chain' (2013/C 227 E/03).

573 Eight different practices (for example, advance payment for accessing negotiation, listing fees, entry fees, shelf space pricing, etc.) are classified in the first group and 24 in the second group (for example, unilateral and retrospective changes to contractual conditions, payment delays, unrealistic delivery terms, unilateral withdrawal of products from store shelves, etc.). See: European Parliament (n 572) 10.

574 European Parliament (n 572) 20.

575 Commission, *Unfair Trading Practices in the Business-to-Business Food and Non-Food Supply Chain in Europe* (Green Paper 2013) COM(2013) 37 final.

576 Commission (n 575) 3.1.

577 Commission (n 575) 3.1.

578 Paredis and Keirsbilck (n 560) 10.

extended to business-to-business relations; in addition, the Late Payments Directive[579] and some sector-specific regulations[580] can be mentioned.[581]

Among the direct effects of unfair trading practices, the 2014 EC Communication[582] mentions "undue costs or lower-than-expected revenues for the trading partner in the weaker bargaining position." In a rather interesting link, the Communication mentions that "unpredictable changes of contract terms may also lead to overproduction and result in unnecessary food waste," and the negative change in the ability or willingness to fund investments on the weaker party's side may also be a long-term disadvantage.[583]

Furthermore, the Communication formulates the definition of unfair trading practices. These are "practices that grossly deviate from good commercial conduct, are contrary to good faith and fair dealing and are unilaterally imposed by one trading partner on another."[584] This definition has been taken over word for word by the final version of the UTP Directive.[585]

In its 2016 report, the European Commission was against the harmonisation of unfair trading practices at the EU level because of the positive developments in certain parts of the food chain as well as owing to the different regulatory approaches needed to handle these practices.[586] On the contrary, a few months later, the European Parliament saw in unfair trading practices "an obstacle to the development and smooth functioning of the internal market," and besides the weaker party which may suffer excessive costs or lower-than-expected revenues, "consumers potentially face a loss in product diversity, cultural heritage and retail outlets as a result of UTPs."[587] Nevertheless, there have been strong criticisms in the literature about the impact of UTPs and the consequences of their regulation. Although the EU documents do not suggest this, *Schebesta et al.* write that "the empirical basis for the prevalence of UTPs, and the effect of their prohibition is relatively dire; the actual effect and effectiveness of the future UTPD is therefore uncertain."[588] The claim with regard to the lack of prevalence of unfair trading practices is contradicted by a finding in a

579 Directive 2011/7/EU of the European Parliament and of the Council of 16 February 2011 on combating late payment in commercial transactions [2011] OJ L48/1 (Late Payments Directive).

580 The Commission mentions Regulation (EU) No 261/2012 of the European Parliament and of the Council of 14 March 2012 amending Council Regulation (EC) No 1234/2007 as regards contractual relations in the milk and milk products sector [2012] OJ L94/38, but it is no longer in force.

581 Commission (n 575) 3.1.

582 Commission, 'Tackling Unfair Trading Practices in the Business-to-Business Food Supply Chain' (Communication) COM(2014) 472 final.

583 Commission (n 582) 4.

584 Commission (n 582) 1.

585 UTP Directive, art 1(1).

586 Commission, 'Unfair Business-to-Business Trading Practices in the Food Supply Chain' (Report) COM(2016) 32 final, 4.

587 European Parliament, 'Unfair Trading Practices in the Food Supply Chain' (Resolution) 2018/C 086/05, K–M.

588 Hanna Schebesta, Tom Verdonk, Kai P. Purnhagen and Bert Keirsbilck, 'Unfair Trading Practices in the Food Supply Chain: Regulating Right?' (2018) 9 European Journal of Risk Regulation 700.

Commission Communication based on empirical research. An EU-wide survey found that "83% of the respondents asserting that they were subject to UTPs said that UTPs increased their costs and 77% stated that UTPs reduced their revenues."[589]

After this rather unclear history, and two years after it considered harmonisation at the EU level to be unjustified, the European Commission submitted its proposal to the European Parliament and the Council.[590] The proposal differs from the final version of the UTP Directive on a number of important points. One of the most important differences is the change in the directive's scope *ratione personae*[591]: while the proposal covered only those cases when a small or medium-sized enterprise (hereinafter referred to as 'SME') as a supplier bargains with a non-SME buyer,[592] the adopted version of the directive establishes turnover thresholds.

As can be seen from the aforementioned EU documents, the rationale for dealing for more than 10 years with unfair trading practices in the agri-food sector lies in the unequal, asymmetrical bargaining power of food supply chain actors. UTPs may occur at every stage of the food chain, but agricultural producers are in the worst situation when it comes to selling their products. Not only the preparatory documents but also the EU legal basis chosen for the adoption of the directive can lead us to the main policy objective behind the adoption of this legal act. The choice that the directive was adopted on the basis of Article 43(2) TFEU[593] is not without concern, however it determines the essence: the UTP Directive was adopted within the framework of developing and implementing the Common Agricultural Policy. The debated legal basis brings to the fore the following issues: (a) the scope *ratione materiae* of the directive exceeds agricultural products in connection with which "measures under the CAP may principally be taken," (b) it is unclear that the principle of proportionality and subsidiarity have been regarded, and (c) there is no chance to expand the UTP rules to other sectors in the same Directive.[594] Thus, the impetus behind the adoption of the UTP Directive has been that agricultural policy objectives formulated in Article 39(1) could be better achieved: without strong empirical foundations, at a theoretical level, the UTP Directive may contribute to ensuring a fair standard of living for the agricultural community, in particular by increasing the individual earnings of persons engaged in agriculture, as well as stabilising markets.[595]

The explanatory memorandum of the proposal emphasises that unfair trading practices may go hand in hand with exclusionary effects when the profits of market participants with weaker bargaining position are put under pressure resulting in a misallocation of resources and causing otherwise competitive players to leave the

589 Commission (n 582) 2.
590 Commission, 'Proposal for a Directive of the European Parliament and of the Council on Unfair Trading Practices in Business-to-Business Relationships in the Food Supply Chain', COM(2018) 173 final.
591 Daskalova (n 559) 282.
592 Commission (n 590), art 1(2).
593 See the UTP Directive: "Having regard to the Treaty on the Functioning of the European Union, and in particular Article 43(2) thereof."
594 Paredis and Keirsbilck (n 547) 17.
595 TFEU, Article 39(1)(b)–(c).

business.[596] This is in strong connection with antitrust law objectives analysed in Chapter 18 in the aspect of whether consumer welfare or total welfare including both of the previous two is an appropriate objective of antitrust law. Covering and aiming to prevent possible exclusionary effects is a feature of both EU antitrust law and the UTP Directive.[597]

A significant number of practices regulated in the UTP Directive are exploitative in nature, and preventing exploitative abuses is an inherent[598] but a debated[599] area of Article 102 TFEU. A marked difference is that Article 102 TFEU only addresses exploitative abuses connected to pricing (unfair high prices, i.e., excessive pricing),[600] and conversely, the UTP Directive covers many more forms of exploitation which go beyond pricing practices and are non-pricing in nature. It seems that the exploitative conducts covered by the UTP Directive not falling under the scope of Article 102 TFEU can be perceived as an extension to Article 102 TFEU in the agricultural and food sector.

14.1.2 UTP Directive: its normative analysis

The directive contains 15 articles, the first three of which are substantive norms; Articles 4 to 15 contain procedural and other provisions. The directive follows a minimum harmonisation approach,[601] that is, Member States may adopt stricter rules than the ones included in the directive. This is in line with Recitals (8) and (9) of Council Regulation (EC) No 1/2003 which allow for Member States to adopt stricter rules than Article 102 TFEU and to prohibit other unfair trading practices, be they unilateral or contractual.[602]

Article 1 of the UTP Directive formulates the definition of unfair trading practices, which has already appeared during the process of preparatory works. The definition has three main elements. It refers to practices which

a grossly deviate from good commercial conduct,
b are contrary to good faith and fair dealing, and
c are unilaterally imposed by one trading partner on another.[603]

596 Commission (n 590) 1.
597 Daskalova (n 559) 281.
598 Whish and Bailey (n 409) 202: "It is clear from its very wording that Article 102 is capable of application to exploitative behaviour: Article 102(2)(a) gives as an example of an abuse the imposition of unfair purchase or selling prices or other unfair trading conditions."
599 *Michal S. Gal* uses the adjectives 'intriguing' and 'controversial' to describe the situation of exploitative abuses, in particular, of excessive pricing in EU competition law. See: Michal S. Gal, 'Abuse of Dominance: Exploitative Abuses' in Ioannis Lianos and Damien Geradin (eds), *Handbook on European Competition Law: Substantive Aspects* (Edward Elgar 2013) 385 and 422.
600 Gal (n 599) 385.
601 UTP Directive, recital (1), (39) and (44).
602 Council Regulation (EC) No 1/2003 of 16 December 2002 on the implementation of the rules on competition laid down in Articles 81 and 82 of the Treaty [2003] OJ L1/1 (Council Regulation 1/2003), recitals (8)–(9).
603 UTP Directive, art 1(1).

These are not alternative building blocks but ones that shall be met simultaneously in order to deem a trading practice unfair. Council Regulation (EC) No 1/2003's Recital (9) already defined the notion of unfair trading practice.[604] The quasi-definition of unfair trading practices in the Council Regulation (EC) No 1/2003 is as follows:

> Accordingly, Member States may under this Regulation implement on their territory national legislation that prohibits or imposes sanctions on acts of unfair trading practice, be they unilateral or contractual. Such legislation pursues a specific objective, irrespective of the actual or presumed effects of such acts on competition on the market. This is particularly the case of legislation which prohibits undertakings from imposing on their trading partners, obtaining or attempting to obtain from them terms and conditions that are unjustified, disproportionate or without consideration.[605]

These provisions correspond to the definition of unfair trading practices formulated in the UTP Directive. Although the first sentence of the cited preamble refers to the possibility of the Member States adopting laws on unfair trading practices, the EU itself with the UTP Directive – almost two decades after the adoption of Council Regulation (EC) No 1/2003 – adopted a legal act on UTPs. The act pursues specific objectives, namely that of the Common Agricultural Policy, and it does not require negative effects on competition. The definition of unfair trading practice in the UTP Directive reflects this approach, as the wording is rather vague with the use of such expressions as 'deviation from good commercial conduct', 'good faith', and 'fair dealing'. It does not say anything about actual or presumed effects on competition. The possible effects of unfair trading practices on competition have rather been indirect considerations during preparatory works, the reason for which is that our understanding of the impact of unfair trading practices on both farmers and consumers is limited.[606] Nevertheless, one of the communications of the European Commission declares that unfair trading practices "may affect the SME's capacity to survive in the market, undertake new financial investments in products and technology, and develop their cross-border activities in the Single Market,"[607] which suggests that unfair trading practices adversely affect innovation.[608] One can see that social objectives and considerations connected to agriculture dominate regarding the directive and the run-up thereto instead of traditional EU competition law objectives. The

604 Ackermann (n 560) 216.

605 Council Regulation 1/2003, recital (9).

606 Jan Fałkowski, 'The Economic Aspects of Unfair Trading Practices: Measurement and Indicators' in Federica Di Marcantonio and Pavel Ciaian (eds), *Unfair Trading Practices in the Food Supply Chain: A Literature Review on Methodologies, Impacts and Regulatory Aspects* (Publications Office of the European Union 2017) 20.

607 Commission (n 582) 3.

608 For the complex relationship between innovation and competition, see: Øystein Moen, Tord Tvedten and Andreas Wold, 'Exploring the Relationship between Competition and Innovation in Norwegian SMEs' (2018) 5 Cogent Business & Management, Article: 1564167.

definition as regards the finding of the existence of an unfair trading practice requires neither competition prevention, restriction and distortion, nor effects on trade between Member States as in Articles 101 and 102 TFEU, which are necessary conditions to be fulfilled by anticompetitive agreements and abuse of dominance.

Of the three elements of the definition, only the third one is evident. The requirement 'unilateral imposition by a trading partner on another' is obviously identical to the characteristic of abuse of dominance, and it deserves no further explanation. On the contrary, the features of 'grossly deviating from good commercial conduct' and 'contrary to good faith and fair dealing' raise a number of questions that cannot be answered satisfactorily. What does the directive mean by the expressions 'gross deviation', 'good commercial conduct', 'good faith' and 'fair dealing'? Presumably, the directive was intended to provide an avenue for Member States to extend regulation to further practices not covered by the directive, if they wished to provide more extensive protection for the vulnerable actors in the food supply chain. However, marking the route for broader regulation in the Member States through this definition is not too successful owing to the vagueness of the definition.

First, let us look at the personal scope of the directive. As already mentioned, it was envisaged during the preparation of the directive that only small and medium-sized enterprises would be protected. The final text of the directive changed this and the scope of protection is linked to the level of annual turnover of the given supplier and buyer in a tiered way. There are turnover thresholds determined to compare the annual turnover of the supplier and of the buyer as to whether the existence of an unequal bargaining power can be found.[609,610] This assessment method is not free of contradictions because of its single-factor nature. The simplified assessment makes the regulation predictable[611] but raises serious concerns. For example: what happens if a supplier which has an annual turnover of EUR 1.999.999 bargains with a buyer which has an annual turnover of EUR 2.000.001?[612] Although this is an extreme example, at a theoretical level it may happen. The turnover threshold in itself may be an appropriate proxy for assessing bargaining power, but the characteristics of any product and geographical market in question may influence not only the (absolute) market power but also the relative market power of market actors bargaining with each other. The fact that the UTP Directive is intended to regulate the market power of two market players vis-à-vis each other does not mean that the general characteristics of the market in question and the position and role of the market players in the respective market do not affect their market power vis-à-vis each other.

Suppliers which have an annual turnover of more than EUR 350.000.000 are not protected against UTPs. However, it is worth recalling, for example, that Coca-Cola

609 See: UTP Directive, art 1(2).

610 See also: Daskalova (n 559) 282.

611 Anna Piszcz, 'EU Directive on Unfair Trading Practices in Business-to-Business Relationships in the Agricultural and Food Supply Chain: Dipping a Toe in the Regulatory Waters?' in Zlatan Meškić, Ivana Kunda, Dušan V. Popović and Enis Omerović (eds), *Balkan Yearbook of European and International Law 2019* (Springer 2020) 117.

612 See this argument and a similar example: Paredis and Keirsbilck (n 560) 33.

has revenues in excess of several billion euros, not only on the global market but also in Europe, and yet there are examples (albeit only in the US) of a retail chain being able to put pressure on the world's biggest beverage company.

> Wal-Mart decided that it did not approve of the artificial sweetener Coca-Cola planned to use in a new line of diet colas. In a response that would have been unthinkable just a few years ago, Coca-Cola yielded to the will of an outside firm and designed a second product to meet Wal-Mart's decree.[613]

The regulation is asymmetric in terms of the direction of protection, and buyers are not protected against suppliers if the latter have superior bargaining power over the former. As with the setting of turnover thresholds, this could also raise concerns. According to *Piszcz*, there is no justification for not providing protection for buyers.[614]

Another important provision to be emphasised is that the UTP Directive also applies in relation to sales of agricultural and food products by suppliers which have an annual turnover not exceeding EUR 350.000.000 to all buyers which are public authorities,[615] therefore public authorities have to respect the UTP Directive in all cases when they bargain with a supplier of agricultural and/or food products whose turnover does not exceed 350 million euros. The directive explicitly declares that it does not apply to agreements between suppliers and consumers.[616] Buying alliances are covered by the directive,[617] since the legal act means by the term 'buyer' also the groups of natural or legal persons who buy agricultural and/or food products.[618]

In order to apply the directive, it is sufficient that only one of the parties be established in any of the Member States of the European Union.[619] It is quite questionable how a supplier outside the EU will be able to bring a case against an EU-based buyer, seeing that the Member States may establish their own framework for the directive's enforcement.

It is also of great importance that not only primary producers are protected but also the intermediaries who function as suppliers from the viewpoint of buyers. Thus, for example, food processors also fall under the scope *ratione personae*. It may be justified with the prevention of the cascading effect[620] to take place, that is to say, covering the whole food supply chain may contribute to a food processor not

613 Wenonah Hauter, *Foodopoly: The Battle Over the Future of Food and Farming in America* (The New Press 2012).
614 Piszcz (n 611) 115.
615 UTP Directive, art 1(2).
616 UTP Directive, art 1(2).
617 Daskalova (n 559) 282–283.
618 UTP Directive, art 2(2).
619 UTP Directive, art 2(2).
620 The term 'cascading effect' is not a legal term. It comes from the field of computer science. "A cascading effect is an unforeseen chain of events that occurs when an event in a system has a negative impact on other, related systems." See: Lucie Langer and Markus Kammerstetter, 'The Evolution of the Smart Grid Threat Landscape and Cross-Domain Risk Assessment' in Florian Skopik and Paul Smith (eds), *Smart Grid Security: Innovative Solutions for a Modernized Grid* (Syngress 2015) 49–77.

passing on possible negative effects to a primary producer, when a buyer conducts an unfair trading practice against a processor.

If one turns to the material scope of the directive, further concerns may be raised. The legal act protects the suppliers of *agricultural and food products*. Article 2 defines what the UTP Directive means by agricultural and food products: products listed in Annex I to the TFEU as well as products not listed in that Annex, but processed for use as food using products listed in that Annex.[621] As a possible risk of excluding nonfood products from the material scope of the directive, the issue of discriminatory treatment of nonfood suppliers may be raised, given that the European Commission also acknowledged the imposition of UTPs on the suppliers of other products. Furthermore, the regulatory approach of exclusively dealing with unfair trading practices in the food sector may cause fragmentation in the legal system of Member States.[622] Nevertheless, the minimum harmonisation nature of the UTP Directive enables Member States to adopt non-sectoral prohibitions, thus broadening the circle of protected suppliers.[623]

The unfair trading practices included in the directive are divided into two groups: there is a black list which consists of the practices prohibited per se,[624] and there is a grey list of those practices which are prohibited unless they have been previously agreed to in clear and unambiguous terms in the supply agreement or in a subsequent agreement between the supplier and the buyer.[625,626] Therefore, the former ones are prohibited, while the latter ones are conditionally permitted practices.[627]

The question arises as to why exactly these trading practices were regulated in the first place. The proposal can provide us with a possible answer.

> [P]ractices that occur after the transaction has started without being agreed in advance in clear and unambiguous terms [are] unlikely to generate efficiencies for the parties. Therefore [the Directive] accommodates contractual arrangements between parties unless they cannot reasonably be seen as creating efficiencies, for instance if they give vague and unspecified powers to the stronger party to unilaterally decide on such practices at a point in time after the transaction has started (unpredictability) or because some practices are by their nature unfair.[628]

As can be seen, the proposal speaks about efficiencies, in the cited part in particular about efficiencies for the parties. Besides, the proposal also mentions the efficiency of

621 UTP Directive, art 2(1).
622 Paredis and Keirsbilck (n 560) 29.
623 Piszcz (n 611) 118.
624 UTP Directive, art 3(1).
625 UTP Directive, art 3(2).
626 See: Daskalova (n 570) 283; Piszcz (n 622) 119–120.
627 Sofie De Pourcq and Evelyne Terryn, 'Prohibited and Conditionally Permitted Unfair Trading Practices' in Bert Keirsbilck and Evelyne Terryn (eds), *Unfair Trading Practices in the Food Supply Chain: Implications of Directive (EU) 2019/633* (Intersentia 2020) 37–60.
628 Commission (n 590) 9.

the food supply chain.[629] These references to efficiency may be considered as infiltrations to the discourse from general EU competition law, given that with the appearance of the more economic approach, most competition lawyers and economists see enhancing economic efficiency as the utmost objective of competition law. A problem, however, emerges in connection with the proposal's and the UTP Directive's references to efficiency: there is no clear-cut and concise content in economics literature as to what we (should) understand by the term 'efficiency'.[630] Actually, these references to efficiency may be underpinned by the declaration of the proposal that the UTP Directive complements, inter alia, common competition rules of the EU,[631] thus – to a certain extent – both the adoption of the directive and EU competition law are motivated by enhancing the efficiency of internal market functioning. Contrary to the horizontal rules of EU competition law, the efficiency-enhancing nature of the directive is limited to the food supply chain. Nevertheless, the question arises as to how the increase in efficiency can be measured in this context.

Let us turn to the blacklist conducts. The first one[632] addresses late payment with regard to agricultural and food products. Given that EU law already includes another directive (hereinafter referred to as 'Late Payment Directive')[633] concerning this type of unfair practice, one has to define the relationship between this provision of the UTP Directive and the Late Payment Directive. Although the Late Payment Directive has been in force since 2011, it has not reached significant results owing to enforcement difficulties. Although market participants are aware of the provisions of the Late Payment Directive, the fear factor is a serious problem which is the main reason for under-enforcement.[634] As *Daskalova* puts it, the provision on late payment of the UTP Directive is not too revolutionary.[635] The relationship between the two legal acts is characterised by the principle of *lex specialis derogat legi generali*: the scope *ratione materiae* of the UTP Directive's respective provision is limited to sales with regard to agricultural and food products, while the Late Payment Directive has general scope. The prohibition on late payments of the UTP Directive shall be without prejudice to the consequences of late payments and remedies as laid down in the Late Payment Directive, which shall apply, by way of derogation from the

629 Commission (n 590) 1 and 13.

630 Damien Geradin, 'Efficiency Claims in EC Competition Law and Sector-Specific Regulation' in Hanns Ullrich (ed), *The Evolution of European Competition Law: Whose Regulation, Which Competition?* (Edward Elgar 2006) 313.

631 Commission (n 590) 28.

632 UTP Directive, art 3(1)(a).

633 See: Directive 2011/7/EU of the European Parliament and of the Council of 16 February 2011 on combating late payment in commercial transactions [2011] OJ L48/1.

634 Commission, 'Ex-Post Evaluation of Late Payment Directive' (Publications Office of the European Union 2015) ENTR/172/PP/2012/FC – LOT 4, 8 and 68: "The main reason for failing to exercise their rights under the Directive is the fear, among creditor firms, of damaging good business relationships. Lack of efficient remedy procedures is another barrier preventing companies from exercising their rights to compensation and interest."

635 Daskalova (n 559) 288.

payment periods set out in that Directive, on the basis of the payment periods set out in this Directive.[636] Concerning the core concept of this provision of the UTP Directive, one has to distinguish perishable products from nonperishable ones. The payment term for perishable products is 30 days, that is to say, it is half of the payment term for nonperishable ones which is 60 days. In comparison, the Late Payment Directive considers 30 calendar days as a starting point for the maximum payment term but also declares that Member States shall ensure that the period for payment fixed in the contract does not exceed 60 calendar days, unless otherwise expressly agreed in the contract and provided it is not grossly unfair to the creditor.[637] It means that the payment term with regard to the sales of perishable agricultural and food products is halved as compared with the Late Payment Directive's default payment term. At the same time, the maximum payment term for nonperishable products did not change as a consequence of the UTP Directive, but there is a significant difference. The 60 days of the UTP Directive is nonnegotiable in nature, while the Late Payment Directive provides an opportunity to lengthen this 60-day period if this is agreed to expressly in the agreement and it is not grossly unfair to the creditor.[638] The starting point for the payment term in the UTP Directive depends on whether the delivery of products takes place on a regular basis[639] or not.[640,641] The prohibition of late payments do not influence the applicability of value-sharing clauses.[642] Since 2018, not only the sugar sector[643] but also all other agricultural sectors have the possibility to apply these clauses as provided in Article 172 of the CMO Regulation.[644,645] Article 3 determines exemptions when the provision of the prohibition on late payment shall not apply. There are three groups

636 UTP Directive, art 3(1).
637 Late Payments Directive, art 3(5).
638 De Pourcq and Terryn (n 627) 43.
639 See: UTP Directive, art 3(1)(a) (i).
640 See: UTP Directive, art 3(1)(a) (ii).
641 De Pourcq and Terryn (n 627) 42.
642 UTP Directive, art 3(1).
643 Commission Delegated Regulation (EU) 2016/1166 of 17 May 2016 amending Annex X to Regulation (EU) No 1308/2013 of the European Parliament and of the Council as regards purchase terms for beet in the sugar sector as from 1 October 2017 [2016] OJ L193/17, art 1.
644 CMO Regulation, art 172a is inserted by Regulation (EU) 2017/2393 of the European Parliament and of the Council of 13 December 2017 amending Regulations (EU) No 1305/2013 on support for rural development by the European Agricultural Fund for Rural Development (EAFRD), (EU) No 1306/2013 on the financing, management and monitoring of the Common Agricultural Policy, (EU) No 1307/2013 establishing rules for direct payments to farmers under support schemes within the framework of the Common Agricultural Policy, (EU) No 1308/2013 establishing a common organisation of the markets in agricultural products and (EU) No 652/2014 laying down provisions for the management of expenditure relating to the food chain, animal health and animal welfare, and relating to plant health and plant reproductive material [2017] OJ L350/15, art 4(17).
645 See also: Jay Modrall, 'EU Competition Policy in the Agriculture Sector' (2017/14) Cultivate: Food and Agribusiness Newsletter 18; De Pourcq and Terryn (n 627) 44–45.

of transactions exempted. The first exemption refers to those payments which take place in the framework of school fruit and vegetables schemes.[646,647] The aim of the introduction of this exemption is to "safeguard the smooth functioning of the school scheme."[648] The second exemption refers to those buyers which are public entities providing healthcare. Nevertheless, these privileged entities shall continue to meet the requirements of the Late Payment Directive, that is, they are covered by a maximum of 60-day payment periods.[649] The third exemption covers supply agreements between suppliers of grapes or must for wine production and their direct buyers, provided that these agreements are or become multiannual, as well as the specific terms of payment being placed in standard contracts which have been made binding and renewed from time to time by the respective Member State. This provision was introduced because of the special characteristics of grape harvesting and wine markets, taking into account that "grapes are harvested only during a very short period but used to produce wine that may be sold several years later."[650]

The second blacklist conduct is short notice order cancellation.[651] The prohibition does not mention and does not cover agricultural and food products which are not perishable, so the scope of this provision is even narrower than that of the UTP Directive in general. It is irrefutably presumed that an order cancellation less than 30 days before the delivery is at short notice. A further condition shall be fulfilled: the supplier cannot reasonably be expected to find an alternative means of commercialising or using those products. Member States are also authorised to set periods shorter than 30 days for specific sectors in duly justified cases. The question emerges as to whether this provision on shorter periods means to provide protection to the most perishable agricultural and food products and this can be considered a duly justified case. I have to mention another confusion. The relationship between the provision on short notice order cancellations and the first grey-list conduct raises practical complications. The latter enables contracting parties to agree (in clear and unambiguous terms) that the buyer may return unsold agricultural and food products to the supplier without paying for those unsold products or without paying for the disposal of those products, or both. Given that this grey-list conduct does not exclude perishable agricultural and food products, a buyer may be better off if it agrees preliminarily with the supplier on the possibility of returning the products. This practical incoherency may bring about – because of the per se prohibition of short notice order cancellations – buyers preferring to seize the opportunity to return the products to the respective supplier.[652] Anyways, in neither

646 CMO Regulation, art 23 contains the provisions on the aid for the supply of fruit and vegetables, processed fruit and vegetables and banana products to children.
647 UTP Directive, art 3.
648 UTP Directive, recital (18).
649 Late Payments Directive, art 4(4)(b). See also: De Pourcq and Terryn (n 627) 45.
650 De Pourcq and Terryn (n 627) 45.
651 UTP Directive, art 3(1)(b).
652 Daskalova (n 559) 289.

case did they have to pay, but cancelling the order at short notice may result in more serious consequences on the buyer's side. The proposal sees short notice order cancellations as expressions of disproportionate allocation of risk in favour of the buyer and as being manifestly unfair.[653]

The third blacklist conduct refers to the prohibition of when the buyer unilaterally changes the terms of a supply agreement for agricultural and food products that concern the frequency, method, place, timing or volume of the supply or delivery of the agricultural and food products, the quality standards, the terms of payment or the prices or as regards the provision of services.[654] These are what Daskalova calls the core terms of the contract.[655] The literature is divided as to whether the provision applies only to retroactive changes[656] or even to nonretroactive changes.[657] Although it seems like a lax and broad provision that provides full protection for suppliers, Recital (21) weakens this protection by declaring that the provision does not apply in situations when there is an agreement between a supplier and a buyer that specifically stipulates that the buyer can specify a concrete element of the transaction at a later stage in respect to future orders.[658] The laxity of this provision, however, lies in the fact that it does not require the existence of market power of the buyer.[659] Nevertheless, this can be traced back to the general difference between the assessment method of EU competition law and of the directive.

The fourth blacklist conduct, which prohibits buyers from requiring payments from suppliers that are not related to the sale of the agricultural and food products of the respective supplier,[660] is broadly formulated, open to interpretation and, thus, may cause problems.[661] The broad scope of this provision is – to a certain extent – narrowed by the payment-related conducts of the grey list. One can conclude from the grey list that the UTP Directive accepts those payments from the supplier to the buyer which are in connection with the advertising or marketing of products and which are charged as a condition for stocking, displaying or listing its agricultural and food products, or of making such products available on the market, or for staff for fitting out premises used for the sale of the supplier's products. The necessary requirement to be fulfilled by these payment-related grey-list conducts is that they have been previously agreed upon in clear and unambiguous terms in the supply agreement or in a

653 Commission (n 590) 13.
654 UTP Directive, art 3(1)(c).
655 Daskalova (n 559) 289.
656 Daskalova (n 559) 290; Ackermann (n 560) 285.
657 De Pourcq and Terryn (n 627) 47.
658 UTP Directive, recital (21).
659 Daskalova (n 559) 290. See also her reference to Case T-83/91 *Tetra Pak International SA v Commission of the European Communities* [1994] EU:T:1994:246.
660 UTP Directive, art 3(1)(d).
661 De Pourcq and Terryn (n 627) 50.

subsequent agreement between the supplier and the buyer. Given that there is no mentioned example in the directive, the question arises

> as to where the grey zone ends and where the "prohibition zone" begins. Assuming that the drafters did not aim to create contradictions, one may understand that any practice listed under Article 3(2) falls outside the scope of Article 3(1)(d).[662]

This provision had not been included in the proposal, therefore it may give the impression that it was incorporated as an auxiliary (and lax) provision to cover those payment-related practices which are not prohibited by other provisions; nevertheless, it makes the systematic interpretation more difficult. However, the European Parliament mentioned the charges for fictious services as one form of the unfair trading practices,[663] and the European Commission also identified as a key category of UTPs when one party asks the other party for advantages or benefits of any kind without performing a service related to the advantage or benefit asked.[664] From a conventional competition law perspective, *Daskalova* writes that both national and EU competition laws cover those conducts which relate to unrelated payments. From the perspective of the EU, not only Article 102 but also Article 101 aims to handle certain forms of these practices which may have either exclusionary or exploitative effects, or both. As can be seen from *Daskalova*'s analysis, unrelated payments are typically, but not exclusively, charged by (food) retail chains.[665] One of the most significant cases will be presented later with regard to the national level of Germany.[666]

The fifth blacklist conduct imposes a ban on the conduct when the buyer requires the supplier to pay for the deterioration or loss, or both, of agricultural and food products that occurs on the buyer's premises or after ownership has been transferred to the buyer, where such deterioration or loss is not caused by the negligence or fault of the supplier.[667] This phenomenon is called 'shrinkage': "theft by consumers or by employees of the retailer, loss and misplacement, consumers tampering with the product or workers damaging the goods in the process of handling."[668] Although interpretation concerns may arise when trying to determine whether the deterioration or loss is caused by the negligence or fault of the supplier,[669] this narrowing aims to balance which risks must be borne by the supplier and which by the buyer.[670] Charging suppliers with these costs is exploitative in nature due to the lack

662 Daskalova (n 559) 291.
663 European Parliament (n 587) F.
664 Commission (n 586) 5.
665 Daskalova (n 559) 291–292.
666 See *Bundeskartellamt*'s decision of 3 July 2014 in case B2–58/09 against EDEKA Zentrale AG & Co. KG.
667 UTP Directive, art 3(1)(e).
668 Daskalova (n 559) 293.
669 De Pourcq and Terryn (n 627) 50.
670 Daskalova (n 559) 293.

of objective commercial justification,[671] and, if the general conditions are met, this conduct can fall under the scope of abuse of dominance.

The sixth blacklist conduct refers to the situation when the buyer refuses to confirm in writing the terms of a supply agreement between the buyer and the supplier when the supplier has asked for written confirmation; this shall not apply when the supply agreement concerns products to be delivered by a member of a producer organisation, including a cooperative, to the producer organisation of which the supplier is a member, if the statutes of that producer organisation or the rules and decisions provided for in, or derived from, those statutes contain provisions having similar effects to the terms of the supply agreement.[672] Written contracts contribute to the higher level of legal certainty, not only in general from the viewpoint of law enforcement but also between contracting parties. It is in suppliers' interest to regulate their relationship with their buyers on the basis of predictable, clear and reliable contract provisions. Encouraging agricultural producers to conclude written contracts first appeared in the milk sector in the early 2010s. The previous and first Single Common Market Organisation,[673] which is no longer in force, was amended by Regulation (EU) No 261/2012.[674] The High Level Group on Milk, which was set up in October 2009, inter alia, recommended the European Commission to enhance the use of formal written contracts concluded in advance.[675] Moreover, the amending Regulation (EU) No 261/2012 provides useful information on the general condition of the milk sector.

> The use of formalised written contracts concluded in advance of delivery containing basic elements is not widespread. However, such contracts may help to reinforce the responsibility of operators in the dairy chain and increase awareness of the need to better take into account the signals of the market, to improve price transmission and to adapt supply to demand, as well as to help to avoid certain unfair commercial practices.[676]

The Regulation (EU) No 1308/2013, the current common market organisation in force, consists of several provisions in connection with the obligation to conclude written contracts. In the milk and milk products sector each Member State may decide whether all delivery of raw milk in its territory by a farmer to a processor of raw milk must be covered by a written contract between the parties and/or may decide that first purchasers must make a written offer for a contract

671 Daskalova (n 559) 293.

672 UTP Directive, art 3(1)(f).

673 Council Regulation (EC) No 1234/2007 of 22 October 2007 establishing a common organisation of agricultural markets and on specific provisions for certain agricultural products [2007] OJ L299/1.

674 Regulation (EU) No 261/2012 of the European Parliament and of the Council of 14 March 2012 amending Council Regulation (EC) No 1234/2007 as regards contractual relations in the milk and milk products sector [2012] OJ L94/38 (Regulation 261/2012).

675 See <https://ec.europa.eu/commission/presscorner/detail/en/IP_10_742> accessed 15 August 2023.

676 Regulation 261/2012, recital (8).

for the delivery of raw milk by the farmers.[677] It can be seen from the provision's wording that a Member State can also decide not to make use of this possibility, but in this case a producer, a producer organisation or an association of producer organisations may require that any delivery in raw milk to a processor of raw milk be the subject of a written contract between the parties and/or be the subject of a written offer for a contract from the first purchasers.[678] If a Member State decides to require written contracts and/or written offers for contracts, as well as if a producer, a producer organisation or an association of producer organisations does so, these contracts have to fulfil several conditions.[679] Furthermore, if a Member State decides that deliveries of raw milk by a farmer to a processor of raw milk must be covered by a written contract between the parties, it shall also decide which stage or stages of the delivery shall be covered by such a contract if the delivery of raw milk is made through one or more collectors.[680,681] If a producer, a producer organisation or an association of producer organisations requires written contracts and/or written offers for contracts, all elements of the respective contracts for the delivery of raw milk concluded by farmers, collectors or processors of raw milk, including price, volume, duration, payment periods and procedures, collecting and delivering and force majeure provisions, shall be freely negotiated between the parties.[682] Notwithstanding this provision, and as a derogation to the principle of contractual freedom, if a Member State decides to make a written contract for the delivery of raw milk compulsory, it may establish (i) an obligation for the parties to agree on a relationship between a given quantity delivered and the price payable for that delivery, and (ii) a minimum duration,[683] applicable only to written contracts between a farmer and the first purchaser of raw milk.[684] As another derogation to the principle of contractual freedom, if a Member State decides that the first purchaser of raw milk must make a written offer for a contract to the farmer, it may provide that the offer must include a minimum duration[685] for the contract, set by national law for this purpose. Including a minimum duration does not mean that the respective farmer cannot refuse this minimum duration, however the refusal shall be done in writing. In case of a refusal, the parties shall be free to negotiate all elements of the

677 CMO Regulation, art 148(1).

678 CMO Regulation, art 148(1a).

679 See CMO Regulation, art 148(2).

680 For the purposes of CMO Regulation, art 148, a "collector" means an undertaking which transports raw milk from a farmer or another collector to a processor of raw milk or another collector, where the ownership of the raw milk is transferred in each case.

681 CMO Regulation, art 148(1).

682 CMO Regulation, art 148(1a) and (4).

683 A minimum duration shall be at least six months, and shall not impair the proper functioning of the internal market.

684 CMO Regulation, art 148(4).

685 A minimum duration shall be at least six months, and shall not impair the proper functioning of the internal market.

contract.[686] The Member States which make use of any of these options shall notify the Commission of how they are applied.[687]

Besides the milk and milk products sector, the CMO Regulation includes a stronger obligation concerning the requirement of written agreements in the sugar sector. While in the milk and milk products sector, Member States only have the possibility to require a written form for contractual relations between operators in the sector, with regard to the sugar sector the CMO Regulation declares that the terms for buying sugar beet and sugarcane, including pre-sowing delivery contracts, shall be governed by written agreements within the trade concluded between, on the one hand, Union growers of sugar beet and sugarcane or, on their behalf, the organisations of which they are members, and, on the other hand, Union sugar undertakings or, on their behalf, the organisations of which they are members.[688]

Not only the milk and milk products sector but also the sugar sector have special provisions with regard to written contract/agreements/offers, but also there are general rules formulated by the CMO Regulation. Member States may decide as regards any sector listed in Article 1(2) of the CMO Regulation[689] that every delivery in its territory of those products by a producer to a processor or distributor must be covered by a written contract between the parties, and/or that the first purchasers must make a written offer for a contract for the delivery in its territory of those agricultural products by the producer.[690] The next option is the same as in the milk and milk products sector: where Member States do not make use of the previous possibilities, a producer, a producer organisation or an association of producer organisations, in respect to agricultural products in the listed sector may require that any delivery of its products to a processor or distributor be the subject of a written contract between the parties and/or be the subject of a written offer for a contract from the first purchasers.[691,692] Where the Member State decides that deliveries of the products covered by this article by a producer to a processor must be covered by a written contract between the parties, it shall also decide which stage or stages of the delivery shall be covered by such a contract if delivery of the products concerned is made through one or more intermediaries.[693]

686 CMO Regulation, art 148(4).
687 CMO Regulation, art 148(5).
688 CMO Regulation, art 125(1).
689 The list includes cereals, rice, sugar, dried fodder, seeds, hops, olive oil and table olives, flax and hemp, fruit and vegetables, processed fruit and vegetable products, bananas, wine, live trees and other plants, bulbs, roots and the like, cut flowers and ornamental foliage, tobacco, beef and veal, milk and milk products, pig meat, sheep meat and goat meat, eggs, poultry meat, ethyl alcohol of agricultural origin, apiculture products, silkworms, other products.
690 CMO Regulation, art 168(1).
691 A special rule applies to micro, small or medium-sized enterprises as first purchasers: the contract and/or the contract offer is not compulsory without prejudice to the possibility for the parties to make use of a standard contract drawn up by an interbranch organisation. See: CMO Regulation, art 168(1a).
692 CMO Regulation, art 168(1a).
693 CMO Regulation, art 168(2).

Nevertheless, the provisions adopted shall not impair the proper functioning of the internal market.[694] In this case, the Member State may establish a mediation mechanism to cover cases in which there is no mutual agreement to conclude such a contract, thereby ensuring fair contractual relations.[695] If a Member State decides to require written contracts and/or written offers for contracts, as well as if a producer, a producer organisation or an association of producer organisations does so, these contracts have to fulfil several conditions.[696] By way of derogation from the requirement of written contracts and/or offers, a contract or an offer for a contract shall not be required where the products concerned are delivered by a member of a cooperative to the cooperative of which he is a member if the statutes of that cooperative or the rules and decisions provided for in, or derived from, these statutes contain provisions having similar effects to the provisions mentioned in Article 168(4). Not only is the principle the same for the general rules as for the milk and milk products sector, i.e., all elements of contracts for the delivery of agricultural products concluded by producers, collectors, processors or distributors shall be freely negotiated between the parties,[697] but also the same exceptions apply: an at least six-month minimum duration can be established by Member States despite the principle of contractual freedom. Nevertheless, this minimum duration can be refused by the farmer in writing.[698] Two further conditions shall be fulfilled by the Member States which make use of these possibilities: the substantial one is that they shall not impair the proper functioning of the internal market, while the procedural one is that they shall notify the Commission of how they apply any of these measures.[699]

All in all, although "[c]ompetition law does not take a stance on the form that agreements take,"[700] the stronger party's refusal to conclude written contracts with the other party is the refusal to ensure predictability of the respective contractual relations. From the perspective of conventional competition law, this refusal and having verbal agreements is not an infringement, however, it shows a possible sign of one party having superior bargaining power over the other. Although, written contracts do not necessarily prevent the party in superior bargaining position to change the content of the contract to the detriment of the weaker party; they prescribe the obligation to conclude written contracts unequivocally, which contributes to fill in an enforcement gap which arises from the fact that the parties concerned have only a verbal agreement. The traditional competition law relevance of the obligation of concluding written agreements is that it reduces the chances of those abusive conducts which are related to the content of the contracts. It must be emphasised, however, that "the European legislator does not require each supply

694 CMO Regulation, art 168(2).
695 CMO Regulation, art 168(3).
696 CMO Regulation, art 168(4).
697 CMO Regulation, art 168(6).
698 CMO Regulation, art 168(6).
699 CMO Regulation, art 168(7).
700 Daskalova (n 559) 293.

agreement to be specified in writing. This is only required if the supplier asks for a written confirmation."[701]

The seventh blacklist conduct is when the buyer unlawfully acquires, uses or discloses the trade secrets of the supplier within the meaning of Directive (EU) 2016/943 of the European Parliament and of the Council.[702] The only strength of this provision is that it involves the misuse of trade secrets into the enforcement mechanism established by the UTP Directive.[703] The acquisition, use or disclosure of trade secrets is a traditional unfair competition law conduct.

> From a policy perspective, the legal protection of trade secrets encourages efficiency and the circulation of R&D and innovation information. Legal protection and contractual protection of trade secrets work as a partial substitute for excessive investments in physical security, and legal protection of trade secrets facilitates disclosure in contract negotiations over the use or sale of know-how that otherwise would not occur in the absence of such protection. Protecting trade secrets is therefore rational from a societal and law and economics perspective since it decreases transaction costs and facilitates that transactions occur.[704]

Although the cited thought says that the legal protection of trade secrets encourages efficiency, and most authors see competition law's primary objective in enhancing efficiency, "little has been said about the application of competition rules to trade secrets."[705] In relation to the United States of America, it becomes apparent that finding the balance between trade secret protection and efficient competition is not an easy task. As *First* puts it,

> [a]lthough the initial Sherman Act cases reveal a careful understanding of the legal properties of trade secret protection and a desire to limit the ability of trade secret holders to use trade secret licenses to restrict competition, once past these early cases the courts have too often fallen into a reflexive pattern of protecting trade secret holders at the expense of competition and consumer welfare.[706]

The balance must be found by the enforcement authorities not only in the United States but also in the EU and at the national level.

701 De Pourcq and Terryn (n 627) 51.
702 UTP Directive, art 3(1)(g).
703 Daskalova (n 559) 294.
704 Henrik Bengtsson, 'International Report' in Pranvera Këllezi, Bruce Kilpatrick and Pierre Kobel (eds), *Abuse of Dominant Position and Globalization & Protection and Disclosure of Trade Secrets and Know-How* (Springer International 2017) 292.
705 Katarzyna A. Czapracka, 'Antitrust and Trade Secrets: The U.S. and the EU Approach' (2008) 24 Santa Clara High Technology Law Journal 208.
706 Harry First, 'Trade Secrets and Antitrust Law' in Rochelle C. Dreyfuss and Katherine J. Strandburg (eds), *The Law and Theory of Trade Secrecy: A Handbook of Contemporary Research* (Edward Elgar 2011) 332–380.

From the food and beverage industry excellent examples can be mentioned for trade secrets: Coca-Cola's secret recipe or Kentucky Fried Chicken's eleven herbs and spices on their fried chicken.[707] These examples are not those which are in the greatest danger against retail chains' misuse, but there are many trade secret holder suppliers who compete with the private label products[708] of supermarkets. This situation is tried to be addressed by the UTP Directive so that buyers could not misuse confidential supplier information to develop their own private label brands.[709] The appearance of private labels is in strong connection with the emerging buyer power of retail chains. In the context of private labels, it is manufacturers rather than producers who are the likely victims of buyer power abuse by retailers. Supermarkets may force manufacturers "to grant ever increasing price reductions (also indirectly, e.g. access fees) or accept the transfer of commercial risks that may threaten their survival and reduce their incentives to innovate." Not only upstream may it have negative effects but also downstream by engaging in exclusionary behaviour.[710] Nevertheless, the assessment of private labels is far too complex from the viewpoint of competition law. Concerning inter-brand competition, it may enhance competition through increasing the available choice of options. It is unlikely that private label products obstruct the innovation of branded products, but retailers with market power may cause competition concerns if they disproportionately encourage the sales of private label products to the detriment of branded products. Private labels may also boost competition between retailers by raising the intensity of non-price competition. Moreover, private label products contribute to the buyer power of retailers when negotiating with their suppliers. If one assumes that the savings made by retailers are passed to the consumers, no concerns arise from a consumer welfare-approached antitrust law. However, abusing buyer power has implications on the prices paid by the abusing retailer's rivals to the suppliers; it may increase the rivals' prices resulting in waterbed effect.[711,712]

A further problem may arise from the fact that the relationship between the UTP Directive and the Directive (EU) 2016/943 is not clear as to which takes precedence over the other. While the latter includes safeguards in detail in the interest of both parties, the former does not. A reasonable solution to unblock this problem would be that the safeguards provided for by the Directive (EU) 2016/943 also apply during the enforcement of the UTP Directive.[713]

707 Bengtsson (n 704) 292.

708 On the antitrust law assessment of private labels, see: Chris Doyle and Richard Murgatroyd, 'The Role of Private Labels in Antitrust' (2011) 7 Journal of Competition Law & Economics 631–650; Hila Nevo and Roger Van den Bergh, 'Private Labels: Challenges for Competition Law and Economics' (2017) 40 World Competition 271–298.

709 Daskalova (n 559) 294.

710 Nevo and Van den Bergh (n 695) 296.

711 For more on the waterbed effect, see: Paul W. Dobson and Roman Inderst, 'The Waterbed Effect: Where Buying and Selling Come Together' (2008) <https://tinyurl.hu/eBbJ/> accessed 30 June 2024; Roman Inderst and Tommaso M. Valletti, 'Buyer Power and the "'Waterbed Effect"' (2011) 59 The Journal of Industrial Economics 1–20.

712 Doyle and Murgatroyd (n 708) 650.

713 De Pourcq and Terryn (n 627) 52.

The eighth blacklist conduct takes place when the buyer threatens to carry out, or carries out, acts of commercial retaliation against the supplier if the supplier exercises its contractual or legal rights, including by filing a complaint with enforcement authorities or by cooperating with enforcement authorities during an investigation.[714] Commercial retaliation includes, for example, "delisting products, reducing the quantities of products ordered or stopping certain services which the buyer provides to the supplier such as marketing or promotions on the suppliers' products."[715] Making use of the possibilities provided for by legal rights and initiating enforcement procedures shall not be thwarted by buyers because this is not in line with the notion of competition on the merits.[716] By this provision, the UTP Directive aims to address the fear factor[717] mentioned several times in the preparatory documents.[718] The fear factor generally describes a deficit of law enforcement or an enforcement barrier. The fear factor is based on the assumption that an undertaking affected by an unfair trading practice will refrain from enforcing its rights despite being aware of them for fear of losing its business relationship with its trading partner or of other reprisals. Since the undertaking concerned is also reluctant to turn to the competition authority in such cases, no official enforcement of the standard can take place for the same reason. Fear factor is known as the *Ross-und-Reiter-Problematik*[719] in German competition law. In order to counteract this, the sixth amendment of *GWB* in 1998 introduced a provision which enables the competition authority to take action ex officio at the request of the complainant. This is intended to ensure that the name of the complainant does not appear in the files of the competition authority as soon as the relevant proceedings are initiated.[720] In the UTP Directive, the fear factor is tried to be overcome by, on the one hand, expanding the categories of rights of action holders, and, on the other hand, encouraging enforcement through the confidentiality of complaints.[721] Complaints and confidentiality are regulated in detail in Article 5 of the UTP Directive. As an innovative element,[722] not only suppliers themselves but also producer organisations,

714 UTP Directive, art 3(1)(h).
715 De Pourcq and Terryn (n 627) 52. See also: Daskalova (n 559) 294–295; UTP Directive, recital 25.
716 Daskalova (n 559) 295.
717 See in detail: Till Göckler, *Angstfaktor und unlautere Handelspraktiken: Eine Untersuchung anlässlich des Grünbuchs der Europäischen Kommission über unlautere Handelspraktiken in der b2b-Lieferkette* (Mohr Siebeck 2017).
718 See Commission (n 590): "A weaker party to a commercial transaction is often unwilling to lodge a complaint for fear of compromising an existing commercial relationship with the stronger party." See also: European Parliament (n 587) U and X; Commission (n 582) 7; Commission (n 575) 7. Commission (n 586) 6 posits that "fear factor can easily obstruct authorities from penalising market operators imposing UTPs because authorities require sufficient information to be able to follow up on a complaint."
719 See more: Georg Küpper, 'Mißbräuchliche Ausübung von Nachfragemacht, insbesondere Lösung des sog. Roß und Reiter-Problems' (1997) 52 Betriebs-Berater 1105–1115.
720 Ackermann (n 560) 218–220.
721 Muriel Chagny, 'Enforcement in the Directive' in Bert Keirsbilck and Evelyne Terryn (eds), *Unfair Trading Practices in the Food Supply Chain: Implications of Directive (EU) 2019/633* (Intersentia 2020) 63–65.
722 Daskalova (n 559) 284.

other organisations of suppliers and associations of such organisations have the right to submit a complaint to the enforcement authority of the Member State in which the supplier is established or to the enforcement authority of the Member State in which the buyer that is suspected to have engaged in a prohibited trading practice is established. Moreover, other organisations that have a legitimate interest in representing suppliers have the right to submit complaints, at the request of a supplier, and in the interest of that supplier, provided that such organisations are independent non-profit-making legal persons.[723] With regard to confidentiality, the UTP Directive declares that Member States shall ensure that, at the request of the complainant, the enforcement authority shall take the necessary measures for the appropriate protection of the identity of the complainant or the members or suppliers and for the appropriate protection of any other information in respect of which the complainant considers that the disclosure of such information would be harmful to the interests of the complainant or of those members or suppliers. The complainant shall identify any information for which it requests confidentiality.[724] However, the right of defence of the possible infringer shall be respected. As the proposal for the directive put it, "[i]n particular for the confidential treatment of complaints, a balance must be struck in relation to the rights of defence."[725] Besides initiating investigations on the basis of complaints, Member States shall also ensure that the respective enforcement authority could initiate and conduct investigations on its own initiative, ex officio.[726]

The ninth blacklist conduct refers to the situation when the buyer requires compensation from the supplier for the cost of examining customer complaints relating to the sale of the supplier's products despite the absence of negligence or fault on the part of the supplier.[727] Here the interpretation concern arises in the same context as in the case of imposing charges on suppliers because of shrinkage: the enforcement authority shall decide whether negligence or fault on the part of the respective supplier took place.

After the ninth blacklist conduct comes the grey list[728]: these practices are permitted when they have been previously agreed to in clear and unambiguous terms in the supply agreement or in a subsequent agreement between the supplier and the buyer.[729] "By taking this approach, [the EU] implicitly accepts that it is fair to stipulate these terms."[730] With the exception of the first practice in the grey list, all practices are related to some kind of payment from the supplier to the buyer.[731]

723 UTP Directive, art 5(1)–(2).
724 UTP Directive, art 5(3). See also: Daskalova (n 559) 284.
725 Commission (n 590) 11. See also: Chagny (n 721) 64.
726 UTP Directive, art 6(1)(a). See also: Piszcz (n 611) 123.
727 UTP Directive, art 3(1)(i).
728 See: Ackermann (n 560) 285–286.
729 It is worth noting in passing that the number of conducts both on the black and grey list in the directive increased in comparison with the proposal. A four-point blacklist and a four-point grey list became a nine-point blacklist and a six-point grey list. See: Piszcz (n 611) 119.
730 De Pourcq and Terryn (n 627) 53.
731 De Pourcq and Terryn (n 627) 53.

The first grey-list conduct is when the buyer returns unsold agricultural and food products to the supplier without paying for those unsold products or without paying for the disposal of those products, or both.[732] It is quite clear that it is in the respective buyer's commercial interest to sell the products purchased by the buyer from the supplier, and if the buyer cannot do so, the main principle is that the buyer should bear the resulting losses. With this prohibition, the directive aims to avoid the buyer being able to buy products he intends to sell without any commercial risk. Nevertheless, it is dubious whether the *conditionally permitted* nature of this provision provides enough protection to suppliers. The basic assumption of the UTP Directive is that there are "significant imbalances in bargaining power between suppliers and buyers of agricultural and food products,"[733] therefore the positive impact of this provision, and also in general of these six grey-list practices, is questionable, given that a stronger buyer will probably be able to force a weaker supplier to accept "clear and unambiguous contractual terms" falling under the scope of these six practices.

The second one on the list is when the supplier is charged payment as a condition for stocking, displaying or listing its agricultural and food products, or of making such products available on the market.[734] If agreed upon clear and unambiguous terms, buyers may make use of the possibility to demand listing fees or slotting allowances[735] from their suppliers.[736]

732 UTP Directive, Article 3(2)(a).

733 UTP Directive, recital (1).

734 UTP Directive, art 3(2)(b).

735 See, for example, in detail: Joseph P. Cannon and Paul N. Bloom, 'Are Slotting Allowances Legal under the Antitrust Laws?' (1991) 10 Journal of Marketing & Public Policy 167–186; Kenneth Kelly, 'The Antitrust Analysis of Grocery Slotting Allowances: The Procompetitive Case' (1991) 10 Journal of Public Policy & Marketing 187–198; Mary W. Sullivan, 'Slotting Allowances and the Market for New Products' (1997) 40 The Journal of Law & Economics 461–494; Gregory T. Gundlach and Paul N. Bloom, 'Slotting Allowances and the Retail Sale of Alcohol Beverages' (1998) 17 Journal of Public Policy & Marketing 173–184; J. Chris White, Lisa C. Troy and R. Nicholas Gerlich, 'The Role of Slotting Fees and Introductory Allowances in Retail Buyers' New-Product Acceptance Decisions' (2000) 28 Journal of the Academy of Marketing Science 291–298; Azzeddine M. Azzam, 'Slotting Allowances and Price-Cost Margins: A Note' (2001) 17 Agribusiness 417–422; Stephen F. Hamilton, 'Slotting Allowances as a Facilitating Practice by Food Processors in Wholesale Grocery Markets: Profitability and Welfare Effects' (2003) 85 American Journal of Agricultural Economics 797–813; Timothy J. Richards and Paul M. Patterson, 'Slotting Allowances as Real Options: An Alternative Explanation' (2004) 77 The Journal of Business 675–696; John L. Stanton and Kenneth C. Herbst, 'Slotting Allowances: Short-Term Gains and Long-Term Negative Effects on Retailers and Consumers' (2006) 34 International Journal of Retail & Distribution Management 187–197; K. Sudhir and Vithala R. Rao, 'Do Slotting Allowances Enhance Efficiency or Hinder Competition?' (2006) 43 Journal of Marketing Research 137–155; Øystein Foros and Hans Jarle Kind, 'Do Slotting Allowances Harm Retail Competition?' (2008) 110 Scandinavian Journal of Economics 367–384; Robert Innes and Stephen F. Hamilton, 'Slotting Allowances under Supermarket Oligopoly' (2013) 95 American Journal of Agricultural Economics 1216–1222.

736 For a nonacademic article, see: Phil Edwards, 'The Hidden War Over Grocery Shelf Space' *VOX* (22 November 2016).

> A slotting allowance is a fee paid by a grocery manufacturer to a grocery retailer at the time of the introduction of a product to the retailer's inventory, ostensibly to reimburse the retailer for the initial expenses it incurs by adopting the product.[737]

The Federal Trade Commission's report broadens the scope of this definition, and it also includes lump sum, up-front payments from *producers* to retailers so that the latter can place the product of the former on its shelves.[738]

The lawfulness of these charges has to be decided on a case-by-case basis. For example, a German judgment by the *Bundesgerichtshof* considered the listing fee[739] in question unfair, while there are also opinions in which these charges are considered lawful when in alignment with "the costs and the potential risks connected to contracting."[740] In the English-language literature, *Sullivan* writes that "slotting allowances are consistent with competitive behavior."[741] *Sudhir and Rao* also find – in spite of the controversial nature of slotting allowances – little support for the anticompetitive rationales in the data.[742] On the contrary, the Guidelines on Vertical Restraints[743] of the EU acknowledges that listing fees and slotting allowances may go hand in hand with exclusionary effects.[744] Obviously, they are primarily criticised by manufacturers and small retailers; nevertheless they are defended by retailers who make use of them as a "risk-transfer mechanism."[745] The reason for treating listing fees and stocking allowances as a conditionally permitted practice may come from the controversial nature of these phenomena. Nevertheless, the general critique can also be formulated against this provision, that is to say, concerns may arise from the weak protection owing to the conditional nature of grey-list conducts.

The third one takes place when the buyer requires the supplier to bear all or part of the cost of any discounts on agricultural and food products that are sold by the buyer as part of a promotion.[746] This provision is complemented by a further requirement: if the buyer initiates a promotion, prior to this, the buyer shall specify the period of the promotion and the expected quantity of the agricultural and food products to be ordered at the discounted price.[747]

737 Kelly (n 735) 187.
738 Federal Trade Commission, 'Slotting Allowances and Other Marketing Practices in the Grocery Industry' (February 2001) 1.
739 In German: *Listungsentgelte* or *Eintrittsgeld*.
740 De Pourcq and Terryn (n 627) 56.
741 Sullivan (n 735) 461.
742 Sudhir and Rao (n 735) 137.
743 Commission, 'Guidelines on Vertical Restraints' (Communication) 2022/C 248/01, paras 379–380.
744 Daskalova (n 559) 296.
745 Gundlach and Bloom (n 735) 173.
746 UTP Directive, art 3(2)(c).
747 UTP Directive, art 3(2). See also: De Pourcq and Terryn (n 627) 56.

The fourth conduct is when the buyer requires the supplier to pay for the advertising by the buyer of agricultural and food products.[748] The fifth one happens when the buyer requires the supplier to pay for the marketing by the buyer of agricultural and food products.[749] As mentioned by *De Pourcq–Terryn*, the UTP Directive

> does not describe how advertising or marketing costs should be understood. The provisions furthermore broadly describe the payment that may be allowed, as they do refer in general to advertising and marketing "by the buyer of agricultural and food products". They do not explicitly refer to advertising of *the* agricultural and food product of the supplier. The exact scope of these provisions is therefore unclear.[750]

The sixth grey-list conduct refers to the situation when the buyer charges the supplier for staff for fitting out premises used for the sale of the supplier's products.[751] This regulated conduct is considered less problematic than the previous two, given that it formulates a clear-cut connection with the products of the respective supplier and establishes "some mutual interest" in relation to the directive.[752]

All in all, the conducts regulated in the UTP Directive have – in many cases – interfaces with EU competition law. According to *Daskalova*, these practices may have not only exploitative but also exclusionary effects. The enforcement gaps of EU competition law, however, are not completely filled in owing to the interpretation concerns raised by the formulation of provisions which may thwart the intended goals of the directive.[753] By contrast, *Piszcz* finds the strength of the UTP Directive in that

> [it] does not base the prohibition of UTPs on any open-ended concept of bargaining power, its abuse or unfairness. All of them, if used, would give the enforcement authority greater flexibility embedded in them. Most importantly, however, the approach adopted by the UTP Directive results in less ambiguity and, consequently, more legal certainty.[754]

In my view, there is no doubt that the conducts included in the list of unfair trading practices raise certain questions of interpretation, but a general prohibition without a detailed and specific assessment method could greatly widen the directive's scope for which it would be up to the law enforcement alone to determine the unlawfulness of a certain conduct. The general prohibition of the assessment method of

748 UTP Directive, art 3(2)(d).
749 UTP Directive, art 3(2)(e).
750 De Pourcq and Terryn (n 627) 57.
751 UTP Directive, art 3(2)(f).
752 De Pourcq and Terryn (n 627) 58.
753 Daskalova (n 559) 296.
754 Piszcz (n 611) 125.

turnover thresholds could constitute a too wide intervention to contractual relations of the respective contracting parties.

Because of minimum harmonisation, a general prohibition would mean that all Member States shall also include a general prohibition in their national laws. It is more reasonable to regulate a list of practices which may go hand in hand with some interpretation concerns than to use a general prohibition. The former can be corrected and interpreted by the enforcement authorities, while the latter can wheel towards enhanced and excessive enforcement activism.

The provisions on enforcement appear in the directive's Articles 4 to 8. Pursuant to Article 4, each Member State shall designate one or more enforcement authorities. If more than one enforcement authority is designated, the Member State shall determine which enforcement authority is the contact point for both cooperation among the enforcement authorities and cooperation with the Commission. The Commission shall be informed about the designation.[755] Member States are not obliged to set up a new authority; they have the possibility to confer the powers mentioned shortly on an existing authority.[756]

We have already mentioned the rules on complaints and confidentiality as well as that the UTP Diretive aims to overcome the fear factor by expanding the scope of persons who are entitled to make a complaint beyond the direct victim of the respective unfair trading practice and by ensuring the confidentiality of complaints.

However, the powers of enforcement authorities are also worth mentioning. The approach taken by the UTP Directive is based on decentralisation, that is, the enforcement is transferred to the Member States' authorities.[757] Similarly to European competition law traditions, the enforcement of the UTP Directive is established in public law proceedings and not in private law proceedings. The public law enforcement of these provisions was likely to be chosen because of the fear factor. If the direct victim of an unfair trading practice should initiate a private law proceeding as claimant against a buyer of the claimant's products as defendant, the objective and the likely positive impacts of the UTP Directive become questionable.

In order for the public enforcement to be effective and professional, Member States shall confer on the enforcement authority the power to initiate and conduct investigations on its own initiative or on the basis of a complaint, to require buyers and suppliers to provide all necessary information in order to conduct investigations of prohibited trading practices, to carry out unannounced on-site inspections within the framework of its investigations, in accordance with national rules and procedures, to take decisions finding an infringement of the prohibitions and requiring the buyer to bring the prohibited trading practice to an end, to impose, or initiate proceedings for the imposition of, fines and other equally effective penalties and interim measures on the author of the

755 UTP Directive, art 4.
756 Piszcz (n 611) 122.
757 Piszcz (n 611) 121.

infringement, in accordance with national rules and procedures, as well as to publish its decisions. The penalties imposed by the enforcement authority shall be effective, proportionate and dissuasive, taking into account the nature, duration, recurrence and gravity of the infringement. The burden of proof is not harmonised within the UTP Directive, that is each Member State has the right to regulate the provisions with regard to it.[758]

However, the infringer's rights of defence shall be respected in accordance with the general principles of Union law and the Charter of Fundamental Rights of the European Union. The respect for the rights of defence shall also be ensured when the complainant requests confidential treatment of information.[759]

Concerning the transposition of the UTP Directive, Member States were obliged to adopt and publish the laws, regulations and administrative provisions necessary to comply with this directive by 1 May 2021 at the latest. These measures shall apply from 1 November 2021 at the latest.[760] By 1 November 2021, the Commission had to present an interim report on the state of the transposition and implementation of the directive to the European Parliament and to the Council, as well as to the European Economic and Social Committee and the Committee of the Regions.[761] Furthermore, by 1 November 2025, the Commission shall carry out the first evaluation of this directive and shall present a report on the main findings of that evaluation to the European Parliament and to the Council, as well as to the European Economic and Social Committee and the Committee of the Regions. Such report shall be accompanied, if appropriate, by legislative proposals.[762]

For the sake of ensuring a sufficient degree of publicity, Member States shall ensure that their enforcement authorities publish an annual report on their activities falling within the scope of the UTP Directive, which shall, inter alia, state the number of complaints received and the number of investigations opened or closed during the previous year. For each closed investigation, the report shall contain a summary description of the matter, the outcome of the investigation and, where applicable, the decision taken, subject to the confidentiality requirements.[763]

14.2 The United States

The most relevant regulation in the United States is the Packers and Stockyards Act of 1921. Furthermore, I will also take a brief look at two other pieces of legislation, namely the Perishable Agricultural Commodities Act of 1930 and the Unfair Trade Practices Affecting Producers of Agricultural Products Act of 1968.

758 UTP Directive, recital (24).
759 UTP Directive, art 6.
760 UTP Directive, art 13(1).
761 UTP Directive, art 12(4).
762 UTP Directive, art 12(1).
763 UTP Directive, art 10(1).

14.2.1 Packers and Stockyards Act of 1921

The aim of the Packers and Stockyards Act of 1921 – as "one of the most comprehensive regulatory measures ever enacted"[764] – is "to insure effective competition and integrity in livestock, meat, and poultry markets."[765] Being a liberally construed remedial legislation and having broader authority than the one established by antitrust laws (Sherman, Clayton, and Federal Trade Commission Acts), the act prohibits "monopolistic, unfair, deceptive, and unjustly discriminatory practices" with an enforcement mechanism of the Secretary of Agriculture which has an authorisation for exercising "complete inquisitorial, visitorial, supervisory, and regulatory power over the packers, stockyards, and all activities connected therewith."[766]

As part of the Fair Trade Practices Program (FTPP) of the Agricultural Marketing Service in the US Department of Agriculture (USDA), the Packers and Stockyards Division is responsible for not only the monitoring of the industries covered by the act's scope but also administering compliance reviews and investigations. There are four ways of handling violations: (a) notice of violations, (b) stipulation agreements, (c) administrative actions and (d) court actions. While notice of violations and stipulation agreements lack formal action, bringing administrative or civil action by the enforcement authority is a more serious step having the possibility to impose stricter penalties on the firm or individual in question. Within the framework of an administrative action, the FTPP files a complaint and the accused party is entitled to have a hearing before an administrative law judge. The decision can be appealed to the USDA Judicial Officer, whose ruling can further be appealed to a US Appeals Court and further to the Supreme Court. An administrative law judge can issue a cease and desist order and/or suspend business operations. Court actions by the USDA can also take place through the Department of Justice before a US District Court. Not only civil but also criminal penalties are available. Regarding the poultry trust provisions, a maximum of $85.150 fine per violation and, while regarding other provisions in the P&S Act and regulations, a maximum of $29.270 fine per violation can be imposed. Even imprisonment can serve as a possible and ultima ratio penalty for violations.[767]

The concentration and consolidation of meat and livestock industries regulated by the Packers and Stockyards Act has not changed since its passage; it has even worsened and the sectors have become more integrated.[768] This implies that the likeliness of unfair and unreasonable practices is still high or even higher than at

764 Donald A. Campbell, 'The Packers and Stockyards Act Regulatory Program' in John Davidson (ed), *Agricultural Law* (Shepards's/McGraw-Hill 1981).

765 The National Agricultural Law Center, 'The Packers and Stockyards Act: An Overview' <https://nationalaglawcenter.org/overview/packers-and-stockyards/> accessed 27 December 2023.

766 Christopher R. Kelley, 'An Overview of the Packers and Stockyards Act' (2003) Arkansas Law Notes 35–36 <http://media.law.uark.edu/arklawnotes/2003/10/15/an-overview-of-the-packers-and-stockyards-act/> accessed 27 December 2023.

767 U.S. Department of Agriculture, 'Packers and Stockyards Enforcement' <www.ams.usda.gov/services/enforcement/psd> accessed 27 December 2023.

768 Kelley (n 766) 37.

the time of the act's adoption. Furthermore, the debate on whether the act goes beyond antitrust laws in terms of the level of protection and whether the act requires proving negative effects on competition still arises periodically.[769] Although these two questions are quite connected to each other, the former one can be answered affirmatively, while, in contrast, the latter one raises serious doubts, as can be read from contradictory court rulings.[770] These questions strongly intertwine with the doubt as to whether the Packers and Stockyards Act is an antitrust statute at all. If it is, adverse effects on competition shall, of course, be required to find a violation; on the contrary, if it is not, no proof shall be presented on negative impacts on competition to find a violation. There are diverging views.[771] In my opinion, not only the general scope of but also the unfairness included in the Packers and Stockyards Act are meant to be different than that of the antitrust laws.[772] Beyond antitrust laws which exclusively concentrate on harms to the overall competitive environment (or, in recent times, rather strictly on consumer welfare), the Packers and Stockyards Act is also concerned with "unjustifiable harm to individual farmers and ranchers" in equitable terms.[773]

Following *Kelley*'s grouping, the act can be divided into four main structural units. There are rules applying to (1) packers, (2) swine contractors, (3) live poultry dealers and (4) stockyard owners, market agencies and dealers.[774]

The term 'packer' is defined by the act as

> any person engaged in the business (a) of buying livestock in commerce for purposes of slaughter, or (b) of manufacturing or preparing meats or meat food products for sale or shipment in commerce, or (c) of marketing meats, meat food products, or livestock products in an unmanufactured form acting as a wholesale broker, dealer, or distributor in commerce.[775]

Therefore, this definition is connected to that of the term 'livestock', reproduced here in full: "[it] means cattle, sheep, swine, horses, mules, or goats – whether live or dead."[776] The definition of live poultry dealer is as follows:

> any person engaged in the business of obtaining live poultry by purchase or under a poultry growing arrangement for the purpose of either slaughtering it

769 Christopher M. Bass, 'More Than a Mirror: The Packers and Stockyards Act, Antitrust Laws, and the Injury to Competition Requirement' (2007) 12 Drake Journal of Agricultural Law 424 and 426. See also: John D. Shively and Jeffrey S. Roberts, 'Competition under the Packers and Stockyards Act: What Now?' (2010) 15 Drake Journal of Agricultural Law 419–454.

770 Bass (n 769) 426–427.

771 Shively and Roberts (n 769) 425.

772 Rosales (n 193) 1511–1514.

773 Michael C. Stumo and Douglas J. O'Brien, 'Antitrust Unfairness vs. Equitable Unfairness in Farmer/Meat Packer Relationships' (2003) 8 Drake Journal of Agricultural Law 92.

774 Kelley (n 766) 41.

775 7 U.S. Code § 191.

776 7 U.S. Code § 182(4).

> or selling it for slaughter by another, if poultry is obtained by such person in commerce, or if poultry obtained by such person is sold or shipped in commerce, or if poultry products from poultry obtained by such person are sold or shipped in commerce.[777]

Respectively, the definitions of the fourth umbrella category are the following: stockyard owner "means any person engaged in the business of conducting or operating a stockyard,"[778,779] market agency "means any person engaged in the business of (1) buying or selling in commerce livestock on a commission basis or (2) furnishing stockyard services,"[780] while dealer "means any person, not a market agency, engaged in the business of buying or selling in commerce livestock, either on his own account or as the employee or agent of the vendor or purchaser."[781]

The act regulates several and various protective pillars regarding the business conduct of packers vis-à-vis livestock sellers. First and foremost, the Secretary of Agriculture may require reasonable bonds from every packer in connection with its livestock purchasing operations to secure the performance of their obligations. Under this provision, only those packers are exempted whose average annual purchases do not exceed $500.000. If the Secretary finds that the packer is insolvent, he may issue an order of suspension or a cease and desist order to prevent the packer from purchasing livestock during insolvency.[782] In addition, the act establishes a statutory trust for livestock[783] which benefits unpaid cash sellers. Given that the assets of the trust are not part of the bankruptcy estate in case of a packer's bankruptcy, "unpaid cash sellers of livestock do not have to compete with the bankrupt debtor's [that is, the packer's] secured creditors for the assets contained in the trust."[784] Moreover, a requirement of prompt payment can also be found on packers,[785] which obligation is regulated in extreme detail, including rules on the methods of payment, the possibility for a waiver by written agreement and disclosure requirements. It is declared that the violation of this obligation is an unfair practice.[786]

Last but not least, an enumeration of unlawful practices appears in the act.[787] Of these practices, the first two are so lax that many interpretation problems may arise. The violation "engaging in or using any unfair, unjustly discriminatory, or deceptive practice or

777 7 U.S. Code § 182(10).
778 7 U.S. Code § 201(a).
779 See 7 U.S. Code § 202(a).
780 7 U.S. Code § 201(c).
781 7 U.S. Code § 201(d).
782 7 U.S. Code § 204.
783 7 U.S. Code § 196.
784 Roger A. McEowen, 'Packers and Stockyards Act Provisions for Unpaid Cash Sellers of Livestock' (*Agricultural Law and Taxation Blog*, 21 March 2019) <https://lawprofessors.typepad.com/agriculturallaw/2019/03/packers-and-stockyards-act-provisions-for-unpaid-cash-sellers-of-livestock.html> accessed 27 December 2023.
785 Kelley (n 766) 44.
786 7 U.S. Code § 228b.
787 7 U.S. Code § 192.

device"[788] has covered, among others, discriminatory pricing, predatory pricing, deceptive advertising as well as false weighing.[789] The second provision prohibits "mak[ing] or giv[ing] any undue or unreasonable preference or advantage to any particular person or locality in any respect, or subject any particular person or locality to any undue or unreasonable prejudice or disadvantage in any respect."[790] Recently, the Agricultural Marketing Service of the Department of Agriculture has issued a regulation on those criteria which shall be considered when determining whether an undue or unreasonable preference or advantage has occurred. These are as follows: the authority aims to explore whether the preference or advantage cannot be justified (a) based on cost savings considerations, (b) based on meeting a competitor's prices, (c) based on meeting other terms offered by a competitor, (d) as a reasonable business decision. It is also noted that "[d]isparate contract terms are not undue or unreasonable just because the terms are not identical. Some disparities in contract terms can be attributed to reasonable business negotiations between contracting parties."[791] The interpretation of these first two practices creates fertile ground to the questions mentioned previously: is the Packers and Stockyards Act an antitrust statute and does it require evidence of adverse impact on competition to find a violation, or does the act go beyond antitrust laws in the level of protection through not requiring any negative effect on competition? By looking at the act's legislative intent, textual and systematic interpretation and earlier case law, opposing views clashed in a case before the Fifth Circuit, which ended with the victory of those who argue for the antitrust nature of the Packers and Stockyards Act and, thereby, the requirement of proving negative effects on competition:

> Once more a federal court is called to say that the purpose of the Packers and Stockyards Act of 1921 is to protect competition and, therefore, only those practices that will likely affect competition adversely violate the Act. That is this holding.[792]

Although it must not be forgotten that the case was then settled which meant that the Supreme Court had no opportunity "to rule on whether the majority or dissenting opinion is correct."[793]

The further enumerated practices do not raise these questions thanks to their wording. The act can also be violated by apportioning the supply and manipulating or controlling prices, as well as conspiring, combining or agreeing to do so, and even aiding or abetting the doing of any of that.[794]

788 7 U.S. Code § 192(a).
789 Kelley (n 766) 44.
790 7 U.S. Code § 192(b).
791 U.S. Department of Agriculture, 'Undue and Unreasonable Preferences and Advantages Under the Packers and Stockyards Act' (2020) 85 Federal Register 79780.
792 United States Court of Appeals, Fifth Circuit, Wheeler v. Pilgrim's Pride Corp, 591 F.3d 355 (5th Cir. 2009).
793 Shively and Roberts (n 769) 427.
794 See: 7 U.S. Code § 192(c)–(g).

Furthermore, there are specific requirements determined for swine packer marketing contracts, mostly referring to obligations of giving contract-related information to the Secretary.[795]

The second group of subjects under the act consists of swine contractors. The previously mentioned unlawful practices also apply to them, but they do not fall under the personal scope of provisions on statutory trust, the bond requirement and the prompt payment requirement.[796]

The third group, live poultry dealers, are subject to the provisions on unlawful practices, however, the enforcement authority has limited powers against them in comparison with packers and swine contractors. The Secretary's main power is seeking injunctive relief. The requirements for statutory trust and prompt payment also apply to live poultry dealers.[797]

The fourth umbrella group includes stockyard owners, market agencies and dealers. While, in the case of meeting the statutory definition of the term 'stockyard', the respective stockyard is posted as such, market agencies and dealers shall obtain a bond prior to registration. The prompt payment obligation mentioned previously also refers to market agencies and dealers.[798] However, there are some differences from the prohibited practices applying to the first three groups. On the one hand, there is a general duty as to stockyard services. Stockyard owners and market agencies shall provide those services reasonably and in a nondiscriminatory way, and services shall not be refused on any basis that is unreasonable or unjustly discriminatory.[799] On the other hand, it is unlawful for any stockyard owner, market agency or dealer to engage in or use any unfair, unjustly discriminatory or deceptive practice or device in connection with determining whether persons should be authorised to operate at the stockyards, or with the receiving, marketing, buying or selling on a commission basis or otherwise, feeding, watering, holding, delivery, shipment, weighing or handling of livestock.[800]

14.2.2 Perishable Agricultural Commodities Act of 1930

It is unambiguous that the most vulnerable farmers are those who produce perishable agricultural commodities. In general, the act was adopted to prevent unfair practices of buyers (commission merchants, dealers and brokers) against their suppliers. The late rejection of the takeover of supplied goods by buyers may cause extreme difficulties for suppliers to sell their products to another buyer because of the limited market alternatives.[801]

The term 'perishable agricultural commodity' means fresh fruits and fresh vegetables of every kind and character, whether or not they are frozen or packed in ice, as

795 See: 7 U.S. Code §§ 198–198b.
796 Kelley (n 766) 47.
797 Kelley (n 766) 53–54.
798 Kelley (n 766) 49 and 51.
799 7 U.S. Code § 205.
800 7 U.S. Code § 213(a).
801 Toulmin (n 194) 207.

well as cherries in brine.[802,803] The unfair conducts are listed in seven heads in technical terms. The condemned practices[804] are greatly summarised by *Heron and Hayes*:

> The[y] range from unfair, unreasonable, discriminatory or deceptive practices in connection with the weighing, counting, or in any way determining the quantity of any perishable agricultural commodity, to the making of a change by way of substitution or otherwise in the contents of a load or lot of any perishable agricultural commodity. In between those two poles other unfair conduct is defined. It includes full rejection of the goods, dumping the goods without just cause, making fraudulent or misleading statements in connection with any transaction, making misrepresentations by any means as to the quality, quantity, size, pack, weight, condition, and degree of maturity, etc., of the goods, and fraudulently tampering with any mark on the container or car containing the goods.[805]

A comprehensive list on unlawful practices is also presented by *Looney*:

> failure to pay fully; rejecting produce without reasonable cause; failure to pay promptly; failure to make good delivery without reasonable cause; failure to account truly and correctly; discarding, dumping, or destroying produce on consignment without rea sonable cause; shipping misbranded or misrepresented produce as to grade, quality, weight, or state of origin; and altering inspection certificates or making false or misleading statements.[806]

802 7 U.S. Code § 499a(4).

803 Pursuant to the regulations of the Department of Agriculture, these definitions are determined in more detail: (u) Fresh fruits and fresh vegetables include all produce in fresh form generally considered as perishable fruits and vegetables, whether or not packed in ice or held in common or cold storage, but does not include those perishable fruits and vegetables which have been manufactured into articles of food of a different kind or character. The effects of the following operations shall not be considered as changing a commodity into a food of a different kind or character: Water, steam, or oil blanching, battering, coating, chopping, color adding, curing, cutting, dicing, drying for the removal of surface moisture; fumigating, gassing, heating for insect control, ripening and coloring; removal of seed, pits, stems, calyx, husk, pods rind, skin, peel, et cetera; polishing, precooling, refrigerating, shredding, slicing, trimming, washing with or without chemicals; waxing, adding of sugar or other sweetening agents; adding ascorbic acid or other agents to retard oxidation; mixing of several kinds of sliced, chopped, or diced fruit or vegetables for packaging in any type of containers; or comparable methods of preparation.

(v) Frozen fruits and vegetables include all produce defined in paragraph (u) of this section when such produce is in frozen form.

(w) Cherries in brine means cherries packed in an aqueous solution containing sulphur dioxide or other bleaching agent of sufficient strength to preserve the product, with or without the addition of hardening agents.

See: 7 CFR 46.2(u) – 7 CFR 46.2(w).

804 See: 7 U.S. Code § 499b.

805 Julian B. Heron Jr. and John C. Hayes Jr., 'Reparations Proceedings under the Perishable Agricultural Commodities Act: Valuable Tool in Need of Change' (1997) 22 South Dakota Law Review 520.

806 J.W. Looney, 'Protection for Sellers of Perishable Agricultural Commodities: Reparation Proceedings and the Statutory Trust under the Perishable Agricultural Commodities Act' (1990) 23 U.C. Davis Law Review 675–676.

The protection of produce sellers has been broadened in 1984 by creating a statutory trust,[807,808] which is similar to that of the Packers and Stockyards Act. Both of these trusts "protect unpaid sellers from delinquent purchasers by elevating the claims of trust beneficiaries above secured lenders and creditors."[809] However, not all agree with this special treatment of produce sellers in connection with their claims against their buyers, by emphasising that "the noble ideal" behind the act's passage no longer applies.[810] Conversely, the standpoint of Congress was that "due to the need to sell perishable commodities quickly, sellers of perishable commodities are often placed in the position of being unsecured creditors of companies whose creditworthiness the seller is unable to verify."[811]

Regarding the enforcement of its provisions, the Perishable Agricultural Commodities Act "establishes a reparation forum for claims that involve Act violations," in those cases which are related to (a) perishable agricultural commodities, (b) interstate commerce, (c) licenses subjected to the act and (d) when the respective petition has been filed within nine months of committing the violation.[812] I do not aim to analyse the procedural rules in more detail, but it must be noted that violation of the act may result in a reparation order issued by the enforcement authority. In the decision, the Department of Agriculture determines the amount of damage and makes an order directing the offender to pay that amount, and orders the losing party to pay the prevailing party, as reparation or additional reparation, reasonable fees and expenses incurred in connection with the hearing.[813]

14.2.3 Unfair Trade Practices Affecting Producers of Agricultural Products Act of 1968

As can be found in the policy declaration regarding the act, the main reason behind its adoption is the creation of the possibility for farmers and ranchers "to join together voluntarily in cooperative organizations as authorized by law." The public interest requires that no interference with this right take place.[814] The prohibited practices of handlers, reproduced here in full, are the following. It is forbidden for

807 Bartholomew M. Botta, 'Personal Liability for Corporate Debts: The Reach of the Perishable Agricultural Commodities Act Continues to Expand' (1997) 2 Drake Journal of Agricultural Law 339.

808 See: 7 U.S. Code § 499e(c).

809 John J. Korbol, 'Current Issues Involving Statutory Trusts under the Perishable Agricultural Commodities Act' (1992) 2 San Joaquin Agricultural Law Review 2.

810 See, for example: Thomas J. Cunningham, 'Amended Perishable Agricultural Commodities Act: Further Concealment of a Lien Already Nearly Invisible' (1999) 116 Banking Law Journal 253–260.

811 Sandra M. Ferrera, 'Perishable Agricultural Commodities Act Affecting Lender's Secured Priority Interest' (1999) 7 University of Miami Business Law Review 355.

812 Looney (n 806) 684–685.

813 7 U.S. Code § 499g(a).

814 7 U.S. Code § 2301.

handlers knowingly to engage or permit any employee or agent to engage in the following practices:

> (a) To coerce any producer in the exercise of his right to join and belong to or to refrain from joining or belonging to an association of producers, or to refuse to deal with any producer because of the exercise of his right to join and belong to such an association; or (b) To discriminate against any producer with respect to price, quantity, quality, or other terms of purchase, acquisition, or other handling of agricultural products because of his membership in or contract with an association of producers; or (c) To coerce or intimidate any producer to enter into, maintain, breach, cancel, or terminate a membership agreement or marketing contract with an association of producers or a contract with a handler; or (d) To pay or loan money, give any thing of value, or offer any other inducement or reward to a producer for refusing to or ceasing to belong to an association of producers; or (e) To make false reports about the finances, management, or activities of associations of producers or handlers; or (f) To conspire, combine, agree, or arrange with any other person to do, or aid or abet the doing of, any act made unlawful by this chapter.[815]

The prohibitions aim to ensure that agricultural cooperatives (associations of producers) could function without external restraints and exercise their rights.

Both the persons aggrieved and the competent attorney general may bring civil action against offenders for preventive relief, including an application for a permanent or temporary injunction, restraining order or other order. Furthermore, the persons injured may sue and recover damages and reasonable attorneys' fees.[816]

Takeaway 8

Similarly to antitrust law, both the European Union and the United States have certain regulatory means that go beyond the competition-related supervision of agri-food markets by antitrust. While the legal act of the EU on the prohibition of unfair trading practices encompasses almost all types of agricultural produce, the US regime has a narrower approach and – beyond antitrust – only addresses certain subsectors within the supply chain, such as meat-packing and perishable commodities.

815 7 U.S. Code § 2303.
816 7 U.S. Code § 2305.

15 Comparison between EU and US law[817]

The aim of this chapter is to compare the approach of the United States with that of the EU towards competition and its regulation in force in agri-food markets. The comparison between the EU and the US makes it possible to outline the key similarities and differences on both sides of the Atlantic.

Both the European Union and the United States have established a legal regime that provides for derogations for the agricultural sector under general antitrust rules. They are also similar in that the exemption is not unlimited; agricultural cooperatives shall respect antitrust rules, however, with some alleviations. The US exemption can be found in Section 6 of the Clayton Act and in the Capper-Volstead Act, while the EU exemption is codified in two EU regulations. The limitedness of the exemptions is ensured in part in different ways. What is similar is that both jurisdictions *expressis verbis* declare which types of activities the agreement shall be related to so that they can be exempted. In the United States, they are the following: collective processing, preparing for market, handling and marketing, as well as common marketing agencies. At the same time, in the EU the agreement shall concern the production or sale of agricultural products or the use of joint facilities for the storage, treatment or processing of agricultural products. What is immediately visible is that the EU exemption also covers agreements related to the production, while it is not referred to in the United States. It is relevant in the case of limiting production which the EU deems permissible within a producer organisation, but the United States does not.

The exemption provided for any association of producers (be it legally recognised, such as a producer organisation, or legally non-recognised, such as a farmers' association, or be it an agricultural cooperative within the US) is based, in part, on the doctrine of a single economic entity. The association is like a parent company that has its own subsidiaries, i.e., its agricultural producer members. The members are not independent undertakings from one another from an antitrust law perspective but constitute a single economic entity. Although, neither the EU nor the US exemption mentions them explicitly – but as a consequence of the single

817 This chapter is, in part, based on Martin Milán Csirszki, 'The Comparison of the US and EU Agricultural Antitrust Exemption' (2022) 15 Yearbook of Antitrust and Regulatory Studies 137–173.

DOI: 10.4324/9781003604747-19

economic entity doctrine even price fixing is permissible to a certain extent based on case law. Indirectly, within the framework of the term 'marketing', which is a legitimate objective to be carried out by an agricultural cooperative, the US case law also means price fixing. Although the EU regulation declares the prohibition of charging identical prices, recent case law in *Endives* shows that this provision only refers to that if a producer organisation prohibits its members from selling their own produce at a price under the minimum fixed price determined within the producer organisation. It is actually in accordance with the requirement that the agreement shall concern the sale of agricultural products.

As to the personal scope of exemptions, there are similarities and differences. The EU and the US regulations are similar in that they do not connect the applicability of the exemption to a certain form of legal entity. It is irrelevant in both jurisdictions whether the undertaking is profit-making or non-profit making, or it is a cooperative or a company. Both the EU and the United States employ criteria, negative or positive, to be fulfilled by the undertaking to be exempted, but the structure of these criteria and their formulation are different. The EU has derogations which can only apply to legally recognised producer organisations (see Article 152(1a) of the CMO Regulation), while there are others which apply in general to farmers and farmers' associations, without giving them a correct definition (see Article 209 of the CMO Regulation and Article 2 of the Agri-Food Competition Regulation). The recognition of producer organisations is regulated in detail, on the one hand, in secondary EU law (in the CMO Regulation itself), and, on the other hand, in national law. These general rules on the recognition of producer organisations constitute a separate area of provisions in the EU, while the US antitrust formulates its negative criteria on associations, which can apply the exemption, directly among the provisions on the exemption. The US negative conditions 'no more than one vote per member', 'dividends not excessing 8 per cent' and 'no dealing to an amount greater in value to nonmembers than to members' do not have EU equivalents, however, the general rule 'one member, one vote' also applies in the EU to producer organisations that are cooperatives. But again, this procedural provision derives from general rules and is not declared among the rules on the agricultural antitrust exemption. Negative requirements are formulated with regard to the undertaking itself in the United States, while the European Union is rather concerned with the economic conduct when formulating negative conditions. The latter declares that the agreement shall not exclude competition, require charging identical prices and jeopardise the objectives of the Common Agricultural Policy. While limiting the exemption in the United States takes place primarily from the standpoint of the undertaking and secondarily from the conduct itself with the prohibition of undue price enhancement, the EU rather aims to limit the exemption by regulating and reaching for certain unwanted effects to be avoided (competition exclusion, identical prices, jeopardised agricultural policy objectives).

Another important distinction can be drawn which sheds light on the diverging focus of the two jurisdictions. The European Union withdraws the protection (exemption) provided for the agreement, if it jeopardises common agricultural policy objectives. It means that the conduct is not only assessed in antitrust terms but also within the framework of agricultural law. Hijacking the assessment method from antitrust law in a direction where other policy objectives are taken into consideration is clearly missing regarding the US agricultural antitrust exemption. This EU approach may seem like folly. It is an antitrust provision, the agreement is related to agricultural products, no competition concerns arise, but it endangers agricultural policy objectives, so it does not deserve the privileged treatment of antitrust law.

The organisational criteria for the application of the exemptions are also similar both in the EU and the United States. The EU only accepts certain derogations if the PO or the APO concerned is legally recognised. The US exemption also establishes the Capper-Volstead criteria to be exempt. In neither jurisdiction can an agreement be exempt from the prohibition, if any of the parties to the agreement does not fulfil the requirements. Both legal regimes only provide protection *below* cooperative level, that is to say, agreements between two separate legal entities *on* cooperative level (between two cooperatives or between two producers' organisations) are not exempt. Producers may join forces in an agricultural cooperative fulfilling the Capper-Volstead criteria in the United States or in a legally recognised producer organisation in the EU, but two separate legal entities shall not cooperate; in case of that the doctrine of single economic entity would be violated and the prohibition should be applied. Furthermore, both legal systems require that only those agreements are exempt which are – in the EU – strictly necessary to achieve the objectives of the respective PO or APO, or which are – in the United States – necessary to carry out any of the legitimate objects. The US legitimate objectives and the EU objectives are analogous in that they make concentration supply possible. The specific aims to be pursued by a producer organisation, which are determined by the CMO Regulation, fit into the toolbox of means to realise the overall Common Agricultural Policy objectives in the EU.

A slight and insignificant difference is that the United States does not determine exact umbrella objectives to be pursued and realised by its agricultural policy, however, it does not change the fact that it treats agricultural cooperatives in the competition environment the same way like the EU. Perhaps the most significant difference between EU and US regulation is that the former also allows supply restrictions, as can be read from the *Endives* judgment. As to the concentration on quantities put on the market, the Court ruled that it escapes the prohibition in Article 101 TFEU, if it is agreed between the members of a legally recognised producer organisation or a legally recognised association of producer organisations and strictly necessary to reach the objective pursued by the respective PO or APO. On the contrary, the United States is rather against limiting production. The CMO Regulation explicitly declares that ensuring that production is planned and adjusted to demand, particularly in terms of quality and *quantity*, is a specific aim which can be pursued by a PO. That is to say, limiting production in the EU by a producer organisation is permissible and may be exempt from the general prohibition, if it takes place within a legally recognised PO. The United States does not address price fixing and supply control as two sides of the same coin, unlike the European Union where both economic activities are lawful from the perspective of the agricultural antitrust exemption. While the US only accepts restrictions which take place *postproduction*, the EU also deems lawful *preproduction* cooperations. The exchange of strategic information is also permissible in both of the jurisdictions.

The economic justification of limited agricultural exemptions lies in the concept of countervailing power. The exemptions, which make it possible for agricultural producers to combine forces, enable them to create countervailing power against the market power of buyers. One significant difference between the EU and US regimes is that the former does not include a control mechanism, if the association of agricultural producers faces a buyer which does not have monopsony power. In that case, the exemption can be misused because of the fact that the unity of farmers does not face a buyer whose economic power should be countervailed to increase efficiency. That is to say, when there is no monopsony power in the hands of a buyer which should be countervailed, the market power of sellers becomes super-vailing power with likely adverse effects on competition. This is attempted to be controlled by the US antitrust provision which prohibits undue price enhancement by agricultural cooperatives. This is missing in EU antitrust. At a theoretical level, producer organisations or associations of producer organisations, if they meet the general criteria determined and bargain with buyers without market power, have at their disposal the possibility to increase sales prices to a level which is not competitive anymore, and thus not efficient, given that their market power is not countervailing but super-vailing in relation to their buyers.

Another significant difference between the EU and US regimes is that the former also provides for a derogation to interbranch organisations. These entities have members at different levels of the food supply chain, that is to say, the competition derogation applies to vertically integrated organisations according to the rules laid down in Article 210 of the CMO Regulation. The derogation is only applicable to recognised entities, contrary to Article 209 of the CMO Regulation and the provisions of the Agri-Food Competition Regulation. Both vertical agreements of interbranch organisations and horizontal agreements for farmers, their associations, POs and APOs are based on self-assessment, whether they are compatible with the rules on the derogation.

From the viewpoint of functional comparison, both the EU and US regulations aim to achieve the same goal with the same legal means. The main function is to increase the bargaining power of producers against their buyers. The realisation of it takes place by excluding certain agreements of agricultural producers from the scope of the general prohibition of anticompetitive agreements. Even the most harmful of all agreements, price cartels, which distort competition by object, are also exempted until they are concluded within a legal entity. In antitrust terms, these would be per se prohibited because they are drawn up with the participation of competitors to fix sale price, however based on the doctrine of the single economic entity these agricultural associations are treated as one undertaking despite the fact that they unite competitors.

The structure of regulation is also similar. The provisions can be found in the legal sources of agricultural law. The US agricultural exemption, the Capper-Volstead Act, is codified in Title 7 of the US Code which consists of the laws related to agriculture. The EU also separates its derogations from general antitrust rules, and codifies them, in part, in the CMO Regulation, and, in part, in a completely separate legal act, the Agri-Food Competition Regulation, which does not cover any other topic beyond the exemption.

As to the trade regulation pillar of agri-food markets, both the European Union and the United States have adopted sector-specific provisions. While the EU collects unfair trading practices in one legal act, namely the Directive (EU) 2019/633, the United States has several federal acts to address the problems of certain agricultural subsectors. The Packers and Stockyards Act regulates livestock, meat and poultry markets; the Perishable Agricultural Commodities Act regulates the markets of fresh fruit and vegetables of every kind and character; the Unfair Trade Practices Affecting Producers of Agricultural Products Act regulates agricultural markets in general in order to ensure that producers can exercise their rights related to associating under statutory possibilities. The UTP Directive of the EU covers agricultural and food products in general, including livestock, meat and poultry, as well as fruits and vegetables. The unlawful practices enumerated in the Unfair Trade Practices Affecting Producers of Agricultural Products Act are mostly covered by Article 3(1)(h) of the UTP Directive which prohibits buyers from threatening to carry out, or carrying out, acts of commercial retaliation against the supplier if the supplier exercises its contractual or legal rights. The Perishable Agricultural Commodities Act has some practices falling under the scope of unfair competition law, such as shipping misbranded and misrepresented produce as to grade, quality, weight or state of origin, and altering inspection certificates or making false and misleading statements. These do not have an equivalent in the UTP Directive. The greatest difference comes to the fore with the Packers and Stockyards Act which is dubious in nature. There are conflicting views as to whether it is an antitrust statute, therefore it requires proof of negative effects on competition, or else it lacks the antitrust character. Recently it has been treated as an antitrust statute, therefore it differs in principle from the UTP Directive, for the latter does not require any adverse effects on competition to be found. The lax formulation of the prohibitions in the Packers and Stockyards Act, however, suggests otherwise. The violation ‘engaging in or using any unfair, unjustly discriminatory, or deceptive practice or device’ seems like a general prohibition of unfair trading practices; nevertheless this provision has covered a wide variety of practices with antitrust or even unfair competition law character, such as discriminatory pricing, predatory pricing, deceptive advertising and false weighing. The Packers and Stockyards Act is hard to explain and compare with any legal act of the EU, since it evolved as a consequence of the extreme consolidation of the American meat-packing industry dominated by five, and recently four, giant meat-packers controlling approximately two-thirds of the market.

Part V

Agricultural policy paradigms on competition and sustainability

After concentrating on the current situation of external ruptures and complex interrelationships between policy areas that have been dealt with in Parts II, III and IV, Part V shifts the focus to the schisms (internal ruptures) within the two public policy areas: competition and agricultural policy. This Part is of utmost importance to recognise that there is a wide variety of differing opinions even *within* the respective policy areas. Competition policy as such is not an area where there is complete agreement as regards values, objectives and/or the methods to represent those values and achieve those objectives. This holds true also for agricultural policy. While competition policy is better off in this regard (competition as such is generally treated desirable), actors in agricultural policy (policy-makers, undertakings, legislators, any other stakeholders) are so diverse that it is challenging to find common points of reference.

Part V aims to scrutinise competition policy and sustainability in agri-food markets in light of the agricultural policy paradigms, in particular of the contesting food sovereignty movement. As mentioned in the Introduction, while Parts II, III and IV are concerned with the current law-and-policy framework of competition, sustainability and the agricultural sector, the focus of Part V lies in the food sovereignty movement's perceptions and demands concerning competition and sustainability. This requires exploring and disentangling the paradigm's theory about a well-functioning agricultural and food supply chain based on the publications of its flagship organisations as well as its renowned scholars. Obviously, I will concentrate on the topics of competition and sustainability, and their possible connections.

DOI: 10.4324/9781003604747-20

16 The prevailing neoliberal paradigm

The preceding parts displayed the current law-and-policy landscape of the interrelationship between the agricultural sector, competition and sustainability. However, it is worth providing here a brief overview about their nexus to see clearly.

The agricultural sector, that is agricultural production, enjoys substantial alleviations even in the prevailing competition policy framework that is embedded in the context of neoliberal political philosophy as well as the underlying economic approach based on neoclassical economics. This alleviation has not only accompanied the development of antitrust law almost since the birth of modern antitrust, but also broken into areas where antitrust enforcement could not be set in motion. It is enough to think of the prohibition of unfair trading practices, which appears in different forms both in the United States and the European Union. Though antitrust law has become more concerned with economic analysis in the last four decades, the sector-specific exemption under the prohibition of anticompetitive agreements has remained intact, not to say that in the EU it has been even broadened in its scope in the 2010s. At the EU level, the same decade also saw the adoption of the UTP Directive based on a minimum harmonisation approach. Even if there had been Member States before that where agricultural producers had not enjoyed an *ius proprium*-like protective pillar from uneven market forces, now they have been obliged by EU law to implement the directive through the adoption of at least such prohibitions that are found in it. This signals that the European Union unequivocally strengthened the protection of agricultural producers in the market.

In the last four decades, the same neoliberal establishment, which not only preserved sectoral antitrust rules applicable to the agricultural sector but also expanded them and introduced new economic regulatory protection beyond antitrust, took a completely different standpoint about agricultural state aid policies. The slogan of 'more market orientation' came with decoupled subsidies that do not mean the same extent of safety net as the heavy, production-based market intervention in the form of intervention prices, import levies and quotas. Shifting the focus from market support to producer support resulted in producers being less protected against whimsical market forces that flow from the nature of agricultural production. As already mentioned, it seems that what the EU has taken away with one hand, it tries to give back to the farmers with the other hand.

DOI: 10.4324/9781003604747-21

Before decoupling, subsidies linked to the production of specific crops did raise the level of income of agricultural producers, irrespective of the fact that it could lead to overproduction. On the contrary, what legislation has given to farmers instead of coupled subsidies and beyond the decoupled ones are the competition-related legal concessions, such as the prohibition of unfair trading practices or newer antitrust exemptions. Nevertheless, they have much more modest contributions to the increase of farmers' living standard, despite that they have been adopted in light of this objective. Simply put, antitrust and competition-related regulations are not designed to distribute wealth and to contribute to social objectives, contrary to subsidies. The earlier means that had helped farmers were not replaced with those new ones that are fully suitable to compensate farmers for losing the more market-interventionist state aid.

US farmers also wittnessed the same trends as regards agricultural subsidies, however, the agricultural sector of the United States – thanks to its different farm structure based on large estates – was better prepared for the market forces growing stronger. As demonstrated in subheading 3 of Chapter 10, the agricultural policy of the New World was always one step ahead of the Old Continent. Though new antitrust and other regulatory provisions have not been adopted throughout these four decades, the priority setting of the enforcement agencies clearly thematised farmers as victims of the ever-concentrating US food economy. Although the Neo-Brandeisians were not extant then, in the first years of the 2010s US antitrust agencies held a series of workshops to scrutinise the problems of agricultural producers from the viewpoint of competition, in particular antitrust, policy. As the wind of change started to blow after Biden's new appointments, the rhetoric intensified once again that farmers shall be protected and the competitive nature of the food supply chain shall be restored.

Turning the attention towards private sustainability initiatives, I mentioned several times that they do not receive direct attention in the United States from a competition policy perspective. Not so in the European Union. What is, however, similar on both sides of the Atlantic is the introduction and continuous expansion of greening criteria in the area of agricultural subsidies. Producers are to an ever higher extent incentivised to implement environmentally friendly farming practices. These are in most cases embodied by so-called conditionalities that have to be fulfilled by farmers to receive the subsidies.

In the European Union, based on legally binding norms, private sustainability initiatives of the agri-food supply chain are handled within an assessment system more favourable than those sustainability agreements which are not in the scope of the *ius singulare*, that is Article 210a of the CMO Regulation. In other words, the agricultural sector enjoys less stringent rules also when it comes to the antitrust assessment of private sustainability initiatives. It was interesting to see that although the general legal framework of sustainability agreements has not been regulated in a legally binding way, the agricultural sector not only achieved but also succeeded in relaxing the horizontal (sector-neutral) assessment criteria based on soft law guidelines, significantly hijacking the logic of antitrust law regarding the individual exemption system.

In light of the aforementioned considerations, it would be wrong to conclude that the prevailing paradigm in competition policy, including antitrust, does not reflect the particular characteristics of the agricultural sector. Actually, it aims at establishing a legal framework that is sensitive to the different nature of agricultural production and to the marketing of agricultural produce. This conclusion holds true both for the European Union and the United States. These frameworks applicable to agriculture are far from following the free-marketer approach characteristic of the neoliberal policy paradigm dominant since the 1980s. Though there was a clear paradigm change from a formalistic to an economics-based viewpoint in antitrust in the respective period, this has not affected agricultural producers adversely, legally speaking.

The doubts and problems of agricultural producers do not flow from a bunch of unfavourable and insensitive legal provisions applicable to the sector. They are the result of economic and market processes from those adjacent areas to which only general antitrust rules apply. These markets both downstream and upstream in relation to agricultural production must be considered as 'industry' in the context of economic duality referring to the confrontation 'industry vs agriculture'. Irrespective of being integral and important parts of the agri-food supply chain, both the input markets to agriculture, such as machinery and fertilisers, and the procurement markets, such as processing, wholesale and trade, are at ease, and function easily in line, with the inherent logic of a free-marketer neoliberal policy design.

The roots of problems of the agricultural sector, thus, lie in its strong dependence on the functioning of its adjacent markets upstream and downstream. This sheds light on a crucial consideration in connection with regulation: though isolated, sector-specific legal provisions may reflect to the complications extant in the agricultural sector and may even serve as a solution to handle these problems, as a consequence of the powerful interdependence between the different levels of the supply chain (between the vertically adjacent markets), industry-wide economic trends, such as consolidation and concentration, may outweigh otherwise effective legal norms. Globalisation with its impetus in the form of neoliberal economic policy design has not attacked the sectoral rules of agriculture, but intensified the sector's independence on, and embeddedness in, the agri-food supply chain. By the same token, in the last four decades, the free-marketer approach dominant in all industries that are engaged in selling inputs to agricultural producers and buying agricultural produce thwarts the attainment of agricultural policy objectives, in particular that of the fair standard of living for farmers, which were to be achieved through agriculture-specific policy tools in the form of *ius singolare* and *ius proprium*.

After these considerations, it is worthwhile to turn our attention to the paradigm of food sovereignty that attempts to establish an alternative way of agricultural production, which is in harsh contrast with the basic assumptions of neoliberal policy design.

Takeaway 9

Despite the free-marketer neoliberal paradigm, which came to the fore about four decades ago, the agricultural sector has preserved, and in the EU even expanded, its privileges in competition policy, contrary to the food sovereignty paradigm contending that the unfairness of agri-food markets are not taken into account. It seems that the level of protection in the competitive process, which has been reduced by creating more market-oriented (decoupled) agricultural state aid schemes on both sides of the Atlantic, is attempted to be redressed through competition policy means, such as the prohibition of unfair trading practices, the extension of antitrust exemptions in scope or intensified attention by antitrust agencies to agri-food markets. Nevertheless, these have much more modest contributions to the increase of farmers' living standard, because antitrust and competition-related regulations are not designed to distribute wealth and to contribute to social objectives, contrary to agricultural state aid programmes.

17 Food sovereignty as the contesting paradigm

In this chapter, I aim to explore those elements of the food sovereignty movement(s) which may provide us with insights into the way competition and sustainability are perceived within its framework. In some aspects, as a conflicting basis for comparison, I use the concept of food security that stands at the centre of the neoliberal paradigm.

The literature is not consistent on the relationship between food security and food sovereignty. Some draw a sharp dividing line between the two and treat them as opposing alternatives. Food security and food sovereignty are construed as a global conflict, for example, by *William D. Schanbacher*,[818] *María Elena Martínez-Torres and Peter M. Rosset*[819] as well as *Philip McMichael*[820] and *Joe J. Wills*.[821] However, the European Union and its institutions do not necessarily take this position. The approach of the EU institutions is neither revolutionary nor new, because the first definition of food sovereignty in 1996[822] and the early literature on food sovereignty also took the view that food sovereignty is a precondition for food security.[823] Some overlaps do exist between these paradigms (for example, culturally appropriate food).[824] Nevertheless, goes the saying, it does not mean that they would not have an irresolvable conflict.

818 Schanbacher (n 141).

819 María Elena Martínez-Torres and Peter M. Rosset, 'Diálogo de saberes in La Vía Campesina: Food Sovereignty and Agroecology' (2014) 41 The Journal of Peasant Studies 979–997.

820 Philip McMichael, 'Historicizing Food Sovereignty' (2014) 41 The Journal of Peasant Studies 933–957.

821 See Chapter 3 entitled 'Food Security vs. Food Sovereignty: The Right to Food and Global Hunger' of Joe J. Wills, *Contesting World Order? Socioeconomic Rights and Global Justice Movements* (CUP 2017) 94–150.

822 La Via Campesina, 'The Right to Produce and Access to Land: Food Sovereignty: A Future Without Hunger' (November 1996).

823 Marc Edelman, Tony Weis, Amita Baviskar, Saturnino M. Borras Jr, Eric Holt-Giménez, Deniz Kandiyoti and Wendy Wolford, 'Introduction: Critical Perspectives on Food Sovereignty' (2014) 41 The Journal of Peasant Studies 914.

824 Edelman, Weis, Baviskar, Borras Jr, Holt-Giménez, Kandiyoti and Wolford (n 823) 914.

DOI: 10.4324/9781003604747-22

A general criticism that is formulated against food sovereignty is "its lack of conceptual clarity."[825] *Clapp* considers broad conceptualisation as a satisfactory solution in the early stages of a movement, however, later the proponents and activists cannot ignore more nuanced articulations of any topic relevant to the concept.[826] It was asserted that, for example, the official position of the food sovereignty movement on trade is enigmatic.[827] It is no different for its standpoint towards competition. This is the reason I attempt to explore its statements and declarations in connection with this issue, and based on these, to draw up a coherent framework.

Furthermore, one of several clearly unanswered questions is the role of the state in food sovereignty, as well as the meaning and nature of sovereignty in food sovereignty itself. This is, in part, the root of many contradictions. The vagueness of food sovereignty supporters and scholars in this aspect is to be eliminated because of its relevance as to "how a food sovereign society will be administered"[828] at all. Basically, there are two strands: some authors argue for a 'multiple sovereignties' approach,[829] while others take a more permissive viewpoint towards conventional, state-centred sovereignty.[830] The meaning of the latter is evident: it means the lack of external intervention into independent states' decision-making in their own territory (for example, the government of a country can, and should, decide and determine its own agricultural policy independently from other sovereign states and supranational organisations, such as the WTO).[831] The former, however, requires some clarification. While the state-centred sovereignty concept is prima facie associated with a kind of external dimension, the 'multiple sovereignties' approach also includes internal fragmentation within a state. According to *Schiavoni*, food sovereignty runs counter to, and cannot be harmonised with, accepting the state as a single sovereign; it is a "redefini[tion] of internal sovereignty."[832] She refers to *Patel* who interprets the call for "nations, peoples, regions, and states to craft their own agrarian policy" as a "concomitant call for spaces of sovereignty."[833] *Schiavoni*

825 Koen Dekeyser, Lise Korsten and Lorenzo Fioramonti, 'Food Sovereignty: Shifting Debates on Democratic Food Governance' (2018) 10 Food Security 223–233.
826 Jennifer Clapp, *Food* (Polity Press 2012) 176.
827 Kim Burnett and Sophia Murphy, 'What Place for International Trade in Food Sovereignty?' (2014) 41 The Journal of Peasant Studies 1065–1084.
828 Marc Edelman, 'Food Sovereignty: Forgotten Genealogies and Future Regulatory Challenges' (2014) 41 The Journal of Peasant Studies 959–978.
829 Alastair Iles and Maywa Montenegro de Wit, 'Sovereignty at What Scale? An Inquiry into Multiple Dimensions of Food Sovereignty' 2015 (12) Globalizations 481–497.
830 Patrick Clark, 'Can the State Foster Food Sovereignty? Insights from the Case of Ecuador' (2016) 16 Journal of Agrarian Change 183–205.
831 Adam Lupel, *Globalization and Popular Sovereignty: Democracy's Transnational Dilemma* (Routledge 2009).
832 Christina M. Schiavoni, 'Competing Sovereignties, Contested Processes: Insights from the Venezuelan Food Sovereignty Experiment' (2015) 12 Globalizations 466–480.
833 Patel (n 54) 668.

points out correctly that, if this approach is taken, these multiple sovereignties compete with one another.[834]

The aforementioned critical considerations can easily be accepted, if one peruses the food sovereignty definitions adopted in different declarations in 1996, 2002 and 2007. In connection with the changing definitions, *Agarwal* draws attention to its continuous broadening. In its 1996 definition, it concentrated on national self-sufficiency, given that food sovereignty was defined as the right of each nation; then, in 2002, it moved in the direction where it is "the rights of people to define domestic production and trade, as well as determine the extent to which they want to be self-reliant,"[835] and subsequently in 2007, it "embraces everyone who is involved in the food chain – from producers to distributors to consumers."[836] The 2007 definition included in the *Nyéléni Declaration* has many more contradictions than the earlier versions. As *Patel* puts it, "[t]he diversity of opinions, positions, issues, and politics bursts through in the text," being a prime example of "big tent politics," in which a wide variety of groups can express their views and interests, resulting in contradictions "a little more fatal."[837] The 1996 definition has a distinctive feature in comparison with the other two: food sovereignty is the right of each *nation*, not of peoples. The 2002 and 2007 definitions spoke about the rights of peoples. This change is of relevance to us, since later I propose for the movement to return to its initial rhetoric in this regard.

Some important findings on food sovereignty's approach towards competition and trade can be collected from these definitions. In 1996, fair trade and respect for the Earth appeared as two aspects that the movement is determined to create for rural economies. Primarily, the criticism rained down on food imports, export dumping and subsidised exports. It was emphasised that the prices which are received by producers must reflect the actual costs of production for the sake of adequate farm incomes. It was also claimed that food trade is based on the economic exploitation of farmers as well as environmental degradation, which must be halted. The control over marketing the agricultural produce must be given back to the producers.[838]

The 2002 version of the definition declares that it does negate trade but aims to promote trade policies and practices serving the rights of peoples to food, hand in hand with safe, healthy and ecologically sustainable production. "[A]dequate remunerative prices for all farmers" must be ensured. Furthermore, in contrast to the neoliberal framework represented by the WTO, an alternative must be established for the sustainable production and trade of agricultural products and food.

834 Schiavoni (n 832).

835 Statement on People's Food Sovereignty, 'Our World Is Not for Sale: Priority to Peoples' Food Sovereignty: WTO Out of Food and Agriculture' (June 2002).

836 Bina Agarwal, 'Food Sovereignty, Food Security and Democratic Choice: Critical Contradictions, Difficult Conciliations' (2014) 41 The Journal of Peasant Studies 1247–1248.

837 Patel (n 54) 666.

838 La Via Campesina, 'The Right to Produce and Access to Land' (November 1996).

Market forces and powerful transnational corporations determine how food is traded and marketed, which goes against sustainable, family-based production.[839]

In 2007, the *Nyéléni Declaration* added further layers to the concept, agreeing with *Patel*, with depressing contradictions. The contention remains that markets and corporations cannot be placed at the heart of food systems, but in the very same sentence it is also mentioned that this role is reserved for those who produce, *distribute* and consume food. Omitting 'distribute' could completely change the meaning of the sentence, because it would become clear that only producers and consumers are the keystones of the supply chain, and not the intermediary distributors, such as wholesalers and retailers, who have become price givers (and not price takers) to the detriment of producers. The document refers to sustainability both implicitly ("defend[ing] the interests and inclusion of the next generation") and explicitly ("environmental, social and economic sustainability-based production, distribution and consumption"). The statement encourages "transparent trade that guarantees just income to all peoples." The *Nyéléni Declaration* clearly acknowledges that food sovereignty defines itself as against, among others, neoliberalism that favours transnational corporations placing profit before people and the environment. The movement sees local and national economies and markets as a solution to counter the neoliberal approach.[840]

Although the paradigm of food sovereignty has emerged most significantly at the international level, and aims to formulate suggestions with regard to international trade in agricultural and food products, it is apparent from its self-determination that it argues against completely free markets lacking the guardian role of state regulation.[841] In general, it defines the state as the protector of farmers,[842] and this need for protection is also to be interpreted regarding the agricultural markets and the role farmers should play therein. It not only refers to international markets but also to regional and national ones. Food security advocates argue for the liberalisation of markets as the one and only means to achieve their objectives. However, at the international level the proponents of food sovereignty represent the view that the World Trade Organization should get out of agriculture because free trade policies and their foundation in the form of neoclassical economics are not suitable to meet the needs of agriculture and the food sector.[843]

As seen from the earlier parts of the book, in the multi-level food supply chain worrisome concerns not only arise from anticompetitive agreements, abuse of dominance and mergers,[844] but also from unfair trading practices against suppliers

839 Statement on People's Food Sovereignty (n 835).

840 Declaration of Nyéléni (February 2007) <https://nyeleni.org/IMG/pdf/DeclNyeleni-en.pdf> accessed 9 September 2023.

841 Michael Windfuhr and Jennie Jonsén, *Food Sovereignty: Towards Democracy in Localized Food Systems* (ITDG Publishing 2005) 29.

842 Mann (n 2) 54.

843 See: Rosset (n 2).

844 See: Organization for Economic Co-Operation and Development, 'Competition Issues in the Food Chain Industry' (2013) DAF/COMP(2014)16.

of agri-food products falling outside the scope of conventional antitrust law instruments. In many cases, the latter remain hidden from the eyes of antitrust authorities, on one hand, because of the lack of normative and prohibitive regulation, and, on the other hand, if there is some kind of regulation, because of the fear factor which discourages suppliers from making a formal complaint against offenders out of fear of commercial retaliation.[845] Both the market behaviours which can be assessed with antitrust law instruments and the unfair trading practices emerging in contractual relations are unacceptable if one uses the food sovereignty paradigm as a benchmark.

Neoclassical economics, attacked by food sovereignty proponents, is also the basis for those antitrust law regimes which consider the goal of economic efficiency as the exclusive aim of antitrust, as in the US in the last four decades with the dominance of the Chicago School. The core principle of neoclassical economics is to maximise allocative efficiency,[846] which – in antitrust terms – is understood as consumer welfare.[847] Consumer welfare is none other than the guiding principle of the Chicago School of antitrust dominating the US antitrust regime from the appearance of Robert Bork's *The Antitrust Paradox*.[848]

Neoclassical economics and its political philosophy background in the form of neoliberalism are condemned by food sovereignty which cannot accept, and argues against, the trait of neoliberalism based on which separate economic, social and political spheres are evaluated according to a single economic logic.[849] With regard to antitrust law, this single-factor nature may lie in the approach that considers consumer welfare as the one and only legitimate objective of antitrust law.

From the perspective of food sovereignty, with regard to agricultural and food products, this can be paralleled with the commodification of food products. From a neoliberal standpoint, regarding competition in agri-food markets, the only considerations to be taken into account should be economic ones, which are against the immanent features of food sovereignty. By challenging the dominance of agribusiness and the unjust trade system[850] and by not negating trade,[851] food sovereignty – on the contrary – puts significant emphasis on social considerations and aims to contribute to a humane market economy which intends to surpass the neoliberal market economy that operates with purely economic terms.

845 Göckler (n 717).
846 Robert D. Atkinson and David B. Audretsch, 'Economic Doctrines and Approaches to Antitrust' (*Indiana University-Bloomington: School of Public & Environmental Affairs Research Paper Series*, 2011) <https://papers.ssrn.com/sol3/papers.cfm?abstract_id=1750259#> accessed 14 October 2023.
847 Dina I. Waked, 'Antitrust as Public Interest Law: Redistribution, Equity, and Social Justice' (2020) 65 The Antitrust Bulletin 88.
848 Robert H. Bork, *The Antitrust Paradox* (Free Press 1978).
849 William Davies, *The Limits of Neoliberalism* (SAGE Publications 2014) 31–32.
850 See: Mann (n 2).
851 Windfuhr and Jonsén (n 841).

In summary, the paradigm of food sovereignty builds upon a mode of competition and a way of market functioning which require the guardian role of the state in the form of legal regulation aiming to protect the interests of agricultural producers and farmers as well as those of small and medium-sized enterprises. It craves extensive and strong competition legislation and enforcement dominated not only by efficiency-based considerations but also non-efficiency-based ones. On the contrary, neoliberals see the solution of ameliorating the situation of agricultural producers (farmers) in having completely free markets of which the state backed out. Pursuant to the understanding by the representatives of neoliberalism, completely free markets make it possible for each and every agricultural producer to enter global markets and, thus, to generate higher profits. Food sovereignty aims to take into account those noneconomic aspects that are overlooked by neoliberal agricultural policy and its food security paradigm.

In my opinion, to achieve the objectives of the food sovereignty paradigm, the movement(s) should return to its 1996 origins, dismiss the 'multiple sovereignties' approach and strictly adopt a state-centred sovereignty concept. As *McMichael* formulated, "the term sovereignty was arguably a form of strategic essentialism, given the override of national sovereignty via WTO trade rules."[852] This would not be the promotion of "reactionary nationalism,"[853] but an acknowledgment of the functioning of modern nation-states that they are – with their legislative powers – capable of transforming broad policy objectives into binding legal rules delivering the wished outcomes. The push for globalisation, thus the more market orientation, of agri-food markets came most intensively from the international level, which even meant an external pressure to reforming EU and US agricultural policy, in particular their state aid programmes. The best self-determination of the food sovereignty paradigm can only take place as an opposition to international influence on the continuous attempt for opening up agri-food markets. The most evident form of it is to strengthen the power of the state and to reclaim as well as accept its sovereignty as the only alternative depository of favourable legislation.

It does not mean that those who are treated now as sovereign in the 'multiple sovereignties' approach are not taken into account. It is an obligation for the state to consider and respect the different values and interests of all groups, also of those who are worthy of protection by the food sovereignty movement. Nonetheless, the state must balance the competing interests, and exclusively the legislative branch of power – with all of its established mechanisms throughout the legislative process – is in the position to determine the public good. This line of thinking about the way of the possible attainment of food sovereignty demands would be the first step to find the method that can help achieve the articulated goals of the food sovereignty movement. Second, the statements and declarations should be converted to feasible policy tools in the form of legal regulations, as I will attempt in Chapter 22. If the actual functioning of policy-making and legislation is accepted and the clearly enunciated policy tools that serve the attainment of food sovereignty

852 McMichael (n 820).
853 McMichael (n 820).

objectives are elaborated, the efforts of any food sovereignty movement should be dedicated to organise its pressure groups and attempt at influencing the outcomes.

Without these three steps, the movement will not achieve any breakthrough. Food sovereignty advocates who idealise that the escape from capitalist market economy could save family farm-based and small-scale agriculture will not help those who are worthy of protection according to them. They show false hope. Clearly articulated and feasible policy tools must be presented to the decision-makers, which implies the acceptance of a state-centred sovereignty concept, or that of when the state voluntarily renounces a well-determined part of its sovereignty in favour of a supranational organisation (for example, the European Union) or of the federal government (for example, the United States). The fact that certain similarly situated groups and communities declare and consider themselves sovereign does not change the way legislation takes place, but obscures reality.

Furthermore, as can be seen, one of the main targets of the food sovereignty paradigm is the free market that has been created globally, and has been seen as ideal, by neoliberal economic thinking. The counterweight to this can only be regulation by the state, which tames untrammelled market forces and supervises the fair functioning of markets, which is endorsed by food sovereignty. This endorsement is also in contrast with the rejection of the state-centred sovereignty concept: it would be difficult to reconcile the demand for protection by the state against market forces and the view towards reducing the power of sovereignty of the state. Then, who would be the 'protector' of farmers?

The practical difficulties arising from the 'multiple sovereignties' concept of food sovereignty are also emphasised by *Clark*.[854] Food sovereignty scholars place much greater emphasis on supranational organisations' ability to influence policy-making than they should, and they tend to endorse local initiatives, resulting in overshadowing the role of the nation-state.[855] Of course, trade liberalisation in the neoliberal spirit took place within the World Trade Organization and was realised through the Agreement on Agriculture, which entered into force in 1995. However, a great extent of policy-making and – obviously – legislation happens at the national level. *Borras* recognises in his analysis on land policy that "central states remain key actors in national–local governance in most parts of the world."[856] The fact that "food sovereignty activists have long worked simultaneously for political change at multiple scales," including "the creation of local markets,"[857] does not – in my opinion – mean that local sovereignties are to be constituted. There are local interests[858] that must

854 Clark (n 830) 186.

855 Clark (n 830) 185.

856 Saturnino M. Borras Jr., 'The Politics of Transnational Agrarian Movements' (2010) 41 Development and Change 781.

857 Annie Shattuck, Christina M. Schiavoni and Zoe VanGelder, 'Translating the Politics of Food Sovereignty: Digging into Contradictions, Uncovering New Dimensions' (2015) 12 Globalizations 425.

858 See, for example: Magali Barreto Ávila, 'The Mayan Indigenous Women of Chiapas: Lekil Kuxlejal and food autonomy' (2011) 54 Development 485–489.

be chanelled into the decision-making processes of the state and of the state's local administration, which should be taken into account.

Though a few nation-states, typically in Latin America, have incorporated food sovereignty into their constitutions and/or regulated some aspects of food sovereignty in statutes,[859] this number is far from many. The impact of these provisions is marginal. Although constitutions are at the top of legal hierarchy, if constitutional provisions are not fulfilled with enforceable content at the lower levels of legal sources, they are not to achieve real breakthrough. One can hardly see legal proposals[860] and legal analysis[861] in connection with the legal feasibility of the food sovereignty paradigm's demands. It is not necessary for legal sources to refer explicitly to food sovereignty. Scholars and policy-makers should translate the demands of the movement into legal provisions that can be readily available to those decision-making bodies which have the highest impact to help attain – through adopting concurrent legislation – objectives formulated by interest groups.

This can be best realised through national parliaments enjoying the highest democratic legitimation in the modern world.

Takeaway 10

The food sovereignty movement's rhetoric in official statements and policy documents revolves around the notions of fair trade and the respect for the natural environment, without further elaboration in many cases. In order to better channel these considerations into the policy-making processes, the food sovereignty paradigm should specify its demands in these regards in a usable way for policy-makers and legislators, and should cling to the state-centred concept of sovereignty, constituting a necessary step to accept the reality of modern states that national legislatures are the primary means to attain favourable policy outcomes for all interest groups. The multiple sovereignties approach represented by many food sovereignty proponents obscures the significant breakthrough that could be achieved through the attempt to influence legislation and achieve advantageous legal provisions with the help of the state's legislative powers.

859 Hannah Wittman, 'Food Sovereignty: An Inclusive Model for Feeding the World and Cooling the Planet' (2023) 6 One Earth 474–478.

860 See, for example, an exception: A. Haroon Akram-Lodhi, 'Accelerating Towards Food Sovereignty' (2015) 36 Third World Quarterly 570.

861 Martin Milán Csirszki, Hajnalka Szinek Csütörtöki and Katarzyna Zombory, 'Food Sovereignty: Is There an Emerging Paradigm in V4 Countries for the Regulation of the Acquisition of Ownership of Agricultural Lands by Legal Persons?' (2021) 2 Central European Journal of Comparative Law 29–52; Martin Milán Csirszki, 'Is There Room for Food Sovereignty Considerations in EU Competition Policy? A Theoretical Framework' (2022) 18 Croatian Yearbook of European Law and Policy 83–106; Gabriela Pechlaner and Gerardo Otero, 'The Neoliberal Food Regime: Neoregulation and the New Division of Labor in North America' (2010) 75 Rural Sociology 179–208.

18 The compatibility of agricultural policy paradigms with competition policy schools of thought

After the introduction of the prevailing neoliberal paradigm and the food sovereignty paradigm in agricultural policy, this chapter studies their compatibility with the schools of thought in competition policy. To examine this, I rely on the objectives of competition, in particular antitrust law, which is a recurring theme among legislators, enforcers and theoreticians.

Simply put, I aim to discover which competition policy framework is the closest to the perceptions of food sovereignty on competition and its regulation. The analysis on food sovereignty in Chapter 17 provides a helping hand in discovering the paradigm's perceptions about competition. If I am aware of its standpoint towards competition, I can identify that competition school of thought which can be brought into line with the considerations of food sovereignty.

First, I share some general findings about antitrust law objectives, then I scrutinise the goals of the EU and US antitrust law, respectively.

18.1 Antitrust law objectives

Concerning the objectives, first, it is worth looking at competition policy in the agricultural sector from two different standpoints.

From the perspective of competition policy, the group of rules, analysed in Part IV, comprising the area of competition law (antitrust rules and rules beyond antitrust) applying to the agricultural sector is a sub-area of a broadly understood competition law, where social objectives in the form of distributional goals hand in hand with the protection of certain market participants sneak into the policy-making process. This results in adopting specific and exemption norms in favour of the market players of agriculture and the food supply chain who possess weak bargaining position and no market power. The inclusion of wealth transfers as a concern is none other than a value decision which competition policy-makers may or may not make[862] in favour of certain sectors, such as agriculture. Nevertheless, the general trend can be observed that – to a certain extent – both the US and the

862 Pinar Akman, *The Concept of Abuse in EU Competition Law: Law and Economic Approaches* (Hart Publishing 2012) 40.

DOI: 10.4324/9781003604747-23

EU provide for specific and exemption norms to handle the agricultural sector and the food supply chain specially.

From the perspective of agricultural policy, the group of rules, analysed in Part IV, is one part of the law where agricultural policy objectives influence and "hijack" the broadly understood competition laws, and these laws serve as an instrument to achieve agricultural policy objectives.[863]

The reason for briefly reviewing the objectives of antitrust law is that they have a crucial impact on the application and interpretation of antitrust laws,[864] thus they are also of paramount importance when speaking of sector-specific regulation. Debates on antitrust law goals are continuous, so much so that one must admit to the arbitrary nature of the question of what antitrust law objectives should be. It would be more exact to pose the question as what we want from markets and antitrust, considering that the answer to the former question "is typically given in terms of what the respondent – invariably an inside player who has already formed a normative view – believes the operational guiding principle should be."[865] This means that most of the positions on the goals of antitrust law are prejudicial because they are preliminarily determined by the respondent's own perceptions of what we aim to strengthen with the help of well-functioning markets.

Antitrust law objectives are rather dynamic and not static in nature.[866] In general, and based on *Akman*'s approach, two main groups of objectives can be identified: one group is connected to the notion of welfare, while the other to notions unrelated to efficiency.[867,868] While the former is dominated by economic considerations (in particular, by the considerations of welfare economics), the latter focuses also on considerations other than different types of welfare. For an even clearer clustering and simpler terminology, one may group antitrust law objectives to efficiency-based and non-efficiency-based goals. However, non-efficiency-based goals do not necessarily mean that efficiency is not taken into account during the enforcement of antitrust laws. For example, the antitrust goal of the protection of the competitive process, or – in other words – the protection of competition as such, does not imply

863 There are other areas of law, such as tax law and property law, where agricultural policy objectives have the same effect.

864 Deborah Healey, 'The Ambit of Competition Law: Comments on Its Goals' in Deborah Healey, Michael Jacobs and Rhonda L. Smith (eds), *Research Handbook on Methods and Models of Competition Law* (Edward Elgar 2020) 12.

865 Eleanor M. Fox, 'Against Goals' (2013) 81 Fordham Law Review 2159.

866 "The goals of competition law evolve over time." See: Roger Van den Bergh, 'The Goals of Competition Law' in Roger Van den Bergh, Peter Camesasca and Andrea Giannaccari (eds), *Comparative Competition Law and Economics* (Edward Elgar 2017) 88.

867 Akman (n 862) 25.

868 The dichotomy of competition law goals is divided into the "Freedom to Compete Approach" and the "More Economic Approach" by Martin Meier, 'Pleading for a "Multiple Goal Approach" in European Competition Law: Outline of a Conciliatory Path Between the "Freedom to Compete Approach" and the "More Economic Approach"' in Klaus Mathis and Avishalom Tor (eds), *New Developments in Competition Law and Economics* (Springer Nature 2019) 51–52.

that consumer welfare, understood as allocative efficiency,[869] is not and cannot be enhanced. "Protecting the competitive process is economically efficient."[870] Nonetheless, a complex assessment would require that not only the process but also the outcome be taken into account.[871]

In the last four decades, debates on the goals of antitrust law have taken a direction where voices echoing the triumph of enhancing efficiency prevail over non-efficiency-based concerns, such as fairness, the protection of competitive processes and the protection of individual economic freedom. The common question which – according to *Nihoul* – always arises in connection with the notion of efficiency is how to measure it: "[s]hould we aim at maximising consumer welfare? Producer welfare? Total welfare?"[872] The adoption of any of these economic welfare standards by enforcement authorities is of particular importance regarding the outcome of decisions.[873,874] Nevertheless, not all authors share the view that these standards are of paramount relevance to enforcement. The picture is nuanced by, for example, *Motta*: "consumer and total welfare standards would not often imply very different decisions by antitrust agencies and courts."[875]

We must not forget, however, that "no welfare test can eliminate the exercise of policy judgment in competition policy."[876] Both *Akman* and *Hovenkamp* acknowledge the importance and influential role of policy choices within antitrust law, be it about whether wealth transfers and social considerations should be taken into account, or whether consumer or total welfare standard should be employed by enforcement authorities. The choice on welfare standard expresses a certain value decision, for by committing ourselves to the total welfare standard one also leaves scope for considering the interests of groups other than consumers. The views of *Akman* and *Hovenkamp* are also consistent with *Fox*'s discussion about antitrust law objectives. *Fox* explicitly states that the goals of antitrust law depend on what one wants from markets and antitrust, thus it is a question of value decision and policy choice. It is convincing when three of the greatest and most renowned antitrust scholars of our time all recognise and acknowledge that antitrust law is – to a significant extent – guided by policy choices and value decisions which inevitably and indirectly have effect on enforcement priorities.

869 Consumer welfare is understood as allocative efficiency by, for example, Waked 2020, p. 88.

870 Anchustegui (n 98) 89.

871 Akman (n 862) 47.

872 Paul Nihoul, 'Choice vs Efficiency?' (2012) 3 Journal of European Competition Law & Practice 315.

873 Pieter Kalbfleisch, 'Aiming for Alliance: Competition Law and Consumer Welfare' (2011) 2 Journal of European Competition Law & Practice 111.

874 For a detailed analysis on the choice between the standard of consumer welfare and total welfare, see: Louis Kaplow, 'On the Choice of Welfare Standards in Competition Law' in Daniel Zimmer (ed), *The Goals of Competition Law* (Edward Elgar 2012) 3–26. In his study, Kaplow finds that "it is more efficient to confine competition law to the maximization of total welfare."

875 Massimo Motta, *Competition Policy: Theory and Practice* (CUP 2004) 19.

876 Herbert J. Hovenkamp, 'Is Antitrust's Consumer Welfare Principle Imperiled?' 45 The Journal of Corporation Law 104.

18.2 The objectives of EU antitrust law

EU antitrust law objectives vary widely.[877] A recent empirical study by *Stylianou and Iacovides* has found that EU competition law follows a multitude of goals and all seven objectives examined have existed from the 1960s until now. The authors call it a risky but not unsubstantiated finding that the competition law goals connected to the ordoliberal school of thought are continuously present; they also conclude that the protection of competition as such, that is, the protection of the competitive process, takes precedence over outcome considerations. Although with fluctuating intensity, the following objectives have been present since the 1960s: efficiency, welfare, the freedom of competition, maintaining market structure, fairness, the European integration and the competitive process.[878]

The ordoliberal impact on EU antitrust law is a heavily debated area, but the majority of authors argues for having such influence.[879] One of the most renowned scholars who argues against the ordoliberal effects on EU antitrust law is *Akman*.[880]

Given that ordoliberal competition policy originates in Germany, it is worth looking at some evolutionary phases of this school of thought in the country.

Since World War II, the dominant school of thought in German economic policy has been ordoliberalism, which finds its roots in Freiburg. Competition law scholars tend to identify ordoliberal competition policy strictly with the first generation of the Freiburg School,[881] but it should rather be perceived as a continuously changing notion which is settled in its constituting elements. Ordoliberalism has undeniably German roots[882] and "has proved singularly influential in shaping the social market economy of post-war Germany."[883] Before World War II, there was no chance for ordoliberalism to influence economic policy[884]; however – thanks to his strong connections with the Freiburg School – Ludwig Erhard's appointment to the position

877 Paul Craig and Gráinne de Búrca, *EU Law: Text, Cases, and Materials* (6th edn, OUP 2015) 1001.

878 Stylianou and Iacovides (n 558).

879 See, for example: David J. Gerber, 'Constitutionalizing the Economy: German Neo-Liberalism, Competition Law and the "New" Europe' (1994) 42 The American Journal of Comparative Law 69; Gerber (n 108) 264; Ignacio Herrera Anchustegui, 'Competition Law through an Ordoliberal Lens' (2015) 2 Oslo Law Review 139; Peter Behrens, 'The Ordoliberal Concept of "Abuse" of a Dominant Position and Its Impact on Article 102 TFEU' (2015) SSRN <https://papers.ssrn.com/sol3/papers.cfm?abstract_id=2658045> accessed 22 July 2023 29; Conor Talbot, 'Ordoliberalism and Balancing Competition Goals in the Development of the European Union' (2016) 61 The Antitrust Bulletin 264–289; Peter Nedergaard, 'The Ordoliberalisation of the European Union?' (2019) 42 Journal of European Integration 229; Peter van Wijck, 'Loyalty Rebates and the More Economic Approach to EU Competition Law' (2020) 17 European Competition Journal 1–17.

880 See: Akman (n 862).

881 Behrens (n 879).

882 Nedergaard (n 879) 215.

883 Malte Dold and Tim Krieger, 'The Ideological Use and Abuse of Freiburg's Ordoliberalism' (2021) 195 Public Choice 341–361.

884 Anthony Nicholls, 'The Other Germany: The "'Neo-Liberals'" in Roger J. Bullen, Hartmut Pogge von Strandmann and Antony B. Polonsky (eds), *Ideas Into Politics – Aspects of European History 1880–1950* (Croom Helm 1984) 171.

of the *Deutscher Wirtschaftsrat*'s[885] chairperson in January 1948 opened the door to ordoliberal views and ideas to be realised in economic and legal policy-making processes.[886] Actually, the intellectual framework of Germany's competition act (*GWB*) still in force[887] was built up by ordoliberal thinkers.[888]

When analysing ordoliberal competition policy, we must take into account that the literature is utterly rich in this respect, and I do not, and could not, aim to fully present this school of thought in general and its competition policy in particular. The Freiburg School, as the original collective of ordoliberals, defined itself in relation to liberalism by stating that "a free-market order is not simply what one would find if and where government is absent, [it is] a political-cultural product, based on a constitutional order that requires careful 'cultivation' for its maintenance and proper functioning."[889] It means that markets cannot determine a system of legal and ethical standards for themselves in order to fulfil their economic policy tasks.[890] In an obituary on *Walter Eucken*, *Leonhard Miksch*, another representative of the Freiburg School,[891] consistently distanced ordoliberalism from neoliberalism by stating that the economic theory for *Eucken* was only a means to design an order that would liberate humanist values from the threatening grip of chaotic, anarchist, collectivist and nihilist forces.[892] According to *Gerber*, *Miksch*'s mention of nihilist forces referred to neoliberalism in its pure Hayekian sense.[893]

The most authentic ordoliberal concept which accurately includes ordoliberal thoughts and ideas is the concept of social market economy with human beings at its centre.[894] However, the model of social market economy is not construed only in one way by different ordoliberal thinkers. For example, not only the concept of

885 In English: German Economic Council.

886 Sigrid Quack and Marie-Laure Djelic, 'Adaptation, Recombination and Reinforcement: The Story of Antitrust and Competition Law in Germany and Europe' (2005) <https://spire.sciencespo.fr/hdl:/2441/26l5o52m2c857apcgdgcplhr3h/resources/2005-djelic-quack-story-of-antitrust-and-competition-law-in-germany-and-europe.pdf> accessed 10 June 2023.

887 Gesetz gegen Wettbewerbsbeschränkungen.

888 Ben van Rompuy, *Economic Efficiency: The Sole Concern of Modern Antitrust Policy? Non-Efficiency Considerations Under Article 101 TFEU* (Kluwer Law International 2012) § 3.03.

889 Viktor J. Vanberg, 'Ordnungspolitik, the Freiburg School and the Reason of Rules' (2013) 15 Annals of the University of Bucharest/Political Science Series 26.

890 Christian Hecker, 'Soziale Marktwirtschaft und Soziale Gerechtigkeit: Mythos, Anspruch und Wirklichkeit' (2011) 12 Zeitschrift für Wirtschafts- und Unternehmensethik 272.

891 Walter Otto Ötsch, Stephan Pühringer and Katrin Hirte, *Netzwerke des Marktes: Ordoliberalismus als Politische Ökonomie* (Springer 2018) 1.

892 Leonhard Miksch, 'Walter Eucken' (1950) 4 Kyklos 279.

893 Gerber (n 108) 240.

894 Martin Dahl, 'Ordoliberal Roots of Ecological Market Economy' (2018) 11 Review of Economic & Business Studies 116.

Eucken[895] in several of its aspects differs from that of *Müller-Armack*,[896] but beyond these versions there are also different shades of the model.[897] This lack of consistency openly shows us that the concept is not an accurately elaborated economic model even at the theoretical level but rather "a cipher for a 'mélange' of socio-political ideas for a free and socially just society and some general rules of economic policy."[898]

The legal framework of social market economy is set up by an economic constitution laying down the principles necessary for markets to function efficiently based on socially protected values.[899] The content of economic constitution is best illustrated by its principles described by *Eucken*, which can be divided into two groups, taking into account that the elements of these two groups complement each other. Although these elements only make sense when applied in parallel at the same time, I only stress the competition-related ones. One group consists of the so-called constituting/structural[900] principles,[901] while the other one the regulating principles.[902,903] "Constitutive principles ensure the establishment of the competitive order [*Wettbewerbsordnung*], regulative principles its continuous functioning."[904] Of the constituting principles the most important one is freedom of contract which, however, can be limited for the sake of well-functioning competition – while of the regulating principles we must emphasise the containment of market power.[905]

The principle of the freedom of contract is highly relevant when speaking about unfair trading practices in the agricultural sector and the food supply chain, while the containment of market power is important because – in most cases – a certain degree of (relative or absolute) market power is necessary to perform unfair trading practices against suppliers. At least a certain extent of relative market power is needed to commit an unfair trading practice, which – from the supplier's (the

895 See Eucken's most famous article which gives us the best insights on his thoughts on competition: Walter Eucken, 'Die Wettbewerbsordnung und ihre Verwirklichung: Erster Teil über die Wirtschaftspolitik der Vergangenheit' (1949) 2 ORDO: Jahrbuch für die Ordnung von Wirtschaft und Gesellschaft 1–99.

896 The spiritual father of the model/concept of social market economy is *Alfred Müller-Armack*.

897 See also: Christian Watrin, 'The Principles of the Social Market Economy: Its Origins and Early History' (1979) 135 Zeitschrift für die gesamte Staatswissenschaft 405.

898 Nils Goldschmidt, 'Alfred Müller-Armack and Ludwig Erhard: Social Market Liberalism' (2012) Freiburger Diskussionspapiere zur Ordnungsökonomik 04/12, 1.

899 Sylvain Broyer, 'The Social Market Economy: Birth of an Economic Style' (1996) Wissenschaftszentrum Berlin für Sozialforschung: Discussion Paper 9.

900 The name 'structural principles' is used by Siegfried G. Karsten, 'The Social Market Economy and the Moral Problem in Modern Capitalism' (1990) 17 International Journal of Social Economics 27–35.

901 In German: *konstituierende Prinzipien*.

902 In German: *regulierende Prinzipien*.

903 Dirk Sauerland, 'Freiburger Schule' Gabler Wirtschaftslexikon <https://wirtschaftslexikon.gabler.de/definition/freiburger-schule-33210> accessed 30 June 2024.

904 Christian Ahlborn and Carsten Grave, 'Walter Eucken and Ordoliberalism: An Introduction from a Consumer Welfare Perspective' (2006) 2 Competition Policy International 203.

905 Ahlborn and Grave (n 904).

abused party's) perspective – in many cases results in the restriction of the principle of freedom of contract, more exactly in the restriction of the freedom to determine the content of the contract. That is, the respective supplier has no choice in determining the terms of the contract, of which he is one of the contracting parties. This comes from the fact that the buyer has relative market power vis-à-vis – and is in a superior bargaining position over – its supplier.

The goals of ordoliberal competition policy are, on the one hand, to protect individual economic freedom to compete, and, on the other hand, to protect competition as such.[906] *Akman* states in a not very positive tone that "for ordoliberals, efficiency is only a possible outcome of competition and not an aim. More importantly, the objective of protecting economic freedom may not always result in welfare-enhancing outcomes," that is, "pursuing economic freedom does not always coincide with consumer welfare, a competition policy that protects economic freedom may in certain circumstances lead to consumer harm."[907] That is, the goal of consumer welfare later presented among the objectives of US antitrust law and prevailing since the 1980s may not be – in some cases – reconciled with the ordoliberal goals.

By adopting an ordoliberal approach towards antitrust law objectives, in certain cases efficiency-based concerns can become secondary. Although ordoliberals are likely to achieve economic efficiency by realising and following the path of the goals of protecting economic freedom and competition as such, the latter ones also include the possibility to take into account non-efficiency-based considerations insofar as they contribute to the protection of economic freedom and of competition as such. It does not mean sacrificing economic efficiency on the altar of non-efficiency-based considerations but bearing in mind that in the middle and long term, exclusively following the path of economic efficiency may result in outcomes detrimental to competition. In the middle and long term, maintaining an economic system based on competition can only be realised by the direct protection of the competitive process and structure and by making competing possible for each and every market player. It has been criticised that it means the protection of (inefficient) competitors and not that of competition, but one must acknowledge that the competitive process and structure are easier to be protected when there are many competitors. If competition takes place among a lot of market players, it is more likely that economic power will not be concentrated in the hands of a few.

By aiming to achieve an increase in or at least the maintenance of the current level of economic efficiency, one may succeed in the short term, nevertheless fail in the middle and long term, if one does not take into account the competitive structure. Only a well-functioning competitive structure is able to produce efficiencies, and ignoring its significance for a long time for the sake of realising economic efficiency at all costs in the short term may result in such a structure which is not competitive anymore. One of the most prominent ordoliberal scholars of our

906 Anchustegui (n 98) 87.
907 Akman (n 862) 49 and 62.

time, *Wernhard Möschel*, also declares that economic efficiency is an indirect and derived goal of ordoliberal competition policy, contrary to "the protection of individual economic freedom of action," or viewed from the other side, contrary to "the restraint of undue economic power," which are direct goals and values.[908]

One of the most important notions of ordoliberalism, the competitive order (*Wettbewerbsordnung*) protected by the economic constitution, is "the key to a prosperous and humane society,"[909] and its essence is that the rules of the game are defined by the state. It means that "[b]usinesses are free to choose what they produce, what technology they use, what raw materials they purchase and what markets they wish to sell on,"[910] however they are bound by the framework set up by the state. It does not open up the possibility for the state to intervene in economic processes directly but it has the chance to establish the framework within which the competitive order can function.

The competitive order is dominantly characterised by the form of competition which ordoliberals call 'complete competition'. In short, complete competition means that "no corporate entity possess[es] the authority to coerce the action of others."[911] Of course, complete competition is not compatible with monopolies and oligopolies. While monopolies are unambiguously opposed by ordoliberals, the issue of oligopolies is a divisive question. The more relevant issue as to the agricultural and food sector is the latter one. As put by *Eucken*, there are two opposing ordoliberal views towards oligopolistic markets. The approach of stronger state intervention and of direct regulation on oligopolies was taken by *Leonhard Miksch*, while another group of thinkers were of the opinion that taking action only against monopolies was enough to prevent that oligopolies could evolve to monopolies, given that it was not worth it for a market participant of an oligopolistic market to aim to get to a monopolistic position, because then it would fall within the scope of antitrust law.[912] In my opinion, the latter approach is slightly naive considering the profit-oriented nature of market players, thus I'd rather follow and accept *Miksch*'s standpoint.

Although it does not exclusively refer to oligopolistic markets becoming monopolistic markets, the *OECD* declared in general that "[i]n recent years, there has been growing concern that a trend has emerged in which markets around the

908 Wernhard Möschel, 'Competition Policy from an Ordo Point of View' in Alan Peacock and Hans Willgerodt (eds), *German Neo-Liberals and the Social Market Economy* (Palgrave Macmillan 1989) 146.

909 Ahlborn and Grave (n 904) 199.

910 See the English translation of Eucken's seminal article: Walter Eucken, 'The Competitive Order and Its Implementation (English Translation)' (2006) 2 Competition Policy International 227.

911 Isabel Oakes and Anselm Küsters, 'Lessons from the Past? How Ordoliberal Competition Theory Can Address Market Power in the Digital Age' (2021) ProMarket <https://promarket.org/2021/11/14/ordoliberal-lessons-competition-tech-platforms-antitrust-germany/> accessed 21 October 2023. See also: Akman (n 862) 58.

912 Eucken (n 910) 244–245.

world are becoming more concentrated and less competitive."[913] It is hard to believe that already concentrated oligopolistic markets do not become more concentrated, as this general finding suggests, just because market players aim to distance themselves from getting to a monopolistic position because of the fear from antitrust law enforcement.

The tendency towards concentration and consolidation is evident especially in the agricultural and food sector, both in Europe[914] and in the United States.[915,916] As a consequence of these, it is more reasonable to follow *Miksch*'s approach which aims to supervise and deal with markets, already in their 'oligopoly' phase. According to *Miksch*, complete competition is achieved, and – in his view – this is the most important feature, when there are a large number of players in a given market.[917] Oligopolistic markets do not fulfil this requirement, therefore they fall under the notion of 'tied competition'[918] which calls for special regulation under state supervision,[919] or as put by *Goldschmidt*, for special competition laws.[920]

In conclusion and in general, the ordoliberal competition policy followed by German antitrust law is not deterred to regulate markets with legal means in order for the competitive structure and competition as such as well as the economic freedom of individuals to be maintained, ensured and preserved. It does not mean direct intervention in economic processes but establishing game rules according to which market players shall organise their economic activity. This approach is greatly aware of not only economic but also social anomalies deriving from markets abandoned by law and lacking legal regulation.

913 Organisation for Economic Co-operation and Development, 'Market Concentration' (2018) DAF/COMP/WD(2018)46, 3.

914 Philippe Chauve and An Renckens, 'The European Food Sector: Are Large Retailers a Competition Problem?' (2015) 6 Journal of European Competition Law & Practice 513.

915 See, for example: www.foodprocessing.com/articles/2021/market-concentration/. "Mary Hendrickson, a professor of rural sociology at the University of Missouri, agrees that antitrust enforcement policy shapes the pace of concentration in the food industry. She points out that vertical integration in the broiler industry – arrangements where processors supply chicks and feed to growers, who are contractually obligated to use them – was common by the 1960s, but it took until the 1980s for claims of unfairness and abuse to be heard. The difference, Hendrickson says, is that *the top four firms had only about 12% of the market in the 1970s; today, it's more than 50%.* With that situation, Hendrickson says, 'antitrust interpretations and enforcement changed greatly in the 1980s.'" [Emphasis put by the author.]

916 See also: Amy Trauger, 'Toward a Political Geography of Food Sovereignty: Transforming Territory, Exchange and Power in the Liberal Sovereign State' (2014) 41 The Journal of Peasant Studies 1133: "The commodification of food, in the second food regime, has resulted in the vertical integration and the concentration of power in a few very large firms [. . .]."; Furthermore: Andree, Ayres, Bosia and Massicotte (n 24) 34.

917 Leonhard Miksch, *Wettbewerb als Aufgabe: die Grundsätze einer Wettbewerbsordnung* (Kohlhammer Verlag 1937) 24.

918 In German: *gebundene Konkurrenz.*

919 Eucken (n 910) 244.

920 Nils Goldschmidt, 'Leonhard Miksch' Soziale Marktwirtschaft: Vordenker und Klassiker 81 <https://bit.ly/3Dnd0aq> accessed 21 October 2023.

By following ordoliberal competition policy, social aspects may be better and more easily implemented when applying the law, given that economic efficiency (the outcome) is not the only relevant factor for law enforcement to concentrate on, but also the process itself is given appropriate consideration. "[E]fficiency is an expected result of competition."[921] However, the greatest strength of ordoliberal competition policy is its willingness to regulate markets in case of market distortions which endanger the competitive structure: it is a suitable policy choice to bring forward the level of protection. This willingness to regulate stems from the holistic viewpoint of ordoliberalism: it acknowledges that markets cannot be dismantled to separate economic, social and political spheres, and markets cannot be limited to economic transactions. Markets as a complex whole inherently unify economic, social and political aspects, and they only make sense when examined comprehensively in an integrated model, such as in the notion of social market economy.

Though the antitrust law of the European Union has gone its own way, the consumer welfare paradigm of the Chicago School has also made an impact on EU antitrust law and policy.[922] Commencing with the statements of the European Commission in the late 1990s and appearing in a legally binding form in the 2004 Merger Regulation,[923] it has infiltrated the discourse on the goals of EU antitrust law as the more economic approach to European antitrust law.[924]

However, the polythematic nature of EU antitrust law has remained. It is summarised well in the holding of the *GlaxoSmithKline* case:

> there is nothing in that provision [Article 81 EC, then Article 101 TFEU] to indicate that only those agreements which deprive consumers of certain advantages may have an anti-competitive object. Secondly, it must be borne in mind that the Court has held that, like other competition rules laid down in the Treaty, Article 81 EC aims to protect not only the interests of competitors or of consumers, but also the structure of the market and, in so doing, competition as such.[925]

921 Akman (n 862) 60.

922 Anne C. Witt, 'The European Court of Justice and the More Economic Approach to EU Competition Law – Is the Tide Turning?' (2019) 64 The Antitrust Bulletin 172–213.

923 Christian Kirchner, 'Goals of Antitrust and Competition Law Revisited' in Dieter Schmidtchen, Max Albert and Stefan Voigt (eds), *The More Economic Approach to European Competition Law* (Mohr Siebeck 2007) 7.

924 See: Schmidtchen, Albert and Voigt (n 923); Roger van den Bergh, 'The More Economic Approach in European Competition Law: Is More Too Much or Not Enough?' in Mitja Kovač and Ann-Sophie Vandenberghe (eds), *Economic Evidence in EU Competition Law* (Intersentia 2016) 13–42; Anne C. Witt, *The More Economic Approach to EU Antitrust Law* (Hart Publishing 2016); Marta Zalewska-Głogowska, *The More Economic Approach under Article 102 TFEU* (Nomos Verlag 2017).

925 Joined cases C-501/06 P, C-513/06 P, C-515/06 P and C-519/06 P *GlaxoSmithKline Services Unlimited v Commission of the European Communities (C-501/06 P) and Commission of the European Communities v GlaxoSmithKline Services Unlimited (C-513/06 P) and European Association of Euro Pharmaceutical Companies (EAEPC) v Commission of the European Communities*

It is, therefore, clear that the market structure and the competitive process are also concerns in the European Union, when it comes to antitrust objectives.

One significant difference must be noted why the consumer welfare paradigm could not become dominant in the EU but could in the USA. The reform of antitrust law was initiated within the judiciary, in particular the Supreme Court in the United States, while in Europe the institution which first adopted and attempted to introduce the more economic approach (the European equivalent of the consumer welfare paradigm) was the European Commission.[926] Given that EU courts stand above the Commission from an enforcement perspective and the Court of Justice of the European Union makes the final judgments, EU courts are in a stronger position to determine their own approach and standpoint towards reform attempts. Moreover, only the Commission is bound by its notices. It does not mean that a trend did not start in the direction of more efficiency- and welfare-based enforcement, however "the freedom- and fairness-based definitions and concepts coined in the 1970s" have remained.[927]

All in all, still an inherent feature of EU antitrust law is that it pursues a multitude of goals and does not limit itself to efficiency-based considerations, thus leaving room for other priorities. EU antitrust law has been influenced both by the German ordoliberal school of thought and the consumer welfare paradigm coming from the United States.

18.3 The objectives of US antitrust law

The academic debate on the aims of antitrust law has a decades-long tradition in the United States. The antitrust law paradigms appearing in the United States have been to a certain extent adopted almost everywhere, with some delays. The literature on US antitrust goals is so immense that my analysis can only be arbitrary concerning the chosen academic works. However, I strive for diversity.

In connection with the Sherman Act and the goals of antitrust, we must start with one of the most, if not the most, influential antitrust lawyers in the United States, namely Robert Bork, a leading figure of the Chicago School. A major breakthrough and a totally different approach towards antitrust was brought to the fore by his article titled *Legislative Intent and the Policy of the Sherman Act*.[928] In this writing, Bork examined the controversies around the Sherman Act, and he concluded with the following:

> My conclusion, drawn from the evidence in the Congressional Record, is that Congress intended the courts to implement (that is, to take into account in the

---

(C-515/06 P) and Asociación de exportadores españoles de productos farmacéuticos (Aseprofar) v Commission of the European Communities [2009] EU:C:2009:610, para 63.

926 Witt (n 922) 173.

927 Witt (n 922) 212.

928 Robert H. Bork, 'Legislative Intent and the Policy of the Sherman Act' (1966) 9 Journal of Law & Economics 7–48.

> decision of cases) only that value we would today call consumer welfare. To put it another way, the policy the courts were intended to apply is the maximization of wealth or consumer want satisfaction.[929]

The die has been cast: it was that moment which brought to light the goal of consumer welfare in antitrust policy. Bork's extremism lies in the fact that he thought of consumer welfare as the one and only objective antitrust should follow.

> In Bork's critique, it seemed an antitrust law driven by anything but consumer welfare was the law of the libertine, degenerate and debauched. Economic analysis was now righteous and self-restrained. As such, Bork managed to embed the culture war into one's method of interpreting the Sherman Act.[930]

Although debates surrounded his views from the 1960s to the 1980s,[931] opposing voices have calmed down in the last four decades to return more intensively in the 2020s with the appearance of the Neo-Brandeisians. As Hovenkamp writes in 2008: "Few people dispute that antitrust's core mission is protecting consumers' right to the low prices, innovation, and diverse production that competition promises."[932]

The paradigm of consumer welfare has been adopted not only by US antitrust enforcement authorities, but also it has penetrated the discourse on the goals of EU competition law.[933] The days of a more economic approach have come to the

929 Bork (n 928) 7.

930 Tim Wu, *The Curse of Bigness: Antitrust in the New Gilded Age* (Columbia Global Reports 2018).

931 Barak Y. Orbach, 'The Antitrust Consumer Welfare Paradox' (2010) 7 Journal of Competition Law & Economics 133–164.

932 Herbert Hovenkamp, *The Antitrust Enterprise: Principle and Execution* (Harvard University Press 2008) 1–2.

933 See, for example: Alberto Pera and Vito Auricchio, 'Consumer Welfare, Standard of Proof and the Objectives of Competition Policy' (2005) 1 European Competition Journal 153–177; Liza Lovdahl Gormsen, 'The Conflict between Economic Freedom and Consumer Welfare in the Modernisation of Article 82 EC' (2007) 3 European Competition Journal 329–344; Pinar Akman, '"Consumer Welfare" and Article 82EC: Practice and Rhetoric' (2009) 32 World Competition 71–90; Anca Daniela Chirita, 'Undistorted, (Un)fair Competition, Consumer Welfare and the Interpretation of Article 102 TFEU' (2010) 33 World Competition 417–436; Roger Zäch and Adrian Künzler, 'Freedom to Compete or Consumer Welfare: The Goal of Competition Law According to Constitutional Law' in Roger Zäch, Andreas Heinemann and Andreas Kellerhals (eds), *The Development of Competition Law: Global Perspectives* (Edward Elgar 2010) 61–86; Kaplow (n 874); Matteo Negrinotti, 'The Single Market Imperative and Consumer Welfare: Irreconcilable Goals? Exploring the Tensions Amongst the Objectives of European Competition Law Through the Lens of Parallel Trade in Pharmaceuticals' in Daniel Zimmer (ed), *The Goals of Competition Law* (Edward Elgar 2012) 295–337; Victoria Daskalova, 'Consumer Welfare in EU Competition Law: What Is It (Not) About?' (2015) 11 The Competition Law Review 131–160; Kevin Coates and Dirk Middelschulte, 'Getting Consumer Welfare Right: The Competition Law Implications of Market-Driven Sustainability Initiatives' (2019) 15 European Competition Journal 318–326; Frédéric Marty, 'Is the Consumer Welfare Obsolete? A European Union Competition Law Perspective' (2020) GREDEG Working Papers 13.

world of US antitrust law and, with some delay, of EU competition law.[934] The more economic approach is connected to the notion of consumer welfare through the fact that consumer welfare is borrowed from the vocabulary of economics, and its measurement is based on consumer surplus. However, it is unclear whether consumer welfare only includes the maximisation of consumers' surplus, or whether it also aims to include the maximisation of producers' surplus.

According to *Hovenkamp*,

> Bork did not use the term "consumer welfare" in the same way that most people use it today. For Bork, "consumer welfare" referred to the sum of the welfare, or surplus, enjoyed by both consumers and producers. . . . A large part of the welfare that emerges from Bork's model accrues to producers rather than consumers.[935]

Nevertheless, one thing is certain: the aim of introducing the concept to antitrust law has not resulted in the expected outcomes with regard to legal certainty and clarity.[936]

This short outlook to the legislative intent of the Sherman Act in the interpretation of Robert Bork is necessary because it has implications beyond itself, and it started a revolution in US antitrust law and, later, in EU competition law. It makes a difference whether one considers consumer welfare as the sole objective of antitrust law or whether one also formulates other objectives that one wants antitrust law to achieve. The narrow interpretation of antitrust law which only contributes to the generating of consumer surplus may have serious side effects on competition in agri-food markets. It determines not only the depth and extent of intervention but also the roles one expects the agricultural sector to play in the economy. A commitment to a narrow interpretation of antitrust law has far-reaching implications for agricultural producers as a whole which is dominated by social concerns.

As regards US antitrust eras, a good starting point is provided by *Barak Orbach* who distinguishes five periods which "began and ended gradually" and not in "sharp turns."[937] These eras mark quite informative aspects on antitrust goals, and more generally, on the then prevailing antitrust policy. The formative era between 1890 and 1911 was the period of developing general standards, the most important of which was that the Sherman Act "prohibits only unreasonable restraints of trade, not all restraints."[938] In the second era from 1911 to 1935 the scope of antitrust was narrowed by developing reasonableness standards, and more than half of the Supreme Court justices as representatives of laissez-faire constitutionalism considered antitrust "a threat to economic liberties." Moreover, in the spirit of

934 See: Witt (n 924).
935 Hovenkamp (n 876).
936 Daskalova (n 933).
937 Barak Orbach, 'The Present New Antitrust Era' (2018) 60 William & Mary Law Review 1444.
938 Orbach (n 937) 1445–1446.

distinguishing "between constructive and destructive collaborations among competitors" the rule of reason standard was developed.[939] The third period, the fairness era, lasted for four decades from 1935 to 1975. The then prevailing economic theories linked market structure with competition. "[H]ostile toward defendants and enforced aggressively," antitrust law was guided by the premises

> that large businesses and vertical arrangements tend to exclude competition, that horizontal market arrangements tend to be collusive, that intellectual property rights convey monopoly power, and that the corporate form defines the boundaries of economic units.[940]

The fourth era, which is still dominant today, came to the fore in 1975. It is to a significant extent connected with the appearance of the Chicago School in antitrust. *Orbach* marvellously summarises the changes taking place in this period:

> Since the mid-1970s, the Supreme Court has persistently narrowed the substantive scope of antitrust law, adopting procedural barriers, and dismantling doctrines associated with the fairness vision. Among other things, the Court moved from glorification to skepticism of the effectiveness of antitrust enforcement, emphasizing concerns regarding the costs of false positives; replaced per se rules with the rule of reason; abandoned exaggerated concerns about exclusionary practices in favor of skepticism of the viability of exclusionary conduct; reversed judicial premises regarding the competitive effects of unilateral conduct and vertical restraints; overruled the intraenterprise conspiracy doctrine; withdrew from the premise that intellectual property rights convey market power; reinterpreted the implied immunity doctrine to trim the reach of antitrust law; and piled up procedural standards that are favorable to antitrust defendants.[941]

As can be seen from *Orbach*'s analysis, the intensity of antitrust enforcement shows cyclical changes: while the first and third era were characterised by strong law enforcement, the second and fourth ones (the two rule of reason eras) were characterised by reluctance to vivid and severe enforcement of laws.

Since the 1978 publication of Robert Bork's *The Antitrust Paradox*, consumer welfare in the US has become "the only articulated goal of antitrust law" and "the governing standard."[942] Though the years have passed, the clear-cut breakthrough has fallen short of consumer welfare and the more economic approach expected in

939 Orbach (n 937) 1449.
940 Orbach (n 937) 1452.
941 Orbach (n 937) 1456.
942 Orbach (n 937) 133.

the aspect of legal certainty and clarity, and this has been voiced in both Europe[943] and the US.[944]

Recently, four decades after its introduction, critics of consumer welfare have become increasingly vocal, and in the words of *Mark Glick*, the "winds of change are blowing,"[945] meaning that "the relative stability of the antitrust consensus has yielded to a sharp rupture."[946] As *Crane* put it: "[i]n the last two years, the self-styled neo-Brandeis movement has emerged out of virtually nowhere to claim a position at the bargaining table over antitrust reform and the future of the antitrust enterprise."[947] The premonition is best exemplified in the United States by the appointment of *Lina Khan* as the chairperson of the Federal Trade Commission.[948] Of course, the appearance of the Neo-Brandeisians – the emerging school of thought which intensively criticises the consumer welfare paradigm – has not been without reaction, and these new "hipster antitrust"[949] proponents are criticised because of their provocative proposals for changes to the antitrust regime directed by the sole objective of consumer welfare, arguing that the proposals lack little to no empirical evidence.[950] At the same time, neither have consumer welfare advocates escaped strong criticism. Some have even called antitrust law based on consumer welfare profound nonsense by arguing that it is built upon "false history, false concepts and false economics."[951]

It would, however, be wrong to identify the last four decades of US antitrust with the exclusive and general acceptance of early Chicago School premises. Even those who try to embed US antitrust enforcement in economic analysis criticise many aspects of 'Chicago economics'. Economic literature has presented compelling

943 See, for example: Daskalova (n 933). She calls it "shocking" that the meaning of consumer welfare is still unclear more than ten years after its adoption in the EU.

944 See, for example: Orbach (n 931): "This article chronicles how academic confusion and thoughtless judicial borrowing led to the rise of a label that 30 years later *has no clear meaning*."

945 Mark Glick, 'American Gothic: How Chicago Economics Distorts "Consumer Welfare" in Antitrust' (2019) SSRN <https://papers.ssrn.com/sol3/papers.cfm?abstract_id=3423081> accessed 24 June 2023.

946 Lina Khan, 'The End of Antitrust History Revisited' (2020) 133 Harvard Law Review 1656.

947 Daniel A. Crane, 'How Much Brandeis Do the Neo-Brandeisians Want?' (2019) 64 The Antitrust Bulletin 531.

948 Lina Khan is one of the most known advocates of the Neo-Brandeis or New Brandeis School. See, for example: Lina Khan, 'The New Brandeis Movement: America's Antimonopoly Debate' (2018) 9 Journal of European Competition Law & Practice 131–132. See also the book of another prominent advocate: Wu (n 930).

949 The labels 'Hipster Antitrust', 'New Brandeisians' or 'Neo-Brandeisians' could be interpreted as judgmental. See: Seth B. Sacher and John M. Yun, 'Some Reactions to "Reactionary Antitrust"' (2020) 4 Concurrences.

950 Joshua D. Wright, Elyse Dorsey, Jonathan Klick and Jan M. Rybnicek, 'Requiem for a Paradox: The Dubious Rise and Inevitable Fall of Hipster Antitrust' (2019) 51 Arizona State Law Journal 314. For more criticism, see: Christopher S. Yoo, 'Hipster Antitrust: New Bottles, Same Old W(h)ine?' (2018) All Faculty Scholarship <https://scholarship.law.upenn.edu/faculty_scholarship/2168/> accessed 14 January 2024.

951 Sandeep Vaheesan, 'The Profound Nonsense of Consumer Welfare Antitrust' (2019) 64 The Antitrust Bulletin 494.

evidence against the self-correcting nature of markets. The economic analysis in antitrust cannot be equated with the ideology of antitrust laws' underenforcement, as many Chicagoans tend to do. This has resulted in rising inequality. Economics cannot be used arbitrarily, only when anti-enforcement is tried to be justified. In many cases it also delivers an answer in favour of strong enforcement because of anticompetitive conduct. This has been often ignored by the Chicago School in the spirit of "opportunistic economics."[952]

One thing is certain in the United States: currently there is an overlapping period[953] between the second rule of reason era characterised by highly moderate antitrust enforcement and an era in which fairness considerations are given more significance.

It is beyond doubt that some changes are taking place. The Neo-Brandeisian contestation of the consumer welfare paradigm, however, suffers from the same problem, as the consumer welfare paradigm experienced in the EU. The paradigm change in US antitrust policy has come to the fore at the level of enforcement agencies, and not at the highest decision-making institution, the Supreme Court. This results in much less influence than the paradigm change of the 1980s when the Supreme Court was the main innovator in antitrust policy.

18.4 Interim conclusions

Antitrust law objectives are important determining factors with regard to the functioning of markets. The right question posed should be what we want from markets and antitrust law. One must acknowledge and recognise the subjective nature of antitrust law objectives, that is to say, that they depend to a significant extent on those public actors who determine them. Goals are undeniably policy questions and value decisions. It is difficult, if not impossible, to take a neutral standpoint. The dividing line between the EU and US approach toward competition and competition policy may have deeper philosophical roots. As put by *Scruton*, the Europeans do not reject market solutions but "pay more attention than their American counterparts to the things that make markets possible: to law, tradition and the moral life."[954]

I am of the opinion that the resistance of antitrust law legislation and enforcement to broader objectives was only credible until the increasing emphasis on sustainability objectives within the framework of antitrust proved that antitrust can focus on and thematise what it wants. For example, environmental sustainability has become a catchword so emphasised in the academic and political discourse on antitrust that more and more amendments to antitrust laws and guidelines are adopted to open the door for taking into consideration sustainability objectives

952 Herbert Hovenkamp and Fiona Scott Morton, 'Framing the Chicago School of Antitrust Analysis' (2020) 168 University of Pennsylvania Law Review 1852.

953 Orbach (n 937) 1463.

954 Roger Scruton, *Green Philosophy: How to Think Seriously about the Planet* (Atlantic Books 2011).

in antitrust law and enforcement.[955] The EU Commission is, too, committed to a more sustainable competition law.[956] The rules of the CMO Regulation, analysed in Chapters 12 and 13, have also been complemented recently with Article 210a which exempts both vertical and horizontal agreements from the prohibition of anticompetitive agreements in case they aim to apply a sustainability standard higher than mandated by Union or national law.[957]

To sum up, it has become apparent once again that antitrust and competition policy and law – if the political and legislative will exists – can contribute to the attainment of objectives other than economic efficiency. If it wants to, it can step out of the narrow paradigm based on consumer welfare. The complete ignorance of efficiency-based considerations is not required, however, a more sensitive balancing between competing interests and objectives is. This is particularly true for the EU.

Based on the analysis of the competition schools of thought, I find that, at a theoretical level, ordoliberal competition policy is much more capable to display those elements in competition-related regulation which food sovereignty considers indispensable in order to attain its objectives.

It results that in the last Part of the book I work with ordoliberal competition policy and the EU which has significantly been influenced by ordoliberal competition policy. That is why, furthermore, in Part VI, I aim to trace the standpoint of ordoliberalism on agriculture, on one hand, and harmonise two apparently conflicting notions (ordoliberalism and food sovereignty), on the other hand. With the harmonisation, I aim to provide an understanding of sovereignty in the notion of food sovereignty since the critique has come forth that it is undertheorised.[958] The attempt to bring into conformity ordoliberalism and food sovereignty is theoretical. Ordoliberalism is chosen as an orientating point for food sovereignty because of the competition policy represented by it: ordoliberalism, through its economic model of social market economy, leaves room for a multidimensional assessment

955 See, for example, the exemption of Austrian antitrust law: Viktoria H.S.E. Robertson, 'Sustainability: A World-First Green Exemption in Austrian Competition Law' (2022) 13 Journal of European Competition Law & Practice 426–434. Nevertheless, it is not true that Austria was the first to adopt a green exemption in antitrust law. In the Hungarian competition act still in force and adopted in 1996, from the outset there is an exemption possibility under the prohibition of anticompetitive agreements, if the respective agreement contributes to the amelioration of the environmental situation. See the guidelines adopted by the Dutch competition authority for sustainability agreements [https://bit.ly/369d2XL (Accessed: 13 March 2022)] and the legal memo titled "What is meant by a fair share for consumers in article 101(3) TFEU in a sustainability context?" [https://bit.ly/3q08LwV (Accessed: 13 March 2022)]. See also: Hungarian Competition Authority, 'Sustainable Development and Competition Law' (2021).

956 Jurgita Malinauskaite, 'Competition Law and Sustainability: EU and National Perspectives' (2022) 13 Journal of European Competition Law & Practice 336–348.

957 See: CMO Regulation, art 210a(1).

958 Sam Grey and Raj Patel, 'Food Sovereignty as Decolonization: Some Contributions from Indigenous Movements to Food System and Development Politics' (2015) 32 Agriculture and Human Values 432.

of competition-related conducts which may be better suited to optimise competition regulation in agri-food markets.

By examining the different viewpoints towards antitrust law objectives, I conclude that the consumer welfare paradigm as the exclusive aim of antitrust, as was followed in the United States for four decades, is not suitable to take into account the special characteristics of the agricultural sector. If antitrust enforcement exclusively concentrates on consumer harm and only aims to increase consumer surplus, vulnerable market players of the food supply chain, in particular agricultural producers, do not compete in such market circumstances within the framework of which they could be able to compete appropriately and efficiently. It does not mean the protection of weak competitors and market players but that of the market structure, competition as such, and the individual economic freedom to compete.

Ordoliberal competition policy can provide such theoretical framework that follows antitrust law objectives appropriate to – indirectly – give protection to agricultural producers. That is, agricultural producers and primary agricultural production are not protected directly from competition but indirectly through the means of adopting ordoliberal antitrust law objectives. Antitrust legislation in the spirit of ordoliberal competition policy makes it possible to adopt the rules of the game in such a manner that certain economic sectors are given specific consideration in light of their specific needs. It means that, on the one hand, legislation takes the standpoint that retaining the competitive structure of certain economic sectors requires special laws, and, on the other hand, even the enforcement of general provisions takes place in a way that makes authorities not limit themselves to a single-factor perspective. They not only consider the change in consumer welfare but take a holistic strategy by handling market structure, the competitive process and the individual economic freedom to compete as objectives worth pursuing for the sake of maintaining competition.

The single-factor economic efficiency approach towards antitrust law in the form of formulating consumer welfare as the exclusive goal takes into account only short-term results resulting in consumer surplus which, simply put, means lower prices to consumers. At the same time, constructing a competition law regime with a broader variety of goals, such as the ordoliberal notions of the protection of the competitive process and of individual economic freedom, goes hand in hand with a more far-reaching standpoint which also respects middle- and long-term results. The dominant US antitrust approach over the past 40 years belongs to the former, while the EU's broader, multipurpose approach belongs to the latter. This is why I aim to conceptualise and theorise food sovereignty within the EU competition policy discourse. However, before that, it is worthwhile to take a brief look at the approach of ordoliberalism towards agriculture.

19 Agriculture from an ordoliberal viewpoint[959]

Although it is a common misconception that ordoliberalism is strictly associated with the first generation of ordoliberal thinkers from the Freiburg School,[960] it may nevertheless be an appropriate starting point when one aims to analyse an issue from an ordoliberal viewpoint. Obviously, ordoliberalism is constantly changing and evolving, and we cannot ignore looking at it using a dynamic approach, but core concepts represented by first-generation ordoliberals are useful benchmark tools. The mainstream and most famous ordoliberal thinkers did not pay particular attention to agricultural issues, but there was one economist whose writings include far-sighted considerations for agriculture. This is *Wilhelm Röpke* who was called "something of an agrarian" by *Friedman*.[961] Röpke was not only an economist but also a prominent philosophical thinker who wanted to adopt a systemic approach. I do not claim that *Röpke*'s thoughts on agriculture can be equated with those of mainstream ordoliberals or, in general, with the basic and insurmountable findings and assumptions of ordoliberalism, but these may be considered when trying to provide an image of such a peripheral issue as agriculture from an ordoliberal standpoint.

Röpke, in his book entitled *International Economic Disintegration*, acknowledges the special features of agriculture. The 'singular character' of agriculture comes from its strong interrelations with nature. The processes of agricultural production are embedded in a system where natural factors are decisive. *Röpke* lists several distinctive characteristics of agriculture which contribute to its peculiar

959 This chapter is based on Martin Milán Csirszki, 'Is There Room for Food Sovereignty Considerations in EU Competition Policy? A Theoretical Framework' (2022) 18 Croatian Yearbook of European Law and Policy 83–106.

960 For example, see the critique formulated by Behrens (n 882). His critique is aimed at *Pinar Akman* and *David J. Gerber*. *Akman* rejects the ordoliberal impact on EU competition law, while *Gerber* limits the ordoliberal school of thought to the Freiburg School.

961 Amity Shlaes, 'The Foreigners Buchanan Calls His Own' (29 February 1996) The Wall Street Journal cited by Samuel Gregg, *Wilhelm Röpke's Political Economy* (Edward Elgar 2010) 2.

DOI: 10.4324/9781003604747-24

nature in contrast with industrial production. He emphasises and lists why agriculture is a special sector of economic life:

> the limits set to mechanization, division of labour and use of machinery; the constant need of soil preservation by a complex combination of measures; the everpresent tendency toward diminishing returns; the irregularity and precariousness of its output; the unchangeable rhythm of seasonal or longer production periods; the difficulties of storage; the usefulness of combining different lines of agricultural production horizontally or vertically; and the tendency toward a lower optimum size of the unit of production than exists generally in industry.[962]

Besides *Röpke*, we can also turn our attention to an internationally less known ordoliberal thinker who was a polymath: *Constantin von Dietze*. He was an agronomist, lawyer, economist and theologian; thus he represented a rich and holistic viewpoint. The translated title of one of his most relevant works is *Agriculture and Competition Order*.[963]

After presenting the differences between agriculture and industry, *von Dietze* submits that farmers are also overwhelmingly driven by profit maximisation.[964] Nevertheless, antedating the EU's approach which provides exemption from the general cartel prohibition for the agricultural sector and harmonising his thoughts with those of *Röpke*, he finds with regard to horizontal agreements that the completeness of the competition cannot be ruled out even by agreements between dozens or hundreds of agricultural suppliers because of the great number of competing farmers. He also considers the entire agricultural sector as a prime example of the realisation of the conditions of complete competition.[965] In *von Dietze*'s opinion, and I must add that these are timeless anomalies related to agricultural production and that is why I mention them, after the prosperous decades from 1820s to 1870s, several problems arose which carried negative effects on the agricultural sector: the rural exodus resulting in fewer and fewer agricultural workers, urbanisation, price fluctuations, as well as monopolisation. The agricultural sector felt that the monopolisation that was taking place in other sectors of the economy through powerful mergers was disadvantageous for its profession, which remained in complete competition. Thus, towards the end of the 19th century, plans were made and efforts exerted almost all over the world to oppose the traders or industrial monopolies with equally strong associations, i.e., to monopolise the supply of important agricultural products as well.[966] What *von Dietze* established 80 years

962 Wilhelm Röpke, *International Economic Disintegration* (William Hodge and Company 1942) 111–112.

963 Constantin von Dietze, 'Landwirtschaft und Wettbewerbsordnung' (1942) 66 Schmollers Jahrbuch 129–157.

964 Von Dietze (n 963) 132.

965 Von Dietze (n 963) 133.

966 Von Dietze (n 963) 140. See, for example, the previously mentioned Granger movement and the *Kornhausbewegung*. See more: Wilhelm Castendyck, *Die Entwicklung der Kornhausbewegung, mit Besonderer Berücksichtigung der Preussischen und der Bayerischen Verhältnisse* (Forgotten Books 2018).

ago is still true today: market actors downstream in the supply chain, such as the market operators of the processing industry and the retail chains, have a negative impact on the pricing of raw materials to the disadvantage of primary agricultural producers.[967] Or, conversely, suppliers of agricultural products face serious challenges because of the significant imbalances in bargaining power, and, as a result, unfair trading practices against them are a common occurrence. *Von Dietze* saw the future of family farming (and, in general, that of agriculture), as well as the preservation of its rural character, in adopting an economic policy according to the constituting and regulating principles of the ordoliberal notion of competitive order (*Wettbewerbsordnung*).[968] The realisation of a competitive order goes not only against the monopolistic and oligopolistic trends taking place downstream in the food supply chain at the level of processing and retailing but also stands up for freedom of contract which should not be used in the competitive order to create dependencies between market players because these dependencies may result in unfair trading practices against agricultural producers.

That is to say, the ordoliberal approach justifies the additional intervention beyond antitrust.

Takeaway 11

Of the existing competition schools of thought, I find that the spirit of ordoliberalism is the closest to fulfilling the demands of the food sovereignty paradigm. The approach of ordoliberal competition policy in general as well as towards the agricultural sector in particular makes it compatible with the perceptions of food sovereignty about competition and sustainability. As a consequence of the European Union having been heavily influenced by ordoliberal competition policy, in contrast with the United States, my proposals are adjusted to the EU.

967 Castendyck (n 966) 147.
968 Castendyck (n 966) 156.

Part VI

Finale

My hypothesis was that the prevailing and mainstream paradigm in economic, and in particular competition, policy as well as the broader neoliberal idea and model of market organisation dominating in the last four decades had reached their limits as regards the agricultural sector, meaning that the regulatory approach these paradigms offer to the sector cannot contribute better to the attainment of (post-) exceptionalist agricultural policy objectives, including that of sustainability.

Based on the previous analysis, my position is that the hypothesis is justified. However, there is a further remark of utter importance that must be made, which gives a much more nuanced stance on the issue. As demonstrated, in the jurisdictions examined (in the Global North) the dominant neoliberal economic paradigm does take into consideration the special characteristics of agricultural production, so the accusation by the advocates of food sovereignty movements that the sector is left to the vagaries of unbridled competition is inaccurate. The legal framework can be developed, but the changes deemed necessary from the standpoint of food sovereignty proponents would be beyond the borders of the prevailing policy paradigm. The demands of food sovereignty movements as regards competition and enhancing sustainability based on cooperation-centred private initiatives would – to a significant extent – stretch the framework of both the EU and the US towards these issues. They would do so, because – as will be seen in my proposals in the context of the EU in Chapter 22 – viable reforms could only be carried out as regards those two pillars of antitrust (abuse of dominance and merger control) which have no sector-specific rules. These antitrust pillars have been influenced most intensively by the considerations of the Chicago School and the efficiency-centred approach, which have been found at odds with food sovereignty expectations. With the food sovereignty-based proposals, I attempt to make ordoliberal competition policy return to its sector-sensitive origins in these regards, as it appeared in the works of Röpke and von Dietze.

As seen, the EU standpoint is much more suitable to include these new considerations coming from the alternate food sovereignty paradigm, laying the groundwork for how, in the following, I work with a focus on the system of the EU. Not only is the prevailing competition school of thought of the European Union, i.e., ordoliberalism, closer to the perceptions of food sovereignty, but so is its agricultural policy that is based on the model of multifunctional agriculture. Furthermore,

DOI: 10.4324/9781003604747-25

as seen in connection with private sustainability initiatives in the agri-food supply chain, the EU attitude towards regulation derives from the mistrust of uncontrolled economic activities, as well as from the feeling of necessity to show the pathway for undertakings.

Though the United States puts much more trust in free markets delivering appropriate outcomes, the agricultural sector enjoys some concessions in competition-related regulation, derogating from general rules. However, US legislators have not felt the need to designate a bespoke legal framework for the assessment of private sustainability initiatives, nor to intervene in *all* subsectors of agriculture in a general way. Beyond antitrust, there are *a few* agricultural subsectors where additional protection is provided to farmers, but these are limited in number (livestock, meat and poultry; perishable commodities) and can be explained by the competitive conditions (very high concentration of meat-packing markets) and special characteristics of the respective subsector (limited marketing alternatives of perishables, for example, after the late rejection of taking over the produce).

What is of utter importance that the neoliberal economic turn in the 1980s and its concurrent repercussions for agricultural policy within global institutions have not resulted, and have not brought with themselves, is that the competition-related rules (antitrust and beyond) of the sector for the protection of producers would have been eliminated. Quite the contrary, more and more protective pillars for agricultural producers have been introduced in the competitive process, such as the prohibition of unfair trading practices or extending the scope of exemption from the prohibition of anticompetitive agreements in the EU.

This shows that the dominant policy paradigm of the last four decades has not resulted in corresponding legal implications. The direction of policy developments, in light of communicated policy objectives, should have pointed towards less legal intervention in agri-food markets. This has not happened. On the contrary: an ever-extending protection has been provided to the agricultural sector as regards the competitive process. Agricultural subsidies are far less distorting now, but when it comes to the relations between market players (and not between the state and producers), legal intervention has intensified for the protection of producers. Direct help through the means of (coupled) agricultural subsidies, which caused harmful oversupply and unsustainable agricultural policy budgets, was ceased. However, legislation has turned its attention to other ways of supporting the producers, such as the intensifying efforts to balance the bargaining power between producers and their buyers, which sacrificed the purely economic considerations of the neoliberal market idea.

However, problems voiced by producers still remain, which can be explained, on the one hand, by the ever-increasing concentration of buyer markets (processing, wholesale, retail) in the same time span. On the other hand, all legislators and policy-makers should be aware that the kind of direct wealth transfers from middlemen to producers cannot be achieved by antitrust and competition-related regulations to such a significant extent as is expected by these laws. Rules in connection with the competitive process and bargaining conditions can be made stricter for the protection of producers to correct some flaws. I look at these possibilities, because the contesting food sovereignty paradigm, despite the several sector-specific protective pillars, still demands more tightened competition-related rules than at present. These would certainly have an impact, but in realising the primary objective of agricultural policy (raising farm income) they are indirect and complementary means.

Stakeholders should, however, turn their attention to other public policy areas to cure the problems of agriculture. Since the agricultural and food system is utterly complex, this would require, in my opinion, a complex approach to solve these issues with the inclusion of all concerned disciplines and their experts. The theoretical framework for this begs another book.

That competition policy does not provide primary means to achieving sustainability objectives is even more evident. Post-exceptionalist agricultural policy places greater emphasis on environmental problems than the earlier exceptionalist framework. As seen, however, the US antitrust approach towards sustainability is of non-interventionist nature. Though the EU has reacted to better integrate sustainability objectives into its competition framework, and has even derogated (and weakened) its general approach to take into account agriculture-specific characteristics by creating sectoral rules for agricultural market players, this has marginal impact on increasing sustainability. Other public policies are more suitable to contribute to sustainability, therefore in the following I do not formulate any reform proposals in this regard. It may sound strange, but adopting specific antitrust assessment criteria for the agricultural sector's sustainability agreements has been a gesture for producers, but real breakthrough will not be achieved by this. Competition policy has not been the obstacle to create a more sustainable agricultural sector.

20 General conclusions

Agri-food markets are governed differently from other sectors. Competition policy providing direction for agri-food markets is not limited to antitrust law but also leaves room for other regulatory means. In other words, agri-food markets are influenced and controlled by both antitrust and regulation. This is manifest both in the European Union and the United States. The dual nature of regulating competition in agri-food markets is primarily based on the policy choice and value decision that agricultural producers deserve additional protection in order for a fair standard of living to be ensured for them and their individual earnings to be increased. From the viewpoint of the primary means of competition policy, that is from the viewpoint of antitrust, this policy choice is deemed inefficient in several cases. Trade regulation rules, such as the prohibition of unfair trading practices, cannot be justified with the grounds and reasons underpinning antitrust. They have their own function which sometimes contradict conventional antitrust considerations, sometimes coincide with them. From an antitrust standpoint, the previous is more frequent, even more so when the objective of consumer welfare is considered the one and only legitimate goal of antitrust. Contradiction may arise, for example, when the buyer of an agricultural product uses its superior bargaining position, depresses the price of the product to the extent that the producer receives no appropriate (even below-cost) payment, but this depressed farm gate price results in a lower price for consumers because of intensive horizontal competition between the respective buyer and its competitors (passing on of the lower price to consumers takes place).

The main purpose of antitrust, to increase efficiency, runs counter to those objectives of agricultural policy that are redistributive in nature, such as ensuring a higher living standard for agricultural producers. The clash of objectives, however, has been settled by declaring that agricultural policy takes precedence over competition rules. It is explicitly proclaimed in EU primary law. Although no similar declaration is found in the United States, the same commitment emerges implicitly by adopting trade regulation rules that do not require the proving of negative effects on competition. These provisions are in many cases contradictory to efficiency-based considerations emphasised by mainstream antitrust, however, they do not prevent antitrust enforcement from coming to the fore.

DOI: 10.4324/9781003604747-26

Their relationship can be drawn as the violation of trade regulation rules not necessarily being covered by antitrust, but the violation of antitrust rules are presumably covered also by trade regulation. For example, an unfair trading practice against a supplier does not trigger antitrust enforcement, but a unilateral and anticompetitive trading practice with adverse effects on competition by a dominant undertaking also falls under the category of unfair trading and could trigger enforcement based on provisions aimed at preventing unfair trading practices. That is, trade regulation extends its protective scope to practices that are not prohibited by antitrust.

Given that the EU is an open proponent of the multifunctional model of agriculture, the policy choice is undeniable. Multifunctional agriculture embodies an approach that goes beyond the view of looking at agriculture as only a sector producing commodities. It craves the protection of rural lifestyle and landscapes and of agricultural producers living in rural areas. Agriculture also serves social, cultural and traditional functions. This approach is reflected in competition-related rules when agricultural producers are provided with antitrust law exemptions and additional market protection based on quite weak economic but satisfactorily strong social arguments.

In general, agri-food markets have become more concentrated horizontally and more integrated vertically; there are less family farms and smallholders, but we see that food prices are still increasing. Small and medium-sized family farms and agricultural producers sell their produce at lower prices than it would be worth for them, but lower prices paid to producers do not appear as lower prices paid by consumers. Somewhere in the food supply chain, at the level of intermediaries (food processors, wholesale dealers, retailers) these amounts get stuck. Intermediaries between producers and consumers pay less but charge more. It should not be even acceptable from a narrow antitrust standpoint. Consumer welfare does not seem increased by rising vertical integration and horizontal concentration of the food supply chain. No surplus is realised by consumers. They pay more for foodstuffs, but producers have to charge less to stay in the business.

The system's beneficiaries are intermediaries: food processors, wholesalers, retailers. The system is shaped like an hourglass. There is one end point with millions of producers, and there is the other end point with billions of consumers. The two end points are connected to each other through a significantly lower amount of intermediaries who are in a winning situation both upstream and downstream. Most foodstuffs are price inelastic. We all eat. Changes in the prices of basic food staples do not change the demand significantly, therefore intermediaries, in particular retail chains, do not have to expect significant decrease in the demand, if they increase the price of basic foodstuffs. Nevertheless, the most diverse types of dependence suffered by producers as suppliers on buyers forces producers to accept terms and conditions dictated by buyers in order for them to remain in the business.

In the EU, intermediaries in the food supply chain are also given preferential treatment as regards their sustainability agreements. As demonstrated earlier, exempting certain agriculture-related sustainability agreements from the prohibition of anticompetitive agreements requires only one party who is an agricultural producer, and, besides this one and only producer, it may happen that other operators downstream (processors and/or traders) join forces to enjoy the advantages of the derogation. Thanks to this lax provision, it is obvious that the intermediaries, who have in many cases superior bargaining position over their suppliers (the producers), can make use of the alleviation, but will not solve the environmental problems caused by the agricultural sector.

21 Conceptualising food sovereignty with ordoliberalism[969]

In view of these considerations, and taking into account that I have already outlined the food sovereignty's approach towards competition, subsequently, I examine whether ordoliberalism can be brought into line with the emerging paradigm of food sovereignty. The starting point for this is the viewpoint taken by the European Union, given that ordoliberalism – both in terms of legislation and enforcement – has had a significant impact on the competition policy of the EU.

Moreover, this chapter aims to add a further layer to the possible interpretation of 'sovereignty' in 'food sovereignty'. While doing so, in parallel I bring to the fore the tenets of ordoliberalism and ordoliberal competition policy, which may serve as potential interfaces between them and food sovereignty.

In Chapter 17, I argued for a state-centred concept of sovereignty, which would be advantageous to food sovereignty movements. This approach is only the substantial aspect of the question. It is based upon the acknowledgement that the modern state with its legislative powers has exclusive authority to adopt legally binding rules that influence each and every aspect of life, including economic relations between market players. If appropriate legal rules are adopted (that is, the legal norms adopted are indeed capable of delivering the desired outcomes), this is the most efficient way to attain policy objectives represented by any interest group. If not, the modern state plays the role of legislator, but a supranational organisation, such as the EU, with the authority to adopt directly applicable and binding legal norms, is derived also from a state-centred sovereignty concept. The state that is a member of the European Union shall voluntarily accept, by signing the accession treaty, that a part of its legislative powers in clearly determined areas is transferred to the supranational level.

The layer I aim to add here to the concept of sovereignty within food sovereignty is of procedural nature. This is closer to the 'multiple sovereignties' approach, however, it does not call into question the exclusivity of the state either in the determination of legal provisions that may deliver the clearly formulated objectives, or

969 This chapter is, in part, based on Martin Milán Csirszki, 'Is There Room for Food Sovereignty Considerations in EU Competition Policy? A Theoretical Framework' (2022) 18 Croatian Yearbook of European Law and Policy 83–106.

DOI: 10.4324/9781003604747-27

in deciding whether a part of its sovereignty is transferred to other organisations. These two pathways are handled as one in the following.

If we accept *Raf Geenens*' interpretation of sovereignty, one of the main goals of ordoliberalism, i.e., ensuring autonomy for citizens against private and public monopoly powers through a constitutional economic framework, can be raised to the level of collective autonomy within the framework of the agriculture and food supply chain. He uses the term 'sovereignty' as "the name for the perspective a community adopts when it sees itself as collectively autonomous."[970] Within the domain of agriculture and food supply chain, food sovereignty can be perceived as the perspective of a collectively autonomous community making a stand for defining their agricultural and food policy. To mention one example, most agricultural producers share the vision that trade in agri-food products and the food chain in general should be fairer, more balanced and more transparent. This demand is one of the most emphasised and important topics in agricultural policy-making processes. Agricultural producers appear as collectively autonomous in fighting for their common goal. By making a stand for certain demands, they aim to define their own agricultural and food policy.[971] Though agricultural producers are to determine the desired outcomes, the attainment of these objectives are placed into the hands of the state through adopting appropriate legal provisions. To be effective, producers must channel their desires into the state machinery's legislative processes.

With this conceptualisation, we have to give up neither the ordoliberal approach of competition, i.e., the claim for setting up the rules of the game through state regulation, nor the concept of food sovereignty. Furthermore, we can seize food sovereignty as a kind of collective autonomy, which can be led back to the notion of individual autonomy as a value to be protected by ordoliberalism. If we accept the ordoliberal viewpoint, and thus the necessity of regulating competition through general rules, and we also accept *Röpke*'s ordoliberal remark on agriculture, which holds that "in this sector . . . a particularly high degree of far-sighted, protective, directive, regulating and balancing intervention is not only defensible, but even mandatory,"[972] the concept of food sovereignty can be easily reconciled with the ordoliberal approach protecting individual autonomy against public and private constraints of competition. It is one step from the individual to the collective level, from the individual autonomy protected by ordoliberalism to the concept of food sovereignty perceived as a collective autonomy of a community with the emphasised aim of challenging the restrictions of competition exercised by agribusiness, i.e., giant food enterprises, be they processors, wholesalers or retail chains.

Geenens pronouncedly builds his theory of sovereignty as autonomy upon the works of *Habermas*. He emphasises that *Habermas* provides "the most elaborate account of sovereignty as autonomy."[973] The remarks of *Habermas* in one of his

970 Raf Geenens, 'Sovereignty as Autonomy' (2017) 36 Law and Philosophy 524.
971 See, for example, the agricultural lobby groups in the EU: https://copa-cogeca.eu/food_chain#b435.
972 Wilhelm Röpke, *The Social Crisis of Our Time* (The University of Chicago Press 1950) 205.
973 Geenens (n 970) 506.

books can be drawn as an exact parallel to the viewpoint of ordoliberalism. He is of the opinion that "basic rights must now do more than just protect private citizens from encroachment by the state apparatus, [p]rivate autonomy is endangered today at least as much by positions of economic and social power."[974] Ordoliberalism has the same approach: it cannot imagine a mode of economy other than the market economy but wants to set up the rules of the game within the framework of which market actors will perform their economic activities. It is coherent with the view of *Habermas*: "it has become impossible to break out of the universe of capitalism; the only remaining option is to civilise and tame the capitalist dynamic from within."[975] The instrument for civilising and taming the capitalist dynamic is none other than creating competition rules within an economic constitutional framework which highlights economic liberties and individual autonomy. Ironically, the aim of competition policy is to save capitalism from itself.[976]

Although it seems paradoxical to support individual autonomy and collective autonomy at the same time, these two types of autonomy are understood by myself as categories in two different spheres. Individual autonomy (individual economic freedom) as protected by ordoliberalism refers to the capacity to live one's life according to reasons and motives that are taken as one's own and not according to manipulative and/or distorting external forces. That is to say, it refers to being economically independent. In its ordoliberal sense, it is economic capacity and one of the most important principles of the economic constitutional framework. At the same time, food sovereignty perceived as a type of collective autonomy is a political term.[977] Individuals can have individual autonomy, that is, they can be independent from an economic point of view, but when stepping up to the political arena, these individuals can determine themselves as collectively autonomous who all fight for their individual autonomy and for remaining independent. They become collectively autonomous through trying to achieve the same goal: maintaining their independence in, and by, determining their own agricultural and food policy. These notions, thus, have the same legal implications and can be connected to each other with a mutual legal objective: protecting agricultural producers, farmers, small and medium-scale enterprises by creating effective competition and trade rules and enforcing them in the same manner.

Ordoliberalism and food sovereignty have another common feature: they both intend to re-introduce and re-emphasise social issues in pursuance of their goals. In general, ordoliberalism aims to combine economic efficiency with a just and stable social order.[978] The fact that ordoliberalism is also known as German neoliberalism

974 Jürgen Habermas, *Between Facts and Norms – Contributions to a Discourse Theory of Law and Democracy* (The MIT Press 1996) 263.

975 Jürgen Habermas, *The Crisis of the European Union: A Response* (Polity Press 2012) 106.

976 Richard Whish, 'Do Competition Lawyers Harm Welfare?' (2020) Concurrentialiste: Journal of Antitrust Law <https://leconcurrentialiste.com/richard-whish-welfare/> accessed 30 October 2023.

977 Windfuhr and Jonsén (n 841) 15.

978 Brigitte Young, 'Ordoliberalism as an "Irritating German Idea"' in Thorsten Beck and Hans-Helmut Kotz (eds), *Ordoliberalism: A German Oddity?* (CEPR Press 2017) 35.

should not mislead anyone: "[a]s a matter of legal and political form, ordoliberalism and neoliberalism are often in tension with each other, as ordoliberalism's rule-based commitments come up against neoliberal discretionary politics."[979] The feature that distinguishes ordoliberalism from neoliberalism is that the latter views the world as a market and tries to govern it as if it were a market, and it refuses the separation of economic, social and political spheres, by "evaluating all three according to a single economic logic."[980] In contrast, the most significant notion of ordoliberalism carries its socially focused nature: social market economy.[981,982] The concept of social market economy brought to the fore by *Müller-Armack* has at least three core concepts: (a) the preservation of the market economy as a dynamic order; (b) social equilibrium, which is subject to the observance of the first sentence; and (c) securing stability and growth through monetary and competition policy.[983] The social market economy is a normative system based on values such as dignity, well-being, self-determination, encouragement, freedom and responsibility of all individuals; it is fully committed to a humane society in which "economic growth and social sustainability are compatible notions."[984]

Contrary to ordoliberalism, neoliberalism lacks the desire to achieve social equilibrium and does not take into account concerns other than economic ones. That is the ground for me to reconcile food sovereignty with ordoliberalism. At the same time, this is the reason which establishes the impossibility for neoliberalism to be in line with food sovereignty. In each aspect, food sovereignty – as it has emerged as a social movement – pursues the aim of having social considerations taken into account during policy-making processes. The trait of ordoliberalism that it does not just consider economic efficiency as the exclusive objective of antitrust law means that other (noneconomic) considerations may be taken into account when adopting and enforcing competition rules in a broad sense.

Therefore, in an ordoliberal concept of competition law, which – as mentioned – does not limit itself to achieving one and only one objective, i.e., consumer welfare through economic efficiency, noneconomic aspects may also appear when deciding

979 Michael A. Wilkinson, 'Authoritarian Liberalism in Europe: A Common Critique of Neoliberalism and Ordoliberalism' (2019) 45 Critical Sociology 1024.

980 Davies (n 849) 31–32.

981 In German: *soziale Marktwirtschaft*.

982 The relationship between ordoliberalism and social market economy can be perceived in a way that "the ordoliberalism of the Freiburg school constituted a major part of the theoretical foundations on which the creation of the social market economy in post-WWII Germany was based." Of course, there are differences in how ordoliberals in general and Müller-Armack perceived the social market economy. Ordoliberalism in general looked at the competitive order as an ethical order in itself, while Müller-Armack submitted that this order has no inherent ethical qualities but shall be made to have these. See Viktor J. Vanberg, 'The Freiburg School: Walter Eucken and Ordoliberalism' (4 November 2004) Freiburger Diskussionspapiere zur Ordnungsökonomik 2.

983 Ralf Ptak, *Vom Ordoliberalismus zur Sozialen Marktwirtschaft: Stationen des Neoliberalismus in Deutschland* (Springer 2004) 227.

984 Doris Hildebrand, 'The Equality and Social Fairness Objectives in EU Competition Law: The European School of Thought' (2017) 1 Concurrences.

whether or not a conduct is harmful to competition. This means that food sovereignty with its social aims is not contrary to ordoliberalism. As the definition provides, food sovereignty does not negate trade but aims to create trade practices which are able to break the dominance of agribusiness. Doing so is motivated by social considerations which also appear in the ordoliberal line of thinking. The ordoliberal approach of adopting the rules of the game through legislation which directs the behaviour of market participants is in accordance with food sovereignty, since the latter also wants a level playing field.

"Food sovereignty promotes the role of the state as protector of farmers' interests"[985] which can only be realised through legislation. This does not mean that inefficient undertakings and market actors will be prioritised, but all operators in the respective market will have equal opportunities as a result of the aim of reaching social equilibrium. In the broadest context, the ultimate goal is that all market participants be part of a humane economy.[986] Criticism may be made that this links competition policy with redistributive objectives, and redistribution is not an aspect with which antitrust law should deal. However, it is worth perceiving redistribution from another approach. Adopting the thoughts of *Fox*, if we refuse to accept that competition policy can, and should, contribute to redistribution[987] and we view antitrust as something that should only deal with economic efficiency, we may also acknowledge that redistribution is taken over from the state by, and positioned in the hands of, giant undertakings.[988] This is in line with food sovereignty's contention that emphasises the problem of decreasing state regulatory power.[989]

The strength of food sovereignty is that it may provide us with answers at different levels,[990] as well as that it has the feature of multi-interpretability.[991] This allows

985 Mann (n 2) 54.

986 See the influential book: Wilhelm Röpke, *A Humane Economy: The Social Framework of the Free Market* (Intercollegiate Studies Institute 2014).

987 It is manifest that the goal of redistribution should be primarily the concern of tax policy and tax regulation, nevertheless there are situations when taxation cannot be seen as an appropriate tool to solve problems. How can tax regulation remedy a situation when as a consequence of exploitative abuses, be it under the notion of abuse of dominance or of other abuse-type conducts, the abused party is squeezed out of the market? As put by *Lianos*: "Other instruments than competition law have traditionally been employed in order to deal with situations of economic, and in particular income and/or wealth, inequality. Welfare and tax systems constitute an obvious example." The traditional tools of taxation and the welfare state intervene ex post, "thus leaving the root cause of the problem unresolved." See: Ioannis Lianos, 'Competition Law as a Form of Social Regulation' (2020) 65 The Antitrust Bulletin 9.

988 The keynote speech given by *Eleanor Fox* at the conference titled 'Should Wealth and Income Inequality Be a Competition Law Concern?' held on 20 May 2021. The title of her speech was 'Antitrust and Inequality: The History of (In)equality in Competition Law and Its Guide to the Future'.

989 Windfuhr and Jonsén (n 841) 29.

990 José Bové and Francois Dufour, *The World Is Not for Sale – Farmers against Junk Food* (Verso 2001) 168.

991 Maarten A. Hajer, *The Politics of Environmental Discourse: Ecological Modernisation and the Policy Process* (Oxford University Press 1995) 61.

us to identify two trends from different directions but leads to the same result. Ordoliberalism emphasises the role of the state in setting the rules of competition in the market (at the national and/or EU level), while food sovereignty seeks to restore the leading role of the state as protector of the agricultural community (at the international level). The result and the conclusion are the same in both cases: the state must take an active role in shaping competition and trade rules. This does not mean direct intervention into the relationship of market participants but signifies establishing those competition and trade rules according to which these market participants operate on the market.

By adopting the approach of ordoliberalism which goes beyond a single-purpose viewpoint towards antitrust law and by choosing the political category of food sovereignty as a possible conceptual framework in policy-making processes, one steps on the path of prosocial[992] competition policy. By prosocial competition policy, I mean a mode of competition, including antitrust, legislation and enforcement that is sensitive to social issues and does not limit itself to achieving economic efficiency. By looking at the primary law of the European Union, Article 9 TFEU includes the horizontal social clause[993] which requires that "social values have to be respected in all policy fields of the EU."[994] Of the few *expressis verbis* provisions on resolving the conflicts between competition and another policy, the subject of my study – agriculture – is one which establishes the specific social objectives to be considered when adopting and enforcing competition laws in the form of the provision formulated in Article 42 TFEU.[995] As described earlier, Article 42 TFEU paves the way for the precedence of Common Agricultural Policy objectives over general competition rules.

The ordoliberal antitrust law objectives, such as the protection of the competitive process and of individual freedom,[996] are *in themselves* appropriate to consider noneconomic factors when deciding whether a conduct is harmful to competition. This does not mean that the notion of prosocial competition policy would argue against the economic efficiency to be achieved by antitrust laws.

992 Although she does not use the term in the exact same sense, the notion of prosocial antitrust is taken over from Miazad (n 378).

993 See in detail: Maria Eugenia Bartoloni, 'The Horizontal Social Clause in a Legal Dimension' in Francesca Ippolito, Maria Eugenia Bartoloni and Massimo Condinanzi (eds), *The EU and the Proliferation of Integration Principles under the Lisbon Treaty* (Routledge 2018) 83–104.

994 Andreas Heinemann, 'Social Considerations in EU Competition Law – The Protection of Competition as a Cornerstone of the Social Market Economy' in Delia Ferri and Fulvio Cortese (eds), *The EU Social Market Economy and the Law: Theoretical Perspectives and Practical Challenges for the EU* (Routledge 2019) 123–146. See also: Dagmar Schiek, Liz Oliver, Christopher Forde and Gabriella Alberti, *EU Social and Labour Rights and EU Internal Market Law* (European Union 2015) 14–15.

995 Heinemann (n 994).

996 Anchustegui (n 879) 139.

As a consequence of adopting a food sovereignty approach, we reject that food be purely commodified,[997] and as a consequence of a socially responsive ordoliberal competition policy positioned in the framework of social market economy, we can take into account those dimensions of competition and trade in agricultural products and food which would remain invisible from a more economic approach limited to the objective of enhancing consumer welfare. As posited by *Trauger*, "[t]he commodification of food . . . has resulted in the vertical integration and the concentration of power in a few very large firms with national governments increasingly tailoring food regulation to the demands of agribusiness."[998]

The food sovereignty movement's demand to break the control and growing power of corporations over the food system[999] is fully in accordance with the thoughts of ordoliberalism's mainstream economist, *Eucken*. As explained in one of his major works, the state's policy should be directed toward dissolving economic power groups or limiting their function.[1000] It is not the only parallel which can be drawn between the key ordoliberal economist *Eucken* and food sovereignty: an overlap may also be found with regard to the requirement of contractual freedom. In *Eucken*'s view, freedom of contract should not be used in the competitive order to create dependencies between market players, that is, freedom of contract may not be granted for the purpose of concluding contracts that restrict or eliminate freedom of contract.[1001] This tenet of *Eucken* may be a basis for regulating unfair trading practices in the food supply chain from an ordoliberal point of view, given that the UTPs, in most cases, constitute certain types of exploitative abuse which restrict the freedom of contract of that contracting party which is vis-à-vis the party having superior bargaining power. To be more exact, the weaker contracting party's freedom to determine the terms of the contract is restricted due to economic dependence, and so this party is put in a position which – from a food sovereignty approach – is unacceptable because of the economic exploitation.[1002] The ordoliberal concept of efficiency also includes "the continuing possibility of choice for the individual,"[1003] of which the aforementioned behaviours deprive the agricultural producers, who are vulnerable in cases of bargaining with buyers being in a superior bargaining position.

997 As *Oliver and Robison* put it: "Commodification is a widely used and inconsistently defined concept." By commodification they mean "a process in which a good from a humanity sphere is relocated in the commodity sphere where instead of being valued for its connections to persons that enable it to satisfy important socio-emotional needs, it is valued for its physical properties that satisfy mostly physical needs." See: Jeffrey R. Oliver and Lindon J. Robison, 'Rationalizing Inconsistent Definitions of Commodification: A Social Exchange Perspective' (2017) 8 Modern Economy 1314–1327.

998 Trauger (n 916) 1133.

999 William D. Schanbacher, *Food as a Human Right: Combatting Global Hunger and Forging a Path to Food Sovereignty* (Praeger Security International 2019) 91.

1000 Walter Eucken, *Grundsätze der Wirtschaftspolitik* (J.C.B. Mohr 1952) 334.

1001 Eucken (n 1000) 278.

1002 Windfuhr and Jonsén (n 841) 46.

1003 Akman (n 862) 56–57.

The characteristic of food sovereignty that it can be interpreted at all levels means that the movement's demand for ceasing unequal trading rules at the international level can be projected at the national and EU levels.[1004] Ordoliberal competition policy and the social market economy constitute an appropriate framework to set up those competition and trade rules which take into account noneconomic (social) factors to provide protection for the weakest actors of the food supply chain, the farmers as well as small and medium-size enterprises. The food sovereignty movement promoting social justice[1005] may find a useful partner in ordoliberal competition policy to establish the set of rules necessary to provide protection for the most vulnerable of the food supply chain. On the one hand, this 'partner-in-crime' role of ordoliberalism comes from the view of ordoliberal thinkers who dealt with agriculture, and on the other hand, from the general constituting principles drawn up by Eucken.

There are two conflicting viewpoints as to how the privileged position of the agricultural sector in relation to competition-related rules can be explained. The first point of view is that the favoured status of the sector is based on strong social and economic considerations and arguments. On the contrary, the second group takes the view that providing exemption from antitrust rules and stronger protection for agricultural producers are none other than the repercussions of strong, well-organised and methodical agricultural lobbying both at the EU and national level. It may be more reasonable to unearth the middle ground: on the one hand, owing to the structural characteristics of agriculture and the factors beyond human control (for example, weather and climatic conditions), and, on the other hand, because of the products of primary agricultural production and food being essential to sustain human life, agricultural lobbyists are in a position to have a great impact on legislation, because their arguments – in many cases – seem quite valid (for example, regarding the weak bargaining position of producers, the struggle to ensure predictable income for themselves, changing weather and climatic conditions, etc.).

This gives justification for their ambition to fight for exemptions from antitrust and sector-specific rules for the agricultural sector not only at the EU but also national level. Although from the standpoint of conventional antitrust law which aims to achieve the highest possible economic efficiency, these arguments are often not satisfactory on the grounds of economics. The more we move away from the single-factor economic approach towards antitrust law and the more non-efficiency-based considerations we open the door for, the more acceptable the arguments of agricultural lobbyists are. The extent to which we commit ourselves to non-efficiency-based considerations in antitrust law determines whether there

1004 Henry Bernstein, 'Food Sovereignty Via the "Peasant Way": A Sceptical View' (2014) 41 The Journal of Peasant Studies 1055 also mentions the regulation of international and *domestic* trade in food commodities as well as the protection of small-scale farming among the demands of food sovereignty. According to our view, the protection may also take place through effective competition law regulation which guarantees that smaller market players could compete within a market where their interests are taken into account.

1005 David M. Kaplan (ed), *Encyclopedia of Food and Agricultural Ethics* (2nd edn, Springer 2019) 99.

will be – and if yes, how many – exemptions and how much protection agricultural producers will enjoy. It can be imagined as a sliding scale whose one end point stands for economic efficiency exclusively and the other end point for non-efficiency-based considerations as an umbrella term. The extent of it is policy choice, therefore it is determined by relevant and current policy-makers. Viewed from another angle, other policies can, and will, undermine antitrust.[1006]

The relative autonomy of competition policy in agri-food markets from general antitrust law trends can be illustrated quite well by the fact that the prevalent antitrust doctrines in the last four decades in the United States (the paradigm of consumer welfare) and in the last 25 years in the EU (the more economic approach) have left untouched the competition-related exception and specific norms provided for agriculture. It is another reason as to why one should perceive competition rules of agri-food markets as an integral part of agri-food law rather than as part of competition law. The way competition in agri-food markets is governed is determined – to a significant extent – by agricultural policy objectives, and – to much less extent – by mainstream antitrust considerations. This is why antitrust lawyers often claim that the efficiency of agri-food markets has been sacrificed on the altar of considerations that have nothing to do with competition, such as ensuring a higher living standard for agricultural producers.

From the perspective of antitrust policy, trade regulation rules in agri-food markets– in many cases – point in the opposite direction than antitrust rules. However, from the perspective of agricultural policy, antitrust and trade regulation rules rather complement each other. While antitrust attacks those conducts that are contrary to economic efficiency, trade regulation attacks those which cannot be reached by antitrust enforcement.

These provisions serve to realise agricultural and food policy objectives, that is to say, they are an instrument in the hands of agricultural and food policy-makers. Their primary aim is to create a competitive environment that reduces the vulnerability of weak market actors in the food supply chain and, thus, raises the income of agricultural producers generated from the sales of their produce. This cannot be justified with the assessment methods of antitrust law without framing antitrust in a context different from the current standpoint. Antitrust exclusively serving the increase of consumer welfare and exclusively triggered by conducts harming economic efficiency is not eligible to take into account the unique competition-related problems in the agricultural and food supply chain. Criticism may be raised that curing sector-specific anomalies is not the task of antitrust, but even if it were, certain problems to be solved remain on the surface. It is also possible that these do not seem to be a problem at all from the single economic logic of antitrust, but the feature of the goods being the object of these trade relations, that is to say, their necessity for life, puts the problem in a different perspective.

In general, by looking at the full picture from a practical standpoint, it is hard, if not impossible, to find any increase in economic efficiency as the consequence

1006 Tóth Tihamér, *Uniós és magyar versenyjog* (Wolters Kluwer 2020) 48.

of the current and mainstream paradigm of competition regulation. I am aware that there are many more factors in the background which overall contribute to the increase of food prices, such as biofuel production, energy prices, weather, speculation, economic growth and changing diets,[1007] but a competition policy exclusively concentrating on economic efficiency in the form of consumer welfare does not seem to mitigate the problems. However, from an agricultural policy standpoint, it does impair important pillars of the rural landscape and lifestyle by not taking into account non-efficiency-based considerations.

The dominance of agribusiness is against the inherent values of traditional and centuries-old agricultural production. This should not be understood as a return to ancestral methods, but as support for viable farmers and family farms that are fit for the 21st century. These market actors significantly contribute to the preservation of the rural landscape and lifestyle, traditions and values foreign to the urban environment, beyond producing food. It does not seem like their exploitation by giant food companies and retail chains would bring about any tangible benefit for consumers, for example, in the form of lower prices. As a consequence of these general considerations, I propose two possible ways for the better functioning of competition in agri-food markets, which – to a certain extent – may cure the current two-component competition regimes. By two components I mean antitrust and trade regulation; the amelioration of agri-food competition is built on these two constituting elements and their interrelationship.

A competition policy, if not limited to increasing economic efficiency, can contribute to the multifunctional model of agriculture, thus by creating balance between competition and agricultural policy. A holistic and integrated view to competition-related issues of agri-food markets does not impede the realisation of the essence of multifunctional agriculture, such as "the management of renewable natural resources, landscape, conservation of biodiversity and contribution to the socio-economic viability of rural areas,"[1008] but facilitates its realisation.

Small farms, though endangered by giant food companies and retail chains, play a crucial role in rural sustainability, as well as support biodiversity and ecological resilience.[1009] One of the purposes of food sovereignty is precisely to express the fact that agriculture does not only consist of agricultural production as economic activity. It is much more. Food sovereignty protects the interest of future generations, empowers family farms, is committed to the three shades of sustainability (environmental, social and economic), aims to guarantee just incomes

1007 Patrick Westhoff, *The Economics of Food: How Feeding and Fueling the Planet Affects Food Prices* (Pearson Education 2010) 4.

1008 Henk Renting, Walter AH Rossing, Jeroen CJ Groot, Jan Douwe Van der Ploeg, Catherine Laurent, Daniel Perraud, Derk Jan Stobbelaar and Martin K van Ittersum, 'Exploring Multifunctional Agriculture: A Review of Conceptual Approaches and Prospects for an Integrative Transitional Framework' (2009) 90 Journal of Environmental Management 112.

1009 Nuno Guiomar et al., 'Typology and Distribution of Small Farms in Europe: Towards a Better Picture' (2018) 75 Land Use Policy 785.

for producers, fights for biodiversity and social relations free of oppression and inequality.[1010] Food sovereignty fully subscribes to the multifunctional model of agriculture and is even more than that. The multifunctional model of agriculture does not say anything about the role states should play in governing markets; the paradigm of food sovereignty, on the contrary, does.

A food sovereignty-based competition policy, on the one hand, acknowledges that agriculture cannot only be interpreted as a necessary production activity to create the 'subject matter' of agricultural and food trade, and, on the other hand, espouses the multifunctional model of agriculture. Moreover, it respects the way food sovereignty addresses competition in agri-food markets: the strong guardian role of the state over the competitive process with an extensive competition regulation and enforcement also leaving room for non-efficiency-based considerations. This approach is manifested in the form of legal regulation which takes into account the unique features of the agricultural sector, either through creating exemption under general antitrust rules (exception norms), or through adopting sector-specific trade regulation rules (specific norms).

1010 Schanbacher (n 999) 49–50.

22 Regulating competition in light of the food sovereignty paradigm

This chapter aims to evaluate the legal regulation in force in light of a food sovereignty-based competition policy. By food sovereignty-based competition policy I mean a mode of controlling competition in agri-food markets which takes into consideration the perceptions of the food sovereignty paradigm on competition.

Patel's statement that the European Union is better off than the United States in terms of food sovereignty[1011] is also correct regarding competition rules. According to *Fairbairn*, food sovereignty could provide the ambition US agri-food movements are currently lacking,[1012] and the food sovereignty-based competition policy may prove to be useful for agricultural policy-makers concerned with antitrust and trade regulation in US agri-food markets.

Agricultural producers in the EU are protected to a greater extent than in the United States. While the US system does not recognise any other legitimate goal for antitrust, the EU does so but with the limitation that the primary objective is still to enhance economic efficiency. However, there are other ancillary goals which are pursued by EU competition policy. These further EU antitrust objectives leave more room for the enforcement authority to manoeuvre in the area of non-efficiency-based considerations which can be beneficial from the standpoint of agricultural policy.

From a food sovereignty approach, the EU exemption under the prohibition of anticompetitive agreements takes better account of agricultural policy, given that it requires the attainment of CAP objectives as a condition for the respective agreement to be exempted. It is missing in US antitrust. Furthermore, given that one of the CAP objectives is the raising of living standards of agricultural producers, which is also an implicit objective of food sovereignty, the EU exemption is more in line with the paradigm than the US one which is only concerned with economic considerations.

A significant difference between US and EU competition regulation is that the latter has a much more intensive protective pillar through trade regulation rules,

1011 Patel (n 54) 668–669.

1012 Madeleine Fairbairn, 'Framing Transformation: The Counter-Hegemonic Potential of Food Sovereignty in the US Context' (2012) 29 Agriculture and Human Values 228.

DOI: 10.4324/9781003604747-28

such as the UTP Directive. The United States has even experienced that, with the appearance of the consumer welfare antitrust paradigm, the interpretation of the Packers and Stockyards Act has shifted in an unfavourable direction from an agricultural policy perspective. Recently it is rather interpreted as an antitrust statute and not as trade regulation. It means that it is much more difficult for claimants to have a violation found, for adverse effects on competition shall be proved.

All in all, the EU system of agri-food competition rules fits better with the food sovereignty's perceptions on competition than that of the United States.

There are two alternatives for regulating competition in agri-food markets. Taken into account that the perceptions of food sovereignty on competition have been found compatible with EU competition policy, I aim to formulate my reform proposals in the context of the European Union, keeping in mind that reforms carried out at the EU level – even those which are soft law in nature – may permeate Member States' legislation and enforcement trends.

My proposals are not formulated in connection with the previously scrutinised legal instruments but abuse of dominance and merger control, which lack agriculture-specific provisions. As I identified, the competition problems of agricultural producers do not come from there being no special rules applicable to primary agricultural production. They are created by the concentration taking place upstream and downstream in relation agricultural production.

Despite the increasing concentration of agri-food markets and the lack of abuse of dominance cases therein, these instruments currently do not serve the attainment of agricultural policy objectives. The gap identified is the inappropriate handling of buyer power from an agricultural policy perspective, which may, however, be narrowed with the review of the rules on abuse of dominance and of merger control. The legal possibility to better align them to the expectations of agricultural policy exists in EU law, taking into consideration the sufficiently broad authorisation to provide derogation for the sector from general competition rules as well as the precedence of agricultural policy objectives over competition policy.

The strength of the food sovereignty-based competition policy drawn up lies in the fact that it concentrates on one sector – the agricultural sector. Calls for a more socially sensitive and inclusive competition policy are mostly formulated in general terms, as seen earlier, applying to all economic sectors. Differently from all other sectors and public policies behind them, agricultural policy objectives – which are specific social objectives – are given priority over competition rules. The policy choice, therefore, is given, and thus the deviation from the general paradigm of competition policy in the context of the agricultural sector does not seem like a radical step. Since it is explicitly declared in the EU context that the specific social objectives of agricultural policy shall be taken into account in relation to competition policy and law, a food sovereignty-based competition policy – which is only interpretable regarding the agricultural sector – is not a profound "shock" for general competition policy. The food sovereignty-based competition policy takes a prosocial view which is in line with the starting point that competition regulation in agri-food markets shall take account of agricultural policy objectives which are social in nature.

The alternatives take into consideration, and aim to sustain, the elements of multifunctional agriculture but also provide more than that. The alternatives are food sovereignty based because they consider it important that competition be supervised and regulated under the watchful eyes of the state. If I took an approach only respecting the model of multifunctional agriculture but not the considerations of food sovereignty, the guardian role of the state would be missing. The constituting feature of food sovereignty that accepts the indirect supervisory role of the state over the competitive process through adopting the rules of the game is in accordance with the existing and influential ordoliberal competition policy. That is to say, no competition policy must be elaborated from scratch but I can insert sector-specific considerations into a contemporary competition policy framework which, as found earlier, is suitable for that.

Food sovereignty-based competition policy means that legislation and enforcement aim to alleviate the situation of agricultural producers in the competitive process of agri-food markets. It aims to target those economic conducts which are not covered by conventional antitrust, in particular harms suffered by agricultural producers as suppliers against their buyers. The means for that are twofold: through adopting either antitrust or trade regulation rules, or both. The proposed modifications are related to those cases when producers are likely victims of buyer power abuses or misuses.

I propose that in cases related to agri-food products, be they unilateral behaviours or mergers and acquisitions, assessing the impacts the conduct may have on procurement markets and evaluating economic dependence of suppliers on buyers should play a key role in deciding the outcome of the respective case. As seen in Part IV, there are no sector-specific antitrust rules for abuse of dominance and merger control.

The consequence of this was already felt in 1899. The *Civic Federation of Chicago* convened and held a conference to address the problem of trusts. Here the fear for the vulnerability of agricultural regions was already mentioned, given that the *Merger Movement* had created companies with market power that could raise the price of manufactured goods while lowering the price of raw materials.[1013] One century passed, and still there is no solution. More than ten years ago, the American Antitrust Institute also proposed that "developing agricultural market guidelines for assessing buyer mergers" and "challenging buyer mergers whenever they are likely to result in the exercise of buyer power" would be necessary.[1014] Furthermore, in a quite radical manner, in the House of Representatives in 2019 and in the Senate in 2022, a bill was introduced titled the Food and Agribusiness Merger Moratorium and Antitrust Review Act. It would have aimed to "place a moratorium on certain acquisitions between large agricultural and retail-related businesses

1013 Martin (n 176) 6.

1014 American Antitrust Institute, 'The Next Antitrust Agenda: The American Antitrust Institute's Transition Report on Competition Policy to the 44th President of the United States' (2008) 283.

and establish the Food and Agriculture Concentration and Market Power Review Commission."[1015]

Since then, there has been no development in that respect, neither in the EU nor in the United States. This is despite the fact that the EU seems to keep its doors open to some kind of agriculture-specific merger control, when it declares in the Merger Regulation's Recital (7) that

> [t]his Regulation should therefore be based not only on Article 83 but, principally, on Article 308 of the Treaty, under which the Community may give itself the additional powers of action necessary for the attainment of its objectives, and also powers of action with regard to concentrations on the markets for agricultural products listed in Annex I to the Treaty.[1016]

It is a confirmation that the declaration of the precedence of agricultural policy objectives over competition rules in Article 42 TFEU may not only guide the EU legislation in connection with anticompetitive agreements (and abuse of dominance) found in EU primary law but also merger control included in EU secondary law.

The alternatives of a food sovereignty-based competition policy do not aim to reform antitrust law in general. They aim to reform antitrust law in agri-food markets, the sectoral competition laws for agri-food markets. In the EU, the policy choice of giving preference to agricultural policy over competition rules is given, therefore competition in agri-food markets rather constitute part of agricultural policy than that of competition policy. It means that my proposals are primarily underpinned by agricultural policy arguments and secondarily by antitrust arguments.

It is another question that ordoliberal competition policy and food sovereignty have been found to be in line with one another, in particular if we concentrate on those ordoliberals who dealt with agricultural issues, such as Röpke. However, with my proposals I do not want to get completely detached from general antitrust considerations; I aim to express my 'sectoral radicalism' with modifications which may seem significant from the standpoint of mainstream antitrust but slight and necessary from that of an alternative agricultural policy, the paradigm of food sovereignty.

Ordoliberal competition policy going beyond efficiency-based considerations and promoting the competitive process as such and individual economic freedom leaves room for the food sovereignty's perceptions on competition. Not being fully detached from general competition policy considerations is tried to be indicated by my finding that there is such competition policy which can be reconciled with food sovereignty, and it is ordoliberal competition policy. Given that ordoliberal

1015 See: www.congress.gov/bill/116th-congress/house-bill/2933 and www.congress.gov/bill/117th-congress/senate-bill/4245.

1016 Council Regulation (EC) No 139/2004 of 20 January 2004 on the control of concentrations between undertakings [2004] OJ L24/1 (Merger Regulation), recital (7).

competition policy has been a determining factor in the competition regime of the EU, I make my proposals in connection with it.

Let us start with the alternative of stretching the reach of antitrust. The mainstream antitrust paradigm aims to define itself as the guardian of consumers. Guarding consumers is attempted to be realised through stepping up against those economic conducts which may result in increased consumer prices. A narrow consumer welfare paradigm does not consider harm done to agricultural producers. This deficiency is primarily a matter of concern in connection with unilateral conducts. Although the association and 'collusion' of agricultural producers within farmers' associations and producer organisations are ensured ex lege without resulting in the antitrust violation of the prohibition of anticompetitive agreements, this possibility and sector-specific exemption only makes sense when agricultural producers are those who would commit an antitrust violation, and not when they are the likely victims of an antitrust violation.

The abuses experienced and voiced by agricultural producers shed light on the shortcomings the current antitrust regimes have when they aim to assess more complex market situations in certain sectors which not only exist for profitability but also have noneconomic contributions. Although *Lianos and Carballa-Smichowski* formulate their finding in connection with the digital economy, their opinion may also be a guide to the agricultural sector. "The traditional concept of market power used by competition authorities cannot engage with th[e] new reality in which (economic) power manifests beyond price and output within a relevant market."[1017] The traditional concept of market power is not only unfit to take into account considerations other than price and output but also unable to acknowledge and prevent the 'dangers' unrelated to efficiency loss. And this is not the concept's fault but it derives from its limitedness. Of course, intermediary market participants between agricultural producers and consumers do not have the sufficient extent of market power which is necessary to have a unilateral antitrust violation found, but they have the power to significantly influence the latitude of agricultural producers in their market behaviour. This necessarily spills over and determines whether the agricultural sector and in particular smallholders and family farms can fulfil their functions beyond production – functions that are given consideration in the framework of the food sovereignty paradigm and the concept of multifunctional agriculture.

As historical experience showed regarding the US market in live animals, sectoral regulation in itself is insufficient to protect suppliers. While the consent decree on the basis of the Sherman Act between the government and the largest meatpackers prevented market concentration after divestiture in the period from 1920 to 1980, as soon as it was terminated, the market started to become concentrated and even rose to a concentration level higher than before the divestiture. It shows that

1017 Ioannis Lianos and Bruno Carballa-Smichowski, 'A Coat of Many Colours – New Concepts and Metrics of Economic Power in Competition Law and Economics' (2022) 18 Journal of Competition Law & Economics 795–831.

sector-specific regulation may lose its function in case general antitrust provisions as a strong hinterland do not support it. Sector-specific rules in force cannot forestall concentration which, however, may multiply the occurrence of anticompetitive unilateral conducts against those market participants who sectoral rules aim to protect. The key to the better functioning of agri-food markets – if the policy choice has already been made that producers should be protected in the competitive process – would be to prevent further concentration of the intermediary stage (processing, wholesale, retail). It could be fulfilled ex ante by a stronger merger control applying to those market participants who buy agri-food products for processing and/or resale.

Agri-food markets already concentrated could become more bearable for producers by sectoral rules on abuse of dominance. I am of the opinion that antitrust rules have more of a deterrent effect than trade regulation rules. Using the features which *Buccirossi et al.* determined as factors influencing the deterrent effect of competition regulations (sanctions and damages, financial and human resources, powers to investigate, quality of the law, independence from political influence, separation of investigative and adjudicatory power),[1018] I render it more likely that an antitrust statute could better serve these aspects and thus could be more efficient in preventing detrimental conducts.

Abuse of dominance has no sector-specific rules which would take into consideration the unique features of the agricultural sector. Typically and generally, the business partners of agricultural producers, i.e., those to whom they sell their products, are not in a dominant position. Agricultural producers as suppliers bargain with buyers (food processors, retailers) who are not in a dominant position, therefore the protective shield of antitrust does not cover these bargains. Article 102 TFEU abuses – such as directly or indirectly imposing unfair purchase prices or other unfair trading conditions, applying dissimilar conditions to equivalent transactions with other trading parties, thereby placing them at a competitive disadvantage, and making the conclusion of contracts subject to acceptance by the other parties of supplementary obligations which, by their nature or according to commercial usage, have no connection with the subject of such contracts – are not interpretable, if no dominance is found.

These practices, however, are common occurrences committed against agricultural producers. No dominance – as understood in the current antitrust regime – is necessary for buyers to engage in and to be able to commit these practices. Obviously, the existence of a dominant position shall be decided on a case-by-case basis. Sectoral differences can be expressed in the respective case, but the question arises as to how far law enforcement is willing to deviate from the general (average) trend when there are only general rules, but the respective product market (sector)

1018 Paolo Buccirossi, Lorenzo Ciari, Tomaso Duso, Giancarlo Spagnolo and Cristiana Vitale, 'Deterrence in Competition Law' in Martin Peitz and Yossi Spiegel (eds), *The Analysis of Competition Policy and Sectoral Regulation* (World Scientific Publishing 2014) 423–454.

under investigation is very different from all other sectors. If we concentrate on one of the most important indicators of dominance and accept the 40% market share as a guide to and starting point for finding a dominant position, is it likely that an undertaking with 25%–30% market share will be found dominant? No. Deviating with 10%–15% from the guiding principle may seem like bravery or folly, a lack of good judgment on the part of the enforcer.

However, if there is a sector-specific rule giving legislative underpinning of the deviation, the situation is totally different. Nevertheless, there is no sector-specific rule regarding abuse of dominance, but it is rare to find any intermediary food buyer, be it a processor or a retailer, which is dominant in conventional terms. They need no dominance in a legal sense to force suppliers into terms and conditions which are not advantageous to them at all. This power is the consequence of the unique features of agri-food markets. The ruling in EU case law that buyer power does not require direct evidence of end consumer harm is an alleviation and seems like a derogation from the narrow consumer welfare paradigm, but this does not affect the prerequisite that dominance shall be found. It leads us to the conclusion that abuse of dominance is not a useful antitrust means in agri-food markets, because food processors and retail chains are not dominant in the conventional sense. This has brought to the fore other regulatory solutions, such as the provisions on relative market power and unfair trading practices which fall outside the area of conventional antitrust.

The third pillar of antitrust, merger control, also has no sector-specific rules applying to the agricultural and food sector. That is to say, mergers and acquisitions between food companies, including processors and grocery retail chains, are assessed pursuant to general rules. This is despite the acknowledged facts that food supply chains are becoming more integrated vertically and their respective levels (e.g., processing and retailing) more concentrated horizontally.

That is to say, two of the three antitrust pillars remain inactive in finding solutions for sector-specific problems. General antitrust rules, without any exception norms adopted for agriculture, are unfit to find answers to sectoral anomalies. Just as the rules on anticompetitive agreements would be inappropriate without a limited agricultural exemption to handle sector-specific features, so are the rules on abuse of dominance and merger control.

As to abuse of dominance and merger control, I aim to present my proposals jointly. In abuse of dominance cases related to agri-food markets, I aim to make a proposal with two elements. Both elements are connected to and both thresholds appeared in the merger analysis in *Carrefour/Promodès*.[1019,1020] I am of the opinion that if a certain market situation may raise concerns to be assessed in a merger analysis,

1019 *Carrefour/Promodès* (COMP/M. 1684) Commission Decision OJ C 359/33 [1999].

1020 See its detailed analysis: Maurice de Valois Turk and Ignacio Herrera Anchustegui, 'Ex Post Assessment of European Competition Policy: Buyer Power in Concentration Cases' (2021) Draft Report prepared for the 2021 Annual Conference of the GCLC.

it should also do so in an abuse of dominance context, and vice versa. As regards Articles 101 and 102, it is established case law that

> [t]he same conduct may give rise to an infringement of both [Article 101 and Article 102], even though they pursue different objectives and have distinct scopes. Those articles may thus apply simultaneously where their respective conditions of application are met. They must, accordingly, be interpreted and applied consistently, although in compliance with the specific characteristics of each of them.[1021]

Merger control also constitutes part of competition law, and serves as one of the pillars to achieve competition law objectives.

As to abuse of dominance, it would be reasonable to consider the introduction of a lower-level intervention threshold in the form of exactly determined market shares as a first proxy regarding food retailers and processors, as it was done in several national legal systems concerning food retailers.[1022] It should not be included in EU secondary law but in a Commission guideline/communication as a reference point to the Commission itself. This 'soft' reform – using soft law instruments instead of formal amendments to competition provisions – would fit the trends of the 21st century's first decade when EU antitrust law was being reformed in all of its three pillars predominantly with guidelines.[1023] As to the institutional aspect of a possible review of competition rules in agri-food markets, it would be welcome to include and give equal role to both the Directorate-General for Agriculture and Rural Development and Directorate-General for Competition. This would be less radical than the establishment of the independent Review Commission proposed in the US bill.

The intervention threshold could be determined in the form of a cascading system consisting of two pillars: the market share of the buyer downstream as processor/retailer and the share of the sales of the supplier in relation to the buyer. That is to say, the threshold referring to the downstream market should be combined with assessing the economic dependence of suppliers on the buyer in the upstream market. Assessing economic dependence could happen on the basis of the so-called threat point. The threat point is reached, if the buyer represents at least 22% of the sales of its supplier, which constitutes de facto economic dependence. While the first element referring to the downstream market is absolute in nature because it assesses the whole market in general (retailing or processing market), the second element referring to the upstream market is relative because it only assesses the relationship between the buyer and the supplier. Both rates are expressed in exact terms and provide for unambiguous legal clarity.

The cascading nature of the system could be the following. (1) A processor/retailer is presumed to be dominant, if it reaches 35% in market shares in the

1021 See, for example: C–333/21 *European Superleague Company* [2023] EU:C:2023:1011, para. 119.

1022 For example, in Finland: Section 4a of No 948/2011: "An undertaking or an association of undertakings with a minimum of 30 per cent market share in the Finnish daily consumer goods retail trade shall be deemed to occupy a dominant position in the Finnish daily consumer goods market. This includes both the retail and procurement markets."

1023 Witt (n 924) 43.

processing/retail market; if it reaches 35%, the threat point should not be examined. (2) A processor/retailer is presumed to be dominant, if it reaches 30% in market shares in the processing/retail market and reaches the threat point, i.e., 22%, in relation to the respective supplier. (3) A processor/retailer is presumed to be dominant, if it reaches 25% in market shares in the processing/retail market and reaches twice the threat point, i.e., 44%, in relation to the respective supplier. These would be presumptions for dominance. The authority should, of course, prove that this dominant position has been abused to the detriment of the undertaking's suppliers of agri-food products.

The lowest level of dominance – 25% of market shares – is based on and taken over from Recital (32) of the Merger Regulation which declares that the impediment of effective competition is not likely when the market share of the undertakings concerned does not exceed 25% either in the common market or in a substantial part of it.[1024] As a rule of thumb, why not examine then the market behaviour of an undertaking with 25% market shares in an abuse of dominance context, if a post-merger entity with 25% market shares may impede effective competition?

The control of mergers and acquisitions related to undertakings engaged in buying agri-food products, in particular to food retail chains and food processors, should follow a similar approach. These previous numerical measures could mean a strict but exactly determined starting point for the assessment of mergers and acquisitions. It would mean that more emphasis is put on the economic dependence of suppliers on buyers post merger caused by the respective merger/acquisition. The Commission's horizontal merger guidelines[1025] do not say a lot about the assessment of mergers creating or strengthening buyer power in upstream markets. In its point 61, it concentrates on monopsony power which may bring about foreclosure effects *on the buyer's rivals* and may harm *consumer welfare*. It does not mention at all the likely impacts the merger/acquisition may have on suppliers. In its point 62, it attempts to shortly describe bargaining power against suppliers which is deemed pro-competitive because of the possible pass-on of cost reductions to consumers in the form of lower consumer prices. That is to say, the merger guidelines do not suppose that the examination should necessarily cover the relationship between the merged entity and its suppliers. It is only concerned with consumer welfare and only condemns buyer power, if it may result in increased consumer prices as a consequence of foreclosing the buyer's rivals. That "[t]he Commission *may* also analyse to what extent a merged entity will increase its buyer power in upstream markets" seems soft, and it does not place emphasis on likely effects which may take place in upstream markets post merger. Concerning agri-food markets, it would, however, be reasonable to do so in light of the policy choice of preferring agricultural policy objectives to general antitrust rules. Although one of the CAP objectives – to ensure that supplies reach consumers at reasonable prices – seems

1024 Merger Regulation, recital (32).

1025 Commission, 'Guidelines on the Assessment of Horizontal Mergers under the Council Regulation on the Control of Concentrations between Undertakings' (2004/C 31/03) OJ C 31/5.

to favour consumers instead of producers, and a balance always needs to be found among CAP objectives, taking into account the intensive competition downstream (for example, between retail chains), I find it unlikely that provisions requiring a stricter assessment of procurement markets would result in higher consumer prices.

That the post-merger situation of suppliers of agri-food products would be given higher focus in the merger control framework is not the devil's work. Sector-specific merger control assessment criteria (such as media pluralism, editorial dependence) have also been adopted as regards media market concentrations.[1026] It is the acknowledgement that not only economic, in particular competition, considerations are to be assessed within this market. The same would be true for the agricultural sector, where agricultural producers provide services that go beyond the aspects of profit-making and have (noneconomic) impacts on rural areas and the environment.

Expanding the reach of antitrust with this method would be a step towards fairness-based antitrust in agri-food markets. However, fairness would be given an exact meaning expressed in intervention thresholds. The advantage of expanding the reach of antitrust is that it intervenes earlier than other regulations could. It intervenes before a higher level of concentration would be created, therefore it mitigates buyer power problems ex ante and does not give the chance for agribusinesses to get to a situation where they can abuse their buyer power.

The advantage and disadvantage of this alternative can be illustrated as follows. By expanding the reach of antitrust regarding abuse of dominance and merger control in agri-food markets, we attempt to hinder the murderer from buying a weapon. Leaving antitrust untouched and waiting for trade regulation to do the work mean that the murderer already has a weapon at his disposal and we attempt to discourage him to use that weapon. From the perspective of agricultural policy, that weapon is buyer power, be it monopsony or bargaining power, abused or misused against agricultural producers.

By lowering the intervention threshold related to abuse of dominance and merger control, food sovereignty-based competition policy may prevent the creation of buyer power to a greater extent than the current antitrust paradigm. With this, from an agricultural policy perspective, producers would be less vulnerable to unfair trading practices, because the root cause of the problem is attempted to be handled.

It would mean a step towards fairness-based competition policy in agri-food markets. The whole issue is a series of policy choices. If competition policy, in particular antitrust, did not want to be concerned about sustainability, it could do that by saying that environmental protection is not about economic efficiency and economically efficient business conducts do not necessarily lead to sustainable solutions, but the latter is not a problem for competition law to deal with. Or it

1026 Regulation (EU) 2024/1083 of the European Parliament and of the Council of 11 April 2024 establishing a common framework for media services in the internal market and amending Directive 2010/13/EU (European Media Freedom Act), art. 22.

could be said that media pluralism, too, is not a concern to assess within the framework of media market concentrations: it is not a competition-relevant factor. And still, a different perspective has been taken. So why does competition policy insist on avoiding and establishing even better assessment criteria when it comes to the objectives of agricultural policy?

Reference list

Bibliography

1. Ackrill R, Kay A and Morgan W, 'The Common Agricultural Policy and Its Reform: The Problem of Reconciling Budget and Trade Concerns' (2008) 56 Canadian Journal of Agricultural Economics/Revue Canadienne D'agroeconomie 393–411.
2. Adamopoulos T and Restuccia D, 'The Size Distribution of Farms and International Productivity Differences' (2011) University of Toronto Department of Economics Working Paper 411, 2 <www.imf.org/external/np/seminars/eng/2013/spr/pdf/restuccia.pdf> accessed 26 June 2024.
3. Aduddell RM and Cain LP, 'A Strange Sense of Deja Vu: The Packers and the Feds, 1915–82' (1982) 11 Business and Economic History 49.
4. Aduddell RM and Cain LP, 'The Consent Decree in the Meatpacking Industry, 1920–1956' (1981) 55 The Business History Review 359–378.
5. Agarwal B, 'Food Sovereignty, Food Security and Democratic Choice: Critical Contradictions, Difficult Conciliations' (2014) 41 The Journal of Peasant Studies 1247–1248.
6. Ahlborn C and Grave C, 'Walter Eucken and Ordoliberalism: An Introduction from a Consumer Welfare Perspective' (2006) 2 Competition Policy International 203.
7. Akhtar R, 'Protests, Neoliberalism and Right-Wing Populism amongst Farmers in India' (2022) 50 The Journal of Peasant Studies 2457–2477.
8. Akman P, '"Consumer Welfare" and Article 82EC: Practice and Rhetoric' (2009) 32 World Competition 71–90.
9. Akman P, *The Concept of Abuse in EU Competition Law: Law and Economic Approaches* (Hart Publishing 2012).
10. Akram-Lodhi H, 'Accelerating towards Food Sovereignty' (2015) 36 Third World Quarterly 570.
11. Alabrese M, 'Agricultural Law from a Global Perspective: An Introduction' in Mariagrazia Alabrese, Margherita Brunori, Silvia Rolandi and Andrea Saba (eds), *Agricultural Law: Current Issues from a Global Perspective* (Springer 2017).
12. Albisinni F, 'Diritto agroalimentare innanzi alle sfide dell'innovazione' (2020) 2 Rivista di BioDiritto 25–42.
13. Alons G, 'Environmental Policy Integration in the EU's Common Agricultural Policy: Greening or Greenwashing?' in Carsten Daugbjerg and Peter Feindt (eds), *Transforming Food and Agricultural Policy: Post-Exceptionalism in Public Policy* (Routledge 2018).
14. Anania G and Pupo d'Andrea MR, 'The 2013 Reform of the Common Agricultural Policy' in Johan Swinnen (ed), *The Political Economy of the 2014–2020 Common Agricultural Policy: An Imperfect Storm* (Centre for European Policy Studies 2015).
15. Anchustegui IH, *Buyer Power in EU Competition Law* (Concurrences 2017).

16. Anchustegui IH, 'Competition Law through an Ordoliberal Lens' (2015) 2 Oslo Law Review 139.
17. Anderson AM, 'Agricultural Cooperative Antitrust Exemption-Fairdale Farms Inc. v. Yankee Milk Inc.' (1981–1982) 67 Cornell Law Review 401–402.
18. Andree P, Ayres J, Bosia M and Massicotte M-J (eds), *Globalization and Food Sovereignty: Global and Local Change in the New Politics of Food* (University of Toronto Press 2014) 34.
19. Antillón GO and others, 'Animal Welfare and the United Nations' Sustainable Development Goals – Broadening Students' Perspectives' (2021) 13 Sustainability <https://doi.org/10.3390/su13063328> accessed 1 September 2023.
20. Atkinson AB, *Inequality: What Can Be Done?* (Harvard University Press 2015) 126–127.
21. Atkinson RD and Audretsch DB, 'Economic Doctrines and Approaches to Antitrust' *Indiana University-Bloomington: School of Public & Environmental Affairs Research Paper Series* (2011) <https://papers.ssrn.com/sol3/papers.cfm?abstract_id=1750259#> accessed 14 October 2023.
22. Atwood JD and Hallam A, 'Farm Structure and Stewardship of the Environment' in Arne Hallam (ed), *Size, Structure, and the Changing Face of American Agriculture* (Routledge 1994) 561–586.
23. Azzam AM, 'Slotting Allowances and Price-Cost Margins: A Note' (2001) 17 Agribusiness 417–422.
24. Baker JB and Salop SC, 'Antitrust, Competition Policy, and Inequality' (2015–2016) 104 Georgetown Law Journal Online 27.
25. Barkley A and Barkley PW, *Principles of Agricultural Economics* (Routledge 2013) 86.
26. Barnes DM and Levine JL, 'Farmer Cooperatives "Take Cover": The Capper-Volstead Exemption Is under Siege' (2021) 74 Arkansas Law Review 16.
27. Barral S and Detang-Dessendre C, 'Reforming the Common Agricultural Policy (2023–2027): Multidisciplinary Views' (2023) 104 Review of Agricultural, Food and Environmental Studies 47.
28. Barreto Ávila M, 'The Mayan Indigenous Women of Chiapas: Lekil Kuxlejal and Food Autonomy' (2011) 54 Development 485–489.
29. Bartoloni ME, 'The Horizontal Social Clause in a Legal Dimension' in Francesca Ippolito, Maria Eugenia Bartoloni and Massimo Condinanzi (eds), *The EU and the Proliferation of Integration Principles under the Lisbon Treaty* (Routledge 2018) 83–104.
30. Bass CM, 'More than a Mirror: The Packers and Stockyards Act, Antitrust Laws, and the Injury to Competition Requirement' (2007) 12 Drake Journal of Agricultural Law 424 and 426.
31. Baumer DL, Masson RT and Abrahamson Masson R, 'Curdling the Competition: An Economic and Legal Analysis of the Antitrust Exemption for Agriculture' (1986) 31 Villanova Law Review 198.
32. Baumgartner M and others, 'Improving Horse Welfare and Environmental Sustainability in Horse Husbandry: Linkage between Turnout and Nitrogen Surplus' (2021) 13 Sustainability <https://doi.org/10.3390/su13168991> accessed 1 September 2023.
33. Baylis K, Rausser GC and Simon LK, 'Including Non-Trade Concerns: The Environment in EU and US Agricultural Policy' (2005) 4 International Journal of Agricultural Resources Governance and Ecology 264.
34. Behrens P, 'The Ordoliberal Concept of "Abuse" of a Dominant Position and Its Impact on Article 102 TFEU' (2015) SSRN <https://papers.ssrn.com/sol3/papers.cfm?abstract_id=2658045> accessed 22 July 2023.
35. Bengtsson H, 'International Report' in Pranvera Këllezi, Bruce Kilpatrick and Pierre Kobel (eds), *Abuse of Dominant Position and Globalization & Protection and Disclosure of Trade Secrets and Know-How* (Springer International 2017) 292.

36. Bernard J, 'Where Have All the Rural Poor Gone? Explaining the Rural–Urban Poverty Gap in European Countries' (2019) 59 Sociologia Ruralis 386–387.
37. Bernstein H, 'Food Sovereignty via the "Peasant Way": A Sceptical View' (2014) 41 The Journal of Peasant Studies 1055.
38. Black CM and Kent Sufrin R, 'Agricultural Cooperatives: Price-Fixing and the Antitrust Exemption' (1978) 11 U.C.D. Law Review 553–554.
39. Blockx J and Vandenberghe J, 'Rebalancing Commercial Relations Along the Food Supply Chain: The Agricultural Exemption from EU Competition Law After Regulation 1308/2013' (2014) 10 European Competition Journal 390.
40. Blockx J, 'The ECJ Preliminary Ruling in French Endives: Two (Too?) Simple Rules to Attune Article 101 TFEU to the Common Agricultural Policy' (2017) Kluwer Competition Law Blog <http://competitionlawblog.kluwercompetitionlaw.com/2017/11/15/ecj-preliminary-ruling-french-endives-two-simple-rules-attune-article-101-tfeu-common-agricultural-policy/> accessed 30 December 2023.
41. Bork RH, 'Legislative Intent and the Policy of the Sherman Act' (1966) 9 Journal of Law & Economics 7–48.
42. Bork RH, *The Antitrust Paradox* (Free Press 1978).
43. Borras SM Jr., 'The Politics of Transnational Agrarian Movements' (2010) 41 Development and Change 781.
44. Botta BM, 'Personal Liability for Corporate Debts: The Reach of the Perishable Agricultural Commodities Act Continues to Expand' (1997) 2 Drake Journal of Agricultural Law 339.
45. Bové J and Dufour F, *The World Is Not for Sale – Farmers Against Junk Food* (Verso 2001) 168.
46. Bradley RL Jr., 'On the Origins of the Sherman Antitrust Act' (1990) 9 Cato Journal 739.
47. Brady M, Kellermann K, Sahrbacher C and Jelinek L, 'Impacts of Decoupled Agricultural Support on Farm Structure, Biodiversity and Landscape Mosaic: Some EU Results' (2009) 60 Journal of Agricultural Economics 580.
48. Bragg LA and Dalton TJ, 'Factors Affecting the Decision to Exit Dairy Farming: A Two-Stage Regression Analysis' (2004) 87 Journal of Dairy Science 3092–3098.
49. Bratspies R, 'Owning All the Seeds: Consolidation and Control in Agbiotech' (2017) 47 Environmental Law 583–560; Manuel A. Hernandez and Maximo Torero, 'Market Concentration and Pricing behavior in the Fertilizer Industry: A global Approach' (2013) 44 Agricultural Economics 723–734.
50. Breustedt G and Glauben T, 'Driving Forces behind Exiting from Farming in Western Europe' (2007) 58 Journal of Agricultural Economics 115–127.
51. Broom DM, 'Animal Welfare Complementing or Conflicting with other Sustainability Issues' (2019) Applied Animal Behaviour Science <https://doi.org/10.1016/j.applanim.2019.06.010> accessed 1 September 2023.
52. Broyer S, 'The Social Market Economy: Birth of an Economic Style' (Wissenschaftszentrum Berlin für Sozialforschung: Discussion Paper 9, 1996).
53. Buccirossi P, Ciari L, Duso T, Spagnolo G and Vitale C, 'Deterrence in Competition Law' in Martin Peitz and Yossi Spiegel (eds), *The Analysis of Competition Policy and Sectoral Regulation* (World Scientific Publishing 2014) 423–454.
54. Buccirossi P, Marette S and Schiavina A, 'Competition Policy and the Agribusiness Sector in the European Union' (2002) 29 European Review of Agricultural Economics 376.
55. Buczacki A, Gładysz B and Palmer E, 'HoReCa Food Waste and Sustainable Development Goals – A Systemic View' (2021) 13 Sustainability, Article 5510.
56. Bullard B, 'Under Siege: The U.S. Live Cattle Industry' (2013) 58 South Datoka Law Review 562.
57. Buller H and others, 'Towards Farm Animal Welfare and Sustainability' (2018) 8 Animals <https://doi.org/10.3390/ani8060081> accessed 1 September 2023.

58. Buller H, 'Integrating EU Environmental and Agricultural Policy' in Andrea Lenschow (ed), *Environmental Policy Integration: Greening Sectoral Policies in Europe* (Earthscan 2001) 103.
59. Buller H, 'The Agri-Environmental Measures (2078/92)' in Floor Brouwer and Philip Lowe (eds), *CAP Regimes and the European Countryside: Prospects for Integration between Agricultural, Regional and Environmental Policies* (CABI Publishing 2000) 216.
60. Bureau J-C and Mahé L-P, 'Was the CAP Reform a Success?' in Johan Swinnen (ed), *The Political Economy of the 2014–2020 Common Agricultural Policy: An Imperfect Stom* (Centre for European Policy Studies 2015).
61. Bureau J-C, Crombez C, Knops L, Matthews A, Swinnen J, Tangermann S and Viaggi D, 'The Common Agricultural Policy After 2013' (2012) 47 Intereconomics 316–342.
62. Burnett K and Murphy S, 'What Place for International Trade in Food Sovereignty?' (2014) 41 The Journal of Peasant Studies 1065–1084.
63. Busse C, 'Die Sonderrechtstheorie im Agrarrecht – Konzeptionelle Überlegungen zu ihrer Weiterentwicklung' in José Martínez (ed), *Reichweite und Grenzen des Agrarrechts: Gedächtnisschrift für Dr. Wolfgang Winkler*. (Nomos 2018) 19.
64. Cahill D, Cooper M, Konings M and Primrose D, 'Introduction: Approaches to Neoliberalism' in Damien Cahill, Melinda Cooper, Martijn Konings and David Primrose (eds), *The SAGE Handbook of Neoliberalim* (SAGE Publications 2018).
65. Campbell CM and Wiles P, 'The Study of Law in Society in Britain' (1976) 10 Law and Society Review 547–578.
66. Campbell DA, 'The Packers and Stockyards Act Regulatory Program' in John Davidson (ed), *Agricultural Law* (Shepards's/McGraw-Hill 1981).
67. Candel JJL, 'The Expediency of Policy Integration' (2021) 42 Policy Studies 346.
68. Cannon JP and Bloom PN, 'Are Slotting Allowances Legal under the Antitrust Laws?' (1991) 10 Journal of Marketing & Public Policy 167–186.
69. Carrozza A, 'L'individuazione del diritto agrario per mezzo dei suoi istituti' (1975) 21 Rivista di diritto civile 107–178.
70. Carstensen P, 'Controlling Unfairness in American Agriculture' in Ignacio Herrera Anchustegui, Ronny Gjendemsjø, Peter C. Carstensen, Johan Hedelin and Antonio Miño López (eds), *Unfair Trading Practices in the Food Supply Chain* (Concurrences 2019) 7.
71. Carstensen P, 'Economic Analysis of Antitrust Exemptions' in Roger D. Blair and D. Daniel Sokol (eds), *The Oxford Handbook of Antitrust Economics*, vol 1 (OUP 2015) 33–62.
72. Castendyck W, *Die Entwicklung der Kornhausbewegung, mit Besonderer Berücksichtigung der Preussischen und der Bayerischen Verhältnisse* (Forgotten Books 2018).
73. Castillo-Díaz FJ, Belmonte-Urena LJ, López-Serrano MJ and Camacho-Ferre F, 'Assessment of the Sustainability of the European Agri-Food Sector in the Context of the Circular Economy' (2023) 40 Sustainable Production and Consumption 408.
74. Castronuovo D, Antonio Doval Pais and Luigi Foffani, *La sicurezza agroalimentare nella prospettiva europea: Precauzione, prevenzione, repressione* (Giuffrè Francis Lefebvre 2014).
75. Čechura L, Žáková Kroupová Z and Benešová I, 'Productivity and Efficiency in European Milk Production: Can We Observe the Effects of Abolishing Milk Quotas?' (2021) 11 Agriculture 835.
76. Cejudo GM and Trein P, 'Pathways to Policy Integration: A Subsystem Approach' (2023) 56 Policy Sciences 9.
77. Chaddad FR and Mondelli MP, 'Sources of Firm Performance Differences in the US Food Economy' (2012) 64 Journal of Agricultural Economics 382–404.
78. Chagny M, 'Enforcement in the Directive' in Bert Keirsbilck and Evelyne Terryn (eds), *Unfair Trading Practices in the Food Supply Chain: Implications of Directive (EU) 2019/633* (Intersentia 2020).

79. Chappell MJ and Schneider M, 'The New Three-Legged Stool: Agroecology, Food Sovereignty, and Food Justice' in Mary C. Rawlinson and Caleb Ward (eds), *The Routledge Handbook of Food Ethics* (Routledge 2017) 424.
80. Chauve P and Renckens A, 'The European Food Sector: Are Large Retailers a Competition Problem?' (2015) 6 Journal of European Competition Law & Practice 513.
81. Chirita AD, 'Undistorted, (Un)fair Competition, Consumer Welfare and the Interpretation of Article 102 TFEU' (2010) 33 World Competition 417–436.
82. Claassen R, Hellerstein D and Wallander S, '2018 Farm Act Retains Conservation Programs But Could Reduce Payments for Land Retirement' (2019) <www.ers.usda.gov/amber-waves/2019/december/2018-farm-act-retains-conservation-programs-but-could-reduce-payments-for-land-retirement/> accessed 30 December 2023.
83. Clapp J, *Food* (Polity Press 2012) 176.
84. Clark P, 'Can the State Foster Food Sovereignty? Insights from the Case of Ecuador' (2016) 16 Journal of Agrarian Change 183–205.
85. Coates K and Middelschulte D, 'Getting Consumer Welfare Right: The Competition Law Implications of Market-Driven Sustainability Initiatives' (2019) 15 European Competition Journal 318–326.
86. Collins WD, 'Trusts and the Origins of Antitrust Legislation' (2013) 81 Fordham Law Review 2280.
87. Colver WB, 'The Federal Trade Commission and the Meat-Packing Industry' (1919) 82 The Annals of the American Academy of Political and Social Science 170.
88. Connor JM, Rogers RT, Marion BW and Mueller WF, *The Food Manufacturing Industries: Structures, Strategies, Performance, and Policies* (D.C. Heath 1985).
89. Coppess J, 'Climate Change and the Farm Bill: A Brief History' (2022) 12 Farmdoc Daily 149.
90. Corsini L and Moultrie J, 'What Is Design for Social Sustainability? A Systematic Literature Review for Designers of Product-Service Systems' (2021) 13 Sustainability, Article 5963.
91. Craig P and de Búrca G, *EU Law: Text, Cases, and Materials* (6th edn, OUP 2015) 1001.
92. Crane DA, 'Antitrust and Wealth Inequality' (2016) 101 Cornell Law Review 1228.
93. Crane DA, 'Antitrust as an Instrument of Democracy' (2022) 72 Duke Law Journal Online 40.
94. Crane DA, 'How Much Brandeis Do the Neo-Brandeisians Want?' (2019) 64 The Antitrust Bulletin 531.
95. Craven R, 'Socio-Legal Studies and Economics' in Naomi Creutzfeldt, Marc Mason and Kirsten McConnachie (eds), *Routledge Handbook of Socio-Legal Theory and Methods* (Routledge 2020) 182.
96. Craymer L, 'New Zealand Farmers Set for Right-Wing Protest Vote over Climate Change Policies' *Reuters* (27 September 2023).
97. Creutzfeldt N, Mason M and McConnachie K, 'Socio-Legal Theory and Methods: Introduction' in Naomi Creutzfeldt, Marc Mason and Kirsten McConnachie (eds), *Routledge Handbook of Socio-Legal Theory and Methods* (Routledge 2020) 3.
98. Cuadros-Casanova I et al., 'Opportunities and Challenges for Common Agricultural Policy Reform to Support the European Green Deal' (2023) 37 Conservation Biology 10.
99. Cunha A and Swinbank A, *An Inside View of the CAP Reform Process: Explaining the MacSharry, Agenda 2000, and Fischler Reforms* (OUP 2011).
100. Cunningham TJ, 'Amended Perishable Agricultural Commodities Act: Further Concealment of a Lien Already Nearly Invisible' (1999) 116 Banking Law Journal 253–260.
101. Czapracka KA, 'Antitrust and Trade Secrets: The U.S. and the EU Approach' (2008) 24 Santa Clara High Technology Law Journal 208.
102. Csirszki MM, 'Competition Law, Sustainability, and Agriculture: Uneasy Complexity' (in press by the Institute of Justice in Warsaw).

103. Csirszki MM, 'Is There Room for Food Sovereignty Considerations in EU Competition Policy? A Theoretical Framework' (2022) 18 Croatian Yearbook of European Law and Policy 83–106.
104. Csirszki MM, 'The Comparison of the US and EU Agricultural Antitrust Exemption' (2022) 15 Yearbook of Antitrust and Regulatory Studies 137–173.
105. Csirszki MM, Szinek Csütörtöki H and Zombory K, 'Food Sovereignty: Is There an Emerging Paradigm in V4 Countries for the Regulation of the Acquisition of Ownership of Agricultural Lands by Legal Persons?' (2021) 2 Central European Journal of Comparative Law 29–52.
106. Dahl M, 'Ordoliberal Roots of Ecological Market Economy' (2018) 11 Review of Economic & Business Studies 116.
107. Danbom DD, 'Romantic Agrarianism in Twentieth-Century America' (1991) 65 Agricultural History 1–12.
108. Das Nair R and Chisoro S, 'Competition, Barriers to Entry and Inclusive Growth: Case Study on Fruit and Veg City' (2015) CCRED Working Paper Series 2015/9 <https://doi.org/10.13140/RG.2.1.1417.8321> accessed 20 January 2024.
109. Daskalova V, 'Consumer Welfare in EU Competition Law: What Is It (Not) About?' (2015) 11 The Competition Law Review 131–160.
110. Daskalova V, 'The New Directive on Unfair Trading Practices in Food and EU Competition Law: Complementary or Divergent Normative Frameworks?' (2019) 10 Journal of European Competition Law & Practice 281.
111. Daugbjerg C and Feindt PH, 'Post-Exceptionalism in Public Policy: Transforming Food and Agricultural Policy' in Carsten Daugbjerg and Peter Feindt (eds), *Transforming Food and Agricultural Policy: Post-Exceptionalism in Public Policy* (Routledge 2018) ch 1.
112. Daugbjerg C and Swinbank A, 'An Introduction to the 'New' Politics of Agriculture and Food' (2012) 31 Policy and Society 259–260.
113. Daugbjerg C and Swinbank A, 'Three Decades of Policy Layering and Politically Sustainable Reform in the European Union's Agricultural Policy' (2016) 29 Governance 265.
114. Davies W, *The Limits of Neoliberalism* (SAGE Publications 2014) 31–32.
115. Davis TD, 'Private Decisions and Public Goods: Trade-Offs in the Conservation Programs in the New Farm Bill: Discussion' (2004) 36 Journal of Agricultural and Applied Economics 435.
116. De Pourcq S and Terryn E, 'Prohibited and Conditionally Permitted Unfair Trading Practices' in Bert Keirsbilck and Evelyne Terryn (eds), *Unfair Trading Practices in the Food Supply Chain: Implications of Directive (EU) 2019/633* (Intersentia 2020) 37–60.
117. de Valois Turk M and Anchustegui IH, 'Ex Post Assessment of European Competition Policy: Buyer Power in Concentration Cases' (2021) Draft Report Prepared for the 2021 Annual Conference of the GCLC.
118. Deconinck K, 'Facts, Interests, and Values: Identifying Points of Convergence and Divergence for Food Systems' in Danielle Resnick and Johan Swinnen (eds), *The Political Economy of Food System Transformation: Pathways to Progress in a Polarized World* (OUP 2023) 32–53.
119. Dekeyser K, Korsten L and Fioramonti L, 'Food Sovereignty: Shifting Debates on Democratic Food Governance' (2018) 10 Food Security 223–233.
120. Deutscher E and Makris S, 'Sustainability Concerns in EU Merger Control: From Output-Maximising to Polycentric Innovation Competition' (2023) 11 Journal of Antitrust Enforcement 350–399.
121. Dobinson I and Johns F, 'Qualitative Legal Research' in Mike McConville and Wing Hong Chui (eds), *Research Methods for Law* (Edinburgh University Press 2007) 18–19.
122. Dobson PW and Inderst R, 'The Waterbed Effect: Where Buying and Selling Come Together' (2008) <https://tinyurl.hu/eBbJ/> accessed 30 June 2024.

123. Dobson PW, Waterson M and Davies SW, 'The Patterns and Implications of Increasing Concentration in European Food Retailing' (2003) 54 Journal of Agricultural Economics 111–125.
124. Dold M and Krieger T, 'The Ideological Use and Abuse of Freiburg's Ordoliberalism' (2021) 195 *Public Choice* 341–361.
125. Donohue III JJ, 'Law and Economics: The Road Not Taken' (1988) 22 Law & Society Review 922.
126. Doukas YE, Salvati L and Vardopoulos I, 'Unraveling the European Agricultural Policy Sustainable Development Trajectory' (2023) 12 Land, Article 1749.
127. Doukas YE, Vardopoulos I and Petides P, 'Challenging the Status Quo: A Critical Analysis of the Common Agricultural Policy's Shift Toward Sustainability' in Andrea Ribeiro Hoffmann, Paula Sandrin and Yannis E. Doukas (eds), *Climate Change in Regional Perspective: European Union and Latin American Initiatives, Challenges, and Solutions* (Springer 2024) 128.
128. Doyle C and Murgatroyd R, 'The Role of Private Labels in Antitrust' (2011) 7 Journal of Competition Law & Economics 631–650.
129. Edelman LB, 'Rivers of Law Contested Terrain: A Law and Society Approach to Economic Rationality' (2004) 38 Law & Society Review 182.
130. Edelman M, 'Food Sovereignty: Forgotten Genealogies and Future Regulatory Challenges' (2014) 41 The Journal of Peasant Studies 959–978.
131. Edelman M, Weis T, Baviskar A, Borras SM Jr, Holt-Giménez E, Kandiyoti D and Wolford W, 'Introduction: Critical Perspectives on Food Sovereignty' (2014) 41 The Journal of Peasant Studies 914.
132. Edwards P, 'The Hidden War over Grocery Shelf Space' *VOX* (22 November 2016).
133. Eichler M, 'Land- und Forstwirtschaftsrecht' in Viktor Heller (ed) *Rechtskunde* (1st edn, Manz 1975).
134. Erjavec E, Lovec M and Erjavec K, 'From "Greening" to "Greenwash": Drivers and Discourses of the CAP 2020 "Reform"' in Johan Swinnen (ed), *The Political Economy of the 2014–2020 Common Agricultural Policy: An Imperfect Stom* (Centre for European Policy Studies 2015).
135. Espinosa-Goded M, Barreiro-Hurlé J and Ruto E, 'What Do Farmers Want from Agri-Environmental Scheme Design? A Choice Experiment Approach' (2010) 61 Journal of Agricultural Economics 259–273.
136. Eucken W, 'Die Wettbewerbsordnung und ihre Verwirklichung: Erster Teil über die Wirtschaftspolitik der Vergangenheit' (1949) 2 ORDO: Jahrbuch für die Ordnung von Wirtschaft und Gesellschaft 1–99.
137. Eucken W, *Grundsätze der Wirtschaftspolitik* (J.C.B. Mohr 1952) 334.
138. Eucken W, 'The Competitive Order and Its Implementation (English Translation)' (2006) 2 Competition Policy International 227.
139. Ezrachi A, 'Sponge' (2017) 5 Journal of Antitrust Enforcement 49–75.
140. Fairbairn M, 'Framing Transformation: The Counter-Hegemonic Potential of Food Sovereignty in the US Context' (2012) 29 Agriculture and Human Values 228.
141. Falconer K and Ward N, 'Using Modulation to Green the CAP: The UK Case' (2000) 17 Land Use Policy 270.
142. Fałkowski J, 'The Economic Aspects of Unfair Trading Practices: Measurement and Indicators' in Federica Di Marcantonio and Pavel Ciaian (eds), *Unfair Trading Practices in the Food Supply Chain: A Literature Review on Methodologies, Impacts and Regulatory Aspects* (Publications Office of the European Union 2017) 20.
143. Farmer M and Swales V, *The Development and Implementation of Cross-Compliance in the EU-15: An Analysis* (Institute for European Environmental Policy 2004) 4.
144. Ferrera SM, 'Perishable Agricultural Commodities Act Affecting Lender's Secured Priority Interest' (1999) 7 University of Miami Business Law Review 355.
145. Finger R and El Benni N, 'Farm Income in European Agriculture: New Perspectives on Measurement and Implications for Policy Evaluation' (2021) 48 European Review of Agricultural Economics 254.

146. First H, 'Trade secrets and antitrust law' in Rochelle C. Dreyfuss and Katherine J. Strandburg (eds), *The Law and Theory of Trade Secrecy: A Handbook of Contemporary Research* (Edward Elgar 2011) 332–380.
147. Fischler F, 'Reform of the Common Agricultural Policy' (May/June 2001) Intereconomics 115–118.
148. Fisk Beach C, *A Treatise on the Law of Monopolies and Industrial Trusts, As Administered in England and in the United States of America* (The Lawbook Exchange 2007) 245.
149. Flavin TJ, 'The Packers and Stockyards Act, 1921' (1958) 26 The George Washington Law Review 161.
150. Fodor L, *Agrárjog [Agricultural law]* (Kossuth Egyetemi Kiadó 2005).
151. Folmer C, Keyzer MA, Merbis MD, Stolwijk HJJ and Veenendaal PJJ, *The Common Agricultural Policy Beyond the Macsharry Reform* (Elsevier 1995) 12.
152. Folsom RH, 'Antitrust Enforcement under the Secretaries of Agriculture and Commerce' (1980) 80 Columbia Law Review 1634.
153. Foros Ø and Jarle Kind H, 'Do Slotting Allowances Harm Retail Competition?' (2008) 110 Scandinavian Journal of Economics 367–384.
154. Foster AD and Rosenzweig MR, 'Are There Too Many Farms in the World? Labor Market Transaction Costs, Machine Capacities, and Optimal Farm Size' (2022) 130 Journal of Political Economy 636–680.
155. Fountain G, 'Land Use Related Restrictions and the Conservation Provisions of the Food Security Act of 1985: Sodbuster and Swampbuster' (1988) 11 University of Arkansas at Little Rock Law Review 554.
156. Fox EM, 'We Protect Competition, You Protect Competitors' (2003) 26 World Competition 149–165.
157. Fox EM, 'Against Goals' (2013) 81 Fordham Law Review 2159.
158. Fox EM, 'Economic Development, Poverty and Antitrust: The Other Path' (2007) 13 Southwestern Journal of Law and Trade in the Americas 211–236.
159. Frederick DA, *Antitrust Status of Farmer Cooperatives: The Story of the Capper-Volstead Act* (U.S. Department of Agriculture 2002) 68.
160. Frenz W, 'Agrarwettbewerbsrecht' (2010) 40 Agrar- und Umweltrecht 193.
161. Friedrich L and others, 'Iceberg Indicators for Sow and Piglet Welfare' (2021) 12 Sustainability <https://doi.org/10.3390/su12218967> accessed 1 September 2023.
162. Gal MS, 'Abuse of Dominance: Exploitative Abuses' in Ioannis Lianos and Damien Geradin (eds), *Handbook on European Competition Law: Substantive Aspects* (Edward Elgar 2013) 385 and 422.
163. Galbraith JK, *American Capitalism: The Concept of Countervailing Power* (Routledge 1993) 139.
164. Gallagher KP, 'Economic Globalization and the Environment' (2009) 34 Annual Review of Environment and Resources 279.
165. Garzón Delvaux PA, Riesgo L and Gomez y Paloma S, 'Are Small Farms More Performant Than Larger Ones in Developing Countries?' (2020) 6 Science Advances 1–11.
166. Garzon I, *Reforming the Common Agricultural Policy: History of a Paradigm Change* (Palgrave Macmillan 2007).
167. Gaviglio A, Bertocchi M, Marescotti ME, Demartini E and Pirani A, 'The Social Pillar of Sustainability: A Quantitative Approach at the Farm Level' (2016) 4 Agricultural and Food Economics, Article 15.
168. Geenens R, 'Sovereignty as Autonomy' (2017) 36 Law and Philosophy 524.
169. Gehring MW, 'Competition for Sustainability: Sustainable Development Concerns in National and EC Competition Law' (2006) 15 Review of European Community & International Environmental Law 172–184.
170. Geradin D, 'Efficiency Claims in EC Competition Law and Sector-Specific Regulation' in Hanns Ullrich (ed), *The Evolution of European Competition Law: Whose Regulation, Which Competition?* (Edward Elgar 2006) 313.

171. Gerber DJ, 'Constitutionalizing the Economy: German Neo-Liberalism, Competition Law and the "New" Europe' (1994) 42 The American Journal of Comparative Law 69.
172. Gerber DJ, *Law and Competition in Twentieth Century Europe* (OUP 1998) 4–5.
173. Germanò A, Maria Pia Ragionieri and Eva Rook Basile, *Diritto agroalimentare: Le regole del mercato degli alimenti e dell'informazione alimentare* (2nd edn, Giappichelli 2019).
174. Gil C, Boluda R, Rodríguez Martín JA, Guzmán M, del Moral F and Ramos-Miras J, 'Assessing Soil Contamination and Temporal Trends of Heavy Metal Contents in Greenhouses on Semiarid Land' (2018) 29 Land Degradation and Development 3344–3354.
175. Gizaw D, Myrland Ø and Xie J, 'Asymmetric Price Transmission in a Changing Food Supply Chain' (2021) 25 Aquaculture Economics & Management 89–105.
176. Glick M, 'American Gothic: How Chicago Economics Distorts "Consumer Welfare" in Antitrust' (2019) SSRN <https://papers.ssrn.com/sol3/papers.cfm?abstract_id=3423081> accessed 24 June 2023.
177. Goldschmidt N, 'Alfred Müller-Armack and Ludwig Erhard: Social Market Liberalism' (Freiburger Diskussionspapiere zur Ordnungsökonomik 04/12, 2012) 1.
178. Goldschmidt N, 'Leonhard Miksch' in *Soziale Marktwirtschaft: Vordenker und Klassiker* 81 <https://bit.ly/3Dnd0aq> accessed 21 October 2023.
179. Göckler T, *Angstfaktor und unlautere Handelspraktiken: Eine Untersuchung anlässlich des Grünbuchs der Europäischen Kommission über unlautere Handelspraktiken in der b2b-Lieferkette* (Mohr Siebeck 2017).
180. Granovetter M, 'Economic Action and Social Structure: The Problem of Embeddedness' (1985) 91 American Journal of Sociology 481–510.
181. Grant W, *The Common Agricultural Policy* (Macmillan Press 1997).
182. Graubner M and Sexton RJ, 'More Competitive Than You Think? Pricing and Location of Processing Firms in Agricultural Markets' (2023) 105 American Journal of Agricultural Economics 784.
183. Greer A, 'Post-Exceptional Politics in Agriculture: An Examination of the 2013 CAP Reform' (2017) 24 Journal of European Public Policy 1585–1603.
184. Grey S and Patel R, 'Food Sovereignty as Decolonization: Some Contributions from Indigenous Movements to Food System and Development Politics' (2015) 32 Agriculture and Human Values 432.
185. Grimes WS, 'Antitrust and the Systemic Bias against Small Business: Kodak, Strategic Conduct, and Strategic Conduct, and Leverage Theory' (2001) 52 Case Western Reserve Law Review 233.
186. Grimm C, *Agrarrecht* (3rd edn, C.H. Beck 2004).
187. Grossi G, Goglio P, Vitali A and Williams AG, 'Livestock and Climate Change: Impact of Livestock on Climate and Mitigation Strategies' (2019) 9 Animal Frontiers 69–76.
188. Groteloh P, 'Grundzüge des Agrarkartellrechts' in Matthias Dombert and Karsten Witt (eds), *Münchener Anwaltshandbuch Agrarrecht* (2nd edn, C.H. Beck 2016).
189. Guiomar N and others, 'Typology and Distribution of Small Farms in Europe: Towards a Better Picture' (2018) 75 Land Use Policy 785.
190. Gundlach GT and Bloom PN, 'Slotting Allowances and the Retail Sale of Alcohol Beverages' (1998) 17 Journal of Public Policy & Marketing 173–184.
191. Guyomard H, Détang-Dessendre C, Dupraz P, Delaby L, Huyghe C, Peyraud J-L, Reboud X and Sirami C, 'How the Green Architecture of the 2023–2027 Common Agricultural Policy Could Have Been Greener' (2023) 52 Ambio 1327–1338.
192. Habermas J, *Between Facts and Norms – Contributions to a Discourse Theory of Law and Democracy* (The MIT Press 1996) 263.
193. Habermas J, *The Crisis of the European Union: A Response* (Polity Press 2012) 106.
194. Hajer MA, *The Politics of Environmental Discourse: Ecological Modernisation and the Policy Process* (OUP 1995) 61.
195. Halmai P (ed), *A Közös Agrárpolitika rendszere* (Dialóg Campus 2020) 17.

196. Hamilton SF, 'Slotting Allowances as a Facilitating Practice by Food Processors in Wholesale Grocery Markets: Profitability and Welfare Effects' (2003) 85 American Journal of Agricultural Economics 797–813.
197. Harrigan K and Charney A, 'Impact of 2018 Farm Bill Provisions on Soil Health' (Soil Health Institute National Sustainable Agriculture Coalition, August 2019).
198. Hart K, 'The Fate of Green Direct Payments in the CAP Reform Negotiations' in Johan Swinnen (ed), *The Political Economy of the 2014–2020 Common Agricultural Policy: An Imperfect Stom* (Centre for European Policy Studies 2015).
199. Härtel I (ed), *Handbook of Agri-Food Law in China, Germany, European Union: Food Security, Food Safety, Sustainable Use of Resources in Agriculture* (Springer 2018).
200. Härtel I, '§ 7 Agrarrecht' in Mathias Ruffert (ed), *Europäisches Sektorales Wirtschaftsrecht* (1st edn, Nomos 2013) 437.
201. Härtel I, 'AEUV Art. 42 [Eingeschränkte Anwendung der Wettbewerbs- und Beihilferegeln]' in Rudolf Streinz (ed), *EUV/AEUV – Vertrag über die Europäische Union, Vertrag über die Arbeitsweise der Europäischen Union, Charta der Grundrechte der Europäischen Union* (3rd edn, C.H. Beck 2018).
202. Harvey DR, 'The US Farm Act: "Fair" or "Foul"? An Evolutionary Perspective from East of the Atlantic' (Conference Paper, 1998) <www.staff.ncl.ac.uk/david.harvey/AEF811/AEF811.5/FAIR1.pdf> accessed 29 June 2024.
203. Haspel T, 'Small vs. Large: Which Size Farm Is Better for the Planet?' *The Washington Post* (2 September 2014).
204. Hauter W, *Foodopoly: The Battle over the Future of Food and Farming in America* (The New Press 2012).
205. Hawke SD, 'Antitrust Implications of Agricultural Cooperatives' (1984) 73 Kentucky Law Journal 1035.
206. Healey D, 'The Ambit of Competition Law: Comments on Its Goals' in Deborah Healey, Michael Jacobs and Rhonda L. Smith (eds), *Research Handbook on Methods and Models of Competition Law* (Edward Elgar 2020) 12.
207. Hearn D, Hanawalt C and Sachs L, 'Antitrust and Sustainability: A Landscape Analysis' (2023) Columbia Center on Sustainable Investment and Sabin Center for Climate Change Law, 8 <https://ccsi.columbia.edu/content/antitrust-and-sustainability-landscape-analysis> accessed 22 June 2024.
208. Hecker C, 'Soziale Marktwirtschaft und Soziale Gerechtigkeit: Mythos, Anspruch und Wirklichkeit' (2011) 12 Zeitschrift für Wirtschafts- und Unternehmensethik 272.
209. Heinemann A, 'Social Considerations in EU Competition Law – The Protection of Competition as a Cornerstone of the Social Market Economy' in Delia Ferri and Fulvio Cortese (eds), *The EU Social Market Economy and the Law: Theoretical Perspectives and Practical Challenges for the EU* (Routledge 2019) 123–146.
210. Heinrichs H and Biermann F, 'Sustainability: Politics and Governance' in Harald Heinrichs, Pim Martens, Gerd Michelsen and Arnim Wiek (eds), *Sustainability Science: An Introduction* (Springer 2016) 129–137.
211. Hendrickson MK and James HS Jr., 'Power, Fairness and Constrained Choice in Agricultural Markets: A Synthesizing Framework' (2016) 29 Journal of Agricultural and Environmental Ethics 945–967.
212. Hendrickson MK and James HS Jr., 'The Ethics of Constrained Choice: How the Industrialization of Agriculture Impacts Farming and Farmer Behavior' (2005) 18 Journal of Agricultural and Environmental Ethics 269–291.
213. Heron JB Jr. and Hayes JC Jr., 'Reparations Proceedings under the Perishable Agricultural Commodities Act: Valuable Tool in Need of Change' (1997) 22 South Dakota Law Review 520.
214. Hildebrand D, 'The Equality and Social Fairness Objectives in EU Competition Law: The European School of Thought' (2017) 1 Concurrences.
215. Hill B, *Understanding the Common Agricultural Policy* (Earthscan 2012) 33.

216. Hirsch S and Gschwandtner A, 'Profit Persistence in the Food Industry: Evidence from Five European Countries' (2013) 40 European Review of Agricultural Economics 752.
217. Hogl K, Kleinschmit D and Rayner J, 'Achieving Policy Integration across Fragmented Policy Domains: Forests, Agriculture, Climate and Energy' (2016) 34 Environment and Planning C: Government and Policy 399–414.
218. Hojnyák D, 'Az agrárszabályozási tárgyak megjelenése az EU tagállamainak alkotmányaiban, különös tekintettel a Magyar Alaptörvényben megjelenő agrárjogi szabályozási tárgyakra [Regulatory Objects of Agricultural Law in the Constitutions of EU Member States, in Particular in the Hungarian Fundamental Law]' (2019) 14 Miskolci Jogi Szemle 58–76.
219. Holmberg J and Sandbrook R, 'Sustainable Development: What Is to Be Done?' in Johan Holmberg (ed), *Policies for a Small Planet* (Earthscan 1992) 19–38.
220. Holmes S and Meagher M, 'A Sustainable Future: How Can Control of Monopoly Power Play a Part?' (2022) <www.ebcam.eu/images/SSRN-id4099796.pdf> accessed 29 June 2024. 07. 04.
221. Holmes S, 'Climate Change, Sustainability, and Competition Law' (2020) 8 Journal of Antitrust Enforcement 379–380.
222. Holmes S, Kar N and Cunningham L, 'Sustainability and Competition Law in the United Kingdom' in Pranvera Këllezi, Pierre Kobel and Bruce Kilpatrick (eds), *Sustainability Objectives in Competition and Intellectual Property Law* (Springer 2024) 219–234.
223. Holzer G, *Agrar-Raumplanungsrecht* (Österreichischer Agrarverlag 1981).
224. Holzer G, 'Agrarrecht heute. Versuch einer Gegenstands- und Standortbestimmung' (1982) Agrarische Rundschau 1.
225. Holzer G, 'Zum Begriff und Standort des Agrarrechts in der österreichischen Rechtsordnung' (1982) Juristische Blätter 11–12.
226. Horváth G, 'A környezetjog és az agrárjog közeledése, találkozása és metszete a magyar jogrendszerben [The Approaching, Meeting and Overlapping of Environmental Law and Agricultural Law in the Hungarian Legal System]' (2007) 48 Állam- és Jogtudomány 333–355.
227. Hovenkamp HJ and Scott Morton F, 'Framing the Chicago School of Antitrust Analysis' (2020) 168 University of Pennsylvania Law Review 1852.
228. Hovenkamp HJ, 'Antitrust Policy and Inequality of Wealth' (2017) Faculty Scholarship at Penn Law <https://bit.ly/3t6leB4> accessed 29 June 2024.
229. Hovenkamp HJ, 'Antitrust's Place in Regulation' (2024) SSRN <https://papers.ssrn.com/sol3/papers.cfm?abstract_id=4841731> accessed 7 July 2024.
230. Hovenkamp HJ, 'Is Antitrust's Consumer Welfare Principle Imperiled?' 45 The Journal of Corporation Law 104.
231. Hovenkamp HJ, *The Antitrust Enterprise: Principle and Execution* (Harvard University Press 2008) 1–2.
232. Hovenkamp HJ, 'The Slogans and Goals of Antitrust Law' (2022) 25 Legislation and Public Policy 705.
233. Hsu S-L, 'Antitrust and Inequality: The Problem of Super-Firms' (2018) 63 The Antitrust Bulletin 112.
234. Huffman M, 'The Shifting Regulation and Competition Interface' (2024) 8 Market and Competition Law Review 15–32.
235. Husa J, 'Comparative Law, Legal Linguistics and Methodology of Legal Doctrine' in Mark Van Hoecke (ed), *Methodologies of Legal Research: Which Kind of Method for What Kind of Discipline?* (Hart 2011) 215–216.
236. Hutchinson T, 'Doctrinal Research – Researching the Jury' in Dawn Watkins and Mandy Burton (eds), *Research Methods in Law* (Routledge 2013) 7.
237. Iacovides MC and Mauboussin V, 'Sustainability Considerations in the Application of Article 102 TFEU: State of the Art and Proposals for a More Sustainable Competition

Law' in Julian Nowag (ed) *Research Handbook on Sustainability and Competition Law* (Edward Elgar 2024).
238. Iacovides MC and Vrettos C, 'Falling through the Cracks No More? Article 102 TFEU and Sustainability: The Relation between Dominance, Environmental Degradation, and Social Injustice' (2021) 10 Journal of Antitrust Enforcement 32–62.
239. Iles A and Montenegro de Wit M, 'Sovereignty at What Scale? An Inquiry into Multiple Dimensions of Food Sovereignty' (2015) 12 Globalizations 481–497.
240. Inderst R and Thomas S, 'Abuse of Dominance and Sustainability' (2024) 15 Journal of European Competition Law & Practice 48–56.
241. Inderst R and Valletti TM, 'Buyer Power and the "Waterbed Effect"' (2011) 59 The Journal of Industrial Economics 1–20.
242. Innes R and Hamilton SF, 'Slotting Allowances under Supermarket Oligopoly' (2013) 95 American Journal of Agricultural Economics 1216–1222.
243. Jaraitė J and Kažukauskas A, 'The Effect of Mandatory Agro-Environmental Policy on Farm Fertiliser and Pesticide Expenditure' (2012) 63 Journal of Agricultural Economics 656–676.
244. Jeronen E, 'Economic Sustainability' in Samuel O. Idowu, René Schmidpeter, Nicholas Capaldi, Liangrong Zu, Mara Del Baldo and Rute Abreu (eds), *Encyclopedia of Sustainable Management* (Springer 2023) 1257–1263.
245. Jongeneel R, van Berkum S, de Bont C, van Bruchem C, Helming J and Jager J, 'European Dairy Policy in the Years to Come: Quota Abolition and Competitiveness' (2010) LEI Report 9.
246. Kalbfleisch P, 'Aiming for Alliance: Competition Law and Consumer Welfare' (2011) 2 Journal of European Competition Law & Practice 111.
247. Kaplan DM (ed), *Encyclopedia of Food and Agricultural Ethics* (2nd edn, Springer 2019) 99.
248. Kaplow L, 'On the Choice of Welfare Standards in Competition Law' in Daniel Zimmer (ed), *The Goals of Competition Law* (Edward Elgar 2012) 3–26.
249. Karsten SG, 'The Social Market Economy and the Moral Problem in Modern Capitalism' (1990) 17 International Journal of Social Economics 27–35.
250. Keeling L and others, 'Animal Welfare and the United Nations Sustainable Development Goals' (2019) Frontiers in Veterinary Science, Article 336.
251. Kelley CR, 'An Overview of the Packers and Stockyards Act' (2003) Arkansas Law Notes 35–6 <http://media.law.uark.edu/arklawnotes/2003/10/15/an-overview-of-the-packers-and-stockyards-act/> accessed 27 December 2023.
252. Kelly K, 'The Antitrust Analysis of Grocery Slotting Allowances: The Procompetitive Case' (1991) 10 Journal of Public Policy & Marketing 187–198.
253. Key N, Lubowski R and Roberts MJ, 'The 1996 Federal Agriculture Improvement and Reform Act: Correcting a Distortion?' (Annual Meeting of the AAEA, Denver, Colorado, August 2004) <https://core.ac.uk/download/pdf/6522852.pdf> accessed 27 January 2024.
254. Khan L, 'The End of Antitrust History Revisited' (2020) 133 Harvard Law Review 1656.
255. Khan L, 'The New Brandeis Movement: America's Antimonopoly Debate' (2018) 9 Journal of European Competition Law & Practice 131–132.
256. Khan LM and Vaheesan S, 'Market Power and Inequality: The Antitrust Counterrevolution and Its Discontents' (2017) 11 Harvard Law and Policy Review 294.
257. Khemani RS, 'Application of Competition Law: Exemptions and Exceptions' (2003) UNCTAD Series on Issues in Competition Law and Policy 32.
258. Kingston S, 'Greening Merger Control? The Role of Environmental Considerations in Merger Analysis' in Ioannis Kokkoris and Nicholas Levy (eds), *Research Handbook on Global Merger Control* (Edward Elgar 2023) 383–401.
259. Kirchner C, 'Goals of Antitrust and Competition Law Revisited' in Dieter Schmidtchen, Max Albert and Stefan Voigt (eds), *The More Economic Approach to European Competition Law* (Mohr Siebeck 2007) 7.

260. Kjeldahl R and Tracy M, *Renationalisation of the Common Agricultural Policy?* (Institute of Agricultural Economics 1994).
261. Komarek AM, De Pinto A and Smith VH, 'A Review of Types of Risks in Agriculture: What We Know and What We Need to Know' (2020) 178 Agricultural Systems, Article 102738.
262. Korbol JJ, 'Current Issues Involving Statutory Trusts under the Perishable Agricultural Commodities Act' (1992) 2 San Joaquin Agricultural Law Review 2.
263. Kornezov A, 'For a Socially Sensitive Competition Law Enforcement' (2020) 11 Journal of European Competition Law & Practice 399–403.
264. Kuch PJ and Ogg CW, 'The 1995 Farm Bill and Natural Resource Conservation: Major New Opportunities' (1996) 78 American Journal of Agricultural Economics 1212.
265. Küpper G, 'Mißbräuchliche Ausübung von Nachfragemacht, insbesondere Lösung des sog: Roß und Reiter-Problems' (1997) 52 Betriebs-Berater 1105–1115.
266. Lafferty W and Hovden E, 'Environmental Policy Integration: Towards an Analytical Framework' (2003) 12 Environmental Politics 1–22.
267. Lande RH, 'Wealth Transfers as the Original and Primary Concern of Antitrust: The Efficiency Interpretation Challenged' (1999) 50 Hastings Law Journal 907–910, 925–926, 945.
268. Landgrebe R, Kaphengst T and Friedrich S, 'German Perspectives on the Current CAP Reform' *Policy Brief for the German Marshall Fund of the United States* (Ecologic Institute 2009) 4.
269. Langbroek P, van den Bos K, Thomas MS, Milo M and van Rossum W, 'Methodology of Legal Research: Challenges and Opportunites' (2017) 13 Utrecht Law Review 2.
270. Langer L and Kammerstetter M, 'The Evolution of the Smart Grid Threat Landscape and Cross-Domain Risk Assessment' in Florian Skopik and Paul Smith (eds), *Smart Grid Security: Innovative Solutions for a Modernized Grid* (Syngress 2015) 49–77.
271. Latruffe L, Diazabakana A, Bockstaller C, Desjeux Y, Finn J, Kelly E, Ryan M and Uthes S, 'Measurement of Sustainability in Agriculture: A Review of Indicators' (2016) 118 Studies in Agricultural Economics 123–130.
272. Lecchi E, 'Sustainability and EU Merger Control' (2023) 44 European Competition Law Review 70–80.
273. Lemon LG, 'The Capper-Volstead Act: Will It Ever Grow up?' (1970) 22 Administrative Law Review 443–444.
274. Letwin W, *Law and Economic Policy in America: The Evolution of the Sherman Antitrust Act* (Randon House 1965) 67–68.
275. Lianos I and Carballa-Smichowski B, 'A Coat of Many Colours – New Concepts and Metrics of Economic Power in Competition Law and Economics' (2022) 18 Journal of Competition Law & Economics 795–831.
276. Lianos I, 'Agriculture & Competition Law: An Overview of EU and National Case Law' (2022) Concurrences.
277. Lianos I, 'Competition Law as a Form of Social Regulation' (2020) 65 The Antitrust Bulletin.
278. Lianos I, 'Polycentric Competition Law' (2019) 71 Current Legal Problems 206.
279. Lindenberg H, 'Will Sustainability and Environmental Considerations Be the Next Big Hit for Shaping the Application of Article 102 TFEU?' (2022) 20 Zeitschrift für Wettbewerbsrecht 320–332.
280. Looney JW, 'Protection for Sellers of Perishable Agricultural Commodities: Reparation Proceedings and the Statutory Trust under the Perishable Agricultural Commodities Act' (1990) 23 U.C. Davis Law Review 675–676.
281. Lovdahl Gormsen L, 'The Conflict between Economic Freedom and Consumer Welfare in the Modernisation of Article 82 EC' (2007) 3 European Competition Journal 329–344.

282. Lovec M, Rac I and Erjavec E, 'External Shocks, Policy Spillovers, and Veto Players: Post(exceptionalist) Common Agricultural Policy and the Case of the 2023–2027 Reform' (2024) 46 Journal of European Integration 433–453.
283. Lovec M, *The European Union's Common Agricultural Policy Reforms* (Palgrave Macmillan 2016) 93.
284. Lowder SK, Skoet J and Raney T, 'The Number, Size, and Distribution of Farms, Smallholder Farms, and Family Farms Worldwide' (2016) 87 World Development 16–29.
285. Lowe P and Baldock D, 'Integration of Environmental Objectives into Agricultural Policy Making' in F. Brouwer and P. Lowe (eds), *CAP Regimes and the European Countryside* (CAB International 2000) 31–52.
286. Lupel A, *Globalization and Popular Sovereignty: Democracy's Transnational Dilemma* (Routledge 2009).
287. Lübbig T, 'Sustainable Development and Competition Policy' (2013) 4 Journal of European Competition Law & Practice 1–2.
288. MacDonald JM, Ollinger ME, Nelson KE and Handy CR, 'Consolidation in U.S. Meatpacking' (U.S. Department of Agriculture, 2000).
289. Malinauskaite J, 'Competition Law and Sustainability: EU and National Perspectives' (2022) 13 Journal of European Competition Law & Practice 336–348.
290. Malone LA, 'The Conservation Title of the 1990 Farm Bill' *Agricultural Law Update* (May 1991) 4.
291. Mamonova N and Franquesa J, 'Right-Wing Populism in Rural Europe: Introduction to the Special Issue' (2020) 60 Sociologia Ruralis 704.
292. Mann A, *Global Activism in Food Politics: Power Shift* (Palgrave Macmillan 2014).
293. Mann S, 'Different Perspectives on Cross-Compliance' (2005) 14 Environmental Values 471.
294. Martin DD, *Mergers and the Clayton Act* (University of California Press 1959) 6.
295. Martínez-Torres ME and Rosset PM, 'Diálogo de saberes in La Vía Campesina: Food sovereignty and agroecology' (2014) 41 The Journal of Peasant Studies 979–997.
296. Marty F, 'Is the Consumer Welfare Obsolete? A European Union Competition Law Perspective' (GREDEG Working Papers, 2020) 13.
297. Mauboussin V, 'Environmental Defences as a Shield from Article 102 TFEU' (2022) 3 Concurrences 30–41.
298. McBeth D, 'Wetlands Conservation and Federal Regulation: Analysis of the Food Security Act's Swampbuster Provisions as Amended by the Federal Agriculture Improvement and Reform Act of 1996' (1997) 21 Harvard Environmental Law Review 221.
299. McEowen RA, 'Packers and Stockyards Act Provisions for Unpaid Cash Sellers of Livestock' (21 March 2019) Agricultural Law and Taxation Blog <https://lawprofessors.typepad.com/agriculturallaw/2019/03/packers-and-stockyards-act-provisions-for-unpaid-cash-sellers-of-livestock.html> accessed 27 December 2023.
300. McMahon JA, 'The Common Agricultural Policy: From Quantity to Quality?' (2001) 53 Northern Ireland Legal Quarterly 15.
301. McMichael P, 'COVID-19 Implications on Our Broken Food System' (2020) <www.isa-agrifood.com/post/covid-19-implications-on-our-broken-food-system> accessed 29 June 2024.
302. McMichael P, 'Historicizing Food Sovereignty' (2014) 41 The Journal of Peasant Studies 933–957.
303. Mehrabi Z, 'Likely Decline in the Number of Farms Globally by the Middle of the Century' (2023) 6 Nature Sustainability 949.
304. Meier M, 'Pleading for a "Multiple Goal Approach" in European Competition Law: Outline of a Conciliatory Path between the "Freedom to Compete Approach" and the "More Economic Approach"' in Klaus Mathis and Avishalom Tor (eds), *New Developments in Competition Law and Economics* (Springer Nature 2019) 51–52.

305. Mestmäcker E-J, '50 Jahre GWB. Die Erfolgsgeschichte eines unvollkommenen Gesetzes' (2008) 58 Wirtschaft und Wettbewerb 19.
306. Mestmäcker E-J, *Der verwaltete Wettbewerb: eine vergleichende Untersuchung über den Schutz von Freiheit und Lauterkeit im Wettbewerbsrecht* (Mohr Siebeck 1984).
307. Meyer C, Matzdorf B, Müller K and Schleyer C, 'Cross Compliance as Payment for Public Goods? Understanding EU and US Agricultural Policies' (2014) 107 Ecological Economics 185.
308. Meyer J and von Cramon-Taubadel S, 'Asymmetric Price Transmission: A Survey' (2004) 55 Journal of Agricultural Economics 581–611.
309. Meyers RL, 'Greening of the Farm Bill' *Washington Watch* (October 1989) 599.
310. Miazad A, 'Prosocial Antitrust' (2022) 73 Hastings Law Journal 1637–1696.
311. Miksch L, 'Walter Eucken' (1950) 4 Kyklos 279.
312. Miksch L, *Wettbewerb als Aufgabe: die Grundsätze einer Wettbewerbsordnung* (Kohlhammer Verlag 1937) 24.
313. Modrall J, 'EU Competition Policy in the Agriculture Sector' (2017) 14 Cultivate: Food and Agribusiness Newsletter 18.
314. Moen Ø, Tvedten T and Wold A, 'Exploring the Relationship between Competition and Innovation in Norwegian SMEs' (2018) 5 Cogent Business & Management, Article: 1564167.
315. Monica JC Jr. and Sandin JC, 'Agricultural Antitrust Pitfalls' (2017) 50 Maryland Bar Journal 19.
316. Morales MB and others, 'Protect European Green Agricultural Policies for Future Food Security' (2022) 3 Communications Earth & Environment, Article 217.
317. Motta M, *Competition Policy: Theory and Practice* (CUP 2004) 19.
318. Moyer W and Josling T, *Agricultural Policy Reform: Politics and Process in the EU and US in the 1990s* (Ashgate 2002).
319. Möschel W, 'Competition Policy from an Ordo Point of View' in Alan Peacock and Hans Willgerodt (eds), *German Neo-Liberals and the Social Market Economy* (Palgrave Macmillan 1989) 146.
320. Nagel C, 'The Origin and Purpose of the Sherman Act' (1930) 15 St. Louis Law Review 323.
321. Nedergaard P, 'The 2003 Reform of the Common Agricultural Policy: Against All Odds or Rational Explanations?' (2006) 28 Journal of European Integration 203–223.
322. Nedergaard P, 'The Ordoliberalisation of the European Union?' (2019) 42 Journal of European Integration 229.
323. Nedergaard P, 'The Reform of the 2003 Common Agricultural Policy: An Advocacy Coalition Explanation' (2008) 29 Policy Studies 179–195.
324. Negrinotti M, 'The Single Market Imperative and Consumer Welfare: Irreconcilable Goals? Exploring the Tensions amongst the Objectives of European Competition Law through the Lens of Parallel Trade in Pharmaceuticals' in Daniel Zimmer (ed), *The Goals of Competition Law* (Edward Elgar 2012) 295–337.
325. Neuenfeldt S, Gocht A, Heckelei T and Ciaian P, 'Explaining Farm Structural Change in the European Agriculture: A Novel Analytical Framework' (2019) 46 European Review of Agricultural Economics 713–768.
326. Nevo H and Van den Bergh R, 'Private Labels: Challenges for Competition Law and Economics' (2017) 40 World Competition 271–298.
327. Nicholls A, 'The Other Germany: The "Neo-Liberals"' in Roger J. Bullen, Hartmut Pogge von Strandmann and Antony B. Polonsky (eds), *Ideas into Politics – Aspects of European History 1880–1950* (Croom Helm 1984) 171.
328. Nihoul P, 'Choice vs Efficiency?' (2012) 3 Journal of European Competition Law & Practice 315.
329. Norer R (ed), *Handbuch des Agrarrechts* (Springer 2005).
330. Norer R, *Handbuch zum Agrarrecht* (Stämpfli Verlag 2017).

331. Norer R, *Lebendiges Agrarrecht – Entwicklungslinien und Perspektiven des Rechts im ländlichen Raum* (Springer 2005).
332. Novak JL, Sanders LD and Hagerman AD, *Agricultural Policy in the United States: Evolution and Economics* (2nd edn, Routledge 2022) 4.
333. Oakes I and Küsters A, 'Lessons from the Past? How Ordoliberal Competition Theory Can Address Market Power in the Digital Age' (2021) ProMarket <https://promarket.org/2021/11/14/ordoliberal-lessons-competition-tech-platforms-antitrust-germany/> accessed 21 October 2023.
334. Offutt SE and Gundersen C, 'Farm Poverty Lowest in U.S. History' (United States Department of Agriculture, Economic Research Service, 2005).
335. Oliver JR and Robison LJ, 'Rationalizing Inconsistent Definitions of Commodification: A Social Exchange Perspective' (2017) 8 Modern Economy 1314–1327.
336. Orbach BY, 'The Antitrust Consumer Welfare Paradox' (2010) 7 Journal of Competition Law & Economics 133–164.
337. Orbach BY, 'The Present New Antitrust Era' (2018) 60 William & Mary Law Review 1444.
338. Orden D, 'Reform's Stunted Crop' (Spring 2002) Regulation 32.
339. Ötsch WO, Pühringer S and Hirte K, *Netzwerke des Marktes: Ordoliberalismus als Politische Ökonomie* (Springer 2018) 1.
340. Page EC, 'The Origins of Policy' in Michael Moran, Martin Rein and Robert E. Goodin (eds), *The Oxford Handbook of Public Policy* (OUP 2008) 210.
341. Paredis E and Keirsbilck B, 'Run-up, Legal Basis and Scope of Application' in Bert Keirsbilck and Evelyne Terryn (eds), *Unfair Trading Practices in the Food Supply Chain: Implications of Directive (EU) 2019/633* (Intersentia 2020).
342. Paroissien E, Latruffe L and Piet L, 'Early Exit from Business, Performance and Neighbours' Influence: A Study of Farmers in France' (2021) 48 European Review of Agricultural Economics 1132–1161.
343. Parr JF and Hornick SB, 'The Evolution of Sustainable Agriculture in the United States: A Recent Historical Perspective' (U.S. Department of Agriculture) <www.infrc.or.jp/knf/PDF%20KNF%20Conf%20Data/C3-8-102.pdf> accessed 23 March 2024.
344. Patel R, 'What Does Food Sovereignty Look Like?' (2009) 36 The Journal of Peasant Studies 663.
345. Pechlaner G and Otero G, 'The Neoliberal Food Regime: Neoregulation and the New Division of Labor in North America' (2010) 75 Rural Sociology 179–208.
346. Peck A, 'The Cost of Cutting Agricultural Output: Interpreting the Capper-Volstead Act' (2015) 80 Missouri Law Review 473.
347. Peeperkorn L, 'Competition Policy Is Not a Stopgap!' (2021) 12 Journal of European Competition Law & Practice 415–418.
348. Penson JB, Capps O Jr., Rosson CP III and Woodward RT, *Introduction to Agricultural Economics* (7th edn, Pearson 2018) 204.
349. Penuelas J, Coello F and Sardans J, 'A Better Use of Fertilizers Is Needed for Global Food Security and Environmental Sustainability' (2023) 12 Agriculture & Food Security, Article 5.
350. Pera A and Auricchio V, 'Consumer Welfare, Standard of Proof and the Objectives of Competition Policy' (2005) 1 European Competition Journal 153–177.
351. Perloff JM and Rausser GC, 'The Effect of Asymmetrically Held Information and Market Power in Agricultural Markets' (1983) 65 American Journal of Agricultural Economics 371–372.
352. Peters WE, 'Agricultural Cooperatives and the Antitrust Laws' (1963) 43 Nebraska Law Review 73–104.
353. Pfenninger A, 'Schweizerisches Agrarrecht: Begriff, Gliederung und Stellung in der Rechtsordnung' (1988) Blätter für Agrarrecht 2.

354. Phillips Sawyer L, 'US Antitrust Law and Policy in Historical Perspective' (2019) Harvard Business School Working Paper 19–110, 2 <www.hbs.edu/ris/Publication%20 Files/19–110_e21447ad-d98a-451f-8ef0-ba42209018e6.pdf> accessed 13 January 2024.
355. Phiri R, Mavinkere Rangappa S and Siengchin S, 'Agro-Waste for Renewable and Sustainable Green Production: A Review' (2024) 434 Journal of Cleaner Production, Article 139989.
356. Pichler P, 'Die Umsetzung der UTP-Richtlinie ins deutsche Recht. Überblick über ein ordnungspolitisches Ungetüm' (2021) 9 Neue Zeitschrift für Kartellrecht 537.
357. Pieralli S, Hüttel S and Odening M, 'Abandonment of Milk Production under Uncertainty and Inefficiency: The Case of Western German Farms' (2017) 44 European Review of Agricultural Economics 425–454.
358. Pietola K, Väre M and Oude Lansink A, 'Timing and Type of Exit from Farming: Farmers' Early Retirement Programmes in Finland' (2003) 30 European Review of Agricultural Economics 99–116.
359. Pietrzak M, Chlebicka A, Kraciński P and Malak-Rawlikowska A, 'Information Asymmetry as a Barrier in Upgrading the Position of Local Producers in the Global Value Chain – Evidence from the Apple Sector in Poland' (2020) 12 Sustainability, Article 7857.
360. Piszcz A, 'EU Directive on Unfair Trading Practices in Business-to-Business Relationships in the Agricultural and Food Supply Chain: Dipping a Toe in the Regulatory Waters?' in Zlatan Meškić, Ivana Kunda, Dušan V. Popović and Enis Omerović (eds), *Balkan Yearbook of European and International Law 2019* (Springer 2020) 117.
361. Poe GL, 'Maximizing the Environmental Benefits per Dollar Expended: An Economic Interpretation and Review of Agricultural Environmental Benefits and Costs' (1999) 12 Society & Natural Resources: An International Journal 571.
362. Ptak R, *Vom Ordoliberalismus zur Sozialen Marktwirtschaft: Stationen des Neoliberalismus in Deutschland* (Springer 2004) 227.
363. Quack S and Djelic M-L, 'Adaptation, Recombination and Reinforcement: The Story of Antitrust and Competition Law in Germany and Europe' (2005) <https://spire.sciencespo.fr/hdl:/2441/26l5o52m2c857apcgdgcplhr3h/resources/2005-djelic-quack-story-of-antitrust-and-competition-law-in-germany-and-europe.pdf> accessed 10 June 2023.
364. Ratcliffe J, 'A Small Step Forward: Environmental Protection Provisions in the 2002 Farm Bill' (2003) 30 Ecology Law Quarterly 637–659.
365. Renting H, Rossing WAH, Groot JCJ, Van der Ploeg JD, Laurent C, Perraud D, Stobbelaar DJ and van Ittersum MK, 'Exploring Multifunctional Agriculture A Review of Conceptual Approaches and Prospects for an Integrative Transitional Framework' (2009) 90 Journal of Environmental Management 112.
366. Ricciardi V, Mehrabi Z, Wittman H, James D and Ramankutty N, 'Higher Yields and More Biodiversity on Smaller Farms' (2021) 4 Nature Sustainability 651–657.
367. Richards TJ and Patterson PM, 'Slotting Allowances as Real Options: An Alternative Explanation' (2004) 77 The Journal of Business 675–696.
368. Ristino L and Steier G, 'Losing Ground: A Clarion Call for Farm Bill Reform to Ensure a Food Secure Future' (2016) 42 Columbia Journal of Environmental Law 92.
369. Robert R and Dean LER, 'An Inquiry into Lowi's Policy Typology: The Conservation Coalition and the 1985 and 1990 Farm Bills' (1994) 12 Environment and Planning C: Politics and Space 71.
370. Robertson VHSE, 'Sustainability: A World-First Green Exemption in Austrian Competition Law' (2022) 13 Journal of European Competition Law & Practice 426–434.
371. Robinson GM, 'Globalization of Agriculture' (2018) 10 Annual Review of Resource Economics 133.
372. Rosales WE, 'Dethroning Economic Kings: The Packers and Stockyards Act of 1921 and Its Modern Awakening' (2004) Wisconsin Law Review 1497–1498.

373. Rosset PM, *Food Is Different: Why We Must Get the WTO Out of Agriculture* (Fernwood Publishing 2006)
374. Roy EW, *Cooperatives: Today and Tomorrow* (2nd edn, Interstate Printers & Publishers 1969) 215.
375. Röhrig M, Ritzenhoff L and Tiffin-Richards M, 'Green Deal and Merger Control Sustainability: A Killer Deal Rationale?' *Brussels à Jour Newsletter* (March 2021).
376. Röpke W, *A Humane Economy: The Social Framework of the Free Market* (Intercollegiate Studies Institute 2014).
377. Röpke W, *International Economic Disintegration* (William Hodge and Company 1942) 111–112.
378. Röpke W, *The Social Crisis of Our Time* (The University of Chicago Press 1950) 205.
379. Ruggerio CA, 'Sustainability and Sustainable Development: A Review of Principles and Definitions' (2021) 786 Science of the Total Environment, Article 147481.
380. Ruhl JB, 'Farms, Their Environmental Harms, and Environmental Laws' (2000) 27 Ecology Law Quarterly 263–350.
381. Russo L, 'Dal diritto agrario al diritto alimentare (e viceversa)' (2011) 5 Rivista di diritto alimentare 2 <www.rivistadirittoalimentare.it/rivista/2011–02/RUSSO>.
382. Sacher SB and Yun JM, 'Some Reactions to "Reactionary Antitrust"' (2020) 4 Concurrences.
383. Sagers C and Cartensen P, *Federal Statutory Exemptions from Antitrust Law* (American Bar Association 2007) 97.
384. Samuel G, *An Introduction to Comparative Law Theory and Method* (Hart 2014) 57–58, 65–120.
385. Sauerland D, 'Freiburger Schule' in *Gabler Wirtschaftslexikon* <https://wirtschaftslexikon.gabler.de/definition/freiburger-schule-33210> accessed 30 June 2024.
386. Schanbacher WD, *The Politics of Food: The Global Conflict between Food Security and Food Sovereignty* (Praeger Security International 2010).
387. Schaub S, Ghazoul J, Huber R, Zhang W, Sander A, Rees C, Banerjee S and Finger R, 'The Role of Behavioural Factors and Opportunity Costs in Farmers' Participation in Voluntary Agri-Environmental Schemes: A Systematic Review' (2023) 74 Journal of Agricultural Economics 617–660.
388. Schebesta H, Verdonk T, Purnhagen KP and Keirsbilck B, 'Unfair Trading Practices in the Food Supply Chain: Regulating Right?' (2018) 9 European Journal of Risk Regulation.
389. Schiavoni CM, 'Competing Sovereignties, Contested Processes: Insights from the Venezuelan Food Sovereignty Experiment' (2015) 12 Globalizations 466–480.
390. Schiek D, Oliver L, Forde C and Alberti G, *EU Social and Labour Rights and EU Internal Market Law* (European Union 2015) 14–15.
391. Schiff DN, 'Socio-Legal Theory: Social Structure and Law' (1976) 39 The Modern Law Review 287.
392. Schinkel MP and Treuren L, 'Green Antitrust: (More) Friendly Fire in the Fight against Climate Change' (2020) SSRN <https://ssrn.com/abstract=3749147> accessed 29 June 2024.
393. Schmalensee R, 'Entry Deterrence in the Ready-to-Eat Breakfast Cereal Industry' (1978) 9 The Bell Journal of Economics 322.
394. Schmidt NM, 'Late Bloomer? Agricultural Policy Integration and Coordination Patterns in Climate Policies' (2019) 27 Journal of European Public Policy 893–911.
395. Schumacher Horneber A, 'Agricultural Cooperatives: Gain of Market Power and the Antitrust Exemption' (1982) 27 South Dakota Law Review 476.
396. Schweizer D, 'Art. 42 AEUV' in Torsten Körber, Heike Schweitzer and Daniel Zimmer (eds), *Wettbewerbsrecht – Band 1: EU. Kommentar zum Europäischen Kartellrecht* (6th edn, C.H. Beck 2019).
397. Schweizer D, 'GWB § 28 Landwirtschaft' in Torsten Körber, Heike Schweitzer and Daniel Zimmer (eds), *Wettbewerbsrecht – Band 2: GWB. Kommentar zum Deutschen Kartellrecht* (6th edn, C.H. Beck 2020).

398. Scown MW, Brady MV and Nicholas KA, 'Billions in Misspent EU Agricultural Subsidies Could Support the Sustainable Development Goals' (2020) 3 One Earth 237–250.
399. Scruton R, *Green Philosophy: How to Think Seriously about the Planet* (Atlantic Books 2011).
400. Sexton RJ and Zhang M, 'An Assessment of the Impact of Food Industry Market Power on U.S. Consumers' (2001) 17 Agribusiness 59–79.
401. Sexton RJ, 'Industrialization and Consolidation in the U.S. Food Sector: Implications for Competition and Welfare' (2000) 82 American Journal of Agricultural Economics 1087–1104.
402. Sexton RJ, 'Market Power, Misconceptions, and Modern Agricultural Markets' (2012) 95 American Journal of Agricultural Economics 209–219.
403. Shapiro C, 'Antitrust in a Time of Populism' (2018) 61 International Journal of Industrial Organization 714–748.
404. Shattuck A, Schiavoni CM and VanGelder Z, 'Translating the Politics of Food Sovereignty: Digging into Contradictions, Uncovering New Dimensions' (2015) 12 Globalizations 425.
405. Sheingate AD, *The Rise of the Agricultural Welfare State: Institutions and Interest Group Power in the United States, France, and Japan* (Princeton University Press 2001).
406. Shelanski H, 'Antitrust and Deregulation' (2018) 127 The Yale Law Journal 1922–1960.
407. Shively JD and Roberts JS, 'Competition under the Packers and Stockyards Act: What Now?' (2010) 15 Drake Journal of Agricultural Law 419–454.
408. Shlaes A, 'The Foreigners Buchanan Calls His Own' *Wall Street Journal* (29 February 1996) cited by Gregg S, *Wilhelm Röpke's Political Economy* (Edward Elgar 2010) 2.
409. Smith VS and Glauber JW, 'The Effects of the 1996 Farm Bill on Food and Feed Grains' (1997) Policy Issues Paper 3 <https://ageconsearch.umn.edu/record/29170/?v=pdf> accessed 27 June 2024.
410. Sodano V, 'Food Policy beyond Neo-Liberalism' in Dennis Erasga (ed), *Sociological Landscape: Theories, Realities and Trends* (IntechOpen 2012) 375–402.
411. Stanton JL and Herbst KC, 'Slotting Allowances: Short-Term Gains and Long-Term Negative Effects on Retailers and Consumers' (2006) 34 International Journal of Retail & Distribution Management 187–197.
412. Steding R, 'Das Agrarrecht: Bedenklichkeiten und Notwendigkeiten seiner Entwicklung' (1994) Neue Landwirtschaft: Briefe zum Agrarrecht 7.
413. Stenmarck Å, Jensen C, Quested T and Moates G, 'Estimates of European Food Waste Levels' (IVL Swedish Environmental Research Institute, 2016).
414. Stiegert KW, Wang S-S and Rogers R, 'Structural Change and Market Power in the US Food Manufacturing Sector' (2009) 25 Agribusiness 164–180.
415. Stigler G, 'The Origin of the Sherman Act' (1985) 14 The Journal of Legal Studies 1–12.
416. Stubbs M, 'Agricultural Conservation in the 2018 Farm Bill' (Congressional Research Service, April 2019).
417. Stubbs M, 'Conservation Provisions in the 2014 Farm Bill' (Congressional Research Service, April 2014).
418. Stumo MC and O'Brien DJ, 'Antitrust Unfairness vs. Equitable Unfairness in Farmer/Meat Packer Relationships' (2003) 8 Drake Journal of Agricultural Law 92.
419. Stylianou K and Iacovides MC, 'The Goals of EU Competition Law: A Comprehensive Empirical Investigation' (2019) SSRN <https://ssrn.com/abstract=3735795> accessed 7 October 2023.
420. Sudhir K and Rao VR, 'Do Slotting Allowances Enhance Efficiency or Hinder Competition?' (2006) 43 Journal of Marketing Research 137–155.

421. Sullivan MW, 'Slotting Allowances and the Market for New Products' (1997) 40 The Journal of Law & Economics 461–494.
422. Sun Y and others, 'Determinants of Animal Welfare Disclosure Practices: Evidence from China' (2021) 13 Sustainability <https://doi.org/10.3390/su13042200> accessed 1 September 2023.
423. Swinbank A, 'New Direct Payments Scheme: Targeting and Redistribution in the Future CAP' (Directorate-General for Internal Policies, 2012).
424. Swinnen J, *The Perfect Storm: The Political Economy of the Fischler Reforms of the Common Agricultural Policy* (Centre for European Policy Studies 2008).
425. Szilágyi JE (ed), *Agrárjog: A magyar agrár- és vidékfejlesztési jogi szabályozás lehetőségei a globalizálódó Európai Unióban [Agricultural Law: Regulatory Possibilities of Hungarian Agricultural and Rural Development Law in the Globalising European Union]* (Miskolci Egyetemi Kiadó 2017).
426. Szilágyi JE, 'Változások az agrárjog elméletében? [Changes in the Theory of Agricultural Law?]' (2016) 11 Miskolci Jogi Szemle 1, 30–50.
427. T.O., 'Agricultural Cooperatives and the Antitrust Laws: Clayton, Capper-Volstead, and Common Sense' (1958) 44 Virginia Law Review 63.
428. Talbot C, 'Ordoliberalism and Balancing Competition Goals in the Development of the European Union' (2016) 61 The Antitrust Bulletin 264–289.
429. Tang S, Wang Z, Yang G and Tang W, 'What Are the Implications of Globalization on Sustainability? – A Comprehensive Study' (2020) 12 Sustainability 3411.
430. Taylor CR, 'Buyer Power Litigation in Agriculture: Pickett v. Tyson Fresh Meats, Inc.' (2008) 55 Antitrust Bulletin 457.
431. The Editors of Encyclopaedia Britannica, 'Granger Movement: American Farm Coalition' <www.britannica.com/event/Granger-movement> accessed 13 January 2024.
432. Thompson RL, 'The US Farm Bill and the Doha Negotiations: On Parallel Tracks or a Collision Course?' (September 2005) IPC Issue Brief 5.
433. Thorelli H, *The Federal Antitrust Policy: Origination of an American Tradition* (Johns Hopkins University Press 1955) 92.
434. Torpman O and Röcklinsberg H, 'Reinterpreting the SDGs: Taking Animals into Direct Consideration' (2021) 13 Sustainability <https://doi.org/10.3390/su13020843> accessed 1 September 2023.
435. Tóth T, *Uniós és magyar versenyjog* (Wolters Kluwer 2020) 48.
436. Toulmin HA, *A Treatise on the Anti-Trust Laws of the United States: And Including All Related Trade Regulatory Laws* (vol 3, W.H. Anderson 1949) 215.
437. Tourkochoriti I, 'Comparative Rights Jurisprudence: An Essay on Methodologies. Special Issue – Comparative Law' (2017) Law and Method 2 <https://doi.org/10.5553/REM/.000030> accessed 30 June 2024.
438. Trauger A, 'Toward a Political Geography of Food Sovereignty: Transforming Territory, Exchange and Power in the Liberal Sovereign State' (2014) 41 The Journal of Peasant Studies 1133.
439. Tullis P, 'Nitrogen Wars: The Dutch Farmers' Revolt That Turned a Nation Upside-Down' *The Guardian* (16 November 2023).
440. Uffer M, 'Competition Law: Sustainability through Competition and Participation' in Birgit Peters and Eva Julia Lohse (eds), *Sustainability through Participation? Perspectives from National, European and International Law* (Brill 2023) 275–280.
441. Umstätter C, Mann S and Werner J, 'A Simple Measure for Workload as a Social Sustainability Indicator for Family Farms' (2022) 14 Environmental and Sustainability Indicators, Article 100180.
442. Ünekbaş S, 'The Resurrection of the Comfort Letter' (2022) 15 Yearbook of Antitrust and Regulatory Studies 37–61.
443. Vaheesan S, 'The Profound Nonsense of Consumer Welfare Antitrust' (2019) 64 The Antitrust Bulletin 494.

444. Vallance S, Perkins HC and Dixon JE, 'What Is Social Sustainability? A Clarification of Concepts' (2011) 42 Geoforum 342–343.
445. van den Bergh R, 'The Goals of Competition Law' in Roger Van den Bergh, Peter Camesasca and Andrea Giannaccari (eds), *Comparative Competition Law and Economics* (Edward Elgar 2017) 88.
446. van den Bergh R, 'The More Economic Approach in European Competition Law: Is More Too Much or Not Enough?' in Mitja Kovač and Ann-Sophie Vandenberghe (eds), *Economic Evidence in EU Competition Law* (Intersentia 2016) 13–42.
447. van der Ploeg JD, 'Right Wing Farmers' Protests in the Netherlands' *Agrarian Conservations* (2 July 2022) <www.peasantjournal.org/news/jan-douwe-van-der-ploeg-on-right-wing-farmers%E2%80%99-protests-in-the-netherlands/> accessed 9 March 2024.
448. Van Hoecke M, 'Legal Doctrine: Which Method(s) for What Kind of Discipline?' in Mark Van Hoecke (ed), *Methodologies of Legal Research: Which Kind of Method for What Kind of Discipline?* (Hart 2011) 4.
449. van Rompuy B, *Economic Efficiency: The Sole Concern of Modern Antitrust Policy? Non-Efficiency Considerations under Article 101 TFEU* (Kluwer Law International 2012) § 3.03.
450. van Wijck P, 'Loyalty Rebates and the More Economic Approach to EU Competition Law' (2020) 17 European Competition Journal 1–17.
451. Vanberg VJ, 'Ordnungspolitik, the Freiburg School and the Reason of Rules' (2013) 15 Annals of the University of Bucharest/Political Science Series 26.
452. Vanberg VJ, 'The Freiburg School: Walter Eucken and Ordoliberalism' (Freiburger Diskussionspapiere zur Ordnungsökonomik 04/11, 2004) 2.
453. Varney CA, 'The Capper-Volstead Act, Agricultural Cooperatives, and Antitrust Immunity' (2010) The Antitrust Source 1.
454. Vedder HHB, 'Competition Law and Environmental Protection in Europe; towards Sustainability?' (PhD thesis 2003).
455. Veljanovski C, 'The Case against Green Antitrust' (2022) 18 European Competition Journal 501–513.
456. Verkuijl C and others, 'Mainstreaming Animal Welfare in Sustainable Development: A Policy Agenda' (2022) <https://euagenda.eu/upload/publications/animal-welfare-stockholm50backgroundpaper.pdf> accessed 1 September 2023.
457. Virtue GO, 'The Meat-Packing Investigation' (1920) 34 The Quarterly Journal of Economics 626–685.
458. von Dietze C, 'Landwirtschaft und Wettbewerbsordnung' (1942) 66 Schmollers Jahrbuch 129–157.
459. Waked DI, 'Antitrust as Public Interest Law: Redistribution, Equity, and Social Justice' (2020) 65 The Antitrust Bulletin.
460. Watrin C, 'The Principles of the Social Market Economy: Its Origins and Early History' (1979) 135 Zeitschrift für die gesamte Staatswissenschaft 405.
461. Weimer S, 'Being Sustainable Doesn't Equate to a Free Pass on Animal Welfare' (2020) <www.thepoultrysite.com/articles/being-sustainable-doesnt-equate-to-a-free-pass-on-animal-welfare> accessed 1 September 2023.
462. Westhoff P, *The Economics of Food: How Feeding and Fueling the Planet Affects Food Prices* (Pearson Education 2010) 4.
463. Whish R and Bailey D, *Competition Law* (7th edn, OUP 2012) 963.
464. Whish R, 'Do Competition Lawyers Harm Welfare?' (2020) Concurrentialiste: Journal of Antitrust Law <https://leconcurrentialiste.com/richard-whish-welfare/> accessed 30 October 2023.
465. White JC, Troy LC and Gerlich RN, 'The Role of Slotting Fees and Introductory Allowances in Retail Buyers' New-Product Acceptance Decisions' (2000) 28 Journal of the Academy of Marketing Science 291–298.

466. Wilkinson D, 'Maastricht and the Environment: The Implications for the EC's Environment Policy of the Treaty on European Union' (1992) 4 Journal of Environmental Law 221.
467. Wilkinson MA, 'Authoritarian Liberalism in Europe: A Common Critique of Neoliberalism and Ordoliberalism' (2019) 45 Critical Sociology 1024.
468. Wills JJ, *Contesting World Order? Socioeconomic Rights and Global Justice Movements* (CUP 2017).
469. Windfuhr M and Jonsén J, *Food Sovereignty: Towards Democracy in Localized Food Systems*. (ITDG Publishing 2005) 29.
470. Winkler W, 'Agrarrecht' in Volkmar Götz, Karl Kroeschell and Wolfgang Winkler (eds), *Handwörterbuch des Agrarrechts, Band I: Abfallbeseitigungsrecht* (Berlin 1981).
471. Winter M, 'Strong Policy or Weak Policy? The Environmental Impact of the 1992 Reforms to the CAP Arable Regime in Great Britain' (2000) 16 Journal of Rural Studies 47–59.
472. Witt AC, 'The European Court of Justice and the More Economic Approach to EU Competition Law – Is the Tide Turning?' (2019) 64 The Antitrust Bulletin 172–213.
473. Witt AC, *The More Economic Approach to EU Antitrust Law* (Hart Publishing 2016); Zalewska-Głogowska M, *The More Economic Approach under Article 102 TFEU* (Nomos Verlag 2017).
474. Wittman H, 'Food Sovereignty: An Inclusive Model for Feeding the World and Cooling the Planet' (2023) 6 One Earth 474–478.
475. Wright JD, Dorsey E, Klick J and Rybnicek JM, 'Requiem for a Paradox: The Dubious Rise and Inevitable Fall of Hipster Antitrust' (2019) 51 Arizona State Law Journal 314.
476. Wrigley N, 'The Consolidation Wave in U.S. Food Retailing: A European Perspective' (2001) 17 Agribusiness 489–513.
477. Wu T, *The Curse of Bigness: Antitrust in the New Gilded Age* (Columbia Global Reports 2018).
478. Yoo CS, 'Hipster Antitrust: New Bottles, Same Old W(h)ine?' (2018) All Faculty Scholarship <https://scholarship.law.upenn.edu/faculty_scholarship/2168/> accessed 14 January 2024.
479. Young B, 'Ordoliberalism as an "Irritating German Idea"' in Thorsten Beck and Hans-Helmut Kotz (eds), *Ordoliberalism: A German Oddity?* (CEPR Press 2017).
480. Zäch R and Künzler A, 'Freedom to Compete or Consumer Welfare: The Goal of Competition Law According to Constitutional Law' in Roger Zäch, Andreas Heinemann and Andreas Kellerhals (eds), *The Development of Competition Law: Global Perspectives* (Edward Elgar 2010) 61–86.
481. Zeballos E, Dong X and Islamaj E, 'A Disaggregated View of Market Concentration in the Food Retail Industry' (U.S. Department of Agriculture, 2023).
482. Zeßner-Spitzenberg HK, *Das österreichische Agrarrecht für Studium und Praxis im Grundriss systematisch dargestellt samt Rechtsquellenverzeichnis* (Agrarverlag 1930).
483. Zweigert K and Kötz H, *An Introduction to Comparative Law* (3rd edn, OUP 1998).

Newspapers

1. *Agra Europe* (25 January 1991) 1–2.
2. Stephanie van den Berg, Toby Sterling and Bart Meijer, 'Angry Farmers Cause Dutch Police to Close Off Parliament Square' *Reuters* (16 October 2019).
3. Bartosz Brzeziński and Paula Andrés, 'Meet the Farmers Who Control One-Third of the EU's Budget' *Politico* (6 October 2023).

4. Camile Gijs and Bartosz Brzeziński, 'Europe's Right Wing Piggybacks on Dutch Farmer Protests' *Politico* (29 July 2022).
5. Catarina Demony and Guillermo Martinez, 'Protesting Spanish Farmers Drive Hundreds of Tractors to Madrid' *Reuters* (21 February 2024).
6. Chris Bockman and Paul Kirby, 'French Protests: Female Farmer and Daughter Killed as Car Hits French Protesters' *BBC News* (24 January 2024).
7. Costas Kantouris and Derek Gatopoulos, 'Greek Farm Protests Are a Sign of Europe's Inflation Anxiety' *AP News* (17 February 2022).
8. 'EU Farmers Protest Low Milk Prices in Belgium' *AlJazeera* (7 September 2015).
9. 'Europe's Grumpy Farmers Are a Symptom of Wider Malaise' *The Economist* (London, 1 February 2024).
10. 'French Farmers Close in on Paris as Government Struggles to Calm Protests' *France24* (31 January 2024).
11. Georgi Gotev, 'Slovak Farmers Drive Tractors into Capital to Protest Alleged EU Subsidy Fraud' *Euractiv* (20 June 2018).
12. Jaroslav Hála, 'Farmers Protest as Czech Agriculture Declines' *Eurofound* (4 February 2010).
13. Jessica Parker in Berlin and Adam Robinson, 'Germany's Far Right Seek Revolution in Farmers' Protests' *BBC News* (15 January 2024); Ajit Niranjan, 'Why Europe's Farmers Are Protesting – and the Far Right Is Taking Note' *The Guardian* (London, 15 January 2024); Nicholas Vinocur and Bartosz Brzeziński, 'How the Far Right Aims to Ride Farmers' Outrage to Power in Europe' *Politico* (26 January 2024).
14. John Vidal, 'Farmer Commits Suicide at Protests' *The Guardian* (London, 11 September 2003).
15. Kate Connolly, 'Thousands of Tractors Block Berlin as Farmers Protest over Fuel Subsidy Cuts' *The Guardian* (Berlin, 15 January 2024).
16. Patrick Schröder and Tim Benton, 'European Farmers' Protests Show the Need for a Just Transition to Net Zero' *Chatham House* (London, 2 February 2024).
17. Peter Teffer, 'Why Are European Farmers Unhappy?' *EUobserver* (7 September 2015).
18. Bart Meijer and Geert De Clercq, 'Police Move to End Dutch Farmer Protests' *Reuters* (6 February 2024).
19. 'Spanish Farmers Protest against Plans to Curb Water Supply for Irrigation' *Reuters* (11 January 2023).
20. Alicja Ptak, 'Thousands of Farmers Protest in Warsaw against EU Climate Policies and Ukrainian Imports' *Notes from Poland* (27 February 2024).

Institutional documents

1. American Antitrust Institute, 'The Next Antitrust Agenda: The American Antitrust Institute's Transition Report on Competition Policy to the 44th President of the United States' (2008).
2. Association of Dutch Flower Auctions, 'Consultation on Sustainability Agreements in Agriculture – Guidelines on the Antitrust Derogation' (2022).
3. Association of Dutch Flower Auctions, 'Consultation on Sustainability Agreements in Agriculture – Guidelines on the Antitrust Derogation' (2022); COPA-COGECA, 'Contribution to the Commission Public Consultation on Sustainability Agreements in Agriculture Guidelines on Antitrust Derogation' (2022).
4. BEUC – The European Consumer Organisation, 'European Commission's Consultation on Sustainability Agreements in Agriculture: BEUC's Comments on the Guidelines on the Antitrust Derogation in Article 210a CMO' (2022).
5. ClientEarth, 'Sustainability Agreements in Agriculture – Guidelines on Antitrust Derogation' (2022) 4.
6. Commission, 'A Better Functioning Food Supply Chain in Europe' (Communication), COM(2009).

7. Commission, 'A Farm to Fork Strategy for a Fair, Healthy and Environmentally-Friendly Food System' (Communication) COM/2020/381 final.
8. Commission, 'A Long-Term Vision for the EU's Rural Areas: Towards Stronger, Connected, Resilient and Prosperous Rural Areas by 2040' (Communication) COM/2021/345 final.
9. Commission, 'EU Biodiversity Strategy for 2030: Bringing Nature Back into Our Lives' (Communication) COM/2020/380 final.
10. Commission, 'Europe's Agenda 2000: Strengthening and Widening the European Union' (Office for Official Publications of the European Communities 1999).
11. Commission, 'Ex-Post Evaluation of Late Payment Directive' (Publications Office of the European Union 2015) ENTR/172/PP/2012/FC – LOT.
12. Commission, 'Mapping and Analysis of CAP Strategic Plans: Assessment of Joint Efforts for 2023–2027' (Publications Office of the European Union 2023).
13. Commission, 'Preparing for the "Health Check" of the CAP Reform' (Communication) COM/2007/0722 final
14. Commission, 'Proposal for a Regulation of the European Parliament and of the Council Amending Regulations (EU) No 1308/2013 Establishing a Common Organisation of the Markets in Agricultural Products, (EU) No 1151/2012 on Quality Schemes for Agricultural Products and Foodstuffs, (EU) No 251/2014 on the Definition, Description, Presentation, Labelling and the Protection of Geographical Indications of Aromatised Wine Products, (EU) No 228/2013 Laying Down Specific Measures for Agriculture in the Outermost Regions of the Union and (EU) No 229/2013 Laying Down Specific Measures for Agriculture in Favour of the Smaller Aegean Islands', COM(2018) 394 final.
15. Commission, 'Tackling Unfair Trading Practices in the Business-to-Business Food Supply Chain' (Communication) COM(2014) 472 final.
16. Commission, 'The Application of the Union Competition Rules to the Agricultural Sector' (Report) COM(2018) 706 final.
17. Commission, 'Unfair Business-to-Business Trading Practices in the Food Supply Chain' (Report) COM(2016) 32 final.
18. Commission, 'Unfair Trading Practices in the Business-to-Business Food and Non-Food Supply Chain in Europe' (Green Paper 2013) COM(2013) 37 final.
19. Committee on Agriculture and Rural Development, 'On the Proposal for a Regulation of the European Parliament and of the Council Amending Regulations (EU) No 1308/2013 Establishing a Common Organisation of the Markets in Agricultural Products, (EU) No 1151/2012 on Quality Schemes for Agricultural Products and Foodstuffs, (EU) No 251/2014 on the Definition, Description, Presentation, Labelling and the Protection of Geographical Indications of Aromatised Wine Products, (EU) No 228/2013 Laying Down Specific Measures for Agriculture in the Outermost Regions of the Union and (EU) No 229/2013 Laying Down Specific Measures for Agriculture in Favour of the Smaller Aegean Islands' (A8–0198/2019).
20. COPA-COGECA, 'Contribution to the Commission Public Consultation on Sustainability Agreements in Agriculture Guidelines on Antitrust Derogation' (2022).
21. CRS Report for Congress, 'The 2008 Farm Bill: A Summary of Major Provisions and Legislative Action' (2008) CRS–14.
22. Declaration of Nyéléni (February 2007) <https://nyeleni.org/IMG/pdf/DeclNyeleni-en.pdf> accessed 9 September 2023.
23. European Court of Auditors, 'Single Payment Scheme (SPS): Issues to Be Addressed to Improve Its Sound Financial Management' (2011) Special Report No 5.
24. European Court of Auditors, 'Special Report No 14/2000 on "Greening the CAP" Together with the Commission's Replies' (2000).
25. European Court of Auditors, 'Special Report: Common Agricultural Policy and Climate: Half of EU Climate Spending But Farm Emissions Are Not Decreasing' (Publications Office of the European Union 2021).

26. European Economic and Social Committee, 'Opinion on the Large Retail Sector: Trends and Impacts on Farmers and Consumers' (2005/C 255/08).
27. European Environment Agency, 'Progress and Prospects for Decarbonisation in the Agriculture Sector and Beyond' (6 October 2022).
28. European Parliament, 'Financing of the CAP: Facts and Figures' (Fact Sheets on the European Union 2024).
29. European Parliament, 'Imbalances in the Food Supply Chain' (2013/C 227 E/03).
30. European Parliament, 'Unfair Trading Practices in the Food Supply Chain' (Resolution) 2018/C 086/05.
31. European Parliamentary Research Service, 'Rural Poverty in the European Union' (European Parliament 2017).
32. EuroStat, 'Farms and Farmland in the European Union – Statistics' (5 September 2023).
33. Federal Trade Commission, 'FTC and Justice Department Listening Forum on First-hand Effects of Mergers and Acquisitions: Food and Agriculture' (28 March 2022).
34. Federal Trade Commission, 'Report of the Federal Trade Commission on the Meat-Packing Industry: Summary and Part I' (Government Printing Office 1919).
35. Federal Trade Commission, 'Slotting Allowances and Other Marketing Practices in the Grocery Industry' (February 2001).
36. Food and Agriculture Organization of the United Nations, 'Water Pollution from Agriculture: A Global Eeview: Executive Summary' (FAO 2017).
37. Independent Group of Scientists appointed by the Secretary-General, 'Global Sustainable Development Report 2019: The Future Is Now – Science for Achieving Sustainable Development' (United Nations 2019).
38. International Food Policy Research Institute, 'The Future of Small Farms: Proceedings of a Research Workshop' (IFPRI 2005).
39. La Via Campesina, 'The Corona Crisis Harms Those Who Feed Us' (28 April 2020) <https://viacampesina.org/en/the-corona-crisis-harms-those-who-feed-us/> accessed 29 June 2024.
40. La Via Campesina, 'The Right to Produce and Access to Land. Food Sovereignty: A Future Without Hunger' (November 1996).
41. La Via Campesina, 'The Right to Produce and Access to Land' (November 1996).
42. LTO Nederland, 'Response to Call for Evidene: Sustainability Agreements in Agriculture – Guidelines on Antitrust Derogation' (2022) 4; EuroCommerce, 'Guidelines on Antitrust Derogations for Sustainability Agreements in Agriculture: Call for Evidence' (2022).
43. Organisation for Economic Co-Operation and Development, 'Agriculture and the Environment: Lessons Learned from a Decade of OECD Work' (2004).
44. Organisation for Economic Co-Operation and Development, 'Food Supply Chains and COVID-19: Impacts and Policy Lessons' (OECD 2020).
45. Organisation for Economic Co-Operation and Development, 'Market Concentration' (2018) DAF/COMP/WD(2018)46.
46. Organization for Economic Co-Operation and Development, 'Competition Issues in the Food Chain Industry' (2013) DAF/COMP(2014)16.
47. Statement on People's Food Sovereignty, 'Our World Is Not for Sale: Priority to Peoples' Food Sovereignty: WTO Out of Food and Agriculture' (June 2002).
48. The National Agricultural Law Center, 'The Packers and Stockyards Act: An Overview' <https://nationalaglawcenter.org/overview/packers-and-stockyards/> accessed 27 December 2023).
49. U.S. Department of Agriculture, 'Packers and Stockyards Enforcement' <www.ams.usda.gov/services/enforcement/psd> accessed 27 December 2023.
50. U.S. Department of Agriculture, 'The Number of U.S. Farms Continues Slow Decline' (2023) <www.ers.usda.gov/data-products/chart-gallery/gallery/chart-detail/?chartId=58268> accessed 16 March 2024.

51. U.S. Department of Justice, 'Assistant Attorney General Jonathan Kanter Meets with National Farmers Union' (12 September 2022).
52. United Nations Brundtland Commission, 'Report of the World Commission on Environment and Development: Our Common Future' (1987).
53. United Nations Environment Programme, 'Why Is Animal Welfare Important for Sustainable Consumption and Production?' (2019).
54. United States Department of Agriculture, 'Farms and Land in Farms: 2019 Summary' (National Agricultural Statistics Service 2020).
55. United States Department of Agriculture, 'The Story of the Capper-Volstead Act' (Cooperative Information Report 2002).
56. World Society for the Protection of Animals, 'Animals: Helping Us Achieve the Future We Want' (2013).
57. Written Submission of Federal Trade Commission Chair Lina M. Khan, 'Poultry Growing Tournament Systems: Fairness and Related Concerns' (Docket No. AMS-FTPP-22-046).

Laws (including soft laws)

1. Agriculture improvement act of 2018.
2. Autoriteit Consument & Market, Guidelines regarding collaborations between farmers [22 September 2023].
3. Commission Delegated Regulation (EU) 2016/1166 of 17 May 2016 amending Annex X to Regulation (EU) No 1308/2013 of the European Parliament and of the Council as regards purchase terms for beet in the sugar sector as from 1 October 2017 [2016] OJ L193/17.
4. Commission, Guidelines on the applicability of Article 101 of the Treaty on the Functioning of the European Union to horizontal co-operation agreements (Communication) [2023] OJ C259/1 (Horizontal Guidelines).
5. Commission, Guidelines on the application of Article 81(3) of the Treaty (Communication) [2004] OJ C101/97.
6. Commission, Guidelines on the assessment of horizontal mergers under the Council Regulation on the control of concentrations between undertakings [2004] 2004/C 31/03 OJ C 31/5.
7. Commission, Guidelines on the exclusion from Article 101 of the Treaty on the Functioning of the European Union for sustainability agreements of agricultural producers pursuant to Article 210a of Regulation (EU) No 1308/2013 (Communication) [2023] OJ C/2023/1446 (Article 210a Guidelines).
8. Commission, Guidelines on vertical restraints (Communication) [2022] 2022/C 248/01.
9. Commission, Notice on agreements of minor importance which do not appreciably restrict competition under Article 101(1) of the Treaty on the Functioning of the European Union (Communication) [2014] OJ C291/1 (De Minimis Notice).
10. Commission, Proposal for a Directive of the European Parliament and of the Council on unfair trading practices in business-to-business relationships in the food supply chain COM [2018] (173 Final).
11. Commission, The definition of relevant market for the purposes of Community competition law (Notice) [1997] 97/C 372/03.
12. Consolidated version of the Treaty on the Functioning of the European Union [2012] OJ C 326/47 (TFEU).
13. Council Regulation (EC) No 1/2003 of 16 December 2002 on the implementation of the rules on competition laid down in Articles 81 and 82 of the Treaty [2003] OJ L1/1 (Council Regulation 1/2003).

14. Council Regulation (EC) No 1/2003 of 16 December 2002 on the implementation of the rules on competition laid down in Articles 81 and 82 of the Treaty [2003] OJ L1/1 (Council Regulation 1/2003).
15. Council Regulation (EC) No 1184/2006 of 24 July 2006 applying certain rules of competition to the production of, and trade in, agricultural products [2006] OJ L214/7 (Agri-Food Competition Regulation).
16. Council Regulation (EC) No 1234/2007 of 22 October 2007 establishing a common organisation of agricultural markets and on specific provisions for certain agricultural products [2007] OJ L299/1.
17. Council Regulation (EC) No 1259/1999 of 17 May 1999 establishing common rules for direct support schemes under the common agricultural policy [1999] OJ L160/113.
18. Council Regulation (EC) No 139/2004 of 20 January 2004 on the control of concentrations between undertakings [2004] OJ L24/1 (Merger Regulation).
19. Council Regulation (EC) No 1782/2003 of 29 September 2003 establishing common rules for direct support schemes under the common agricultural policy and establishing certain support schemes for farmers and amending Regulations (EEC) No 2019/93, (EC) No 1452/2001, (EC) No 1453/2001, (EC) No 1454/2001, (EC) 1868/94, (EC) No 1251/1999, (EC) No 1254/1999, (EC) No 1673/2000, (EEC) No 2358/71 and (EC) No 2529/2001 [2003] OJ L270/1.
20. Council Regulation (EEC) No 1765/92 of 30 June 1992 establishing a support system for producers of certain arable crops [1992] OJ L181/12.
21. Council Regulation (EEC) No 2078/92 of 30 June 1992 on agricultural production methods compatible with the requirements of the protection of the environment and the maintenance of the countryside [1992] OJ L215/85.
22. Council Regulation (EEC) No 2328/91 of 15 July 1991 on improving the efficiency of agricultural structures [1991] OJ L218/1.
23. Directive (EU) 2019/633 of the European Parliament and of the Council of 17 April 2019 on unfair trading practices in business-to-business relationships in the agricultural and food supply chain [2019] OJ L111/59 (UTP Directive).
24. Directive 2011 /7/EU of the European Parliament and of the Council of 16 February 2011 on combating late payment in commercial transactions [2011] OJ L48/1 (Late Payments Directive).
25. EEC Council Regulation No 26 applying certain rules of competition to production of and trade in agricultural products [1962] OJ L993/129.
26. Farm security and rural investment act of 2002.
27. Federal agriculture improvement and reform (FAIR) act of 1996.
28. Federal Trade Commission and the U.S. Department of Justice, Antitrust guidelines for collaborations among competitors [2000].
29. Food, agriculture, conservation, and trade act of 1990.
30. Food, conservation, and energy act of 2008.
31. National agricultural research, extension, and reaching policy act of 1977.
32. President Joseph R. Biden Jr., Executive order on promoting competition in the American economy [9 July 2021].
33. Regulation (EC) No 178/2002 of the European Parliament and of the Council of 28 January 2002 laying down the general principles and requirements of food law, establishing the European Food Safety Authority and laying down procedures in matters of food safety [2002] OJ L31/1.
34. Regulation (EU) 2016/679 of the European Parliament and of the Council of 27 April 2016 on the protection of natural persons with regard to the processing of personal data and on the free movement of such data, and repealing Directive 95/46/EC [2016] OJ L119/1 (GDPR).
35. Regulation (EU) 2021/2115 of the European Parliament and of the Council of 2 December 2021 establishing rules on support for strategic plans to be drawn up by member states under the common agricultural policy (CAP Strategic Plans) and financed by the

European Agricultural Guarantee Fund (EAGF) and by the European Agricultural Fund for Rural Development (EAFRD) and repealing Regulations (EU) No 1305/2013 and (EU) No 1307/2013 [2021] OJ L435/1.
36. Regulation (EU) 2022/1925 of the European Parliament and of the Council of 14 September 2022 on contestable and fair markets in the digital sector and amending Directives (EU) 2019/1937 and (EU) 2020/1828 [2022] OJ L265/1 (DMA).
37. Regulation (EU) No 1306/2013 of the European Parliament and of the Council of 17 December 2013 on the financing, management and monitoring of the common agricultural policy and repealing Council Regulations (EEC) No 352/78, (EC) No 165/94, (EC) No 2799/98, (EC) No 814/2000, (EC) No 1290/2005 and (EC) No 485/2008 [2013] OJ L347/549.
38. Regulation (EU) No 1307/2013 of the European Parliament and of the Council of 17 December 2013 establishing rules for direct payments to farmers under support schemes within the framework of the common agricultural policy and repealing Council Regulation (EC) No 637/2008 and Council Regulation (EC) No 73/2009 [2013] OJ L347/608.
39. Regulation (EU) No 1308/2013 of the European Parliament and of the Council of 17 December 2013 establishing a common organisation of the markets in agricultural products and repealing Council Regulations (EEC) No 922/72, (EEC) No 234/79, (EC) No 1037/2001 and (EC) No 1234/2007 [2013] OJ L347/671 (CMO Regulation).
40. Regulation (EU) No 261/2012 of the European Parliament and of the Council of 14 March 2012 amending Council Regulation (EC) No 1234/2007 as regards contractual relations in the milk and milk products sector [2012] OJ L94/38.
41. Regulation (EU) No 261/2012 of the European Parliament and of the Council of 14 March 2012 amending Council Regulation (EC) No 1234/2007 as regards contractual relations in the milk and milk products sector [2012] OJ L94/38 (Regulation 261/2012).
42. The general assembly of illinois – an act to regulate public warehouses and the warehousing and inspection of grain, and to give effect to art. 13 of the Constitution of this State (approved 25 April 1871).
43. Treaty establishing the European Economic Community.
44. U.S. Department of Agriculture, Undue and unreasonable preferences and advantages under the packers and stockyards act [2020] 85 Federal Register 79780.
45. U.S. Department of Justice, *Antitrust Division Manual* (5th edn, DOJ 2021).

Cases

1. *Abbott Labs. v. Portland Retail Druggists Ass'n, Inc.*, 425 U.S. 1, 11 [1976].
2. *Bankamerica Corp. v. United States*, 462 U.S. 122, 147–148 [1983].
3. Bundeskartellamt's Decision of 3 July 2014 in Case B2–58/09 against EDEKA Zentrale AG & Co. KG.
4. C–209/07 *Competition Authority v Beef Industry Development Society Ltd and Barry Brothers (Carrigmore) Meats Ltd* [2008] EU:C:2008:643.
5. *Carrefour/Promodès* (COMP/M. 1684) Commission Decision [1999] OJ C 359/33.
6. Case 123/83 *Bureau national interprofessionnel du cognac v Guy Clair* [1985] EU:C:1985:33.
7. Case 139/79 *Maizena GmbH v Council of the European Communities* [1980] EU:C:1980:250.
8. Case 27/76 *United Brands Company and United Brands Continentaal BV v Commission of the European Communities* [1978] EU:C:1978:22.
9. Case 48/74 *Charmasson v Minister for Economic Affairs and Finance* [1974] EU:C:1974:137.
10. Case 61/80 *Coöperatieve Stremsel- en Kleurselfabriek v Commission of the European Communities* [1981] EU:C:1981:75.
11. Case 71/74 *Nederlandse Vereniging voor de fruit- en groentenimporthandel, Nederlandse Bond van grossiers in zuidvruchten en ander geimporteerd fruit "Frubo"*

v Commission of the European Communities and Vereniging de Fruitunie [1975] EU:C:1975:61.

12. Case 85/76 *Hoffmann-La Roche & Co: AG v Commission of the European Communities* [1979] EU:C:1979:36.
13. Case 8–72 *Vereeniging van Cementhandelaren v Commission of the European Communities* [1972] EU:C:1972:84.
14. Case C–101/07 P *Coop de France bétail and viande v Commission* [2008] EU:C:2008:741.
15. Case C–137/00 *The Queen v The Competition Commission, Secretary of State for Trade and Industry and The Director General of Fair Trading, ex parte Milk Marque Ltd and National Farmers' Union* [2003] EU:C:2003:429.
16. Case C–137/00 *The Queen v The Competition Commission, Secretary of State for Trade and Industry and The Director General of Fair Trading, ex parte Milk Marque Ltd and National Farmers' Union* [2003] EU:C:2003:429.
17. Case C–252/21 *Meta Platforms Inc and Others v Bundeskartellamt* [2023] EU:C:2023:537.
18. Case C–280/93 *Federal Republic of Germany v Council of the European Union* [1994] EU:C:1994:367.
19. Case C–311/94 *IJssel-Vliet Combinatie BV v Minister van Economische Zaken* [1996] EU:C:1996:383.
20. Case C–399/93 *Oude Luttikhuis and Others v Verenigde Coöperatieve Melkindustrie Coberco BA* [1995] EU:C:1995:434.
21. Case C–456/00 *French Republic v Commission of the European Communities* [2002] EU:C:2002:753.
22. Case C–671/15 *Président de l'Autorité de la concurrence v Association des producteurs vendeurs d'endives (APVE) and Others* [2017] EU:C:2017:860.
23. Case C-68/12 *Protimonopolný úrad Slovenskej republiky v Slovenská sporiteľňa a.s.* [2013] EU:C:2013:71.
24. Case T–217/03 *FNCBV and Others v Commission* [2006] EU:T:2006:391.
25. Case T-61/89 *Dansk Pelsdyravlerforening v Commission of the European Communities* [1992] EU:T:1992:79.
26. Case T-83/91 *Tetra Pak International SA v Commission of the European Communities* [1994] EU:T:1994:246.
27. *Fed. Mar. Comm'n v. Seatrain Lines, Inc.*, 411 U.S. 726, 733 [1973].
28. *French Beef* (Case COMP/C.38.279/F3) Commission Decision 2003/600/EC [2003] OJ L209/12.
29. *Grp. Life & Health Ins. Co. v. Royal Drug Co.*, 440 U.S. 205, 231 [1979].
30. Joined cases C-501/06 P, C-513/06 P, C-515/06 P and C-519/06 P *GlaxoSmithKline Services Unlimited v Commission of the European Communities (C-501/06 P) and Commission of the European Communities v GlaxoSmithKline Services Unlimited (C-513/06 P) and European Association of Euro Pharmaceutical Companies (EAEPC) v Commission of the European Communities (C-515/06 P) and Asociación de exportadores españoles de productos farmacéuticos (Aseprofar) v Commission of the European Communities* [2009] EU:C:2009:610.
31. *New potatoes* (Case IV/31.735) Commission Decision 88/109/EEC [1987] OJ L59/25.
32. *Scottish Salmon Board* (Case IV/33.494) Commission Decision 92/444/EC [1992] OJ L246/37.
33. U.S. Supreme Court, *United States v. Borden Co.*, 308 U. S. 206 [1939].
34. U.S. Supreme Court, *Munn v. Illinois*, 94 U.S. 113 [1876].
35. U.S. Supreme Court, *Case-Swayne Co., Inc. v. Sunkist Growers, Inc.*, 389 U.S. 384 [1967).
36. U.S. Supreme Court, *Maryland and Virginia Milk Producers Assn., Inc. v. United States*, 362 U.S. 458 [1960].

37. U.S. Supreme Court, *National Broiler Marketing Association, Petitioner, v. United States*, 436 U.S. 816 [1978].
38. U.S. Supreme Court, *United States v. Borden Co.*, 308 U.S. 188 [1939].
39. *Union Labor Life Ins. Co. v. Pireno*, 458 U.S. 119, 126 [1982].
40. *United States Court of Appeals, Fifth Circuit, Wheeler v. Pilgrim's Pride Corp*, 591 F.3d 355 (5th Cir.) [2009].
41. United States District Court, *E.D. Pennsylvania: In Re Mushroom Direct Purchaser Antitrust Litigation*, 621 F. Supp. 2d 274 [2008].
42. United States District Court, *E.D. Pennsylvania: In Re Processed Egg Products Antitrust Litigation*, 206 F. Supp. 3d 1033 [2016].
43. *United States v. Masonite Corp.*, 316 U.S. 265, 280 [1942].
44. *United States v. McKesson & Robbins, Inc.*, 351 U.S. 305, 316 [1956].

Index

FSC
www.fsc.org
MIX
Papier | Fördert gute Waldnutzung
FSC® C083411

Kolibri 360 GmbH
Ferdinand-Jühlke-Straße 7
99095 Erfurt, Deutschland
produktsicherheit@kolibri360.de